HIDDEN ASPECTS OF WOMEN'S WORK

HIDDEN ASPECTS OF WOMEN'S WORK

EDITED BY
CHRISTINE BOSE,
ROSLYN FELDBERG,
AND NATALIE SOKOLOFF
WITH THE WOMEN AND WORK
RESEARCH GROUP

WOMEN AND WORK RESEARCH GROUP

CHRISTINE BOSE
CAROL BROWN
PEGGY CRULL
ROSLYN FELDBERG
NADINE FELTON
MYRA MARX FEREE
AMY GILMAN
EVELYN NAKANO GLENN
AMY KESSELMAN
SUSAN LEHRER
NATALIE SOKOLOFF
CAROLE TURBIN

New York
Westport, Connecticut
London

Library of Congress Cataloging-in-Publication Data

Hidden aspects of women's work.

Bibliography: p.
Includes index.
1. Sex discrimination in employment—
United States—History   2. Sex role in the
work environment—United States—History.
3. Sex discrimination against women—
United States—History.   4. Women—Employment—
United States—History.   I. Bose, Christine E.
II. Feldberg, Roslyn.   III. Sokoloff, Natalie J.
IV. Women and Work Research Group.
HD6060.5.U5H53   1987   331.4'133'0973   87-2449
ISBN 0-275-92415-7 (alk. paper)

Library of Congress Catalog Card Number: 87-2449
ISBN: 0-275-92415-7

First published in 1987

Praeger Publishers, 1 Madison Avenue, New York, NY 10010
A division of Greenwood Press, Inc.

Printed in the United States of America

The paper used in this book complies with the Permanent
Paper Standard issued by the National Information Standards
Organization (Z39.48-1984).

10 9 8 7 6 5 4 3 2

Contents

Preface

This collection of articles can best be understood by locating it in the context of the larger process of the Women and Work Research Group. In March 1979 a dozen women interested in studying women and work began meeting together on a regular basis. Initially funded by a grant from the American Sociological Association, we were predominantly sociologists with members from a variety of other fields--history, anthropology, psychology, and economics--and several different settings--universities, the government, and women's organizations. We were originally inspired to meet and work together because we recognized that theories about women and work had been dominated by assumptions used for studying men in the work force. We began by discussing our individual research projects, and moved on to search as a group for new concepts to highlight and challenge male-based assumptions. We developed an interdisciplinary approach to the study of women's work at home, in the paid labor force, and in the community. Along the way, we observed that our individual research and group analysis frequently highlighted features of women's work that are hidden from casual observation and obscure women's place in the economy. That was the start of the common framework we have been developing since, through meeting twice yearly and exchanging papers in between. The process has resulted in this book, Hidden Aspects of Women's Work.

Some of our early members--Mary Blewett, Heidi Hartmann, Alice Kessler-Harris, and Dorothy Remy--have left the group; others have joined us; and one of our current members was unable to have a chapter included. Yet each of these women has made important contributions that have left their imprint on this volume. Others, not group members, have been very helpful in completing this volume. Hal Benenson and Ronnie Steinberg read an earlier draft and provided comments that make our ideas more accessible and greatly improved several of the chapters. Lynda Sharp and Alison Bricken, Praeger editors, believed in us and helped usher the book through completion. We thank all of them for their time and effort. Finally, the three coeditors—Chris Bose, Roz Feldberg, and Natalie Sokoloff—shared equally in the diverse tasks required by and for the collective to complete this volume.

Acknowledgments

The authors gratefully acknowledge permission to reprint the following material:

"Racial Ethnic Women and Work: Toward an Analysis of Race and Gender Stratification," by Evelyn Nakano Glenn. A revised version is reprinted by permission of Westview Press (Boulder, Colorado) from Social Power and Influence of Women, edited by Liesa Stamm and Carol D. Ryff. Copyright [1984] by the American Association for the Advancement of Science.

"Technology and Work Degradation: Effects of Office Automation on Women Clerical Workers," by Roslyn L. Feldberg and Evelyn Nakano Glenn. The original version of this article, here revised and updated, was published in Machina Ex Dea: Feminist Perspectives on Technology, edited by Joan Rothschild (New York and Oxford: Pergamon Press, 1985), pp. 59-78. Copyright [1983] by Joan Rothschild. Reprinted with permission.

"'Cogs to the Wheels': The Ideology of Women's Work in Mid-Nineteenth Century Fiction," by Amy Gilman. The original version of this article, here revised, was published in Science and Society 47, no. 2 (Summer 1983). Copyright (1983) by Science and Society, Inc. Reprinted with permission.

"Reconceptualizing Family, Work, and Labor Organizing: Working Women in Troy, 1860-1890," by Carole Turbin. The original version of this article, here revised, was

1

Introduction: Considerations in the Study of Women and Work

The Women and Work Research Group

We have called our collection <u>Hidden Aspects of Women's Work</u>. The question immediately arises: What is hidden, and from whom is it hidden? Each woman who works to maintain her family with limited income knows of the central role of her ability to save, manage, organize, and make do in the survival of her children, her partner, her parents, and, at times, her siblings who are "having trouble." Each woman who works in an office knows of the fatigue and headaches caused by a day spent before the new computerized equipment. Each woman who works in an old industrial factory knows the pervasive fear of a sudden plant closing and the exhaustion of working overtime at reduced pay "to keep the company from folding." And each woman knows from experience and shared stories the crude language and unwanted gestures and touches of male coworkers and bosses.

What is hidden from both women and men is the systematic nature of women's daily experience. Isolated by nuclear families, ad hoc child care arrangements, and dispersed work places, most women internalize their experiences and perceive them as a result of their personality or their "unique" history. Yet the routinization of women's work, barriers to employment or to better employment, sexual harassment, and the links between life on the job and life at home are all the consequences of systematic power differentials that result from a person's class and race, as well as gender. Each of the chapters in this volume reveals some of these hidden aspects of women's work.

1

In different ways, the studies reported here point to the pervasiveness of gender as an organizing principle in the world of employment. Different chapters show how gender affects the ways in which women are included in the labor force (Sokoloff, chapter 2), the impact of work technologies (Feldberg and Glenn, chapter 4), the threat of sexual harassment (Crull, chapter 11), government policy toward workers (Lehrer, chapter 10), the accessibility of labor organizations (Feldberg, chapter 14), the ability to protest collectively (Kesselman, chapter 13), and employed mothers' attitudes toward their work lives as related to the division of labor at home (Ferree, chapter 8).

While gender stratification is pervasive and women often blame themselves for their structurally induced problems, it is also true that women develop a consciousness of these problems and sometimes collectively resist them. Many articles in this collection discuss conditions under which such consciousness is realized, shared, and organized around--Turbin (chapter 9) discusses Troy, New York, collar workers in the 19th century, and Sokoloff (chapter 2), more current labor struggles; Feldberg (chapter 14) examines union organizing over time; Kesselman (chapter 13) interviews women shipyard workers on their desire to keep their jobs after World War 11; and Ferree (chapter 8) looks at conditions under which housewives will demand housework of their families. Such resistance is particularly dramatic because popular literature (Gilman, chapter 6) and even the census (Bose, chapter 5) present a distortion of reality to society at large.

This volume develops these ideas in thematic sections that enable us to pursue three important goals: identifying the dimensions and patterns of women's work experience, examining the links between labor in and out of the home, and exploring the hidden aspects of women's culture and resistance.

THEMATIC CONCERNS

The first goal of this collection is to identify the systematic and institutionally created and reinforced dimensions of women's work experience. The section entitled "Structures, Patterns, and Ideologies" discusses these issues. First, Sokoloff (chapter 2) explains how a narrow focus on Reaganomics can hide the discrimination against

women that is embedded in our society and can obscure
the historical pattern of women's movement in and out of
the wage labor force since 1900. Next, in a more theoretical vein, Glenn (chapter 3) analyzes how the dynamic relationship among race, class, and gender creates different
work experiences among women. She shows how race and
gender are not merely additive, but interconnected so that
they restructure each other. This process is elaborated on
by Feldberg and Glenn (chapter 4) as they describe how
technology can degrade rather than upgrade women's jobs,
but with various effects on different groups of women. In
a different context, Feldberg and Glenn explain which technological changes influencing work structures are uniquely
contemporary, and they suggest possible strategies to confront the attendant problems.

These effects of the labor force on women's lives
are not only a product of economic and technological
changes over time. By examining the persistent government undercount of women's employment, Bose (chapter 5)
illustrates how the very categories of census data and descriptions used to document women's occupations distort
our perceptions. She discusses how more appropriate
categories would change our analysis and world view.
Gilman (chapter 6) illustrates how the ideology incorporated
in 19th-century popular fiction has obscured the nature of
women's work. Thus the final chapters of the first thematic section examine how recording methods and popular
culture, along with economic, political, and technological
changes, have shaped women's lives.

A second goal is to explore the complex links between productive labor in the home and out of the home.
The articles in the section entitled "Links Between the Public and Private Spheres" analyze such interactions between
work and home life. The section begins with an article
by Brown (chapter 7) that examines the changing locus of
patriarchy, or male power, in the public and private
spheres over time. She also notes how these spheres reinforce each other.

This section continues with three chapters that move
from an examination of the private sphere of home life to
a discussion of how home roles have influenced legislation
in the public world outside the home. As Bose indicated
in chapter 5, all too often work within the home done for
pay, such as sewing, doing laundry, caring for boarders,
or caring for unrelated children, has been either lumped

with housework or ignored. This has made it appear that there is a forced choice between paid work and family work, all the while that women have often been required to do both. Ferree (chapter 8) describes what happens when women do both tasks, as epitomized in the role of the superwoman. She analyzes how women's resistance to the ideology of the superwoman role can be seen in their struggles to get family—especially husbands'—aid in housework.

The next two chapters illustrate how the family and the work place are each organized on the basis of the other. Turbin (chapter 9) shows how family relationships among female and male Irish workers enhanced successful work place organizing for unionized women collar workers and male iron molders in 19th-century labor unions of Troy, New York. Lehrer (chapter 10) draws the links between sex role ideology and the battle over minimum wage legislation.

The links between the public and private aspects of life emerge as subthemes in other sections as well. For example, Gilman's (chapter 6) study of images of women workers in fiction, Feldberg's (chapter 14) study of women's union involvement, and Kesselman's (chapter 13) discussion of World War II women workers' attempts to retain skilled industrial jobs can be viewed in this light.

A third goal is to examine the hidden aspects of culture, consciousness, and resistance as they affect women and their work. This is the subject of our third section, "Consciousness and Resistance," which explores several examples of inadequate or misleading popular conceptions of women's place in the work force, and women's efforts to resist or change those traditional images. The section opens with Crull's (chapter 11) analysis of the causes of sexual harassment, which she uses to develop a theory of the relationship between sexuality and work. Her paper is unique in its systematic discussion of the tension between sexuality and hostility as men face women's declining subordination in the work place. This chapter can usefully be read parallel to Brown's (chapter 7) discussion of patriarchy, in which she reconceptualizes male power.

Glenn (chapter 12) illustrates how ethnicity and class affect the consciousness of Japanese-American domestic workers. Her case study shows how paid work can both reinforce traditional gender roles and also be liberating for women.

In chapter 13, Kesselman uncovers aspects of women's post–World War 11 individual and unorganized resistance to reentering traditional female jobs. Ferree's superwomen (chapter 8) also seek individual, rather than collective, solutions to their problems. Finally, Feldberg (chapter 14) asks how unions marginalize the culture and needs of their female workers, and deals with the effects of male power on union organizing and policies. Her study on the inaccessibility of unions to women is a counterpoint to Turbin's (chapter 9) exploration of women's labor union activism and to Sokoloff's (chapter 2) emphasis on women's labor struggles today.

Some chapters in other sections also deal with the issues of consciousness and conflict, illustrating the many aspects of this theme. For example, both Bose (chapter 5) and Gilman (chapter 6) look at the determinants of public consciousness in the larger society through their respective analyses of U.S. census data and popular fiction. In contrast, Turbin (chapter 9) analyzes how family ties among women reinforced their shared consciousness as workers even to the point of maintaining that consciousness when they were not currently employed.

While we chose to include historically based papers, such as the latter three, within each substantive section, it is also possible to read this book in historical order. Certainly all studies need not be historical in focus, but awareness of historical processes is important. This is true because all situations of the present are the result of previous developments and current changes not only in gender relations but also in race relations, capitalism, technology, type of work, worker organizations, workers' rights, forms of struggle, and family forms.

For those who would prefer to read these chapters historically, 19th-century women workers are discussed by Turbin (chapter 9) and Gilman (chapter 6). Changes and continuity throughout the 20th century are described by five chapters: Bose (chapter 5), comparing 1900 and 1980 censuses; Lehrer's (chapter 10) analysis of the development of minimum-wage legislation between 1910 and 1925; Glenn's (chapter 12) case studies of Japanese-American domestic workers between 1905 and 1940; Kesselman's (chapter 13) examination of women workers immediately after World War 11; and Feldberg's (chapter 14) historical analysis of the role of unions throughout the 20th century.

Sources of conflict in the present are discussed in the remaining chapters. Sokoloff (chapter 2) provides an overview of the issues; Glenn (chapter 3) presents a theoretical critique focused on the racial stratification of women's work; and Brown (chapter 7) elaborates on the changing conditions of male dominance. Three other chapters focus on specific contemporary sources of work-related conflicts: technology and clerical work (Feldberg and Glenn, chapter 4), sexual harassment in the work place (Crull, chapter 11), and attitudes toward the division of labor at home (Ferree, chapter 8).

Within the framework of each historical period, it is possible to see the hidden aspects of women's work, the interrelations of public and private spheres, and the development of women's consciousness and resistance. However, the exact dynamics of each vary across time.

WOMEN'S RELATIVE ECONOMIC POSITION

The analyses in this volume span more than 130 years. While much has changed during this time, it is clear that within each historical period women's relative economic status seems to have improved very little despite apparently large changes in opportunities for employment. This surprising fact led us to identify several specific ways in which improvement in contemporary women's status has been slowed down or undermined.

First, as Sokoloff (chapter 2) and Glenn (chapter 3) show, race and sex segregation in the work force are major factors impeding progress. Women, especially racial ethnic minorities, are still much more likely than white men to have dead-end jobs in which there is little opportunity for training and promotion. One of the continuing characteristics of such low-paid work is that the skills that go into it are not recognized by the culture and by the industry. This is particularly true of women's work. Indeed, because the skills are seen as something women "naturally" pick up in the home, they tend not to be recognized, valued, or compensated, as is shown by data emerging in the debates about comparable worth.

Second, although technology has made much "heavy" work lighter, it has not always improved women's status. Rather, technology has been used to break down jobs into small component tasks and to intensify the division of labor (described for the clerical field by Feldberg and Glenn in chapter 4). Technological change has also increased the numbers of people who can utilize services like bank accounts, insurance policies, credit cards, higher education, and hospital care. On the positive side, these industries have had to expand their work forces and to draw on women and racial ethnic men to fill jobs as tellers, insurance agents, and professors. On the negative side, in order to do more business without cutting profits, these industries have utilized technology to decrease their labor needs while lowering the status and pay of jobs servicing the public. Thus, recent changes have resulted in mixed progress.

Third, while sex discrimination laws and affirmative action policies were initially expected to move women into higher positions in the work force, there are ways in which they have often been manipulated by employers, undermined by the government, and even turned against women under the guise of reverse discrimination (Sokoloff, chapter 2). (These reactions are not new, as Lehrer's chapter 10 discussion of opposition to the minimum wage illustrates.) Some jobs that women have been able to obtain, following vigorous affirmative action efforts, have been eliminated by automation (Hacker 1979). Other industries have actually used sex discrimination laws to eliminate women from jobs by combining seniority lists. Sexual harassment is covered by affirmative action laws, yet, as Crull (chapter 11) shows, women frequently face situations in which their sexuality is used against them. Even if a woman is able to maintain her job without being fired, having to quit, or losing a raise under these circumstances, she loses productivity and enjoyment of her work. Although sex discrimination laws and affirmative action can be used in the spirit intended, they need to be continually struggled for and defended by those who stand to gain from them.

Finally, one of the most complex mechanisms in maintaining the current status quo for women is the relationship between women's work on the job and their work in the home. It is easy to think of women's work in the market (public sphere) and their work in the home (private sphere) as separate but, as Brown (chapter 7) indicates, they are part of the same system, each organized on the basis of the other. Ironically, the ideology that women are responsible for home and children gives them no more power in the private sphere than in the public sphere, although some strategies suggested by Ferree's (chapter 8) analysis might do so.

Certainly an understanding of all the economic, legal, and social mechanisms that undermine women's relative status is key to finding a strategy to improve it. Effective social change will also require an adequate theory of women's position, and a framework for its development is a goal of this volume.

ISSUES THAT CROSSCUT THE THEMES

Although the book is divided into major thematic sections, several crosscutting issues that were hidden by early research on women and work are uncovered by each author. Many of these issues are essential to the development of an adequate theory of women's work.

First, we found that theoretical models of work are often based on either men's or women's experience. Too often male workers are seen as totally separate from their home lives and women workers are seen as totally immersed in them (Feldberg and Glenn 1979b). Both views are erroneous. New paradigms are needed that accurately take into account family and other nonlabor force relations for both sexes. This issue is directly addressed by Brown (chapter 7) and Glenn (chapter 3), who seek to reformulate existing theories of patriarchy and racial stratification, respectively, as well as by Ferree's (chapter 8) analysis of housework and Glenn's (chapter 12) analysis of domestic work.

Next, we found that women are portrayed in many studies as either self-actualized actors or as victims. On the one hand, women are portrayed as powerless, as passive victims of forces outside themselves. On the other hand, women are often portrayed as choosing whether to enter the labor force or to stay at home, as if they were free agents outside the context of the social controls and social pressures that affect men. Neither view gives the full picture. It is our double-sided responsibility to study the economic, social, and political forces that limit women's behaviors as they do men's, and at the same time to recognize the active role women play in shaping those forces through both personal struggle and organization. In chapters by Crull (chapter 11) on sexuality, by Lehrer (chap-

ter 10) on the family wage, by Feldberg (chapter 14) on
women in unions, and by Glenn (chapter 3) on racial/
ethnic divisions we explore some of those limits; Ferree
(chapter 8), Glenn (chapter 12), and Kesselman (chapter
13) explore personal, and Turbin (chapter 9) and Sokoloff
(chapter 2) collective, change strategies.

Third, we found that the two interacting systems of
capitalism and patriarchy must be considered. Studies of
women's work sometimes look only at the relations between
work and family, without reference to the type of economic
system in which the women are working and the families
are living. Or they focus an analysis of contemporary
problems on recent policies, demographic trends, or economic cycles, without seeing the larger picture. Yet, as
Sokoloff (chapter 2) illustrates, it is important to do so
and to understand the basis of our economy. Further, the
patriarchal relationship of the gender "men" to the gender
"women" permeates all institutions in any economy (see
Brown, chapter 7; Sokoloff, chapter 2; and Glenn, chapter
3). In studies in a capitalist economy like that of the
United States, theories and research on women's work must
take into account the effects of class, and class theory
must take into account the effect of male power.

Such studies will improve our understanding of who
controls and benefits from women's labor at home and in
the market. Individual men, men as a group, and different classes or racial groups of men stand in a complex
relationship to the spectrum of women's labor (Brown,
chapter 7). Particularly important, both politically and
sociologically, is an understanding of whether and how individual men of a given class have control of, or derive a
benefit from, the unpaid and paid work of women from
their own (presumed) class (Ferree, chapter 8). The importance of unpaid labor as a component of women's home
work raises the issue of unpaid labor generally. In her
chapter on undercounted, unpaid labor, Bose (chapter 5)
indicates that women have not really changed the extent
of their working but have merely changed the form of their
economic contribution, with unpaid labor being counted
somewhat more consistently since 1940. Sokoloff (chapter 2)
further finds that women as a group now have less economic power than is popularly believed.

The remaining crosscutting issue is of particular
concern to the general population: technology. Capitalist
industrial organizations are oriented toward cutting costs

and controlling the work process through rationalization and automation. Yet these technological changes are often touted as a means of providing new jobs requiring a more skilled work force. As Feldberg and Glenn (chapter 4) reveal, the majority of new jobs are often deskilled and repetitive, and pay less than the ones they replace. This outcome is not the result of scientific necessity, but of corporate priorities. Technological development never occurs independently of other forces—technological choices are made within a social context.

Finally, this volume uncovers some issues we were not able to fully explore. We find that not enough attention has been paid to the relationship between objective work conditions and workers' satisfaction with the job. This issue is sometimes phrased as "Why do so many women put up with such lousy jobs?" We do not know if women and men share the same job expectations, or to what extent their perceptions are shaped by their respective places in the overall economy. Glenn (chapter 12) and Kesselman (chapter 13) begin to address these issues, but more research is necessary.

The role of sexuality is another issue not frequently included in studies of work. We all know it is there, and that it has an important influence on reality, as well as on hopes and fears. But most studies of women and work either ignore sexuality or focus on it exclusively. Considerations often tend to be moral rather than theoretical: on the job, it's bad; off the job, it's good. A much better theoretical understanding of the relationship of sexuality to other factors is needed, and Crull (chapter 11) points us in this important direction.

All too frequently, prior research has assumed the perspective of middle-class white women. While recent research has tried to avoid class bias, there is still far too little research on structured racial/ethnic differences in our social system. Much research tends to focus only on class, race, or gender, while the interactions of the gender-race-class systems are ignored. Studies such as Glenn's (chapters 3 and 12) or Sokoloff's (chapter 2) are the exception to the rule. It is clear that much more exploration of the experience of a variety of racial/ethnic women and the interactions of race with gender and class is absolutely necessary. Such research will build on the beginnings developed here to analyze systematically the way class and gender relations are shaped by, and shape, the meanings of race and ethnicity in our society.

NOTE

This introduction outlines the combination of forces that prevent economic progress for women and the issues that need to be addressed for theoretical and research progress.   It demonstrates the importance of looking at many factors rather than single events, industries, or trends before judging the effectiveness of strategies for change.   By identifying issues and the impediments to change, the three thematic sections make visible what was previously hidden from many groups of people.   This opens possibilities for more effective research, theory, and action both by those who are directly affected and by their allies.

PART I
STRUCTURES, PATTERNS, AND IDEOLOGIES

2

What's Happening to Women's Employment: Issues for Women's Labor Struggles in the 1980s–1990s

Natalie J. Sokoloff

INTRODUCTION

The Reagan administration (1980–1988) introduced two sets of policies that have been widely recognized as having negative consequences for almost all women, as well as for racial/ethnic minority men, those in poverty, and those in the working class. First, policies to dramatically increase defense spending have eliminated many kinds of jobs, services, and hard-won protections. Second,

The author gratefully acknowledges the supportive criticisms and helpful comments of a variety of people at various stages of the development of this chapter. It was initially presented at the Johns Hopkins University conference "Feminism and the Critique of Capitalism" in 1981. Revised versions were presented at the Society for the Study of Social Problems meetings in San Francisco in 1982 and at the New York University conference "Women in the Human Services" in 1983. These audiences provided thoughtful questions. Throughout its development, members of the Women and Work Group have been most helpful, particularly Chris Bose, Myra Marx Ferree, Roslyn Feldberg, Nadine Felton, and Peggy Crull, who gave special time to this project. In addition, other people were instrumental in making this a better article: Fred Pincus, Jayne Dean, Berenice Fisher, Elizabeth Higginbotham, Lourdes Benería, Laurie Nisonoff, Ronnie Steinberg, and Hal Benenson.

policies aimed at transferring responsibility from the federal government to more conservative states and localities under the rubric of "the new federalism" have weakened both funding for and enforcement of sexual and racial anti-discrimination laws and regulations. The impact both sets of policies have had on women's abilities to earn a living for themselves and their families (whether they are single parents or members of households with more than one adult) is of particular concern. The list of attempts to dismantle gains made by women since the 1960s includes women's basic right to control their own bodies, their right to an equal education, and their access to jobs equal to those of men, as well as decent pay at whatever job they work.[1] Such policy changes represent a genuine setback.

However, the erosion in the quality of many aspects of women's employment is not unique to the Reagan administration. On the contrary, it is part of a long-term secular trend in the U.S. economy. To be sure, the Reagan administration intensified this process, leading to even greater hardships for women and their families. However, it is too easy to focus an attack on Reagan and the conservative right forces--as if liberals getting into political office would solve the nation's problems. Effective opposition to these policies demands understanding the underlying structural trends that have been at work and will continue to operate in our society--albeit not in exactly the same way--even under more liberal administrations. In short, the first part of this chapter attempts to identify the long-term processes contributing to the acute problems facing women in the U.S. economy in the latter part of the 20th century.

The second section of this chapter discusses certain specific concerns and issues facing women workers in the 1980s–1990s, as more conservative policies augment these broader economic trends. These labor struggles include unemployment, underemployment, renewal of "home" work, occupational sex segregation, the international division of labor, and racism. These areas of struggle for women are selected as illustrative, rather than as inclusive, of all aspects of the problem.

The third and fourth sections of this chapter begin to explore two key issues. The first is Reagan administration policies that threaten women's livelihoods (here we focus on the severe undermining of affirmative action); the second focuses on forms of resistance to a variety of these policies.

STRUCTURAL CONDITIONS AFFECTING
WOMEN'S EMPLOYMENT

Several trends in women's labor force experience
have been significant throughout the 20th century, especially since World War II. While important social gains
have provided new opportunities for women, blacks and
other minorities, and working-class people through their
respective struggles and liberation movements, much of the
inequality by race, sex, and class is actually the basis
on which our society has been built--not an aberration
from it. Thus, the Reagan administration has been able
to build on past inequalities structured into the very fab-
ric of our social, political, and economic system, although
it has also greatly increased those inequalities. (For a
more detailed analysis of processes outlined below, see
Sokoloff 1980, 1982.)
The twin growth of low-wage occupations and low-
wage industries is the major source of employment growth
for women, at least since World War II. For example,
Rothschild (1981) found that 40 percent of new jobs in the
private sector between 1973 and 1980 emerged in three sub-
sectors of the services and retail trades: eating and
drinking places, hospital services, and business services.
These "new industries" have short hours, temporary and
part-time workers, a heavily female work force, and dead-
end jobs, are labor intensive, and offer less protection
and fewer benefits than other industries. Most important,
they have the shortest hours and the lowest wages. This
finding is supported by Rytina (1982), who reveals that
occupations and industries in which women workers are
concentrated tend to rank much lower in terms of earnings,
while men dominate in higher-paid occupations and industries.
Elsewhere we have suggested the need to look at
the kinds of jobs and sectors of the economy where women's
employment has occurred if we are to understand women's
increasing inclusion in the 20th-century U.S. labor market
(Sokoloff 1980, 1982). In the case of the types of jobs,
one must understand something about the cheapening, degradation, and deskilling of jobs in which women have been
employed; in the case of sectors of the economy, one must
understand the relationship between women's increasing
participation in services and in less than full-time and
year-round employment. In both cases, sex segregation of

employment continues to be a key issue. In addition, the
way in which women have been employed in contemporary
U.S. monopoly capitalism is important to our understanding
of their secondary position in the job market today: they
are structurally incorporated as a reserve of labor for
capital at the same time they are employed in wage labor
and continue to have primary responsibility for home and
family. Let us look at each of these issues briefly.

Degradation and Deskilling of Work
or Women's Jobs Are "Bad Jobs"

With regard to the changing nature of work and
women's employment, women have increased their employment in occupations that have been "in brief, bad jobs"
(Dubnoff 1979). According to Dubnoff's analysis of U.S.
female employment between 1940 and 1970, which is a continuation of patterns established earlier in the century
(see Scharf 1980), women became more numerous in jobs
that were "undesirable by every measure considered here.
Females were deployed in occupations which were low in
educational training and requirements, as measured by the
functional nature of the work rather than educational attainment of incumbents, occupations which were low in
autonomy, high in supervision, and above all in occupations which were low paid" (Dubnoff 1979, p. 17). The
persistence of women's employment in low-wage jobs is
documented throughout the 1970s (Serrin 1984b; Norwood
1982) and is projected to continue well into the 21st century (Reskin and Hartmann 1986).
Many of the jobs in which women are employed are
called "deskilled" and "degraded" by Braverman (1974),
who describes the processes by which jobs are broken down
into smaller, more specialized, and more simplified parts
during the period of developing monopoly capitalism. This
deskilling and degradation of labor is said to have certain benefits for capital: (1) it decreases the cost of
labor while (2) increasing productivity and (3) increasing
management's control over the labor process. Women are
paid so little, according to Dubnoff, that they are paid
"below cost": "The growth of women's employment was,
above all an expansion of low wage work, of work which
does not pay the social cost of reproducing the next generation of workers" (Dubnoff 1979, p. 18).

However, it also should be clear that while much of women's work is low-wage and low-status, it is not necessarily unskilled. Phillips and Taylor (1980) and work on comparable worth (Treiman and Hartmann 1981) have shown that job descriptions assume women's work is unskilled, rather than objectively evaluating it as such. For example, studies of the transformation of clerical work appear to involve the establishment of a new alleged hierarchy of skills, with women again assigned to the bottom, regardless of the indispensability of their work, or their absolute or relative skill levels in any objective sense (see Davies 1975). In short, on the one hand, the expansion of jobs at the bottom of the occupational hierarchy encourages the inclusion of more female employees; on the other hand, bringing women into a job allows that job to be deemed unskilled and thus underpaid in other instances. Both processes operate, but in different jobs at different times over the 20th century (Reskin and Roos 1987).

The fact that it is in these kinds of low-wage jobs in low-wage industries that women have been employed during the 20th century goes a long way toward explaining the increase in female employment in the United States since 1900, especially since World War II. Moreover, even where women have gained limited access to higher-status and better-paying traditionally male jobs, many of these gains are not so good as they appear on the surface.[2] Finally, as these processes occur, the sex segregation of the labor market, the recruitment of men into supervisory and professional positions newly created by the reorganization of labor in typically female occupations, and the increasing representation of men in higher levels of both lower- and higher-status "female" occupations either are intensified or emerge in new and different ways. In short, the patriarchal relations of the labor force are maintained, if not strengthened.[3]

Women and Service Sector Jobs

A second way of looking at the inclusion of women in the 20th-century labor force, and particularly since World War II, is to look at the growing nature of service work in the country.

In 1900, seven out of ten workers were in goods production (agriculture or manufacturing). By 1980, seven

out of ten workers were employed in service sector jobs
(Montagna 1977; "Service Producing Industries . . .,"
1981). However, according to Montagna (1977), service
sector jobs are those characterized by instability, little advancement, limited training, a dead-end nature, poor working conditions, little job security, and low pay--or what
are called secondary (less desirable) as opposed to primary (more desirable, stable, with career ladders) market
jobs.

It is precisely in these service sector jobs that
women have increasingly been employed. Moreover, these
are heavily secondary sector jobs: In 1970, 70 percent of
all white women, 83 percent of all black women, and 80
percent of all Latina women were employed in the secondary
labor market--in contrast with only 38 percent of all white
men, 64 percent of all black men, and 50 percent of all
Latino men (Montagna 1977). During the 1970s, 90 percent
of all new jobs for women were in the service industries.
By the end of the decade, more than four out of five employed women worked in service-producing industries ("Service Producing Industries . . .," 1981; Urquhart 1984).
The reasons for these increases are several and include
the need to (1) absorb workers who had worked in or had
sought goods-producing jobs, (2) expand new areas of
profitability for capital, and (3) limit pressure on profits
during economically difficult times (Sokoloff 1982). (In
addition, see Sokoloff 1982 for a discussion of the various
definitions of service work: service trades vs. service
industries vs. service-producing sector of the economy.)

The Importance of "Part-Time" Work

As low-wage, unstable service sector jobs multiplied,
so did female employment in less than full-time and year-
round work.

Until the 1970s, the ideology surrounding women's
employment was that women did not work; if they did, it
was as marginal workers for "pin money"; which was best
done part-time. Since 1970-1975 it has becomemore acceptable to see women as full-fledged, stable, and regular
members of the labor force. For example, in 1980, seven
out of ten employed women worked full-time: women workers are said to be part-time workers no more (U.S. Dept.
of Labor, Bureau of Labor Statistics 1980). Thus, their

permanent attachment to the labor force has been argued. However, the most recent figures indicate that only 45 percent of all women worked both full-time and year-round (in sharp contrast with men 25-54 years old) (U.S. Dept. of Labor, Bureau of Labor Statistics 1983). Therefore, distinguishing data by part-time versus full-time (the way typically done by the census and reports based on its data) severely underestimates industries' discouragement of women's more permanent attachment to the labor force. Most important, less than full-time, full-year employment and low wages maintain women as cheap workers unable to care for themselves and their children in a decent way.

Capital of course benefits from women's less than full-time employment in a variety of ways: "part-timers" are paid 29 percent less per hour, on the average, than full-time workers in the same job (U.S. Dept. of Labor, Women's Bureau 1980); 35 percent of wages spent on fringe benefits (in addition to wages) are not expended by business when women do not work full-time and year-round (Flint 1977; Barko 1986); part-timers are said to be eager workers, hard to organize, able to increase productivity as well as office morale, and able to make control of workers easier (Flint 1977; Samuelson 1977; Fowler 1980; for a recognition of many of these trends, see Serrin 1986).

In short, employing women as less than full-time and year-round workers (1) makes them cheap workers; (2) keeps them attached to their homes, and their domestic and child-rearing responsibilities; (3) makes them dependent on men; and (4) keeps them attached to the labor force but simultaneously available for greater inclusion (or exclusion) as needed by capital.

Since World War II, rapid growth in employment in service industries has provided the bulk of work in part-time jobs during the past decades. And the fastest growth rates within services are in those very industries with the highest percentage of voluntary part-time jobs (low-level services, finance, insurance, real estate, wholesale and retail trade), which have large numbers of female employees. Thus, while in 1940, prior to the huge expansion of service sector jobs, men far outnumbered women in part-time work, today the opposite is true (see Leon and Bednarzick 1978). (However, the number of men working part-time in 1940 may have been affected by the Depression as well as by the rise in the service sector.) Moreover, in the recession of the early 1980s, the number of part-time people who want full-time work but cannot find it is the fastest-growing category in the government's battery of job statistics (Peterson 1982).[4]

If we look at job increases for women in the 1970s and 1980s that were made prior to the Reagan administration, we find that in the 1970s, increases in women's employment were greatest in low-level, white-collar service jobs (clerical work), but that in the 1980s, the greatest job increases are predicted (for men and women alike), first, in low-level services (35 percent of new jobs) and, second, in clerical and sales work (28 percent increase in each). What is so illuminating is that the places of greatest expected increase in the 1980s have the highest percentage of less than full-time and year-round work, and are heavily female. Thus, low-level, part-time service jobs have mushroomed in female-dominated sectors of the economy to such an extent that in 1978, among low-level service workers, three-fourths were part-time workers. Likewise, sales work was three-fourths part-timers, and clerical work had half of its workers in part-time jobs (U.S. Dept. of Labor, Women's Bureau 1980; Nardone 1980; for more recent speculations on future trends in sex segregation in part-time jobs, see Reskin and Hartmann 1986). (See Table 2.1.)

In sum, women's employment has increased as part of a long-term secular trend--in low-wage, sex-segregated, often deskilled jobs in low-wage industries with predominantly male supervisors. Further, women increasingly have been recruited into service jobs offering less than full-time and year-round work. This has occurred as men's wages have been eroded by capital, and thus allows capital to recruit a readily available supply of female labor to these jobs at the same time that it keeps women--especially married women and young mothers--as a "reserve" of labor.

Most important, these conditions are part of a set of historical processes that appeared long before the Reagan administration came into power in 1980, even as it severely intensifies many of these processes. This summary sets the stage for a better understanding of some of the labor struggles women face in the 1980s–1990s. Here we will discuss six basic areas that help us to understand the above economic and structural conditions and their impact on women's work lives: (1) increased levels of unemployment, (2) renewed increases in "home" work, (3) the internationalization of women's work, (4) intensification of occupational sex segregation, (5) problems of underemployment, and (6) racism in the job market.

Table 2.1. Percent Employed Women Working Year-Round and Full-Time in Each Occupation, 1960 and 1978

| | Percent Employed Women Working Year-Round and Full-Time | |
	1960	1978
Professional-technical	42*	54
Manager-administ.	62	66
Sales	26	26
Clerical	51	51
Craft	57	49
Operatives, including transport	38	44
Nonfarm laborers	32	31
Service (not including private household)	30	28
Private household service	19	12
Farm	9	22
TOTAL	37	44

*42% of all women employed as professional and technical workers worked both full-time and year-round in 1960; therefore, 58% did not.

Source: U.S. Department of Labor, Bureau of Labor Statistics, 1980, Table 19.

WOMEN'S LABOR STRUGGLES IN THE 1980s-1990s

Increased Levels of Unemployment

Of the several major problems confronting women in the 1980s-1990s job market, the first is the threat of severe unemployment. Here we will first mention overall unemployment rates, then go on to elaborate threats to employment, especially from the rationalization of industry.

First, between 1969 (the year before contemporary unemployment rates started to rise) and January 1983, female
unemployment increased from 4.7 percent to 10.0 percent.
For black women, the situation is much worse. Their official unemployment rate increased from 7.8 percent in 1969
to 16.5 percent in 1983 (U.S. Dept. of Labor, Bureau of
Labor Statistics 1980; <u>Monthly Labor Review</u> 1984). Significantly, as the economy goes through periods of "improvements" between recessions, the unemployment rates remain
high in the 1980s. For example, in 1980, considered a
"growth" year, 6.9 percent of all men and 7.4 percent of
all women were unemployed. This is an unemployment rate
for women more than 50 percent higher than the 1969 rates--
and much higher than what has been considered "acceptable"
since World War II.

Second are the dire predictions of job losses in the
low-wage, labor-intensive, female-dominated, service-producing sector of the economy as reindustrialization--begin-
ning with the Carter administration and restructured under
the Reagan administration--has evolved. In this process,
existing services are increasingly automated and newer areas
are restructured. Let us look at some of the predictions.

The largest segment of the employed female population will continue to be clerical and office workers. (Over
50 percent of the 20 million new jobs projected through
1990 will be in white-collar managerial, professional, technical, sales, and clerical categories.) However, these jobs
will represent a smaller proportion of the female labor
force. Numerous reports have warned that the cost of running offices--wages--is taking too much of the corporations'
income because office productivity has not increased. Management has responded by looking to computer-based technologies as the mechanism for rationalizing offices.

The development of low-cost microchip technology
makes rationalization of the office economically feasible.
As office employment and wage costs have soared, the price
of office automation equipment has been falling by about
10 percent per year (Counter Information Services n.d.,
p. 8). As microchips become smaller, even less expensive,
and more reliable, it becomes more attractive to the corporations to buy machines than labor--especially women's
labor.

The microprocessor is, in fact, the basis of the
plan to "reindustrialize" the advanced capitalist world--
clearly something we heard before Reagan but that has

been intensified under "supply side" economics' benefits to private industry, especially large-scale corporations. It is as significant in its implications as was industrialization a century ago. A microprocessor is "a complete computer smaller than a postage stamp usually on a chip of silicon, also called a 'micro-computer' or 'mini-computer.' Microprocessors make it possible to use computers economically for very complex purposes, particularly advanced wordprocessing" ("Race Against Time . . ." 1980, p. 2). Thus, for example, costs of computation on computers have decreased 100,000-fold since 1960. And during the 1970s alone, what cost $10,000 to compute could be achieved for less than $8.00 (Zimmerman 1981).

European estimates of the employment impacts of office automation by 1990 are staggering. In West Germany, Siemens, a high-technology firm, estimates 40 percent of today's office work is suitable for automation, which would result in a permanent reduction of 25–30 percent in the current office labor force. In France, the Nora report to the French Ministry of Industry (1978) predicted a 30 percent loss of jobs for clericals in banking and insurance; and in Great Britain, Curnow and Barron concluded that office automation could lead to 20 percent permanent unemployment in that country. While ten other countries have initiated major studies on the possible effects of office automation, ". . . the US Department of Labor [says it] has no method for calculating the impact of automation on employment projections" ("Race Against Time . . ." 1980, p. 19). However, the Siemens report suggests that of the estimated 3.5 million offices in the United States, 1.5 million are ripe for some form of automation. Moreover, more recent reports in the United States and in Canada predict clerical employment will decline by 27 to 46 percent by 1995–2000 (Moroney 1983; Serrin 1984a).

At a public meeting this author attended in late 1979, representatives from one of the largest banks and one of the biggest insurance companies in the United States proudly announced they were eliminating the bank teller and secretary, respectively, in their companies. The bank representative said that "less boring jobs" would be found for the women, but gave no indication as to where. The insurance representative said women would be tracked into two jobs: word processing operator and word processing administrator. No change in salary was anticipated. However, even when current workers are retained, jobs for

new employees are lost. Citibank reported that the introduction of an automated system in 1,000 offices so far
(with 5,000 more to go) has resulted in "better customer
relations, 50 per cent better productivity, and a 40 per
cent reduction in staff" (as quoted in "Race Against
Time . . ." 1980, pp. 16-17; emphasis added).

Rationalization of offices threatens women's jobs.
Simultaneously it cheapens women's wages. Thus, rationalization of women's clerical and office work can lead not
only to massive female unemployment but also to further
difficulties of women being able to care for themselves and
their families.

Renewed Increases in "Home" Work

A second problem facing women in the job market of
the 1980s-1990s is that of employer reductions in the number of hours of paid employment.

We have already indicated how profitable women's
part-time work in the service sector is for corporations.
Home work also is appealing to married women because of
the lack of child care services available to employed women.

In the recent past, there have been attempts to increase the amount of work done by women in their homes--
and not only in traditional types of jobs like sewing and
knitting. Rather, there has been a rise in home work in
banking, insurance, telecommunications, and computer work
(see Zimmerman 1981; "Race Against Time . . ." 1980; an
optimistic view of this trend is presented in the futuristic
predictions by Alvin Toffler in his popular book The Third
Wave [New York: Bantam, 1980]). In fact, in 1981 a
long-standing ban on all industrial work at home was
lifted by the Reagan administration, especially for knitters
in rural parts of the country. The goal of this legislation was to extend it to all types of work, including female
clerical, office, and service jobs (Shabecoff 1981; "Home
Knitters' Victory Reported" 1981).

Such a move can greatly cut costs for companies:
workers are paid for exactly the amount of work they do--
on a piece rate basis; employers need not pay for office
space--it comes out of the employee's rent. And since most
of these workers are not considered full-time, they do not
get fringe benefits. They must pay for their own terminals,
paper, and phone bills. And if any of the equipment

breaks down, the worker not only loses hours of work but also must pay the cost of repairs (Pollack 1981). Most important, this practice is being instituted at a time when office workers are organizing--but it is very difficult to organize isolated women working in their own homes.

Christensen (1985) summarizes several studies on home work. They reveal that women prefer to work at home, mainly to care for their children, rather than not to work at all. However, home-based work is <u>not</u> ideal, according to the women. Christensen continues: "When women work at home as a way of balancing work and family they report feeling socially isolated and stressed; if they are professionals, they feel they are sacrificing their careers" (p. 57). Further, while home-based clerical workers continue to care for their children themselves (whether because they cannot afford other arrangements or because the structure of their work allows them to do so), professional women are more likely to use supplemental child care.

Finally, one set of experts on home-based care report that whatever the occupational status of the home-based worker, men working at home are far less likely to be responsible for child care than are women working at home (Johnson and Johnson 1984). Working at home is a way of combining income-producing activities with child care--for women only. It appears to provide the much-sought "flexibility" for men rather than for married women and mothers with children.

The Internationalization of Women's Labor

The third area of labor struggles for women in the 1980s-1990s has to do with understanding the international division of labor and how women in particular are affected by this phenomenon. When we discuss the problems that U.S. women face in the labor market today, there is a tendency to ignore the place of the U.S. market in the context of the world economy. We know that although multinational corporations began growing in the 1950s, it was not until the 1960s and 1970s that there was an increased employment of Third World women in particular (see Nash and Fernandez-Kelly 1983). Benería and Roldan (1987) argue that this occurred because of the increasing segmentation and fragmentation of the labor process since

1960. This allowed capital to send abroad the more labor-intensive stages of the production process—facilitated particularly by the lowering of transportation costs, at least until very recently. For example, it is cheaper to fly data from the United States to Mexico and the West Indies and back for keypunching than to do this part of the process in the United States (Elson and Pearson 1980).

Women have increasingly been brought into this labor process because of their incredibly cheap wages in Third World countries, and because of the short-term contracts given to them, which allow international capital to pick up and leave virtually whenever it wants. The women who are employed in Third World countries are overwhelmingly young. Many are riddled with health problems by the time they reach age 25—for instance, in the semiconductor industry, women who assemble and connect microchips under microscopes lose much of their vision by that age (Grossman 1979; Elson and Pearson 1980; Ehrenreich and Fuentes 1981).

The world economic crisis affects these women greatly, and must therefore be key in the understanding of the problems facing women in the U.S. labor force today. In 1974, with the fall in world demand leading to massive employment cutbacks in many world market factories, one-third of all electronics workers in Singapore, almost all women, lost their jobs (Grossman 1979). More threatening today, however, is the possibility that many women (and men) in Third World countries will lose their jobs to the new, improved, more rationalized, and more competitive jobs of a reindustrialized U.S. economy. Thus, Elson and Pearson (1980) argue

> there is still the possibility of a resurgence of competition from firms located in developed countries. The very success of world market factories has made them vulnerable to retaliation. So far this has mainly taken the form of the growth of restrictions on imports of manufactures, particularly of consumer goods like textiles, garments and shoes. More recently, there have been signs of fresh attempts to revolutionize the production process in developed countries, to eliminate the advantage which cheap labour gives to world factories

in the production of labour intensive goods
(p. 30).

With high unemployment rates created in part by
the increasing rationalization processes in the United States,
it is not impossible that racist U.S. policies will channel
employment to people in the First World at the expense of
people in Third World countries—so long as there is this
cheapening of labor in the United States, too. In fact,
argues Joan Hoffman (personal communication 1982), the internationalization of the division of labor under capitalism
has been a major force in the weakening of U.S. unions and
a significant lowering of the social wage for both men and
women workers.

Intensified Occupational Sex Segregation

A fourth area of real concern for women in the
1980s–1990s is sex segregation and patriarchal relations in
the job market.
Patriarchal relations are defined here as the relationship of women to men as a group, and how women either
suffer more than men workers or are used and treated as
threats to men's labor. Let us begin by saying that we
usually talk about the patriarchal nature of the labor market when we talk about men and women's labor (see Sokoloff
1980, 1982). By this we mean that the work women do in
the market benefits men materially and ideologically: Because women are more likely to work in low-paying, low-
status, less powerful jobs, men generally are freed to work
in the higher-paying, more prestigious, stable, and powerful
jobs relative to the women of their socioeconomic class.
Likewise, since women are treated as "secondary" workers
in wage labor, it is still women who are structurally and
emotionally encouraged to devote their time to child care
and housework, thereby freeing men from so many of these
wageless and devalued activities and responsibilities.
This, however, is a contradictory process. On the
one hand, because of patriarchal dominance in the market,
men get higher wages and better jobs than women. However, none of the estimated $63 billion to $109 billion that
women would have received if they had been paid wages
equal to those of men in the same occupational categories
went to individual male workers (Blakkan 1971). It went,

instead, to the capitalist class--who often used these mon-
ies in explicit attempts to control workers. So while men
get more benefits and higher wages than women, capital's
ability to keep women's wages down acts, on some levels,
to depress men's wages, too. Likewise, men's jobs have
also become degraded and deskilled over time, though not
as much as women's, according to Dubnoff (1979). Moreover, the economic crises of the 1970s and 1980s have dealt
a severe blow to many relatively more protected male workers in heavy industry. After periods of high unemployment, many of these men have had to take jobs with far
less income and benefits even though they still average
higher wages than women ("Displaced Workers . . ." 1985).
On the one hand, men as a group are better off than
women; on the other hand, most men's jobs suffer, too.

In attempts to protect themselves from the long-term
negative effects on their jobs, men often wrongly blame
women--instead of the changing capitalist system--for many
of their problems. However, it is generally not women who
"take jobs away" from men. (For a comparison of the Depression with contemporary economic crises, see Sokoloff
1984.)

Within this context, the problems of occupational
sex segregation can be understood. First, men and women
do not work in the same jobs: they are employed in sex-
segregated job markets that have remained rather stable
throughout the 20th century. Between 1900 and 1970, the
Index of Sex Segregation varied only between .66 and .69
(Gross 1971; Blau and Hendricks 1979). In 1980, the index
was about .60; that is, about six out of ten employed
women (or men) would have to change jobs for men and
women to be working in the same kinds of jobs (Beller
1984; Bianchi and Rytina 1984). Of course, this is not
happening and there are no such predictions in the near
future (see Blau and Hendricks 1979; Bianchi and Rytina
1984; for a review of the sex segregation literature, see
Reskin and Hartmann 1986; Sokoloff 1986).[5] Further, because of the sex-segregated nature of the labor market,
women are primarily a reserve of labor for women's jobs
on the whole, not for men's (see Milkman 1976). (For
further evaluation of this problem and some of its complexities, see Sokoloff 1980, ch. 3; 1984.)

Next, in the rationalization process, women are
often used by men as scapegoats for capital. It is important for men to begin to understand this and fight

against the white-male capitalist class from rationalizing labor in a way detrimental to workers, rather than attacking or blaming women workers. If they do not, everyone-- men as well as women--will lose out. As an example, Hacker (1979) shows how women, who were trying to break down barriers of sex segregation, were blamed by male workers for the loss of their craft jobs at AT&T under an affirmative action order begun in 1972. However, according to Hacker's evidence, the industry knowingly recruited the women into these typically male craft jobs because these jobs were scheduled to be automated out of existence. So as women learned to climb poles, AT&T shifted to micro- wave and laser (fiber optic) transmission systems; as women learned to install phones, "clip and take" customer installations and phone stores appeared. And where women made their strongest inroads into male protected jobs, in the semiskilled and crafts position of frame work, these jobs became slated for total automation in the near future. Thus, women were blamed for taking away men's jobs through affirmative action, causing great bitterness among the male workers, but were quickly eliminated--along with the men--by the new technology. Everyone lost. Ironical- ly, many more men than women gained jobs through these new technological and social arrangements during a period of intensive affirmative action--women lost even more than men![6]

Despite these setbacks, affirmative action has been found to be instrumental in opening up jobs previously denied to women and racial/ethnic minority men.[7] Within this context, one final example of the struggles centering on intensified occupational sex segregation that women will have to deal with in the 1980s and 1990s is the channel- ing of women away from jobs that were just beginning to open up through hard-fought affirmative action suits, and back to traditional women's work. This is equally true in terms of high-status male professions in white-collar work as it is in high-status craft jobs in blue-collar work. In the first instance, ever since the late 1970s, we have been warned that a "glut" of lawyers (Barbanel 1980) and physicians (Rheinhold 1980) means that we need to discourage men and women from entering these fields. But at the same time, we are being told that after a decline in jobs available in teaching and nursing, there is in the 1980s a "shortage" in these two areas (Watkins 1981; Maeroff 1980; Span 1981). Under such conditions, and with a tight economy, it is very possible women will be more likely to seek training in the more available traditional female professions. This might well lead to accusations that, to the degree women do not enter male-dominated professions or their more prestigious and demanding specialties, women will be blamed for not wanting to prepare for them. The problem, however, is not women's motivations so much as the structure and organization of work that needs to be changed.

With regard to blue-collar craft jobs, women (and their fetuses) are said to be "protected" from occupational hazards by excluding them from higher-paying "heavy" industrial jobs. This process protects neither men nor women adequately while it channels women away from better, and into lower-status, lower-paying, ghettoized female, jobs (Carlton n.d.; Evanoff 1979). This is happening as industrial jobs for men fail to increase. Ironically, women are said to be "protected" from the hazards of the better-paying male-dominated jobs—but there is rarely a cry to "protect" women from the lower-paying, traditional female jobs filled with severe hazards and risks to them and their children—a classic example of which is nursing (Chavkin 1979).

Problems of Underemployment

Fifth are problems of underemployment of women in addition to the increased loss of jobs.

Let us look at one group of women in our society (college graduates) to see how problems of underemployment, as well as threats of unemployment and serious cutbacks, affect them (and other women).

Approximately half of both women college graduates and women Ph.D.s in the 1980s are expected to be employed in jobs that are not commensurate with their years of training (Rosenbaum 1979; Jaffee and Froomkin 1978). For college graduates, one study showed that in the 1960s, 73 percent of all college graduates obtained professional and technical jobs. But during the 1970s, this dropped to less than half of all college graduates (46 percent) (S. Brown 1979). For the women in particular, this had a twofold effect: a large number of women college graduates had to take jobs as clerical workers—thereby underemploying the better-educated women and unemploying many of the less-educated women. One researcher argues:

> By 1980, a greater proportion of young
> female college graduates·were working in
> clerical jobs than 20 years earlier. . . .
> While the 1960's had improved opportunities
> for women, declining opportunities in the
> 1970's all but eliminated those gains.
>   Over all, female college graduates in
> 1980 were worse off than graduates in
> 1960. (Rumberger, as quoted in Magarrell
> 1983, p. 12; see also Rumberger 1981, 1983)

During the 1970s, these changes were said to occur because as more women got an education (as they were told to do), there was a decrease in the traditional jobs available to women college graduates (elementary school teachers and nurses) without a sufficient opening up of jobs for women in traditionally male professions to absorb these excess female college graduates (Jaffee and Froomkin 1978; Patterson and Engelberg 1978). This is in part because, as Montagna (1977) explains, there has not been so much an increase in professional service jobs as an increase in the health-education-research-government service-producing sector of the economy. It is this increase that has led to a greater number of professional and technical jobs in the service industries as much as any general increase in high-level jobs.[8]

In addition, title inflation has hurt women. Many women college graduates received such job titles as "ad= ministrative assistant"--with little or no difference in tasks, training, and rewards from clerical workers, and with hardly any mobility possibilities. Men college graduates, in contrast, as administrative assistants were placed in entry-level management positions (Ronnie Steinberg personal communication, 1986).

Further, it is very important to remember that professional and managerial women have been heavily employed not by private industry but by government. Thus, between 1960 and the mid-1970s, Erie and Brackman (n.d.) report, the federally subsidized expanding human services industry accounted for 62 percent of all professional and managerial job gains for white women and 79 percent for black women. (The respective figures for white men were 28 percent and for black men 37 percent.) And during the 1970s, the bulk (nearly two-thirds) of professional and managerial women still worked in the publicly supported human services sector.

This all happened prior to the Reagan administration. With huge decreases in expenditures for services and government workers by the Reagan administration, a severe blow to women professional and technical workers has been dealt.

But poorer and less-educated women lower down the occupational hierarchy also have been severely hit: these women are losing their jobs—both inside and outside government, being pushed out of government-funded job programs (such as CETA and WIN), and becoming unable to receive such basic services as welfare, subsidized housing, and food stamp benefits. Thus, the loss of government-funded services often means the loss of employment for better-off professional women along with the loss of basic and essential services, as well as jobs, for poorer, non-professional, and minority women.

Racism in the Job Market

While we are trying to better understand women's struggles in the 1980s and 1990s, how these problems intensify for women of color is of major concern. Problems of racism faced specifically by women of color in the U.S. labor market is the sixth and final issue addressed.

It was only in the 1970s that significantly more black women were employed in clerical work than in private household work (Aldridge 1975; U.S. Dept. of Labor, Bureau of Labor Statistics 1980). For example, in 1979, 29 percent of all employed black women worked in clerical jobs and only 8 percent in private household jobs. However, as recently as 1970, as many black women were employed in private household work (19 percent) as in clerical work (19 percent), with the largest place of black female employment in low-level service work (29 percent in 1970 and 27 percent in 1979). Black women are finally moving into traditional white-collar "female" jobs just as these jobs become increasingly threatened with automation! (See "Increased Levels of Unemployment," above.)

Likewise, the struggle for black women to obtain professional and technical jobs is reflected in comparing their representation with that of white women. Between 1910 and 1979, white professional women increased from 12 percent to 16 percent of all white female employees—white women's level has been relatively high and stable. Black

professional women increased from 2 percent to 13 percent
of all black female employees over the course of the 20th
century (Aldridge 1975; U.S. Dept. of Labor, Bureau of
Labor Statistics 1980).

Now that black women's professional representation
is relatively more equal to that of white women, the
threats of government cutbacks seriously affect them.
Moreover, most of these black women are employed in traditional female professions or semiprofessions—such as
teaching, nursing, social work, and library work—very
often in black communities (see Higginbotham 1983, 1987).
In 1970, only 2 percent of all black women employed in
private industry worked as professionals, but 34 percent
of all black women employed by the government did so
(Shea et al. 1970). By 1980, reports Higginbotham (1987),
using a different statistic, little had changed: two-thirds
of all black professional and managerial women are employed in the public sector. The few who found themselves
in the highest-level "male" professions are likewise more
likely to be employed in government, and therefore are
subject to budget cuts just like women in typical female
professions (Higginbotham 1987). Finally, by the late
1970s, racial/ethnic people were already experiencing a
decline in enrollments in graduate and professional schools
(Hechinger 1980; Sullivan 1982).

In addition, the genuine gains of black women and
greater occupational similarity between black and white
women obscure several continuing structural and economic
differences: one is the racial stratification between black
and white women; another is the economic differences between the two groups. In the first case, Malveaux (1981)
sums up the problem thus: "The difference between black
and white women . . . is that black women work in the
bottom strata of those [female] stratified jobs" (p. 43).
Several studies have shown black women are employed lower
on the occupational hierarchy than are white women in
domestic service work (Douglas 1980), clerical work (Douglas 1980; Malveaux 1981), nursing (Cannings and Lazonick
1975), and management (Malveaux 1981, 1984). In addition,
Higginbotham (1987) found black professional and managerial women were racially restricted not only to the public
sector but also to serving mainly black clients, who are
generally poor and working-class.

In terms of incomes, black women have improved
enormously. They have become much more equal to white

women: between 1960 and 1980 black women increased
from making 62 percent of what white women make to 93
percent (Amott 1985).   However, white women are an economically disadvantaged group in U.S. society, making
only about 60 percent of what white males have made at
year-round, full-time employment.   In addition, black
women's recent parity in income has been found to be due,
in large part, to the fact that black women have worked more
than white women.   For example, black women are likely
to have been in the labor force for a longer period of
time than white women, to work more hours, and to work
full-time, as well as full-time, full-year (see P. Wallace
1980; Malveaux 1985).

In addition, Amott (1985) argues for measuring economic standing not by individual incomes alone but by
family incomes, since most people live in families.   By
this measure, the economic condition of the black community, including its women, has not improved nearly as
much as the data on individual women's incomes would indicate.   Amott finds that while black family incomes improved between 1960 (when they were 55 percent of white
family incomes) and 1975 (when they were 62 percent of
white incomes), by 1982 they were back down to where
they were in 1960.

The greater economic parity of black and white
women is also questioned when one looks at poverty rates.
In 1982, over one-third of black Americans, and half of
black families headed by women, lived in poverty.   And
poverty rates are much higher for black women than for
white women.   In 1981, over 61 percent of unmarried black
women supporting two children lived in poverty, compared
with about 40 percent of white women in similar family
structures.   "The key to this greater risk of poverty [in
black families] can be found in the different and changing
family structures in black and white communities and in
the high unemployment faced by black men, women, and
youth" (Amott 1985, p. 7).

THE REAGAN ADMINISTRATION AND
AFFIRMATIVE ACTION

Up to this point we have looked at both long-term
structural trends, and concerns and issues women must
face during the 1980s and 1990s as more conservative

policies have impacted on these trends. Here we will discuss specific policies of the Reagan administration that
have undermined many positive changes that groups had
fought for prior to this administration, thereby intensify-
ing women's labor struggles as well as resistances to
those policies.

Some feminist critics have argued that what has
happened to women under the Reagan administration is not
so much a policy directed against women as it is part of
an overall attempt to restructure the economy in the face
of persistent economic crisis (Power 1984; Jayne Dean personal communication, 1983). They demonstrate that poor
and minority women in particular are disproportionately
hurt by these policies. Thus, attacks on women are said
to be primarily due to the "particular positions women fill
in the U.S. economy, rather than the result of a conscious,
coherent position on women by the Reagan administration"
(Power 1984, p. 32).

Other feminist critics argue that the Reagan administration has tried to "stabilize patriarchy as much as it
tries to fight inflation and stabilize capitalism" and that
"the politics of society is as self-consciously directed to
maintaining the hierarchical male-dominated sexual system
as to upholding the economic class structure" (Z. Eisenstein 1982, pp. 585-586). In both cases, the specific policies of the Reagan administration are distinguished from
the long-term structural trends. These policies--whether
directly or indirectly, whether consciously or unconscious-
ly--have impacted on women's lives, creating inordinate
hardships for them--as a group, as well as differentially
for women of different racial/ethnic and class groups.
(For a list of policies specifically pursued during the
Reagan administration that tried to take away earlier
gains, particularly of women, see note 1.) The policies of
the Reagan administration provide political, economic, and
ideological support for capital and the "free" market, for
weakening the power of labor and redistributing profits
toward the rich, for patriarchal and racist systems of social relations and control in the home as well as in the
market.

Thus, under Reagan, each of the labor market struggles women faced because of the broad economic trends mentioned earlier intensified. Because of space limitations,
we will focus on only one set of policies affected by the
overall economic program of the Reagan administration:

those of affirmative action. Affirmative action is one of
the many important policies influencing women's socially
and economically disadvantaged position in the job market.[9]
Under Reagan, the increasing offensive against women and
racial/ethnic minorities is exemplified by the movement of
the federal government away from affirmative action. Affirmative action is a policy primarily developed by black
civil rights and women's movement activists to prevent employers, including the federal government and its contractors, from discriminating against women, blacks, Hispanics,
and other racial/ethnic minorities. Further, it requires
employers to take affirmative action to ensure more equitable treatment of women and minorities in hiring, recruitment, training, and upgrading of workers. (See Reskin
and Hartmann 1986, ch. 4, for a summary of affirmative
action laws and regulations.)

Affirmative action created some important opportunities for women and minorities in education and work. In
fact, to whatever degree occupational sex and race segregation declined, much of that decline, it has been argued,
can be attributed to affirmative action (Pear 1983a; see
also note 7). However, this policy was weakened during
the later years of the Carter administration and was
directly attacked by the Reagan administration as "reverse
discrimination." As a result, far less decline in occupational sex segregation has been predicted for the 1980s
(Beller 1984).

By 1983, Reagan had fired commissioners who sharp-
ly criticized his civil rights policies and had reconstituted
the U.S. Commission on Civil Rights to represent the position that civil rights should be narrowed to "legal and
political rights while excluding social and economic claims"
(Pear 1985b). "Equality of opportunity--a fair shake" for
everyone (which does not take historical discrimination
into account)--is to replace attempts at defining civil
rights in terms of the opportunity for "equality of results--
a fair share" for all groups, according to Morris Abrams,
one of Reagan's appointees to the Civil Rights Commission.

Reagan-appointed top officials, such as attorneys
general William French Smith and Edwin Meese, as well as
William Bradford Reynolds, director of the Justice Department's Civil Rights Division, have actively campaigned
against civil rights and affirmative action legislation (see
S. Taylor 1986). They have proposed eliminating all federal requirements for numerical hiring goals and Labor

Department regulations under which those contracting with the government must strive to hire and promote women, blacks, Hispanics, and other historically discriminated-against minorities, in rough proportion to the numbers of available qualified candidates in a given labor market (see Power 1984 for discussion of affirmative action policies under Reagan; see also Shennon 1985 for more recent attacks).

They have twisted the meaning of affirmative action legislation by denying, in particular, the historical and structurally embedded systems of racism and sexism. Their argument has been that "true" fairness in hiring exists only when race and sex are ignored altogether—not by giving preferential treatment to equally qualified women and racial/ethnic minorities over white males. The difficulty with the Reagan administration's position is articulated by Mary Frances Berry, a member of the Civil Rights Commission and a staunch critic of Reagan's affirmative action policies: "'Civil Rights laws were not passed to give civil rights protection to all Americans,' but rather out of a recognition that 'some Americans already had protection because they belonged to a favored group,' while minorities and women were confined to 'disadvantaged groups'" (quoted in Marable 1986, p. 2).

Statistical evidence of job discrimination in lawsuits was deemed unacceptable by the Reagan administration. Rather, to prove discrimination, employer intent had to be explicitly shown, and its direction against a particular individual evidenced, almost impossible tasks today. Not only did the Reagan administration change the rules on how to define civil rights and discrimination; the Justice Department actually aligned itself with white male employees against women and minorities to claim affirmative action plans were discriminatory against the white men in those very companies and agencies that the federal government, under earlier administrations, had said discriminated against women and/or minorities, and for whom affirmative action plans had been required (Davidson and Watkins 1985; Pear 1985a).

While many more issues and much more evidence could be amassed to demonstrate Reagan's attempts to destroy affirmative action, suffice it to say that the message given throughout his term of office has come through loud and clear to the business community: "they needn't worry too much about hiring women and minorities, and . . .

they can even ignore laws that are on the books" (Power 1984, p. 44).

Many groups have resisted these harmful policies. For example, in 1984 the Supreme Court ruling in the Grove City College case narrowed federal law prohibiting sex discrimination in educational institutions receiving federal financial assistance. Immediately after that ruling a group emerged to resist it. A coalition of civil rights groups has fought for the restoration of anti-discrimination enforcement powers through the Civil Rights Restoration Act (Williams 1986a). County officials, state and local governments, and certain businesses have opposed proposed changes in the presidential order under which federal contractors would be required to set numerical goals for hiring women and racial/ethnic minorities (Williams 1986b; Fisher 1985).[10]

Resistance to a wide variety of policies of the Reagan administration that negatively impact on women's employment has been active in many cases. This has been true in such areas as affirmative action policies for women and racial/ethnic minorities, equitable pay for women and minorities working in jobs of comparable worth, women's rights to abortion and control over their bodies, cutbacks proposed by the Reagan administration in provisions for welfare and food stamps, and voting rights for black citizens. It is to a few such examples of resistance that we now turn.

RESISTANCE TO CONTEMPORARY CONSERVATIVE POLICIES

We conclude this chapter by suggesting that while differences between groups of people (women vs. men, racial/ethnic minority women vs. white women, poor and working-class women vs. professional and managerial women) are very real and always in need of direct attention (see Malveaux 1985; Dill 1983; Power 1984), there is a compelling need for us also to identify our common interests and work together to pursue them. All too often, groups of people tend to see their own interests as quite divergent from those of other groups. In times of economic and political crises, in particular, groups can easily be turned against one another when, in fact, they often have much in common. In the final section of this chapter we hope to provide some bases for development of more unified responses to economic crises that challenge sex, race, and class hierarchies and divisions in our society by exploring collective acts of resistance to the destructive policies of the Reagan administration.

To begin, women in the 1980s job market are joining together and resisting by organizing unions as well as by developing professional associations that fight for the rights of those workers who often are said not to need such protections. In the first case, office workers at Yale and Columbia universities went out on strike against their employers to win better treatment and fairer wages for the predominantly women office workers, many of whom were women of color (see Geron 1986); in the second case, both unionized and non-unionized nurses have begun to organize, as have human service workers (such as AFSCME), to protect their jobs and prevent further deterioration of services to the public. Nurses' associations have sponsored lobbying days for their members in pursuit of their goals and of raising both nurses' and legislators' consciousnesses (E. Taylor 1983). And even within conservative teachers' unions, which have failed many women workers, rank-and-file members are organizing to seriously challenge the entrenched ways of certain unions that do not work effectively in the members' interests. Further, there are numerous progressive organizations of predominantly female professions, such as the Radical Alliance of Social Workers, continually working to roll back the destructive actions of the Reagan policies as they affect both workers and the general public.

On another level, support systems for women emerge on particular job sites around specific issues that are used to organize the women as well as to increase their knowledge about these issues. Thus, on the issues of sexual harassment (see Carothers and Crull 1984), and occupational health and safety (see Chavkin 1984), women have demonstrated, agitated, and organized for personal and legal changes. Not only women's groups within a particular industry, but often unions in these industries, work toward eliminating sex discrimination in the work place so it will be a safer place for female employment.

In addition, each year when the Reagan administration's budget appears, the Women's Research and Education Institute does an analysis of the disproportionate impact these budgets have on women, and how this affects women of different economic and racial/ethnic backgrounds. At

one point in the early 1980s, a group of 50 women's organizations collectively organized to oppose the cutbacks
in the Reagan budget and its emphasis on the military
buildup as damaging to women throughout the country.

Even in the mid-1980s, when the Reagan administration policies have intensified the hardships for women,
working people, and people of color, a "blue ribbon panel"
at Yale University proposed a federally supported policy
on the availability of mandatory leaves for childbirth and
infant care, income replacement for wages that would have
been earned, and continuation of employee benefits and job
security during childbirth leaves. Behind this recommen-
dation is, according to Dr. T. Berry Brazelton—a pedia-
trician and member of the panel—"a grass roots movement
among parents that no one can resist" (Brozan 1985).

Finally, just as the oppressive forces of the Reagan
administration came into power in the 1980s, women, minority, union, and other groups intensified their efforts to
establish the principles of pay equity. Pay equity, or
comparable worth, has been described as "the women's issue of the 1980s." By 1985 some 131 school districts,
towns, cities, counties, states, agencies, and universities
had taken steps toward implementing pay equity. Even
"[t]he federal government, over the Administration's objec-
tions but at Congressional insistence, may also reexamine
its policies to see if discrimination exists. Companies in
the private sector, too, have acted" (Delatiner 1985, p. 25).
While pay equity is most typically talked about in terms
of greater equality for women, it is also essential to eliminating racial disparities (see Steinberg and Haignere
1987; see also note 9). Agitation and organization by
these groups has led some states and municipalities to be
ordered by the courts to establish equitable pay schemes
(for instance, Washington state), while others have voluntarily established such systems. For example, the state
of Minnesota voluntarily instituted a major pay equity
scheme for state employees. It went even further by man-
dating local governments to develop similar programs, which
must be submitted to the state for approval. Even Reagan's
home state of California has had two important comparable
worth decisions: most recently in Los Angeles (1985), and
earlier (in 1982) in San Jose (Yoshihashi 1985).

To be sure, employed women have been more effective in organizing around certain social issues embedded
in many of the long-term structural trends in U.S. society.

Questions of comparable worth, sex segregation in occupations, and cutbacks by the Reagan administration in social services appear to have been most salient in women's consciousness and in some organized actions. On the other hand, problems of racial inequality and the international exploitation of women workers (including questions of competition and tariffs in the textile and shoe industries most recently) have been more difficult to respond to for the majority of U.S. workers (particularly nonracial/ethnic minority men and women). All these areas require organized action involving varied groups of people, and better understanding of the meaning and impact of broader structural and economic trends, as well as the particular consequences of the Reagan administration's actions, if we are to better the working conditions of all women, racial/ethnic groups, and classes of people.

NOTES

1. Early on, it was clear what the Reagan administration was trying to take away from women. It included legislation that would severely hamper or eliminate the Equal Employment Opportunities Commission, the Pregnancy Discrimination Act, the Women's Educational Equity Act, the Vocational Educational Amendments (with far-reaching sex equity provisions), Title IX and all kinds of affirmative action rulings, women's right to control their own bodies (through attempts to eliminate women's right to abortion and increasingly to abuse women by sterilizing them, and through the Human Life Bill and Amendment), our right to teach children with nonsexist and nonracist materials (through the Laxalt Bill and the Family Protection Act), along with basic provisions in welfare, CETA jobs, food stamps, busing for integration and quality education, and the Voting Rights Act for black citizens (see Fields 1981a, 1981b; Stuart 1981; "New Congress . . ." 1981; Women Employed Advocates 1981, 1982; Huber 1981; Women's Research and Education Institute 1981; see also the following complete issues of Spokeswoman: January-April and December 1981).

2. A striking example of this process is given in an analysis of women's employment in traditional high-status male professions (physicians, lawyers, and college professors) by Carter and Carter (1981). Using a socio-

historical framework, they conclude that women have made gains in these professions only as the nature of work in them has become more routinized, they have less power and prestige, and more limited control is exerted over the profession by its members and their associations. They suggest that there has developed a split in the professions between (1) prestige jobs with good pay, autonomy, and opportunities for growth and development, and (2) a new class of more routinized, poorly paid jobs with little autonomy and no connections via promotion ladders to prestige jobs in the profession itself. It is precisely in these new, more routinized jobs that women are overwhelmingly concentrated. Carter and Carter conclude: "Women's entry into the professions should be seen as something of a hollow victory: women will make gains, but the 'professional' jobs they enter will be such in name only" (p. 478; see also Serrin 1984b; Reskin and Hartmann 1986; Sokoloff 1986, 1987; Reskin and Roos 1987).

3. The fact that men have been increasingly represented at higher levels (often newly created through the routinization process) of both lower- and higher-status "female" occupations is documented for clerical and office work (Feldberg and Glenn 1979a, 1980), the communications industry (Hacker 1979), the banking industry (Shanahan 1976), the insurance industry (Feldberg and Glenn 1980), and the data processing industry (Greenbaum 1979) in the United States, as well as in a variety of industries in England (Phillips and Taylor 1980). On how men benefit from this process, see Sokoloff (1980, 1982).

4. Clearly, many women have increasingly wanted part-time work so they can combine paid employment with their family responsibilities. (Who else will assume them?) However, when women want full-time and/or year-round employment, it is usually not available. For example, fully three-fourths of all unemployed women want full-time work but cannot find it (U.S. Dept. of Labor, Bureau of Labor Statistics 1980).

5. While the largest decline in the sex segregation index did occur in the 1970s—about ten percentage points—the prediction for the 1980s is for a lower decline, estimated at between two and eight percentage points. This is consistent with other variations in the index over the 20th century, where such limited decreases and increases occur each decade (see Sokoloff 1986; Reskin and Hartmann 1986).

6. According to Hacker (1979), overall, more men (16,300) gained formerly women's work than women (9,400) gained formerly men's work during the three years of affirmative action studies (1972-1975). Thus, despite the fact that the women's jobs may have been of poorer quality than the men's jobs that were eliminated, planned technological change eliminated more jobs for women than affirmative action provided.

7. Even in a newspaper account of unpublished studies conducted by the Reagan administration, the Department of Labor concluded that "affirmative action of the type criticized by President Reagan has been highly effective in promoting the employment [and upward mobility] of blacks, women and Hispanic people" (Pear 1983a, p. 16). Accordingly, the Labor Department study of 77,000 businesses between 1974 and 1980 found minority employment grew 20.1 percent in companies covered by affirmative action requirements but by only 12.3 percent where no government contractors were involved. For women, the figures were 15.2 and 2.2 percent, respectively. Moreover, with affirmative action programs, black "officials and managers" increased 96 percent, while women in that category rose by 73 percent and white men by only 6 percent. In companies without affirmative action programs, blacks and women in high-level jobs also increased, but not as much: 50 percent for blacks, 36 percent for women, and 7 percent for white men (Thornton 1983).

8. The number of professional/technical jobs increased greatly during the 1970s, as did women's relative representation in male-dominated professions (see Herbers 1983; Sokoloff 1987). However, in 1980, white males still overwhelmingly dominated traditional male professions, to the tune of 85 to 90 percent. Moreover, the evidence strongly suggests that women are neither recruited into the higher levels or specialties of these professions nor allowed to advance to them (see Carter and Carter 1981; Reskin and Hartmann 1986).

9. According to one expert (Roslyn Feldberg personal communication, 1986), affirmative action and comparable worth should be seen as necessary companions if we hope to improve the work lives of all women. Affirmative action directs itself to the entrance of women and racial/ethnic minorities into sex- and race-segregated occupations and industries. Comparable worth addresses itself to the issue of equitable treatment and pay for the vast majority

of women already employed in lower-paid, primarily female-dominated occupations (see Treiman and Hartmann 1981). Feldberg suggests that sometimes black women see affirmative action as more important to their cause: it not only helps them enter male-dominated jobs from which women have been excluded; it also allows them access to employment and promotions in jobs traditionally held by white women. Comparable worth, in contrast, is sometimes seen as more important to white women, since the vast majority of women—the "80 percent"—are employed in jobs where women are concentrated. Improving these jobs, therefore, would affect a larger proportion of women. However, it should be clear that both avenues are important for women of color and for white women: not only is access to male-dominated jobs important to white women, but pay equity is increasingly important to black and other minority women who have paralleled white women's occupational experiences since about 1970. Again, there is a tremendous need for black and white women to work together to change the system, as well as to focus on their differences.

10. Some of these organizations, like big businesses, have very mixed motives in supporting affirmative action. For example, if the administration's attempt to make goals and timetables (even voluntary ones) illegal wins, ". . . the immediate effects will include badly impaired morale among women, blacks, and Hispanics. The longer-term effects will almost certainly include a big increase in litigation as employees who considered themselves discriminated against [primarily white males] turn to the famous Title VII. Under Title VII, preference is legal as a remedy for a person who has been discriminated against as an individual" (Fisher 1985, p. 30; see also Pear 1983b).

3

Racial Ethnic Women's Labor: The Intersection of Race, Gender, and Class Oppression

Evelyn Nakano Glenn

The failure of the feminist movement to address the concerns of black, Hispanic, and Asian-American women is currently engendering widespread discussion in white women's organizations. Paralleling this discussion is a growing interest among racial ethnic[1] women in articulating aspects of their experiences that have been ignored in feminist analyses of women's oppression (for instance, oral histories by Elasser, MacKenzie, and Tixier y Vigil 1980; Kim 1983; Sterling 1979; and social and historical studies by Mirande and Enriquez 1979; Hooks 1981; Davis 1981; Dill 1979; Jones 1984).

As an initial corrective, racial ethnic scholars have begun research on racial ethnic women in relation to employment, the family, and the ethnic community, both historically and contemporarily (Mora and Del Castillo 1980; M. Melville 1980; Rodgers-Rose 1980; Acosta-Belen 1979; Tsuchida 1982). The most interesting of these studies de-

This paper grew out of studying with members of the Inter-University Group Researching the Intersection of Race and Gender: Bonnie Dill, Cheryl Gilkes, Elizabeth Higginbotham, and Ruth Zambrana. I am also grateful to members of the Women and Work Study Group for their contributions to my thinking. Finally, I thank Nancy Breen, Gary Dymski, Betsy Jameson, Bill James, and Laurie Nisonoff for their careful critiques. An early version was presented at the meetings of the American Association for the Advancement of Science, Washington, D.C., January 1982.

scribe the social world and day-to-day struggles of racial
ethnic women, making visible what has up to now been invisible in the social sciences and humanities. These concrete data constitute the first step toward understanding
the effects of race and gender oppression in the lives of
racial ethnic women.

A necessary next step is the development of theoretical and conceptual frameworks for analyzing the interaction of race and gender stratification. Separate models
exist for analyzing race, ethnic, or gender stratification.
Although the "double" (race, gender) and "triple" (race,
gender, class) oppressions of racial ethnic women are widely acknowledged, no satisfactory theory has been developed
to analyze what happens when these systems of oppression
intersect. A starting point for developing such a theory
would appear to lie in those models which view race and
gender stratification as part of a larger system of insti-
tutionalized inequality. During the 1970s two models that
view race and gender divisions as embedded in, and helping to maintain, an overall system of class exploitation
came to the fore: the patriarchy model developed by Marxist feminists to explain the subordination of women (H.
Hartmann 1981b; Weinbaum and Bridges 1979; C. Brown
1981; Sokoloff 1980) and the internal colonialism model developed by activists and scholars to explain the historic
subordination of blacks, Hispanics, Asian Americans, and
other people of color in the United States (Clark 1965;
Carmichael and Hamilton 1967; Moore 1970; Barerra, Munoz,
and Ornelas 1972; Blauner 1972).

At the center of the Marxist feminist analysis is the
concept of patriarchy, which may be defined as a hierarchical system of power that enables men as a class to
have authority and power over women (H. Hartmann 1976;
Brown 1975; Sokoloff 1980). In this model the main mechanism by which control is achieved and maintained by men
is the sexual division of labor, which places men in positions of authority over women and permits them to reap
disproportionate benefits. Similarly, at the center of the
internal colonialism model is a system of power relations
by which subordinate minorities are kept politically and
economically weak so they can be more easily exploited as
workers. The main mechanism by which economic dependency is maintained is a colonial labor system, characterized by a segmented labor market, discriminatory barriers
to desirable jobs, and separate wage scales. This system

ensures that people of color are relegated to the worst jobs: insecure, low-paying, dangerous, dirty, and dead-end.

Neither model explicitly recognizes the specific situation of racial ethnic women. The patriarchy model ignores differences among women based on race. When race is discussed, it is treated as a parallel system of stratification: an analogy is often made between "women" and "minorities," an analogy that involves comparison of the subordinate status of white women and minority men. Minority women are left in limbo. Similarly, the internal colonialism model ignores gender by treating members of colonized minorities as undifferentiated with respect to gender. Analyses of racial ethnic labor have generally focused only on male workers. Yet these studies also assume that the detrimental impacts of the labor system on men are synonymous with the impacts on the group as a whole, men and women alike.

Despite the focus on only one axis of stratification, the patriarchy and internal colonialism models have some important commonalities. Each focuses on explaining the persistence of inequality and sees gender/race stratification as dynamically related to the organization of the economy. Thus, each implies a historical perspective, one that traces changes in the relations between dominant and subordinate groups in relation to the development of capitalism. Each emphasizes institutional arrangements that ensure control by the dominant group over the labor of the subordinate group. There thus seems to be some common ground for developing a more integrated framework by combining insights from the two perspectives.

This chapter is a preliminary effort to identify aspects of the two models that might contribute to an integrated framework. I will start by briefly reviewing the Marxist feminist analysis of women's subordination. I will then review racial ethnic women's experience as members of colonized minorities in the United States. In light of this experience, I will examine the paid and unpaid work of Chinese, Mexican American, and black women from the mid-19th century to the present, showing how they diverge from those presumed to be typical of white women. In the concluding section, suggestions are made for revision of Marxist feminist theory to be more inclusive of the race-gender interaction.

MARXIST FEMINIST ANALYSIS

The Marxist feminist perspective views women's subordination as a product of two interacting systems: patriarchy and capitalism.[2] While generally adhering to the
Marxist analysis of class exploitation, Marxist feminists
diverge by giving equal importance to patriarchy, which,
they argue, existed prior to capitalism, though interacting
with it as capitalism developed. According to this analysis, the main mechanism by which patriarchy was established and is maintained today is the sexual division of
labor. The assignment of certain tasks (usually the more
onerous and/or less valued) to women, and others (usually
the more highly valued) to men, is considered more or less
universal.

Under capitalism the sexual division of labor takes
a particular form due to the separation of production of
goods, and then services, from the household. As production was industrialized, the household became increasingly
privatized, and its functions reduced to consumption--that
is, shopping and negotiating for services (cf. Weinbaum
and Bridges 1979)--and biological and social reproduction,
including child care, cleaning, preparing food, and providing emotional support for the breadwinner. As capital
took over production, households became increasingly dependent on the market for goods and, therefore, on wages
to purchase goods and services needed for survival. During the 19th century--in part because men could be more
intensively exploited as wage laborers, while women could
benefit capital as full-time consumers and reproducers--a
specialization developed whereby women were assigned almost exclusive responsibility for household consumption and
reproduction, and men were allocated responsibility for
publicly organized production. This division became prescribed in the mid-19th century with the development of
the cult of domesticity, which idealized the woman as the
center of home and hearth (Welter 1966). This division of
labor contributed to the subordination of women by making
them economically dependent on a male wage earner. Simultaneously the domestic code controlled women's behavior
by threatening those who deviated from it with the loss of
their feminine identity.

The ideal of separate spheres was, of course, unattainable for many women whose fathers or husbands were
unable to earn a family wage and who therefore had to

engage in income-producing activities to support themselves and their families (Lerner 1969; Easton 1976). Yet the conception of women as consumers and reproducers affected them, too, depressing their position in the labor market. Women were defined as secondary workers, a status maintained by a sexual division in the labor market (occupational segregation). Jobs allocated to women were typically at the bottom of the authority hierarchy, low in wages, dead-end, and frequently insecure. The secondary position of women in the labor force meant that they had little leverage to shift the burden of household work onto husbands, so they continued to be responsible for the domestic sphere. Moreover, because of low wages and insecure jobs, women, even when employed, remained dependent on additional wages of the male earner (H. Hartmann 1976; Kessler-Harris 1982).

This analysis has much to offer. It permits us to view women's subordination as part of a larger framework of economic exploitation. It also draws connections between women's domestic work and their work in the labor force, and shows how subordination in one sphere reinforces subordination in the other. It is intended as a general analysis that encompasses all women. Yet it is built on class- and race-bounded experiences. To what extent do the concepts developed in the Marxist feminist model apply to the experiences of racial ethnic women? To what extent does the private-public split and women's association with the domestic sphere exist for racial ethnic women? To what extent has economic dependence on men been an important basis for racial ethnic women's subordination? To what extent do struggles over allocation of household labor create gender conflict in racial ethnic households?

In order to begin addressing these questions, we need to examine the impacts of race stratification on racial ethnic women's work, both paid and unpaid. For this, I draw on both earlier and more recent research on the labor histories of "colonized minorities." Because histories of the various peoples in different regions of the country vary and because of the limited size and scope of this chapter, I will limit my examination to three case studies for which there is comparable information from the mid-19th century to the present: Mexican Americans in the Southwest, Chinese in California, and blacks in the South.

COLONIZED MINORITIES IN
INDUSTRIALIZING AMERICA

The United States started out as a colonial economy
that offered raw resources and land to European and
American capitalists. In order to develop the economic
infrastructure and extract resources, capitalists needed
labor, which was always in short supply. The presence
of racial ethnic groups in this country is tied to this demand for labor. Most were brought to this country for
the express purpose of providing cheap and malleable
labor (Cheng and Bonacich 1984).

Although European immigrants were also welcomed as
a source of low-wage labor, they were incorporated into
the urban economies of the North. Racial ethnics were recruited primarily to fill labor needs in economically back-
ward regions: the West, Southwest, and South (Blauner
1972). In the late 19th and early 20th centuries, Chinese
men constituted from a quarter to a third of the work
force (reclaiming agricultural lands, building railroads,
and working in mines) and 90 percent of the domestic and
laundry workers in California (Saxton 1971). During this
same period, native Chicanos and Mexican immigrants
(Mexicanos) were employed as miners, railroad hands, and
agricultural laborers in the western states (Barrera 1979).
In the years following emancipation, blacks were concentrated in agriculture, as well as in heavy construction
labor and domestic service, in the South (Cheng and Bonacich 1984). All three groups helped build the agricultural
and industrial base on which subsequent industrial development rested, but were excluded from the industrial jobs
that resulted.

Racial ethnic labor was cheaper for infrastructure
building in two senses: racial ethnics were paid less
(including lower benefits) and provided a reserve army to
be drawn on when the economy expanded or labor was
needed for a short-term project, and pushed out when the
economy contracted or the particular project ended. Their
cheapness was ensured by institutional barriers that undercut their ability to compete in the labor market. The
labor market itself was stratified into separate tiers for
whites and racial ethnics. The better-paying, more
skilled, cleaner, and secure jobs in highly capitalized industries were reserved for white workers, leaving the low-
paying, insecure, dangerous, seasonal, and dead-end jobs

in competitive (as opposed to monopolistic) industries for people of color. A dual wage system was also characteristic of the colonial labor system; wages for racial ethnics were always lower than for whites in comparable jobs (Barrera 1979). White workers benefited because better jobs were reserved for them. The dual labor system also was a buffer for them against the effects of periodic depressions, since racial ethnics took the brunt of layoffs and unemployment.

Further, racial ethnics were prevented from competing for better work and improved conditions by legal and administrative restrictions. Restrictions on their rights and freedoms began at the time of entry or incorporation into the United States. While the exact forms of entry for the three groups differed, in all cases an element of subordination was involved. The most striking instance of forced entry was that of blacks, who were captured, torn from their homelands, transported against their will, and sold into slavery. This institution so structured their lives that even after emancipation, former slaves were held in debt bondage by the southern sharecropping system (Painter 1976). Equally involuntary was the incorporation of Mexicans residing in territories taken over by U.S. military conquest. Anglo settlers invaded what is now California, Texas, Arizona, New Mexico, and Colorado. When the United States seized the land, native Mexicans living in those areas were reduced to agricultural peons or wage laborers (Barrera 1979). An intermediate case between forced and free entry was that of the Chinese. Their immigration was the result of the economic and political chaos engendered at least in part by western colonial intrusion into China (Lyman 1974). Many Chinese men entered the United States as contract laborers so they could support destitute kin in their home villages. Under the credit ticket system, they signed away seven years of labor in exchange for their passage (Ling 1912).

These unfree conditions of entry imposed special liabilities on racial ethnics. Blacks were not citizens, and counted in the census as only three-fifths of a person; Mexicans were defined as second-class citizens; and Chinese were aliens ineligible for citizenship. All three groups were placed in separate legal categories, denied basic rights and protections, and barred from political participation. Thus, they could be coerced, intimidated, and restricted to the least desirable jobs, where they were especially vulnerable to exploitation.

The process of entry and incorporation into the labor system had profound effects on the culture and family systems of racial ethnics. Native languages, religion, and other aspects of life were constrained, destroyed, or transformed, and kin ties and family authority were undermined. As Blauner (1972, p. 66) notes, "The labor system through which people of color became Americans tended to destroy or weaken their cultures and communal ties. Regrouping and new institutional forms developed, but in situations with extremely limited possibilities."

We are most familiar with assaults on family ties of blacks under slavery due to sale of individuals regardless of kin ties, slave master control over marriage and reproduction, and the brutal conditions of life. Scholars and policy analysts in the past argued that slavery permanently weakened kin ties and undermined the conjugal household, thereby creating a legacy of family pathology (Frazier 1939; Moynihan 1965). More recently, revisionist historians have argued that slaves resisted assaults on family integrity, and managed to maintain conjugal and kin ties to a greater extent than previously believed (Gutman 1976; Fogel and Engerman 1974; Blassingame 1972). Gutman (1975) found that a large proportion of slave marriages were of long standing and that many couples legalized their marriages when given the opportunity to do so after emancipation. Black families showed great strength in the face of assaults on kin networks, though their survival required great struggle and exacted great costs.

Less well known are the assaults on the culture and family lives of Chicanos and Chinese Americans. In both groups households were broken apart by the demand for male labor. Many Mexican American men were employed in mining camps and on railroad gangs, which required them to live apart from wives and children (Barrera 1979). This was also true for male migrant agricultural workers until the 1880s, when the family labor system became the preferred mode (Camarillo 1979). In the case of the Chinese, only prime-age males were recruited as workers, and wives and children had to be left behind (Coolidge 1909). The Chinese Exclusion Act of 1882 not only prohibited further entry of Chinese laborers but also barred resident laborers from bringing in wives and children (Lyman 1974; Wu 1972). This policy was aimed at preventing the Chinese from settling permanently once their labor was no longer needed.

Given these conditions, what was the work of racial/ethnic women in the 19th and early 20th centuries?

RACIAL ETHNIC WOMEN'S WORK IN INDUSTRIALIZING AMERICA

The specific conditions of life experienced by the three groups of women differed. However, they shared some common circumstances due to their similar positions in the colonial labor system and the similar difficulties the system created for their families. All three groups had to engage in a constant struggle for both immediate survival and the long-term continuation of the family and community. Because men of their groups were generally unable to earn a family wage, the women had to engage in subsistence and income-producing activities both in and out of the household. In addition, they had to work hard to keep their families together in the face of outside forces that threatened their integrity.

Chinese American Women

Perhaps the least is known about Chinese American women in the 19th and early 20th centuries. This may be due to the fact that very few working-class Chinese women actually resided in the United States then. For most of the period from 1860 to 1920, the ratio of men to women ranged from 13 to 20 males for every female. As late as 1930 there were only 9,742 females aged 10 or over in a population that included 53,650 males of the same age (Glenn 1983). It is estimated that over half of the men had left wives in China (Coolidge 1909). Although most of these wives never came to the United States, their lives must be considered as part of the experience of American racial ethnics, for they raised subsequent generations who went to America, often with false papers. Little research has been done on what women did in their home villages or how they survived. The available evidence, based partly on some family history interviews I conducted and partly on other sources (Hirata 1983; Kingston 1977), suggests the following: The wife often resided with the husband's parents or other kin, who received remittances from the husband, acted on his behalf, and oversaw the household. She took care of children, performed household work under the direction of the mother-in-law, and helped in subsistence farming. Her sexual chastity was carefully guarded, as was her overall behavior. She might never see her husband again or, if lucky, see him once or twice over the course of 20 or 30 years, during his rare visits home.

In the late 19th century, aside from wives of merchants, who were still allowed entry into the United States, the only notable group of Chinese women were prostitutes (Hirata 1979; Goldman 1981). The unbalanced sex ratio created a demand for sexual services. Except for a few years when some women were able to immigrate on their own as free entrepreneurs, Chinese prostitutes were either indentured servants or outright slaves controlled by Chinese tongs or business associations. They had been sold by their parents or kidnapped and involuntarily transported. The controllers of the trade reaped huge profits from buying and selling women, and hiring out their services. Women who ran away were hunted down and returned to their captors, usually with the collusion of the police and courts. Unable to speak English and without allies, the women could not defend themselves.

Initially the Chinese were dispersed throughout the West in mining towns, railroad camps, and agricultural fields. They were subjected to special penalties, such as a foreign miner's tax in California, that rendered it difficult for them to make a living. During the economic depression of the 1870s, the Chinese were forcibly driven out of many areas (Nee and Nee 1972). They congregated in urban Chinatowns, so that by the 1880s the Chinese were a largely urban population. In place of households, the men formed clan and regional associations for mutual welfare and protection (Lyman 1977). By the early 1900s some Chinese men were able, with minimal capital, to establish laundries, restaurants, and stores, thereby qualifying as merchants eligible to bring over wives (Lyman 1968). These small businesses were a form of self-exploitation; they were profitable only because all members of the family contributed their labor and worked long hours. Living quarters were often in back of the shop or adjacent to it, so that work and family life were completely integrated. Work in the family enterprise went on simultaneously with household maintenance and child care. First up and last to bed, women had less leisure than the rest

of the family. Long work hours in crowded and rundown
conditions took its toll on the whole family. Chinatowns
had abnormally high rates of tuberculosis and other
diseases (Lee, Lim, and Wong 1969).

It is unclear what proportion of women laboring in
family laundries and shops were counted as gainfully employed in the census. They undoubtedly were severely
undercounted (see Chapter 5). In any case, some sizable
proportion of women was employed as independent wage
workers. As employees, Chinese women were concentrated
in ethnic enterprises because of color bars in white-owned
businesses. Nearly half of all gainfully employed women
in 1930 worked in jobs that were typical of Chinese enterprise. Out of a work force of 1,559, garment operatives
and seamstresses accounted for 11.7 percent; sales and
trade for 10.6 percent; laundry operatives for 7.3 percent;
waitresses for 8.2 percent; and clerical workers for 11.2
percent. The only major form of employment outside the
ethnic community was private household service, which accounted for 11.7 percent of Chinese women (U.S. Census
Bureau 1933). (For broad occupational distributions, see
Table 3.1.)

Table 3.1. Occupational Distribution of Employed Black,
Chinese, Mexican, and White Women, 10 Years of Age
and Over, 1930

Occupation	Black	Chinese	Mexican	White
Professional	3.4	11.3	3.0	16.5
Trade	0.8	15.3	9.0	10.7
Public service	0.1	0.0	0.1	0.2
Clerical	0.6	11.2	2.6	22.4
Manufacturing	5.5	20.4	19.3	20.0
Transportation	0.1	1.1	0.5	3.1
Agriculture	26.9	1.5	21.2	4.5
Service, exc. servants and laundresses	35.4	27.6	13.5	20.1
Servants/laundresses	27.2	11.7	30.8	2.5
TOTAL	100.0	100.1[a]	100.0	100.0

[a]Rounding error.

Source: U.S. Census Bureau, Fifteenth Census of the
United States: 1930, Population, vol. 5: General Report on Occupations, Ch. 3, "Color and Nativity of Gainful Workers,"
tables 2, 4, and 6 (Washington, DC: U.S. Government Printing
Office).

Mexican American Women

The information on the work of Chicanas in the late 19th century is also sparse. Barrera (1979) suggests that prior to the 1870s, Chicano families followed the traditional division of labor, with women responsible for household work and child care. Thus, Mexican American women worked largely in the home. Under the conditions of life among working-class and agricultural families, this work was extensive and arduous (Jensen 1981). In rural areas the household work included tending gardens and caring for domestic animals. Many Chicano men were employed in extracting industries that required them to live in work camps and company towns in unsettled territories. If a wife remained with the children in the home village, she had to engage in subsistence farming and raise the children on her own. If she joined her husband in camp, she had to carry on domestic chores and child rearing under frontier conditions, forced to buy necessities in company stores that quickly used up meager wages. Even in the city the barrios often had no running water, and unsanitary conditions added to women's burdens of nursing the sick (Garcia 1980).

By the 1880s, Mexican American women were increasingly being brought into the labor force. In cities such as Los Angeles, Santa Barbara, and El Paso, Chicanas were employed as servants, cooks, and laundresses (Camarillo 1979; Garcia 1980). An economic depression in the 1880s forced more women to seek outside wage work, not only in private households but also as washerwomen in commercial laundries, and as cooks, dishwashers, maids, and waitresses in hotels and other public establishments. In this same period women entered the agricultural labor market. Prior to that time prime-age male workers were preferred for seasonal and migratory field work. In the 1880s whole families began to be used, a pattern that accelerated during World War I (Camarillo 1979, p. 91). By the 1920s family labor was common throughout the Southwest. Describing the situation in Colorado, Paul Taylor (1929) noted that landowners felt that families, despite their lower productivity per unit, were preferable because they were a more stable work force that could be counted on to return year after year.

These trends are reflected in occupational patterns of Chicana women. Between 1880 and 1930, they tended to be employed in two main types of situations. A large part of the Chicana work force, 20 percent officially, was employed as farm laborers (Barrera 1979). Many of these were part of the piece rate system in which entire families worked and moved with the crops (Fisher 1953; P. Taylor 1937; McWilliams 1971). Under this system women had to bear and raise children, cook, and keep house while also working long hours in the field or packinghouse. Infants accompanied their parents to the fields, and children started working at an early age. Living conditions in migrant camps were extremely harsh. Adults rarely lived past 55, and infant and child mortality was high. Children had no regular schooling because of constant movement and the need for their labor. Schools were geared to fit agricultural schedules and provided minimal training (P. Taylor 1929). Once in the migrant pattern, it was almost impossible for families or individuals to break out.

The second type of employment for Chicanas, primarily those in cities and towns, was in unskilled and semiskilled "female" jobs. The distribution of jobs varied in different areas of the Southwest, but the most common occupations in all areas were service positions (household servants, waitresses, maids, cooks, and laundry operatives), which accounted for 44.3 percent of all employed Chicanas in 1930, and operatives in garment factories and food processing plants, which together employed 19.3 percent in 1930 (see Table 3.1). The latter industries also employed Anglo women, but Chicanas were given the worst jobs and the lowest pay. They were victims of both occupational stratification and a dual wage system. Their plight was revealed in testimony by employers before the Texas Industrial Welfare System in El Paso in 1919. F. B. Fletcher, a laundry owner representing the owners of the four largest laundries in El Paso, testified that almost all the unskilled labor was performed by Mexican women, while the skilled positions as markers, sorters, checkers, supervisors, and office assistants went to Anglo women. Further, Mexican women were paid an average of $6 a week, while Anglo women received $16.55. "This difference indicates that in this industry, the minimum wage can be fairly fixed for Mexican female help and for the American entirely different and distinct" (Garcia 1981, p. 91). Only by combining their wages with those of husbands and older children could Mexican American women survive.

Whether engaged in subsistence farming, seasonal migratory labor, agricultural packing, laundry work, domestic service, or garment manufacturing, Chicanas had to raise their children under colonized conditions. As part of the continued legal and illegal takeover of land by Anglos in Texas and Colorado from 1848 to 1900, the Chicanos became a conquered people (McLemore 1973, 1980). Defined and treated as inferior, they saw their language and culture become badges of second-class status. Through their daily reproductive activities women played a critical role not only in maintaining the family but also in sustaining Mexican American ways of life.

Black Women

Perhaps more than any other group of women, black women were from the start exempted from the myth of female disability. They were exploited on the basis of their gender as breeders and raisers of slaves for plantation owners (Genovese 1974). Their gender also made them liable to a special form of oppression, sexual assault. Nevertheless, their gender did not spare them from hard physical labor in the fields (Jones 1984). Hooks (1981) claims plantation owners often preferred women for the hardest field work because they were more reliable workers. In addition, black women did the heavy housework and child care for white women; in that role they were subject to abuse and even physical beatings at the hands of their mistresses. As Angela Davis (1969) notes, under conditions of plantation slavery, staying alive, raising children, and maintaining some semblance of community were forms of resistance.

After emancipation, life for rural blacks remained harsh under the sharecropping system. Blacks found themselves held in debt bondage. Hooks (1981) suggests that landowners preferred sharecropping to hiring labor because black women were unwilling to be employed in the fields once slavery was abolished. With sharecropping, women's labor could be exploited intensively, since women had to work hard alongside the men in order to pay off the ever-mounting debt to the owner. One observer of black farmers noted that these women "do double duty, a man's share in the field, and a woman's part at home. They do any

kind of field work, even ploughing, and at home the cooking, washing, milling, and gardening" (Lerner 1973, p.
247).

Although there were some independent black farmers,
it became increasingly difficult for them to make a living.
Jim Crow laws deprived blacks of legal rights and protections, and national farm policies favored large landowners.
Independent black farmers were increasingly impoverished
and finally were driven off the land (Painter 1976).

Aside from farming, the next largest group of black
women was employed as laundresses and domestic servants.
Black women constituted an exclusive servant caste in the
South, since whites refused to enter a field associated with
blacks since slave times (Katzman 1978). As servants,
black women often worked a 14- to 16-hour day and were
on call around the clock (J. Brown 1938). They were allowed little time off to meet their own domestic responsibilities, despite the fact that the majority of black domestics
had children. A married domestic might see her children
once every two weeks, while devoting night and day to the
care of her mistress's children. Her own children were
left in the care of husband or older siblings (Katzman
1978). Low wages were endemic. They had to be supplemented by children taking in laundry or doing odd jobs.
Many black women testified that they could survive only
through the tradition of the service pan--the term for left-
over food that was at the disposal of the colored cook
(Lerner 1973, p. 229).

Manufacturing and white-collar jobs were closed to
black women, though some of the dirtiest jobs in industry
were offered them. They were particularly conspicuous in
southern tobacco factories, and to some extent in cotton
mills and flour manufacturing. In the cotton mills black
women were employed as common laborers in the yards, as
waste gatherers, and as scrubbers of machinery. The actual manufacturing jobs were reserved for white women
(Foner and Lewis 1981). Regarding black women in the
tobacco industry, Emma Shields noted in a pamphlet she
prepared for the Women's Bureau in 1922:

> Conditions of employment throughout the
> tobacco industry are deplorably wretched,
> and yet conditions for Negro women workers
> are very much worse than those for white
> women workers. . . . Negro women are

employed exclusively in the rehandling of
tobacco, preparatory to its actual manufacture. Operations in the manufacture of
cigars and cigarettes are performed exclusively by white women. Negro women workers are absolutely barred from any opportunity for employment in the manufacturing
operations. . . . It is not unusual to
find the white women workers occupying
the new modern sanitary parts of the factory, and the Negro women workers in the
old sections which management has decided
to be beyond any hope of improvement.
(quoted in Lerner 1973, p. 253)

World War 1 saw increasing migration of blacks to
the urban North and, simultaneously, the entrance of
blacks into factory employment there. As late as 1910,
90.5 percent of all black women were farm laborers and
servants, but between 1910 and 1920, 48,000 black women
entered factory work (Lerner 1973). Most were employed
in steam laundries, the rest in unmechanized jobs in industry as sweepers, cleaners, and ragpickers (Foner and
Lewis 1981).
     During the entire period from 1870 to 1930, black
women, regardless of rural or urban residence, were notable for their high rates of labor force participation, particularly among married women. In 1900, 26.0 percent of
married black women were in the labor force, compared
with 3.8 percent of married white women (Pleck 1979).
They thus had to contend with the double day long before
this became an issue for a majority of white women. Moreover, although their wages were consistently lower than
those of white women, their earnings constituted a larger
share of total family income, due to the marginal and low-
wage employment of black men (Byington 1974). Finally,
they had to perform their double duty under poor and
crowded living conditions, an educational system that provided inferior schooling for their children, uncertain income, and other trials.

RACIAL ETHNIC WOMEN'S WORK
IN THE CONTEMPORARY PERIOD

     All three groups are predominately urban today, a
process that began in the late 19th century for the Chinese,

during World War I for blacks, and after World War II
for Chicanos. All have experienced dramatic changes in
occupational distributions since 1930.

Chinese Women Since World War II

The main change in circumstances for Chinese women
was that they were allowed entry into the United States in
large numbers for the first time after World War II. Many
separated wives were able to join their spouses under the
provisions of the Walter-McCarran Act of 1953, and whole
family units were able to enter after passage of the liber-
alized 1965 immigration law (Li 1977; U.S. Department of
Justice 1977). Since World War II female immigrants have
outnumbered males, and the sex ratio of the Chinese population now approaches equality, with the remaining imbal-
ance existing only in the older age categories (U.S. Census
Bureau 1973). Women who have joined spouses or arrived
with husbands are adapting to the postwar urban economy
by entering the paid labor force. Handicapped by language,
by family responsibilities, and by gender and race discrimination in the skilled trades, both husbands and wives
are employed in the secondary labor market--in low-wage
service and competitive manufacturing sectors. The most
typical constellation among immigrant families is a husband employed as a restaurant worker, store helper, or
janitor and a wife employed as an operative in a small
garment shop. The shops are located in or close to Chinatowns and are typically subcontracting firms run by Chinese. They often evade minimum-wage laws by using an
unofficial piece rate system (Nee and Nee 1972).

An examination of the occupational distribution of
Chinese American women reveals a bimodal pattern. In
1970 (see Table 3.2) Chinese women were concentrated in
clerical (31.8 percent) and professional (19.4 percent)
white-collar work, and in the operative category (22.5
percent). While the high proportion in white-collar fields
indicates considerable success by second-, third-, and
fourth-generation women, generational mobility may be less
than these figures suggest, since many professionals are
actually recent immigrants of gentry origin rather than
working-class Chinese Americans who have moved up.
Working-class Chinese women continue to be relegated to
operative jobs in the garment trade. What Chinese women
of all classes share is a higher than average rate of labor
force participation (U.S. Census Bureau 1973).

Table 3.2. Occupational Distribution of Black, Chinese
American, Mexican American, and White Women in
the United States, 1970 (percent)

Occupation	Black	Chinese American	Mexican American	White[a]
Professional	11.3	19.4	6.4	16.6
Managerial	1.4	3.8	1.9	4.0
Sales	2.6	5.1	5.7	8.1
Clerical	20.7	31.8	25.9	37.0
Craft	1.4	1.2	2.3	1.8
Operative	16.5	22.5	25.8	13.7
Laborers exc. farm	1.5	0.9	1.8	0.9
Farming, inc. farm labor	1.2	0.5	4.0	0.7
Service	25.5	12.8	20.6	15.3
Private household workers	17.8	2.0	5.5	1.9
TOTAL	99.9[b]	100.0	99.9[b]	100.0

[a]All women minus those of black and Spanish origin.
[b]Rounding error.
Sources: U.S. Bureau of the Census, Subject Reports of
the 1970 Census: PC (2)-1B, Negro Population, table 7; PC (2)-
1C, Persons of Spanish Origin, table 8; PC (2)-1F, Japanese,
Chinese, and Filipinos in the United States, table 22 (Washington, DC: U.S. Government Printing Office, 1973); U.S. Bureau
of the Census, Census of the Population: 1970, Detailed Characteristics of the Population, PC (1)-D1, U.S. Summary, table
226 (Washington, DC: U.S. Government Printing Office, 1973).

Postwar economic changes have undercut family enterprises such as laundries and small stores, so that
working-class families today typically engage in dual wage
earning. They encounter difficulties due to the long work
hours of parents, and crowded and run-down housing.
Working mothers are responsible for not only the lion's
share of domestic chores, but often raise their children
almost single-handedly. Husbands are frequently employed
in the restaurant trade, which requires them to be at
work from 11 in the morning until 10 in the evening or
even midnight. Thus, they are rarely around while their
children are awake. The women's own work hours are

often prolonged because they leave work during the day to cook meals or pick up children. They make up the time by returning to the shop for evening work or by taking materials home to sew at night (Ikels and Shang 1979). Their energy is entirely absorbed by paid employment and domestic responsibilities. The one ray of light is their hope for their children's future.

Mexican American Women

The Chicano population is still characterized by continued migration back and forth between Mexico and the United States. In 1970, 16 percent of the resident population in the United States was foreign-born (Massey 1982, p. 10). Not surprisingly, Chicanos remain concentrated in the Southwest, with 76 percent residing in California and Texas in 1979 (Pachon and Moore 1981). Contrary to their image as rural people, four out of five (79 percent) resided in metropolitan areas. In line with the urban shift there has been a sharp reduction in the percentage of men and women engaged in agriculture. The proportion of women employed as farm workers fell from 21.2 percent in 1930 to 2.4 percent by 1979 (see Tables 3.1 and 3.3). As a result of mechanization of agriculture, which caused a sharp decline in the total number of farm workers, however, Chicana women constituted a higher proportion of women in agricultural labor in 1979 than they did in 1930. For those still involved in migrant labor, conditions remained harsh, with extensive exploitation of children despite child labor laws (Taylor 1976).

The period from 1930 to the present has seen a steady rise in the occupational status of Mexican Americans. As with other racial ethnic groups, the occupational dispersion of Chicanos is related to labor shortages during wars, especially World War II. After the war, rising numbers of Chicanas found employment in clerical and sales jobs, though they still lagged behind white women, especially in sales. The lower rates in white-collar jobs were matched by overrepresentation in blue-collar and service occupations. Mexican American women were concentrated in operative jobs, principally in garment factories, laundries, and food processing plants, which together accounted for 25.0 percent of their employment in 1979 (Table 3.3). These enterprises tended to be small

Table 3.3. Occupational Distribution of Employed Black, Mexican, and White Women 16 Years of Age and Over, 1979

Occupation	Black[a]	Mexican	White
Professional	14.2	6.4	16.4
Managerial	3.4	3.5	6.8
Sales	3.1	5.1	7.4
Clerical	29.0	31.1	35.9
Crafts	1.2	1.8	1.9
Operatives	15.3	25.0	11.0
Laborer, exc. farm	1.6	1.3	1.3
Farming, inc. farm labor	0.8	2.4	1.3
Service, inc. private household	31.5	23.4	18.1
TOTAL	100.1[b]	100.0	100.1[b]

[a]Category consists of "black and other."
[b]Rounding error.
Sources: U.S. Bureau of the Census, Current Population Reports, Series P-20, no. 354, Persons of Spanish Origin in the United States: March 1979, table 10 (Washington, DC: U.S. Government Printing Office, 1980); U.S. Bureau of Labor Statistics, Employment and Earnings 27, no. 1 (1980): table 22.

competitive firms that paid minimum wages and often were seasonal. Another 23.4 percent of all employed Chicanas were in service jobs, including private household work.

Mexican American women have traditionally had among the lowest rates of labor force participation among racial ethnic women (Almquist and Wehrle-Einhorn 1978). However, in the 1970s they rapidly entered the labor market, so that by 1980 their rates were similar to those of whites, though lower than those for black and Asian American women (Massey 1982). The lower rates may be related to two other circumstances that usually depress employment: education and family size. Chicanas have the lowest education levels of the three groups and the largest number of children. These factors mean that when Chicanas are in the labor force, they are at a great disadvantage. In 1976 nearly one-third (31.5 percent) of all employed Chicanas had eight years of education or less; the comparable figure for blacks was 14.1 percent and for whites 7.6 percent (U.S. Department of Labor 1977).

In short, though Mexican American women have achieved greater employment parity with Anglo women, they continue to have lower educational levels and heavier family burdens. In addition, they encounter racial barriers to white-collar employment.

Black Women

Black women have also experienced shifts in employment since World War II. The postwar period has seen a great decline in domestic service as a major category of women's work. Because black women were so concentrated in it, they have shown the most dramatic decline. Whereas in 1940 three out of five (59.5 percent) employed black females were in domestic service, by 1960 that proportion had dropped to a little over a third (36.2 percent), and by 1980 to one out of fourteen (7.4 percent) (U.S. Census Bureau 1943, 1973; Westcott 1982). Partially replacing service in private households has been service employment in public establishments, particularly in food service and health care, where the number of low-level jobs has proliferated. These jobs accounted for 25.4 percent of black female employment in 1980, compared with 16.0 percent for white women (Westcott 1982).

U.S. census data (Table 3.3) show that black women are also overrepresented in the operatives category, where 15.3 percent were employed in 1979, in contrast with 11.0 percent of whites. As in the past, there is a stratified labor market and a dual wage system. Baker and Levenson (1975a) examined the careers of black, Hispanic, and white graduates of a New York City vocational high school, and found that black and Hispanic women were disproportionately tracked into lower-paying operative jobs in the garment industry, while better-paying jobs outside the garment industry were reserved for white graduates. Years later the difference in pay and mobility was even greater as black and Hispanic women were progressively disadvantaged (Baker and Levenson 1975b).

The last barrier to fall was white-collar employment. A dramatic increase in professional-technical, clerical, and sales employment took place after 1950. By 1979, the former accounted for 14.2 percent of black female employment; the latter two together, for 32.1 percent. Differences remained, however, in that white-collar employment accounted

for over 69 percent of white women's jobs, but less than
half of black women's employment. In addition, within
white-collar jobs, black women were concentrated in lower-
level jobs. For example, in 1980 black women constituted
10.8 percent of all clerical workers, but they made up
over 15 percent of such lower-level positions as file clerks,
mail handlers, keypunchers, and office machine operators,
and less than 6 percent of more skilled positions, such as
secretaries, bank tellers, and bookkeepers (Glenn and
Tolbert 1987). In effect, though black women have experienced desegregation at the level of broad occupations,
they have been resegregated at the finer level of detailed
job categories.

Other measures also show continued disadvantage
for black women. They have a 50 percent higher unemployment rate and somewhat lower earnings (U.S. Department of Labor 1977). The largest gap is in terms of
median family income, due to discrimination against black
men. Even with the mother in the labor force, the median
family income for black families with children under 18
was $14,461 in 1975, compared with $17,588 for similar
white families (U.S. Department of Labor 1977). Even
though they could not raise family income to white levels
by being employed, black women's wages made a bigger
difference to overall family income. The gap between
blacks and whites was even greater if the mother was not
employed: the median for black families without the
mother in the labor force was $8,912, compared with $14,796
for whites (U.S. Department of Labor 1977). Regardless of
income level, the economic fate of the black conjugal family rested on an economic partnership between men and
women. Moreover, even among relatively affluent black
families, the need to combat racism was a theme that in-
fused daily life and absorbed the energy of parents in
socializing their children (Willie 1981). Women's role as
nurturers required them to combat the daily assaults on
their children's self-esteem and to be vigilant in protect-
ing them from psychic injury.

IMPLICATIONS FOR FEMINIST ANALYSIS

The history of racial ethnic women's work in the
United States reveals their oppression not just as women
but also as members of colonized minorities. As members

of colonized minorities, their experiences differed fundamentally from those used to construct Marxist feminist theory. Thus, concepts within that framework require reformulation if it is to generate analyses that are inclusive of racial ethnic women. I will briefly examine three concepts in Marxist feminist theory that need to be redefined to take into account the interaction of race and gender. These are the separation of private and public spheres, the primacy of gender conflict as a feature of the family, and the gender-based assignment of reproductive labor.

The growing separation of public and private spheres with industrialization was central to early Marxist feminist analyses of women's oppression under capitalism. However, recent historical and comparative research has called into question the extent to which private and public constituted separate and bounded spheres for all classes and groups. Scholars note that in industrializing societies, working-class women engage in many income-earning activities, such as doing piecework at home, taking in boarders, or trading on the informal market, that cannot be easily categorized as private or public (Jensen 1980). Moreover, industrial wage work and family life have been found to interact in complex ways, so that, for example, women's family roles may include and overlap with their roles as workers (Hareven 1977). The examination of racial ethnic women's work adds to the critiques growing out of this research.

The nature of the split, and the extent to which women are identified with the public sphere, seem to vary by class and ethnicity; differences among groups in women's relationship to public and private spheres need to be examined. Like many other working-class women, racial ethnic women were never out of public production. They were integrated into production in varying ways. Black women were involved in agriculture and waged domestic service from the time of slavery. Chinese American women frequently engaged in unpaid labor in family enterprises, where there was little separation between public and private life. Mexican American women were initially more confined to household-based labor than were the other groups, but this labor included a great deal of actual production, since men's wages were insufficient to purchase the necessities of life. Thus, a definition of womanhood exclusively in terms of domesticity never applied to racial ethnic women, as it did not to many working-class women.

Where racial ethnic women diverge from other working-class women is that, as members of colonized minorities, their definition as laborers in production took precedence over their domestic roles. Whereas the wife-mother roles of white working-class women were recognized and accorded respect by the larger society, the maternal and reproductive roles of racial ethnic women were ignored in favor of their roles as workers. The lack of consideration for their domestic functions is poignantly revealed in the testimony of black domestics, who were expected to leave their children and home cares behind while devoting full time to the care of the white employer's home and children. Similarly, Chinese and Mexican American women and children were treated as units of labor, capable of toiling long hours without regard to their need for private life. This is not to say that racial ethnic women did not see themselves in terms of their family identities, but that they were not so defined by the larger society, which was interested in them only as workers.

Another area of divergence is in the scope of what is included in the "private" sphere. For racial ethnic women the domestic encompasses a broad range of kin and community relations beyond the nuclear family. Under conditions of economic insecurity, scarce resources, and cultural assault, the conjugal household was not self-sufficient. Racial ethnic peoples have historically relied on a larger network of extended kin, including fictive relatives and clan associations, for goods and services. This means that women's reproductive work in the "private" sphere included contributions to this larger circle, within which women took care of each other's children, loaned each other goods, and helped nurse the sick. Beyond the kin network, women's work extended to the ethnic community, with much effort being expended in support of the church, political organizing, and other activities on behalf of "the race" (la raza). Women were often the core of community organizations, and their involvement was often spurred by a desire to defend their children, their families, and their way of life (Gilkes 1982; Yap 1983; Elasser et al. 1980). In short, race, as organized within a colonial labor system, interacted with gender (patriarchy) and class (capitalism) to determine the structure of private and public spheres, and women's relationship to these spheres.

A second aspect of Marxist feminist theory that requires reformulation in light of race is the concept of the family as a locus of gender conflict. The Marxist feminist analysis of the family is a response to traditional approaches that treat the family as an entity with unitary interests; in particular it challenges the functionalist view of the division of labor as complementary rather than exploitative. By focusing on inequality--the economic dependence of women and the inequitable division of labor--some Marxist feminists see members of the family as divided in their interests, with conflict manifested in a struggle over resources and housework (H. Hartmann 1981a; for contrasting view see Humphries 1977; Thorne 1982). In this view the conjugal family oppresses women; the liberation of women requires freeing them from familial authority and prescribed roles.

Examination of racial ethnic women's experiences draws attention to the other side of the coin--the family as a source of resistance to oppression from outside institutions.[3] The colonial labor system made it impossible for men of color to support their families with their labor alone, and therefore ruled out economic dependence for women. The issue for racial ethnic women was not so much economic inequality with husbands but, rather, the adequacy of overall family income. Because racial ethnic men earned less, women's wages comprised a larger share of total family income in dual wage-earner families. In the case of family enterprises, common among Asian Americans, family income depended on the labor of men and women equally. Thus, in both dual wage-earner and small business families, men and women were mutually dependent; dependence rarely ran in one direction.

As for the division of household labor, Marxist feminist analysis sees it as benefiting men, who receive a greater share of services while contributing less labor. In the racial ethnic family, conflict over the division of labor is muted by the fact that institutions outside the family are hostile to it. The family is a bulwark against the atomizing effects of poverty and of legal and political constraints. By transmitting folkways and language, socializing children into an alternative value system, and providing a base for self-identity and self-esteem, the family helps to maintain racial ethnic culture. Women do a great deal of the work of keeping the family together and teaching children survival skills. This work is experienced as a form of resistance to oppression rather than as a form of exploitation by men. In the colonial situation

the common interest of family members in survival, the
maintenance of family authority, and the continuation of
cultural traditions is emphasized. This is not to say that
there are no conflicts over the division of labor, but
struggles against outside forces take precedence over
struggles within the family. Thus, the racial stratification system shapes the forms of intrafamilial and extra-
familial conflicts, and determines the arenas in which
struggle occurs.

A third concept in Marxist feminist theory that
would benefit from consideration of race oppression is the
very useful notion of reproductive labor. Following an
early, brief formulation by Marx, Marxist feminists identified two distinct forms of labor, production and reproduction (Sokoloff 1980). "Reproduction" refers to activities
that re-create the labor force: the physical and emotional
maintenance of current workers, and the nurturing and
socializing of future workers. In other words, people as
well as things have to be produced. Although both men
and women engage in production, women are still the ones
who carry out most of the reproduction. In large part
this is because much reproductive work remains at the
household level, which is women's domain. In considering
the situation of racial ethnic women, it is useful to recognize the existence of a racial as well as a sexual division
of reproductive. labor. Historically, racial ethnic women
have been assigned distinct responsibilities for reproductive labor.

In the early industrial period, racial ethnic and
immigrant women were employed as household servants,
thereby performing reproductive labor for white native
families. The labor of black and immigrant servants made
possible the woman belle ideal for white middle-class
women. Even where white immigrant domestics were employed, the dirtiest and most arduous tasks--laundering
and heavy cleaning--were often assigned to black servants.
There was a three-way division of labor in the home, with
white middle-class women at the top of the hierarchy, followed by white immigrants, with racial ethnics at the bottom. In the late industrial period, as capital took over
more areas of life, reproductive activities were increasingly taken out of the household and turned into paid services that yielded profits (Braverman 1974). Today, such
activities as caring for the elderly (old age homes), preparing food (restaurants and fast food stands), and pro-

viding emotional support (counseling services) have been brought into the cash nexus. As this has happened, women have been incorporated·into the labor force to perform these tasks for wages. Within this female-typed public reproduction work, however, there is further stratification by race. Racial ethnic women perform the more menial, less desirable tasks. They prepare and serve food, clean rooms, and change bedpans, while white women, employed as semiprofessionals and white-collar workers, perform the more skilled and administrative tasks. The stratification is visible in hospitals, where whites predominate among registered nurses, while the majority of health care aides and housekeeping staff are blacks and Latinas. Just as white women in tobacco manufacturing benefited by getting cleaner and more mechanized jobs by dint of the dirty preparation work done by black women, so white women professionals enjoy more desirable working conditions because racial ethnic women perform the less desirable service tasks. The better pay white women receive allows them to purchase services and goods that ease their reproductive labor at home.

This point leads to a final consideration. It may be tempting to conclude that racial ethnic women differ from white women simply by the addition of a second axis of oppression, race. It would be a mistake, though, not to recognize the dialectical relation between white and racial ethnic women. Race, gender, and class interact in such a way that the histories of white and racial ethnic women are intertwined. Whether one considers the split between public and private spheres, conflict within the family and between the family and outside institutions, or productive and reproductive labor, the situation of white women has depended on the situation of women of color. White women have gained advantages from the exploitation of racial ethnic women, and the definition of white womanhood has to a large extent been cast in opposition to the definition of racial ethnic women (cf. Palmer 1983). Marxist feminist theory and the internal colonialism model both recognize white men as the dominant exploiting group; however, it is equally important to emphasize the involvement of white women in the exploitation of racial ethnic people, and the ways in which racial ethnic men have benefited from the even greater exploitation of racial ethnic women.

NOTES

1.   The term "racial ethnic" designates groups that
are simultaneously racial and ethnic minorities. It is
used here to refer collectively to blacks, Latinos, and
Asian Americans, groups that share a legacy of labor exploitation and special forms of oppression described in the
body of this chapter. It is offered as an alternative to
more commonly used designations—minority groups, people
of color, and Third World minorities—each of which is
problematic in some way.

2.   Sokoloff (1980) points out that whereas earlier
Marxist feminists viewed gender oppression as a by-product
of capitalism, what she calls "later" Marxist feminists developed the concept of patriarchy as a separate system
that predated capitalism and that interacts with class exploitation under capitalism.

3.   This general line of argument may also apply
to white working-class families. However, 1 would assert
that there were crucial differences in the historical experiences of white working-class and racial ethnic families. The family system of the white working class was
not subject to the institutional assaults, such as forced
separation, directed against black, Chicano, and Chinese
families. Moreover, white working-class women were accorded some respect for their domestic roles.

4

Technology and Work Degradation: Effects of Office Automation on Women Clerical Workers

Roslyn L. Feldberg
and Evelyn Nakano Glenn

Following World War II, when computers were introduced into the office, their potential for revolutionizing office work was widely proclaimed. Both managers and social researchers expected widespread worker resistance to the changes that would take place. As a result, numerous studies were undertaken to assess workers' responses to the new technology.

Much of this research was predicated on a belief among technological optimists that worker resistance was irrational, since computerization would, in the long term, benefit workers as well as managers. We call this the consensual research model.

Other researchers, drawing a parallel to the tendency of mechanization to reduce and deskill jobs in manufacturing, predicted largely negative consequences for

---

Research for this chapter was supported in part by a grant (#MH-30292) from the Center for Work and Mental Health, National Institute of Mental Health. An earlier version was presented at the meetings of the American Sociological Association, New York, 1980. We thank Natalie Sokoloff and Sally Hacker for detailed comments. The chapter also benefited from readings by Sharon Strom and Chris Bose, from discussions of the Women and Work Study Group originally sponsored by a grant from the American Sociological Association Problems of the Discipline Program, and from a careful review by Joan Rothschild.

workers. This position has been developed most systematically in theoretical and empirical work on the labor process (Braverman 1974; Edwards 1979; Stone 1975). We call
this the critical research model.

In this chapter, we argue first that the critical
model, which emphasizes the social relations within which
technology is developed and used, offers a better framework for assessing the impacts of office technology than
does the consensual model. It more accurately portrays
what has happened to clerical work over time.

As new jobs are created, others are lost, and much
of the remaining work becomes increasingly subdivided,
specialized, and standardized. Our argument is supported
through a detailed examination of shifts in the numbers
and types of jobs within clerical work from 1960 to 1980.

Second, we argue that the critical model has serious
limitations: (1) Analysts using the model concentrate solely on the division between capital and labor, ignoring the
divisions within each. Workers are assumed to be homogeneous, with a common relation to work and therefore
similarly affected by technology. (2) Further, Braverman
and others following his lead assume that the workers who
were in previously skilled jobs end up in the newly subdivided and standardized jobs. This implies that workers
employed in the newly degraded jobs experienced the
changes as a downgrading of their work.

Neither assumption is warranted. Workers are not
in fact homogeneous and interchangeable. The work force
is divided into segments based on sex, race, age, class,
education, and previous employment.[1] These segments
have access to different types of work, so workers with
specific characteristics tend to be concentrated in particular job categories. As a result, technological change affects groups differently. New opportunities are opening up
for one group at the same time that positive features of
work are lost by another. When jobs undergo deskilling,
a different segment of workers (such as minority women)
may replace the previous group (such as white women), so
that individual workers may not themselves experience
downgrading.

Most research on technological change, whether from
a consensual or a critical perspective, has obscured the
variation in effects in two ways. First, many studies
focus on the aggregate level, analyzing the relationship
between new technologies and skill level, and using statis-

tics for a total labor force at the national or industry level. These studies usually do not investigate whether the same relationship holds at the firm or work process level, nor do they examine whether the effects are systematically different for particular segments of the work force, such as men vs. women, white vs. minority workers. Second, studies of technological change in particular industries or firms usually focus on industries in which white men are the primary labor force. The findings of such studies are treated as if they depicted trends affecting all industries and all workers. For example, many researchers have studied the automobile industry; the experience of its workers is treated as if it were representative of mechanization in industry as a whole. In fact, however, the automobile assembly line is characteristic of only a fraction of industry, involving primarily one segment of the labor force, white males. To understand the meaning of technological change for other segments, such as women, researchers need to look at the industries and work processes in which those groups are concentrated.

An accurate assessment of technological impacts requires identifying the social divisions within the labor force, describing the impacts for each group, and analyzing the connections between what happens to one group and what happens to another group. We offer this kind of analysis for women in clerical work. We focus on the gender hierarchy as a fundamental division, arguing that men and women have different relations to the labor market. These relations are shaped by the interaction of gender hierarchies in the family, and gender stratification and related structures in the labor market (Feldberg and Glenn 1979b). Because men and women are in different positions in the labor market, they are differentially affected by changes in technology.

THE MODELS

The dominant research model in the early years of office automation was developed within a consensus framework that saw no fundamental opposition between the interests of workers and management. In this model, technology was viewed as a politically neutral tool contributing to progress, for the welfare of all. This optimistic view rested on the assumption that technology would benefit management by increasing productivity and efficiency, and workers by relieving them of boring, routine tasks and by upgrading their jobs. Numerous studies were carried out to assess the responses of workers to automation and to evaluate programs for changeover (Cheek 1958; Hardin et al. 1961). A few studies tried to assess the effects of automation on the occupational structure. They reported that job loss was concentrated among low-skilled jobs, while relative and absolute increases occurred in higher-skilled jobs. The observation, though accurate, was misleading. It implied an upgrading of lower-skilled workers and drew attention away from job loss and displacement among some groups of workers (Faunce et al. 1962; Shepard 1971; Wolfbein 1962). As a result, such studies provided little insight into the transformation of clerical work or the impacts of automation on clerical workers.

The critical research model was developed within a conflict framework that posits an opposition between the interests of workers and management. In this framework, technology is viewed as a resource of the capitalist class, which owns and controls its development (see Noble 1977). Technology is used by management to increase productivity through greater efficiency and rationality, often at the expense of the workers. This position had been partially articulated earlier by Mills (1956) but has been more fully developed in recent years by Marxist analysts of the labor process (Braverman 1974; Edwards 1979). Technology is viewed as one mechanism used by managers to increase control over the work process through centralizing knowledge in the hands of management, thereby reducing dependence on qualified, intelligent, committed workers. By implication, the impact of technology within capitalism is inevitably to displace and downgrade workers.

Analysts in this tradition have spelled out the downgrading argument clearly and have compiled evidence to support it. In line with our criticism of this model's limitations, we contribute to its development by attending to differential impacts on men and women. We argue that gender hierarchies and related practices, in both the labor market and the family, structure the way in which men and women are allocated to jobs created around that technology. We find that in the technological transformation of the office during this period, women are likely to remain in lower-paid jobs with few opportunities for mobility.

In assessing the models, we examine effects on work and workers at three levels: (1) the aggregate labor force and overall occupational structure, (2) the labor force and the work process in an organization, and (3) the workers and work process in particular jobs.[2] Too frequently, analysts fail to differentiate these levels. Change at one level is assumed to indicate parallel change at another; for example, the increase of new technical jobs in the occupational structure (level 1/2) is taken to mean that there has been an upgrading of the work done in all jobs (level 3). There is no necessary connection. Indeed, other jobs are as likely to remain unchanged or to be simplified as they are to be upgraded by such a shift in the occupational structure.

LEVEL 1: OCCUPATIONAL STRUCTURE

We turn first to changes in the occupational structure that have occurred since the introduction and spread of automation.

Assessing the impacts of office technology on the occupational structure is complicated by other economic and organizational changes that occur simultaneously. Some of the latter may have effects on the size and distribution of the clerical labor force equal to or greater than those of technology. These diverse forces can have effects in opposite directions. For example, while new technology reduces the number of workers needed to carry out a given volume of activity, a firm may grow so rapidly that more workers are needed to take care of the expanded work load. The period of increasing automation was also a time of proliferating record keeping and communication as organizations became larger and more complex, and as the service and financial sectors of the economy grew disproportionately (see Glenn and Feldberg 1977). Hence clerical functions expanded to counterbalance job loss due to spreading automation.

As Table 4.1 shows, for the period 1960–1981, employment in clerical and kindred occupations doubled. From the table we can identify categories that grew more quickly than average (more than doubled) and those that grew more slowly (increased less than twofold). Two expected patterns appear. First is dramatic growth in the categories associated with the new technology. For example,

Table 4.1. Employed Persons in Selected Office Occupations by Sex 1960–1981

Selected Occupations	1960[1]			1970[1]			1981[1]		
	Men	Women	Total	Men	Women	Total	Men	Women	Total[2]
Computer Specialists	8,528	765	9,293	204,656	49,945	254,601	457,083	169,917	627,000
Programmers	5,970	2,170	8,140	124,991	36,391	161,382	259,102	107,898	367,000
Systems Analysts	2,558	˙722	3,280	68,293	11,748	80,041	158,046	54,954	213,000
Bank Tellers	39,725	93,205	132,930	34,439	215,037	249,476	36,985	532,015	569,000
Billing Clerks	8,039	35,091	43,130	18,838	87,347	106,185	18,054	134,946	153,000
Bookkeepers	153,559	773,980	927,539	277,214	1,259,443	1,536,657	174,529	1,786,471	1,961,000
Cashiers	112,275	373,955	486,230	136,954	695,142	832,096	229,080	1,430,920	1,660,000
Clerical Assist.									
Social Welfare	—	—	—	261	942	1,203	—	—	—
Clerical Supervisor	28,393	25,824	54,217	64,391	48,389	112,780	73,000	177,000	250,000
Collectors, Bl. & Act.	26,137	6,485	32,622	32,947	18,537	51,484	34,038	48,962	93,000
Counter Clks., Except Food	47,483	74,156	121,639	76,584	152,667	229,251	84,960	275,040	360,000
File Clerks	23,426	121,591	145,017	65,221	294,678	359,899	51,030	263,970	315,000
Messengers	49,659	8,766	58,425	46,206	11,225	57,431	71,004	25,996	97,000
Office Machine Oper.	80,706	230,488	311,194	145,477	408,001	553,478	255,024	710,976	966,000
Bookkeeping/Billing	5,432	45,951	51,383	6,720	56,629	63,349	5,978	43,022	49,000
Calculating	671	36,406	37,077	3,071	31,880	34,951	—	—	—
Computer/Peripheral Equipment	671	1,257	1,928	83,072	34,241	117,313	204,168	359,832	564,000
Duplicating	8,066	5,650	13,716	8,788	11,609	20,397	—	—	—
Keypunch	43,691	117,376	161,067	27,964	244,957	272,921	16,120	231,880	248,000
Tabulating	18,143	7,530	25,673	4,128	4,042	8,170	—	—	—
Office mach. nec.	4,030	16,318	20,350	11,734	24,643	36,377	—	—	—
Payroll, Timekpg.	43,920	63,681	107,601	48,622	107,364	155,986	43,890	187,110	231,000
Receptionists	11,018	145,709	156,727	16,046	288,326	304,372	18,225	656,775	675,000
Secretaries	42,607	1,424,166	1,466,773	64,608	2,640,740	2,705,348	35,253	3,881,747	3,917,000
Statistical Clks.	59,042	78,124	137,166	89,204	160,492	249,696	72,890	297,110	370,000
Stenographers	11,625	258,554	270,179	8,097	120,026	128,123	11,026	62,974	74,000
Typists	25,468	496,735	522,203	57,272	922,804	980,076	38,147	992,853	1,031,000
Misc./Not Specified	448,521	1,085,922	1,534,443	201,255	610,017	811,272	451,836	1,504,164	1,956,000
All Clerical and Kindred[3]	2,921,912	6,203,858	9,125,770	3,452,281	9,582,440	13,034,691	3,619,980	14,944,020	18,564,000

Sources: for 1960 and 1970, U.S. Census Bureau 1970; for 1981, U.S. Department of Labor 1982.
[1] For 1960 and 1970, 14 years of age and over; for 1981, 16 years of age and over.
[2] Rounded to nearest thousand.
[3] Including all clerical occupations listed in census, but excluding computer specialists. This total includes occupations not listed above.

Table 4.2. Distributions of Employees in Selected Occupations in Offices of Life Insurance Carriers in Thirteen Selected Areas of the U.S.[1]

	1961			1966			1971			1976			1980
	Men	Women	Total	Men	Women	Total	Men	Women	Total	Men	Women	Total	Total*
Actuaries	983	83	1,066	499	18	517	527	35	562	755	100	855	1,090
Assemblers	56	1,294	1,350	44	1,002	1,046	—	—	—	—	—	—	—
Claims Approvers	—	—	—	391	338	729	402	491	893	363	866	1,229	1,882
Clerks, Accounting	346	3,174	3,520	278	2,702	2,980	202	3,530	3,732	—	3,887	3,887	4,261
Clerks, Correspondence	782	1,322	2,104	427	1,409	1,836	228	1,659	1,887	—	1,964	1,964	2,121
Clerks, File	156	4,637	4,793	99	4,494	4,593	55	3,725	3,780	—	3,629	3,629	3,218
Clerks, Policy Evaluation	144	1,397	1,541	89	1,045	1,134	43	945	988	—	951	951	935
Clerks, Premium Ledger	25	1,654	1,679	16	780	796	3	553	556	—	263	263	344
Console Operators	131	10	141	417	53	470	—	—	—	—	—	—	—
Computer Operators	—	—	—	—	—	—	1,765	481	2,246	2,104	257	2,361	2,315
Keypunch Operators	2	3,072	3,074	5	3,489	3,494	7	3,458	3,465	—	2,955	2,955	2,813
Premium Acceptors	62	672	734	9	518	527	5	606	611	—	570	570	563
Programmers	503	112	615	1,011	355	1,366	1,935	942	2,877	2,255	1,242	3,497	4,148
Secretaries	—	—	—	—	—	—	5	6,413	6,418	—	7,532	7,532	7,855
Stenographers	—	3,586	3,586	16	3,867	3,883	—	2,336	2,336	—	1,286	1,286	703
Systems Analysts	335	30	365	470	80	550	1,465	345	1,810	1,914	790	2,704	3,596
Tabulating Machine Operators	1,789	1,344	3,133	992	895	1,887	459	421	880	—	—	—	—
Tape Librarians	—	—	—	32	39	71	59	134	193	48	137	185	198
Transcribing Machine Typists	—	—	—	—	—	—	2	1,021	1,023	—	993	993	791
Typists	3	6,389	6,392	2	6,514	6,516	˙ 4	5,327	5,331	—	4,098	4,100	3,252
Underwriters	1,156	404	1,560	1,154	410	1,564	1,119	555	1,674	1,004	657	1,661	2,088

Sources: U.S. Department of Labor 1961, 1966, 1971, 1981. For each year, source is Average Weekly Earnings, Selected Occupations.
* No breakdown by sex given in 1980.
[1] The following metropolitan areas: Atlanta, GA, Boston, MA, Chicago, IL, Dallas–Fort Worth, TX, Des Moines, IA, Hartford, CT, Houston, TX, Jacksonville, FL, Los Angeles–Long Beach, CA, Minneapolis–St. Paul, MN, Newark, NJ, New York, NY, Philadelphia, PA.

computer/peripheral equipment operators (found under the heading office machine operator) grew more than 200-fold during this period, while computer specialists grew 50-fold. In part, this dramatic growth reflects the small size of these occupations in 1960; but even in the years 1970-1981, these categories continued to experience faster-than-average growth. Second is a drastic decline in or complete elimination of categories that are displaced by the computer. Noncomputer machine operators, such as tabulating or calculating machine operators, disappeared and stenographers fell to less than one-third of their 1960 total.

Alongside these expected changes are several anomalies. File clerks, expected to disappear with the growth of central data banks, declined only slightly. Other groups that were expected to decline have grown instead. It was thought that the spread of new technology such as word processing and semiautomatic dictating equipment would lessen the demand for secretaries. However, the number of women employed as secretaries grew more rapidly than clerical workers as a whole. One might speculate that the personal service and assistance rendered by secretaries remained critical to the operation of offices, as well as to the comfort and prestige of managers. These services may have had particular importance in the expanding field of personal, professional, and business services. Similarly, the number of receptionists and typists continued to grow—despite automated and semiautomated correspondence and telephone systems—due to continued expansion of communication in large organizations.

Finally, one interesting indicator of change in the office structure was the disproportionate growth in the number of clerical supervisors. This pattern may also be related to automation. Larger capital investment per worker and potentially greater productivity may stimulate attempts to increase managerial control of the work process.

As these varying patterns indicate, the impacts of technology on the occupational structure are not homogeneous. Technology may increase productivity in certain areas, but the volume of activities can increase even more rapidly, thus offsetting declines in employment. At the level of occupational structure, with data from different industries—some expanding and some shrinking, some undergoing change and others stagnating—it is impossible to separate the effects of technology from other factors. In addition, technology may be used to reorganize work so that, although a job category remains stable or grows, the actual work activity may be transformed. If the same title does not necessarily mean the same work activity or the same place in the social relations of the work place, then it is difficult to state precisely the degree of change or continuity occasioned by new technology.

To control for some of these factors (such as changing business patterns among industries), we examined the aggregate pattern of occupational changes in a single industry—insurance. The Bureau of Labor Statistics conducted wage surveys of over 200 insurance companies in 13 metropolitan regions in 1961, 1966, 1971, 1976, and 1980. Using these data, we can examine changes in detailed occupational categories (see Table 4.2).

For the most part, the data in Table 4.2 for the insurance industry correspond to the data for the clerical and related occupations in all industries. The fastest-growing occupations in the insurance industry were the "professional technical," the EDP (electronic data processing)-related programmers and systems analysts, most of whom were men. Other computer operators increased after 1966, but leveled off with improvements in the systems that increased capacities, and speeded up and decentralized processing. The positions displaced included those involving hand or mechanical processing: for example, tabulating machine operators had disappeared by 1976. Clerks involved in record keeping, transcribing premium payments, assembling records, calculating values of policies, and handling remittances (assemblers, policy evaluation clerks, ledger clerks, and premium accepters) were reduced in number, again despite an increase in the volume of activity.

In the meantime, most other positions dealing with transactions and communication remained at a stable level, including clerks in accounting and correspondence, while underwriters increased slightly in response to greater volume. Stenographers were rapidly disappearing and typists were becoming fewer; the new category of transcribing machine typist, who worked with dictating machines, made up for only some of the loss of these jobs. Although data on secretaries were not presented in 1961 and 1966, there was a substantial increase in secretaries between 1971 and 1976.

A related trend, not shown in either table, is the increased differentiation of levels within occupations. For example, in the 1961 insurance industry survey, file clerks were differentiated into A and B categories based on degree of autonomy/responsibility (U.S. Dept. of Labor 1961, 1966, 1971). By 1966, there were three levels of file clerks. Similarly, in EDP occupations, the levels of programming and systems analysts increased from two to three by 1971.[3] These finer differentiations probably reflect greater rationalization of office procedures and more explicit definitions of duties, changes consistent with the analysis of the critical model (Kraft 1977; Greenbaum 1979).

Examining changes in the distribution of women and men in the various occupations within the insurance industry reveals a striking pattern. With the exception of keypunchers, all of the EDP-related positions, including that of computer operators, began and remained overwhelmingly male. In contrast, most of the shrinking and stable positions that began as mostly female became increasingly feminized. Traditional clerical occupations (such as accounting clerks, correspondence clerks) that had a fairly sizable minority of men in 1961 had almost none by 1976. According to Hacker (1979), jobs in which females are concentrated, or have recently been allowed to enter, are most likely to be displaced by technology. The evidence in this case supports this claim. Although the largest category eliminated by automation, tabulating machine operators, had slightly more men than women in 1961, the other five occupations that declined 25 percent or more between 1961 and 1976 were occupations in which women were at least 90 percent of the 1961 labor force. As these occupations shrank, all five became virtually 100 percent female. Overall, with the exception of underwriting, the occupational structure in the insurance industry became more sex-segregated between 1961 and 1976, with the technical EDP jobs developing as male provinces, especially at the highest levels, while the routine clerical work became increasingly female.

Taking data on both the broad occupational structure and the distribution in one industry, what can we conclude about the relationship between office automation and the occupational structure? First, the introduction of the new technology was labor-saving--fewer workers were needed to accomplish certain tasks and some occupations were eliminated completely. Second, the continued expansion of clerical activity more than offset savings in labor; thus, the clerical labor force grew slightly overall. However, in insurance, a steadily growing industry that relies heavily on both automation and clerical labor, the number of traditional clerical jobs fell dramatically. Third, the new technology has been used not only to reduce the total number of jobs but also to reorganize the work, with the result that many occupations are narrower, more specialized, and more standardized, and rely less on workers' detailed knowledge of the particular office or business. Fourth, the expansion of computer-related occupations has increased the total number of jobs and has created some new, higher-paid occupations. However, the workers displaced by automation do not appear to benefit: the new jobs are defined as technical and are largely held by males. Women rarely move from traditional clerical jobs into these jobs. Instead, a new layer of largely male workers, supplemented by some college-educated women, has been recruited from outside and inserted into the office.

The critical model correctly directs attention to the reorganization of the occupational structure with new jobs for some groups, displacement for others, and more routinized work for still others. It is clear that what benefits management--the savings in labor costs--does not benefit workers as a whole, who undergo displacement or job degradation. However, it is also clear that different segments of workers experience different kinds and degrees of advantage and disadvantage from these changes. One segment, women, benefits less and loses more. They don't move into newly created or expanding technical jobs in the same proportion as men, and they suffer greater displacement and degradation as the occupations in which they are concentrated are reduced or routinized by automation.

LEVEL 2: THE ORGANIZATION

Our analysis of the aggregate level offered a picture of the changing national occupational structure. In order to see how these changes interrelate--how changes in one occupation are linked to changes in another--we must now look at particular firms. Unfortunately, there are few studies that provide detailed information on the changing occupational structure within firms. Most studies at the organizational level deal with the problems managers face during the introduction of automation, especially with

workers' attitudes toward automation.[4] Two early studies
(Helfgott 1966; Rothberg 1969) that present full before-and-
after pictures of the occupational structure in particular
firms will be reviewed to see what light they shed on the
relationships between technological change and the changes
in the clerical occupations, including differential effects
on men and women. We then review findings of two more
recent studies (Cummings 1977; Hacker 1979) that suggest
how patriarchal relations in the labor market interact with
technological innovations to produce the occupational structure in particular firms.

Helfgott (1966), in a case study of a large insurance
company, shows that the number of clerks involved in tasks
such as sorting, calculating, verifying, recording, and
maintaining records was markedly reduced following the
introduction of computers. In 1960, the company home office employed 4,475 clerical workers, accounting for two-
thirds of the total employment there. By 1964, that number had dropped to 3,872--a loss of 603 positions. In
addition, the 1964 figure included the new job of key-
puncher, which represented 154 new jobs (4 percent of the
clerical category). Thus, a total of 757 traditional clerical jobs (16.9 percent) had been eliminated. At the same
time, the company had added new technical employees (programmers, computer operators, systems analysts) and expanded the ranks of supervisory employees so that the combined category increased by 275 jobs (15 percent). Managerial staff increased during this period by 78 jobs (20
percent).[5] By 1964, clerical workers had dropped from the
original two-thirds to three-fifths of the work force in the
home office.

How did these changes affect the sex composition of
the office? Since traditional clerical jobs were almost entirely female, while the growing technical, supervisory,
and managerial jobs were held largely by men,[6] there was
a marked decline in female employment in the home office
between 1960 and 1964. This decline was coupled with increased dominance of men in the upper levels of the office
hierarchy.

Rothberg's (1969) report on automation in a branch
of the Internal Revenue Service shows similar outcomes
even in a context of expanding clerical employment. Before automation, the routine jobs were held primarily by
women (80-95 percent, depending on the job), and the administrative jobs were held primarily by men (over 90

percent). During automation, the total labor force grew
by 80 percent.[7] A large percentage of the increase occurred in traditionally female jobs. Examining and statistical jobs and sorting, classifying, and filing jobs, which
together accounted for 30 percent of employment under the
old system, rose to 50 percent of employment in the new
larger system. In addition, keypunch and other machine
operators doubled in number. However, the new, upper-
level, technical jobs created during automation were filled
almost entirely by men (95 percent). Although women continued to predominate in the total work force, men's domination of the higher levels of the office increased. Thus,
with increasing automation, male/female stratification in
the office became even more pronounced.

Change in the firm's occupational structure reduced
opportunities for upward mobility. Many high-level, complex clerical jobs disappeared early in computerization
(U.S. Department of Labor 1963). Their elimination com-
pressed the occupational hierarchy, cutting off mobility
for employees in certain departments or specialties. Similarly, middle-level jobs, previously viewed as training
positions, were eliminated or changed in ways that reduced
training opportunities. As a result, these jobs and the
ones below them became virtual dead ends. Similar blocks
to mobility of clerical workers after automation are found
in other studies of the insurance industry (Cummings 1977;
U.S. Department of Labor 1965), the cost accounting department in a steel company (Weber 1959), and other types of
firms (Hoos 1961; Shepard 1971). Overall, women who already hold traditionally female clerical jobs are least
likely to benefit from the changes accompanying automation. The available evidence indicates that these workers
are more likely to find their work unchanged or to experience negative consequences, such as loss of employment,
"deskilling," or diminished opportunities for advancement.

In addition to the overall effects on the occupational structure and the composition of jobs, technological
changes can have different and sometimes contradictory effects on particular segments of the clerical labor force. A
study by Cummings (1977) hints at the complex process by
which gender hierarchies are incorporated into technological
changes and work reorganization. In 1960, one unit of a
large insurance company employed approximately 400 clerical workers, male and female. Men were concentrated in
the higher-level jobs; women, in the lower-level jobs.

Over the next 15 years, the work process was reorganized and new technology was introduced. The result was a more standardized work procedure, a lessening of specific knowledge required by the workers, and a loss of approximately 175 jobs. At the end of the period, the unit was 95 percent female. As the jobs were reorganized and downgraded, they were made available to women.

The consequences are complex. On the one hand, the reorganized jobs held by women were lower in salary, prestige, autonomy, and opportunity for advancement than the men's jobs that were eliminated. On the other hand, the new jobs were better on these dimensions than most of the jobs previously held by women. The final ambiguity is that management is now planning to reorganize the work further—to eliminate over 100 additional jobs and to rationalize the remaining ones. It appears that the women were being used as a transitional labor force.[8] It is not clear whether management plans to transfer some of these women into the further rationalized jobs, or to draw on a new labor pool, such as minority men or women, for whom even these jobs might represent an improvement over previous employment opportunities.

A similar process in which technological change disadvantages women is described in Hacker's (1979) analysis of employment shifts at AT&T. Here, significant technological changes were taking place while the company was under a court order to carry out affirmative action. The combination of technological change and the shift of women from "female" to "male" occupations resulted in women being a smaller proportion of the company's labor force. In addition, both minority and white women were most often hired for jobs in which technological change was eroding job security and skills. The women were unable to resist being used as pawns in technological displacement, in part because male-dominated unions and individual husbands and fathers undermined their organizing efforts. For example, at one meeting of a union local, a discussion of women's issues on the agenda was put off until after a film on hunting and fishing was shown. Meetings of one group of women ended abruptly when the organizer's husband, himself a union member, decided his wife's activities were taking too much time from the family. Thus, patriarchal practices in the family, the unions, and the work organization influenced the way technological change affected specific segments of the work force.

LEVEL 3: THE WORK PROCESS

Finally, we turn to the impacts of technology at the work process level as experienced by the individual worker. Researchers of the consensus school (Blauner 1964; Shepard 1971) have pointed out that automation makes it possible to bring together in a single job functions previously separated out and divided among several jobs under mechanized technology. The presumption is that the resulting job is a more integrated one that gives the worker greater autonomy and reduces alienation. Unfortunately, this claim has never been properly assessed in relation to clerical work. The major published investigation during this period (Shepard 1971) deals with the topic primarily by examining the workers' attitudes. If workers in an automated office sound less alienated on a number of dimensions, Shepard infers that their jobs are more integrated and allow more autonomy; yet he fails to look at the actual content or organization of those jobs.

In contrast, those working within the critical tradition point out that bringing together several rationalized tasks does not necessarily increase autonomy; it may be a form of speedup (Rinehart 1978). Here, the argument is that automation requires the use of standardized formats, which means greater rationalization of work procedures and a loss of workers' autonomy in many aspects of the task (Braverman 1974; Glenn and Feldberg 1977, 1979; Hall 1975; Rico 1967). The argument is presented as if it were uniformly applicable across jobs and segments of the labor force. However, the way jobs are reorganized around new technology is not a given. What technologies are selected, how they are used, and how the work process is structured to fit the technology are decisions, conscious or unconscious. These decisions affect autonomy in two ways: by shifting the areas in which workers have latitude and by determining which segments gain or lose autonomy.

An example of these two types of effects comes from our own research on the reorganization of the "customer service" function in a public utility. Before the computer system was fully developed, customers called separate departments for specific types of questions. Clerks in each department provided information on a specific area: sales, bills, service/repair. Separate files were maintained in each office, and a complex question might require several phone calls to track down information. With computerization, the files were centralized. Now, one set of clerks, using computer terminals, has access to all the information. The clerks who answer these phones can look up a customer's account and explain a billing problem, set up appointments for service calls, or tell a customer the balance due on a special service. The clerk can also enter into the terminal any new information provided by the customer: the time someone will be home for the service call, the type of problem, a change in address, or other billing information.

The job involves a broader scope of information, but it is also more closely supervised. Under the old system, supervisors monitored clerks by occasional "listening in" on an extension. Decisions made in writing were reviewed periodically for quality and volume. Under the new system, machines automatically and continuously monitor the work done by each clerk. An automatic call distributor allots phone calls, recording the number of calls answered and lost (by customers hanging up) on each line. The clerk's code, entered into the computer terminal with every transaction, provides a tally of transactions and an error count. In this more rationalized system, each part of the job must be handled according to explicit procedures and within a specified time frame. Although the clerk now has access to information for all areas of the company, less knowledge of the procedures in each area is required than previously. Thus, she is less able to judge what constitutes a reasonable modification of these procedures. Management is also attempting to make greater use of slack time. Clerks are being asked to do part of the work of their previous position, entering routine billing data into customer accounts through their terminals during hours when there are few calls. Finally, the clerk no longer moves around to find records, but is tied to her desk/terminal all day.

It is difficult to evaluate whether there has been an increase or decrease in worker autonomy with reorganization. On the one hand, standardized procedures must be followed for taking care of routine customer requests. The clerk is also subject to close, though unobtrusive, supervision through machine counts. On the other hand, the clerks have broader information and are allowed more leeway in negotiating bill complaints/payments with customers. Management permits this discretion because it increases the likelihood that bills will be paid without addi-

tional expenditure. Since that is the ultimate goal of the
company, this discretion will be maintained as long as it
appears to contribute to that end. In this example, workers gain autonomy in negotiating with customers, but lose
autonomy in deciding what procedures to use and how to
pace the work.

Not only do the areas of autonomy change, but also
which groups of workers gain autonomy in particular areas.
The reorganization of customer service brought about a
shift from predominantly male to predominantly female
clerks. In the process, the job itself changed. When men
were in the positions, the customer service clerk was the
top position in a job ladder that began with outside work,
which was a completely male specialty. The male customer
service clerks, because of their previous work experience,
were knowledgeable about the physical equipment and often
advised customers on problems they were having with appliances. When women were brought into the job, they
were specifically told not to give such advice. In any
case, the new female clerks, coming from positions in accounting and bookkeeping, have not had any experience
with the equipment and are given no training in this area;
they are, therefore, not prepared to discuss these matters
with customers. Thus, discretion in this area has been
reduced. However, because of their experience in accounting, they are better prepared to discuss charges and payments, an area in which the male clerks had little expertise. Thus, autonomy in the financial area has been
increased. Whether knowledge of the billing system represents a greater or a lesser "skill" than knowledge of appliances is debatable. At the moment, the job remains at
the top of the nonmanagerial pay scale.

Given the change in company policy of discouraging
customer clerks from discussing equipment problems, it
might seem that the men remaining in the job, who constitute about a third of the category, have lost their area
of autonomy, while the newer women clerks have gained
autonomy. From our observations, this does not appear to
be the case. It is true that the men's special knowledge
has been declared "off-limits" and the areas of discretion
have shifted to those in which they have little expertise
and previous experience. However, because their practical
knowledge remains useful, and because they have the most
seniority, they continue to use this knowledge unofficially.
Indeed, their "special" knowledge of the equipment and

their longer experience in the job, reinforced by the cultural assumption that males are more authoritative, have combined to make the men informal consultants to the women. As a result, the men are viewed as the experts who "help the girls out" when they get a difficult question. At the same time, the men's lack of experience with billing has freed them from the obligation to do routine billing in slack time, presumably because they do not understand the system well enough to do it.

This example suggests that social characteristics of the workers, in this case "being male," may have an effect independent of the impact of technological change. The effect of sex is also evident in differences in closeness of supervision. One woman complained, "When we come back from lunch or break a few minutes late, it's: 'Come on, girls, let's go,' shouted out across the floor. When the men do it, nothing is said." Observation corroborated her account on at least two occasions. The difference in discipline in the utility company is consistent with the stricter enforcement of rules for women employees found in other settings by Langer (1972) and by Acker and Van Houten (1975). It is also noteworthy that the accounting system, in which the women are expected to be most knowledgeable, is the aspect of the work process that is now subject to closest supervision. Thus, it appears that the impacts of a technologically based reorganization of work on workers' autonomy may differ according to the social characteristics of the workers.

CONCLUSIONS

Review of evidence at three levels--the occupational structure, the industry, and the work process--leads to the conclusion that women have been more negatively affected than men by the reorganization of office work around automated systems. More women than men have lost jobs or had their jobs downgraded; women more than men have found their jobs closely monitored and externally paced. These differences reflect the different positions men and women occupied in offices at the start of the reorganization. Women clerks were affected more negatively and earlier in the process of automation than male professionals and managers.

However, we must be aware of varying effects among women. Reorganization has had different effects on different clerical occupations, and women are not distributed randomly across these occupations. Women with particular race, age, and educational characteristics are concentrated in particular clerical specialties. Hence, a given impact is often linked to a specific group of women, as the examples below indicate. Furthermore, as these examples also show, what benefits one group of women may harm another.

While the research reviewed in this chapter does not systematically examine all the segments within the female labor force, the available data indicate a complex pattern of consequences. Rothberg's (1969) analysis is the final stage of a longitudinal study. In an earlier, more detailed report about the beginning of the automation process, the Bureau of Labor Statistics (U.S. Department of Labor, Bureau of Labor Statistics 1963) indicated that over half (53 percent) of the women being displaced were over 45 years old, while 80 percent of the men entering new jobs were under 45 years old. Pictures accompanying the article suggest that the displaced workers were white, while two black women were employed in new keypunch positions. Hacker's (1979) study of affirmative action in the context of technological change indicates that white women declined most steeply as a proportion of the total AT&T work force, while minority women increased most steeply. However, the minority women who were hired were largely college-educated, while thousands of high school-educated black women telephone operators lost their jobs.

In our own research we found that the new telephone inquiry jobs provided opportunities for women with higher than average educational qualifications or seniority, but the consolidation of all telephone work into that job eliminated some jobs and removed public contact from all other positions.

In addition, we found that a job itself could be affected in contradictory ways. As we indicated, the telephone inquiry job was more integrated and higher-paid than the jobs it replaced, but it was also more externally paced and more closely monitored. It is difficult to say whether it was a "better" job or a "more stressful" one.

Is it important to analyze those varying meanings of technological changes? Does such detailed appreciation of variations affect the way we think about work and its relation to social structure? We think the answer to both questions is "yes." In an earlier period, many researchers assumed that the changes associated with the industrial revolution took place simultaneously, in a uniform fashion, across whole populations. With such a faulty picture of the nature and conditions of work, and the changes people were experiencing in their lives, these researchers found it difficult to understand why there were not more sustained uprisings by people whose entire lives were supposedly uprooted by the industrial revolution. Work such as Strumingher's (1979) shows that men and women were affected differently by changes in the technology and the work organization of the French textile industry during the 19th century. This is a clue to the absence of uniform response by workers. In similar fashion, the new technologies associated with computers are being hailed or decried as the basis of a new revolution. Yet now, too, the extent and direction of change differ by industry, by work process, and by segment of the labor force. Unless we study the pattern and process of change, we will make erroneous predictions of workers' responses and, having done so, will misinterpret their actual responses.

We have seen that the effects of work reorganization are often specific to particular segments within the female clerical labor force. So, too, are their responses. Women whose jobs are displaced may press demands for retraining or for new jobs. Those in new jobs that are higher-paid but more stressful may become more interested in upward mobility and, at the same time, more concerned about gaining control over the pace of the work. Those who work continuously at computer terminals may organize around the health effects of the new technology.

Only if we study the actual changes taking place in particular industries, firms, and work processes, and analyze the concrete way these changes affect specific segments of the labor force, will we understand the complex meanings of technological change, as well as the problems they create. With that understanding we can begin to interpret the variation in workers' responses.

NOTES

1. Our use of the concept of segment of the labor force differs from that associated with labor market segmentation theory (Barron and Norris 1976; Piore 1975). The labor market segmentation theorists stress the division of employment possibilities (the labor market) into two distinct types, representing different conditions of labor (core/primary vs. periphery/secondary). Our analysis stresses the division of the work force itself into distinct segments on the basis of social characteristics, with membership in a particular segment affecting the conditions of work that workers face, even in the same industry.

2. This point, derived independently, parallels Kasarda's in his analysis of the relationship between expanding size and administrative structure for three levels of social system. His research showed that the correlation between size and structural components differed for each of the three levels (Kasarda 1974, p. 24).

3. See Kraft (1977) and Greenbaum (1979) for analyses of this growing differentiation as a consequence of the "deskilling" of computer programming.

4. The case study literature was published primarily between 1955 and 1968, when the introduction of computers was expected to have dramatic effects on office employment. The chief concerns during this period were workers' reactions and personnel problems resulting from geographic and occupational shifts. This literature does not provide basic information about changes in the tasks or the working conditions of specific occupations or about the numbers of people displaced. Thus, we found these studies of little value for our analysis.

5. Increase in the size of the managerial staff following the introduction of computers has been noted by several researchers (Helfgott 1966; Hoos 1961). Various reasons are suggested: each worker produces more and, therefore, needs to be more carefully supervised; new kinds of jobs require new kinds of supervision that need to be tied into the administrative hierarchy; and, as the remaining clerical tasks become "more qualitative and less quantitative," some of the work shifts to administrative personnel—this last according to one administrator of Inland Steel Company.

6. It is interesting that most jobs related to computer processing, such as computer operator, are classified

as technical, but that keypunchers are classified as clerical. Perhaps the fact that keypunchers are overwhelmingly female influenced the classification, since existing female office jobs are defined as clerical.

7. Almost 30 percent of the labor force "chose" to retire or to quit during the transition period, and another 109 people accepted downgrading as an alternative to relocating. Thus, 36.7 percent of the original labor force was displaced. The previous occupation, sex, race, and age distributions are not given.

8. The practice of using women as a transitional labor force has been documented at least since the early introduction of electronic data processing. Mann and Williams (1960) note that employers believe women would have higher rates of (voluntary) attrition and consequently would hire them to fill temporary jobs during the change-over.

5

Devaluing Women's Work: The Undercount of Women's Employment in 1900 and 1980

Christine E. Bose

It is popularly assumed that during the 20th century there has been a "dramatic" increase in women's paid labor force participation. Census data, which indicate that 20 percent of all women were gainfully employed in 1900 and that 54.5 percent of all women participated in the labor force during 1985, appear to bear out this assumption. However, there are several reasons to doubt the "obvious" conclusion. First, the technical definition of employment has changed since 1900, becoming more inclusive of women's work since 1940. Second, it is generally agreed by researchers that an undercount of women's work occurred at the turn of the century (Jaffee 1956; Long 1958; Smuts 1960; Durand 1968), although only one researcher has attempted to calculate the extent of this problem (Ciancanelli 1983). In fact, even today, with better census definitions, certain forms of women's employment, such as home child care or off-the-books domestic work, remain uncounted or under-counted.

An exploration of the census undercount of women's work is important for several reasons. First, by correcting

I would like to thank the University of Washington Center for Studies in Demography and Ecology for making the 1900 Census Public Use Sample, used in the data analysis for this paper, available to me. Their aid in developing a tape format suitable for my purposes was invaluable.

the historical record, we gain a better understanding of women's lives. For example, there is a tendency to assume that men have always been continuously employed throughout their lives, and that until recently women contributed only discontinuously to a household's economy. An analysis of the undercount of women's work reveals that women's contributions to the household have always been fairly continuous. Second, because the process of estimating the undercount is based on an analysis of the income strategies chosen by households, uncovering previously hidden work illustrates the importance of the connection between work and position in family life. For example, married women were frequently assigned to economic roles that were not publicly visible, and their contributions were therefore more likely than men's (or single women's) to be hidden. Third, we improve our understanding of changes in the U.S. economy when we can accurately pinpoint the changes in women's work patterns. Finally, a discussion of the reasons that women's employment was undercounted reveals the role of ideology in shaping census definitions of work. In fact, changes over time and cross-national comparisons prove that different methods have been, and can be, used to count similar forms of labor. Thus, an analysis of census methods illustrates that the route to an improved count of women's work is not merely a technical question, but involves a more positive valuation of women's work.

In this chapter, we argue that the increase in women's employment in the 20th century is due, in large part, to shifts in the definitional ability of that work to be counted. Further, based on new data for 1900, we argue that there was a change in the locus of married women's work from home-based employment in a spouse's farm or business, taking in boarders, or doing factory outwork to employment at sites away from home, which increased the ability of women's work to be counted as the century progressed. Using knowledge of factors inhibiting women's countable employment in 1900, the research reported here uncovers an estimated actual labor force participation rate of between 48.5 and 56.7 percent when more contemporary definitions of employment are utilized. This rate is very similar to the 54.5 percent of women counted as employed in 1985.

The section below explains the census definitional and coding changes that have occurred during the 20th

century and account for our result. These changes were
not merely technical, and the second section illustrates
how definitions of employment reflected ideas about women's
proper role and the political needs of the U.S. government.
With this background, the projected recount of women's
work, no longer shrouded in turn-of-the-century ideology,
is presented. Of course, even today, with a different
locus of work and new census definitions, certain forms of
women's employment remain uncounted, reflecting contemporary ideology. Therefore, in the concluding section the
importance of uncovering the ideology underlying any census count is discussed, as are the implications of finding
similar, rather than increasing, women's work rates in
1900 and 1980.

THE U.S. CENSUS UNDERCOUNT
IN 1900 AND 1980

In certain ways, women's productive participation
is structured by the same considerations today as in 1900,
with many women employed in ways compatible with their
family life or spouse's job. However, in 1900 more of the
locus of this employment was in the home--a place where
it was less likely to be reported--and more men were self-
employed, making use of unpaid family labor that was also
largely uncounted. Some of this undercount problem is
embedded in census definitions of employment, and affects
the records of women's work in 1900 more than in 1980.
Correcting this will raise the earlier count of women's
work while leaving contemporary data relatively untouched.
However, other problems have resulted in the underreport-
ing of women's work both in 1900 and more recently.
In order to address these problems, we first examine
the definitions of employment used in each period. The
census definition of "gainful employment" used from 1870
through 1930 did not encourage the recording of women's
work. The term "gainful worker" defined those persons
aged ten and over who reported an occupation as "employed," whether or not they were working or seeking work
at the time of the census. By 1890, a person's occupation
was considered to be that "work upon which he chiefly depends for support, and in which he would ordinarily be
engaged during the larger part of the year" (Wright 1900).
Although one did not have to explicitly work for pay until

1910, housework was always explicitly excluded, and enumerator instructions later made it clear that women's homework in taking in boarders, for instance, was not to be counted as employment unless it provided the majority of her economic support (Ciancanelli 1983). The impact of these census methods on married women was tremendous, but was probably not quite as large for single women, who, if employed, were more likely to work in locations outside of the home where their work would be counted.

In contrast, the 1980 definition separates the civilian labor force into two components, the employed and the unemployed. People are considered employed if they are 16 years old or over and work for pay during the week of the survey; work 15 hours or more as unpaid workers in a family business; or have a job but are not working for such reasons as illness, bad weather, or vacation. Further, to be considered unemployed by 1980 standards, one has to be both not working during the survey week and to have made specific efforts in the preceding four weeks to find a job.

There are many obvious differences between the 1900 and 1980 definitions of employment, as well as several more subtle ones, that affect the counting of women's work. First, the age limit for inclusion among the employed has been raised from 10 to 16 years. This reflects the prevalence of mandatory school attendance laws, but also means that the contemporary work of young (primarily female) teenagers in baby-sitting or other tasks is not counted as employment.

Second, and more important, the current definitions separate the employed from the unemployed and from those not in the labor force. This results in a concise picture of who actually holds a job at a given point in time. At the turn of the century, the customary job was entered, whether or not a person was currently working or even seeking work. However, women's part-time remunerative work caring for boarders, selling eggs, and the like was not counted as work by the census unless it provided the bulk of their economic support. Such tasks were culturally viewed as a natural extension of women's service work for their families (Bernstein 1984). As a result, the amount of recorded home-based work was very low and involved only 14.1 percent of all employed women in 1900, including seamstresses, laundresses, and boardinghousekeepers (Matthaei 1982). Thus, in 1900 unemployed men and even those out of the labor force, such as the retired, could be recorded as having an occupation, while women who worked at home, part-time, or in a family business were usually recorded as housewives. In 1980, part-time workers are counted as employed and women's home-based work is supposed to be recorded. The latter jobs, in their contemporary equivalents, would include home day care; selling Tupperware, Mary Kay cosmetics, or Undercoverwear at house parties; and doing consignment computer work at home.

A third, related issue is how unpaid work is recorded. The current stipulation is that one be working for pay, unless one is occupied in a family business. This excludes a considerable amount of women's volunteer work, which could have been counted in 1900. In the gainful worker census series (1870 to 1930), one did not explicitly have to work for pay to be recorded as employed until 1910. However, studying and housework were explicitly excluded, the latter resulting in a bias against women's usual work. More important, although unpaid work could legitimately be counted in 1900, the census definitions encouraged women to report their prime role as housewife because the work they "chiefly" did was housework. Even if they actually worked 15 or more hours in a family business (which is considered employment by current standards) or were employed "temporarily," married women were usually recorded as housewives. This resulted in what we will demonstrate to be a severe undercount of women's work, particularly on family farms and in family businesses.

In 1900, when 37 percent of the population lived on farms and 53 percent lived in rural areas of under 1,000 people, women had more opportunity than in the 1980s (with only 3 percent of the population on farms in 1978) for the unpaid family work that is now explicitly included as labor force participation. Thus a great number of women who would now be enumerated as workers were not counted at the turn of the century. Ironically, when the census used a better definition, as part of a major reorganization of its job classifications in 1910, and encouraged enumerators to "never [take for] granted, without inquiry, that a woman, or child, has no occupation," it later bemoaned the "overcount" for women's work that was produced. This occurred particularly because women who regularly did outdoor farm work on family farms for no

wages were recorded as farm laborers. Government farm
experts had wanted this result to show that most farms
were family-run, but the net result was that demographers
discounted this 1910 "aberration" in the rates of women's
gainful employment (Ciancanelli 1983).

Undoubtedly part of the reason that women's unpaid
labor remained unrecorded in 1900 was that it was hidden
by male self-employment. Since women's contributions to
the family enterprises were unpaid and were done alongside
housework tasks, they were less socially visible. As Anderson (1987) indicates, the Victorian definition of the
homemaker obscured her economic function at the same time
that men's new absence from the home made women's domestic labor less visible. Since men no longer associated the
home with work for themselves, it was difficult for them to
associate women with work. Similarly, Ciancanelli (1983)
feels that women's work status, and not their marital
status, was the problem.

A final contrast between the census of 1900 and
those of more recent times is that the former explicitly applied a double standard in counting men's and women's
work. This difference is clear in the instructions to
enumerators. While men could report their usual employment and have their statements accepted, women's reports
were subject to additional criteria. Although men were recorded with their usual occupation, whether or not they
were currently engaged in it, married women who reported
gainful employment were asked if the work was done at
home and if it was only occasional employment. These
criteria were used to exclude women (and not men) from
the labor force totals. Thus, the presumption was that
married women workers were rare. Further, unpaid family
labor, performed primarily by adult women and children,
was not considered an occupation; and self-employment in
the form of taking in boarders was not included unless
women solely relied upon it to "eke out a living."

How do we explain this census double standard for
counting women's and men's work at the turn of the century, or the changing definitions of employment and the
modifications in enumeration methods since 1900? The origins of these different counting procedures not only are
technical but also reflect different ideological perspectives.

THE CENSUS AND IDEOLOGIES OF WORK

Ideology and the Census: The Turn of the Century

The international debate among census statisticians that occurred at the end of the 19th century, as described by Deacon (1985), confirms that the methods of reporting female and child labor were subject to political ideology and social influences. The British census of 1851 and the censuses of England and Wales of 1861 and 1871 were based on classical liberal doctrines that saw women as productive workers in the home, whether they were housewives or workers in a family occupation. Production of human capital through unpaid domestic work was seen as equally important as other occupations, and female relatives of farmers and small businessmen were automatically put in their own separate occupational category. The ideological goal of including women was to present a picture of Britain as a community of workers and a strong nation. However, the Australian colonies began to modify this approach. In 1871, New South Wales stopped automatically assuming women were assisting in family enterprises, while Victoria counted the wives and daughters of farmers and the wives of small businessmen in the husband's/father's category. In 1890 the conflict between these two colonies was resolved in a conference that defeated the liberal point of view. The new Australian classification became even more conservative than the newly revised British one. The Australians divided the whole population into breadwinners and dependents, the latter including women doing domestic work and unpaid workers in the home, as well as children and the infirm. The intent was to provide an image of a country where everyone did not need to work, and thus to appear to be a good place for British investment.

While the United States was not interested in attracting British investment through its enumeration of workers, the censuses of 1870 to 1930 did reflect an ideology popular in the second half of the 19th century that has been variously called "the cult of domesticity" or the "cult of true womanhood." These ideas served to justify a drive to achieve dual spheres, or the predominance of men in paid work and of women in the home. The cult of domesticity tried to elevate the social activity of mothering to an important task and women's homemaking into a profession, albeit a profession whose goal was for a woman to subordinate herself to the needs of the family (Matthaei 1982). This ideology was similar in substance, although different in goals, to that reflected in the new Australian census.

In part, the American ideology was a response to competitive capitalist society and an emotional need to keep the home as a "haven in a heartless world" (Kessler-Harris 1982). But it also served to solidify the new economic structure: male household heads had to work hard to support a family, since a working wife meant that the husband had failed. Further, women employed outside the home had to justify themselves even when their families needed the additional income, yet by 1900 it became harder to do remunerative work within the home. Many minority women objected to these new role constraints, and indeed they, along with working-class women, found the new family model unattainable because their families needed their earnings; but the majority of middle-class women supported the ideology.

The belief in the existence of dual spheres and the cult of domesticity helped to support the goals of patriarchy or of (white) men in the aggregate (Sokoloff 1980; Jensen 1980; see also ch. 10). For example, Sokoloff, Jensen, and Lehrer all point out that among the working class the dual spheres concept was one of the bases on which male unionists argued for women's protective legislation and for the family wage at the beginning of the 20th century. The outcome of protective legislation was to reduce women's ability to compete for better-paid jobs, while a single wage supporting one family meant that a second income would be unnecessary, thus reinforcing women's dependence upon men. The family wage was never attained by all working men, but it remained a strong trade union ideal. While the dual spheres concept, as concretized in the middle-class cult of domesticity and in working-class trade union goals, may have envisioned the sexes as different but equal, each heading its own sphere (Matthaei 1982), the reality was that women's sphere was to become economically dependent upon men's sphere.

This development paralleled a rise in racism at the end of the 19th century. The South moved to disenfranchise blacks and there was an epidemic of lynchings. In 1896, in the Plessy v. Ferguson decision, the Supreme Court announced its "separate but equal" doctrine, which

sanctioned the developing legal systems of racial segregation (Davis 1981). Thus two types of separate-but-equal
concepts arose. One urged white women to serve as
"mothers of the race" and leave the labor force, while the
other segregated and physically forced black men and
women into the lowest-paying jobs within the work sphere.
Southern and eastern European immigrant women were also
occupationally concentrated, since those native-born white
women who were employed sought occupations "socially
superior to factory work" done by ethnic women (Kessler-
Harris 1982, p. 137). These ideologies had clear economic
usefulness to middle-class white men, the group that had
the social power to promote them.

These ideologies were reflected in the enumeration
procedures used by the U.S. Census Bureau from 1870
through 1930 (with the possible exception of the 1910 census) and in the verification procedures instituted beginning
in 1890, when the census introduced machine tabulation
procedures (Conk 1981). In 1900, the census began systematically checking the accuracy of the new coding and
punching procedures by examining cards for blacks in the
North, foreign-born persons in the South, women in men's
jobs, and men in women's jobs. When such "unusual" cases
were encountered during the verification procedures, there
was undoubted pressure to change some occupational codes.
As Conk (1981, p. 68) indicates, "The punching clerks were
aware that their work would be rejected if they coded men
into 'female' occupations and women into 'male' occupations, even if they were true to the schedules. . . .
From the clerk's point of view, it would perhaps be better
to use a non-controversial occupation code in the first
place and avoid having one's work scrutinized." Further,
when the new census occupational classifications of 1910
loosely defined jobs according to levels of skill, the divisions between categories were more social than technical.
Essentially, skilled workers were in the crafts, semiskilled
workers were those who used machinery (operatives), and
laborers were included in the residual category of unskilled
(Braverman 1974). Women and minorities were presumed never
to be skilled and, under Alba Edwards' leadership at the
Census Bureau, those classifying individuals' occupations
were advised to take into account cultural information
about people. As a result, the status of some occupations
was lowered from skilled to semiskilled merely because
many women and children held those jobs (Conk 1978).

Thus, in its methods of assigning individuals to occupational categories and occupational categories to levels of skill, the census reinforced ideologies about the sexual and racial division of labor by determining certain occupations were "wrong."

In addition, and parallel to the Australian census, much of women's work was simply not counted. In both countries, this occurred because the census was intended to reflect the general social division of labor, the larger economic categories into which the population fell. In contrast, contemporary census definitions, initiated in 1940 because of the Depression, were intended to obtain an exact occupational distribution of the employed and unemployed at one particular point in time (Ciancanelli 1983; Conk 1978). The very definition of gainful employment used at the turn of the century, focusing on one's usual task, encouraged most wives to indicate their prime employment as housewife--even if temporarily working for pay or permanently working part-time. Since women did so many kinds of work--housework, factory outwork, employment in a family business, taking in boarders--nothing was really women's prime activity. In this way the census encouraged an undercount of women's work and a parallel overcount of employment by men, who were recorded in their usual job even when currently unemployed.

Second, when women were engaged in productive work, its location was frequently at home, rather than "outside," where it might more easily have been recorded as gainful employment. Some of their alternatives brought money into the household, but other women contributed by performing unpaid work on family farms or in small businesses. In the latter case, men's self-employment "hid" the unpaid work of wives and daughters, because throughout the census gainful worker series (with the exception of 1910) enumerators were instructed to record women working in a family business or on a family farm as housewives, rather than as employed. Their work was uncounted, devalued, and not taken seriously.

Ciancanelli (1983) argues that women's participation in such patriarchal or male-dominated household production units made their work invisible, and that the historical movement of women's work away from home-based units made their work more countable. Prior to this change, the male head of the household directly appropriated the income associated with his wife or children, so that their individ-

ual contributions were unrecorded. The move to "outside"
work and a separate paycheck was undoubtedly helpful in
making women's work visible. However, we argue that by
entering the labor force, women did not escape male domi-
nation--men hold the highest-status, highest-paid jobs.
Therefore, the greater undercount of women's work in the
past was not caused by a greater strength of patriarchy
in 1900, nor is there less patriarchy in the 1980s. Rather,
the form of patriarchal institutions has changed, as have
the census enumeration methods useful to them. Early
20th-century census methods reflected the then-common assumption that work was men's sphere, and women in the
home performed only housework. From 1870 through 1930,
support for the concept of dual spheres was built into the
census categories by which work was defined, excluding
home-based labor unless it was the major source of income.
Usage of these categories both reflected the pervasiveness
of the ideology of domesticity and simultaneously provided
data that supported the perception of dual spheres. They
assumed, rather than tested, the dual spheres concept.
Consequently, what we now consider to be women's dramatic
increase in employment in the United States since World
War 11 primarily represents a shift both in census definitions and in the locus of women's work so that it is once
more classified as such.

Ideology and the Census: Recent Trends

        In 1940 the U.S. Census Bureau dramatically changed
its definition of employment, developed a new occupational
coding scheme, and modified its verification procedures.
The Depression and New Deal social welfare legislation of
the 1930s meant that considerable political pressure was
placed on the census to provide accurate information on
the U.S. work force. For example, the Social Security Administration needed to know how many people were unemployed, and among the employed how many were workers
versus owners or self-employed (Conk 1981). Thus, the
earlier definition of gainful employment as based on one's
usual occupation was replaced by a definition of labor
force participation that includes those actually working or
actively looking for work during the census week. The
new definition excludes disabled and retired workers, thus
reducing the percentage of men reporting an occupation.

It also tends to exclude seasonal or "casual" workers such as women and minorities, although the former generally had not been included anyway. In total, the new definition reduced the size of the work force by 1.2 million people (Durand 1968). At the same time, a focus on the week of the census forced working wives--who previously might have claimed housewife as their primary role--and new workers, who had not yet found jobs, to be counted among the labor force. By 1945 the Census Bureau estimated that its continued revisions had added 2.25 million workers who had been incorrectly recorded as not in the labor force (Durand 1968).

The occupational classification system was also overhauled, changing from the 9 economic sectors of the 1910 census to 11 occupational divisions in 1940. The change was in response to the shift away from a craft and farming economy to an industrial one. The new categories separated head and hand (or white-collar and blue-collar) work, and then subdivided hand work by skill. There was also an attempt to make the divisions represent some rank order of social or economic class: professionals, farmers, proprietors, clerical workers, craftsmen, operatives, domestic service, protective service, other service, farm laborers and foremen, and laborers. Obviously, the social and economic purposes of the Census Bureau were rather entangled (Conk 1978).

The U.S. entry into World War II inadvertently instigated another modification in the 1940 census procedures, this time affecting the verification system. As part of the war effort, the government was encouraging women to enter jobs previously nontraditional for them, and information was needed on the success rate of these efforts. In order to speed up tabulations, and because of the new questions and procedures, the Census Bureau hired many new statisticians. These people were not well schooled in the prior verification methods that checked for women and minorities in "wrong" occupations. As a result, the published detailed census statistics of the fall of 1941 included many women and youths in occupations that were "unusual" for them and from which they had been excluded in previous censuses. Census Bureau director Alba Edwards feared this would give the false impression that the occupational structure for women and youths had greatly changed since 1930 (Conk 1981).

The figures were already published, and it was too late to go back and "check" the occupational codes against the original reports, so Edwards decided to modify only some of the figures. He chose nine occupations in which gender changes were most dramatic and recoded all of the women workers in those jobs to another category within the same occupational group. Women railroad conductors became officials of lodges or societies; women employed as baggagemen became clerical and kindred workers; locomotive engineers, locomotive firemen, and mechanics at railroad and car shops became tailoresses; railway brakemen and switchmen became operatives and kindred workers for railways; and women serving as firemen or soldiers, sailors, marines, and coast guard members were reclassified as guards, watchmen, and doorkeepers. Conk (1981) estimates that 6,110 women, one-third of them in the armed services, were reclassified. Thus, the sex-typed verification procedures initiated at the beginning of the century were not carried out in 1940, although new changes were made that were clearly wrong. Yet, while nine occupations were modified, other occupations, such as machinist, blacksmith, and boilermaker were not, and women workers remained counted in them; women were eliminated only from firefighting and railroad work.

When the final statistics appeared in 1942, newspaper and government reports expressed delight with the success of the war effort, which had drawn so many women into most traditional male occupations. The U.S. government helped to support on-site child care for such women, and in England working mothers could obtain time off for shopping and child care. Suddenly, the dual spheres ideology changed to encourage married women's employment, legitimizing their being counted as workers. The census inconsistencies between 1930 and 1940 went unnoticed, and the need for changing women's occupational codes diminished. Ideologically, the increased numbers of women reported in "men's jobs" inadvertently helped to support the image of patriotic "Rosie the Riveter," who had suddenly entered the labor force as her part of the war effort and later would happily return home. However, we should remember that some of these women had been in such jobs all along, although they had been counted in another category.

The definitional changes introduced in 1940 have continued, with minor modifications, as the basis of the contemporary census terms that were described earlier. These new definitions have several advantages for increasing the visibility of women's work; unpaid family work is explicitly included when 15 or more hours of work per week are involved, work for pay is counted even if it is home-based, and women are to report their current occupation regardless of what they usually do. But ideology continues to influence the U.S. census count of women's employment, and the enumeration is still not fully accurate.

First, the requirement that someone without a job be looking for work in order to be considered unemployed tends to undercount women's (and male minority) labor force representation. On the surface, this seems a reasonable requirement. However, there are large numbers of women who are interested in employment but do not look for it because they know there is none available near their home or with schedules to match their child care needs. While the government has now begun to estimate their numbers under the heading of "discouraged workers," they are not included as members of the labor force, as the unemployed are.

Second, most contemporary census reports do not separate full-time and part-time workers. The advantage is that women employed part-time are no longer primarily recorded as housewives. The drawback is that a false image is created: it appears that men and women are rapidly approaching labor force parity because 54.5 percent of all women and 76.3 percent of men were employed in 1985. Yet only half (50.2 percent) of the female labor force works full-time and year-round, the remainder working part-time, part-year, or both; in contrast, 74 percent of men work full-time year-round (using 1978 data). Prior to 1940, men were the majority of part-time workers, but since then women have become the majority. Thus, much of the "new equality" comes from counting previously uncounted work, and from part-time work moving out of the home. As explained in the next section, by estimating figures for female part-time, home-based work and unpaid family work in the 1900 census enumeration, we can show that the increase in women's labor force participation over the century is not as dramatic as current ideology would have it. Because the new definitions are not comparable with pre-1940 census counts, they have made historical comparisons difficult and create false impressions.

Third, since the census count focuses on one week, usually in March or April, those working seasonally at other times of the year are not counted. This particularly affects unpaid family farm workers, who are employed primarily in the summer and fall. This problem is not currently a large one for women because of the declining number of family farms, but it does influence the employment rate of minority farm workers—male and female alike.

Finally, much of women's remunerative home-based work is still not counted. Such employment is in what economists variously refer to as the underground, informal, irregular, and sometimes illegal economy. It includes multiple jobholding, usually by married men with families (De Grazia 1982); illegal employment in narcotics, gambling, and prostitution; and "off-the-books" work frequently done by illegal aliens, minority men, or women needing extra money. In the last category it is likely that women are the majority of workers engaged in home child care, off-the-books domestic work, factory outwork, and "sweated labor," or in giving piano lessons, running garage sales, selling home products, or having an illegal rental unit in the house (De Grazia 1982; Molefsky 1982). Molefsky reports that the underground economy is growing and may represent as much as 14 percent of the 1980 gross national product, but most of the research in this area is concerned with the effect on measures of the economy or on tax evasion (Humphreys 1985), and has relatively little focus on women per se. Nonetheless the Internal Revenue Service, the U.S. Department of Labor, and the Census Bureau are definitely interested in trying to count this work.

On the whole, the contemporary U.S. Census Bureau definitions of work are clearly very different from the earlier concept of gainful employment. While the modifications were most directly generated by the political pressures of the Depression, they also occurred because of the long-term transformation from an agricultural to an industrial economy and the parallel change in dual spheres sex role ideology. Such changes are not unusual, as the discussion of the Australian census indicates, nor are contemporary international census counts uniform in their methods. But in all cases the outcomes are fairly similar: census definitions, enumeration, and verification methods can be molded to conform to, and thus support, gender- or race-related ideologies. In fact, even internationally, variations in method affect the count of women's work more than that of men (Durand 1975; Benería 1982); but because people believe in the census's objectivity, the undercount of women's work (as well as that of minority men) is hidden by Census Bureau methods.

REEVALUATING WOMEN'S WORK IN 1900

In order to compensate for the male/female double standard embedded in the 1900 census, a recalculation and analysis of the amount of turn-of-the-century women's work is presented in this section. Although work that was never recorded cannot be fully recaptured, it is possible to modify the concept of gainful employment to count both unpaid work in a family enterprise and some forms of part-time paid work done at home. While this process does not take ideology out of the census, it does remove some aspects of the dual spheres perspective and makes the 1900 and 1980 definitions more comparable.

In the 1980s, it is common for an adult woman to seek employment outside of the home in order to keep a child in school and out of the labor force, but in 1900 the reverse was true. Families needing a second income might send adolescents or related single adults out to work while keeping adult women at home to supervise the household, take on some paying work, or both. The 1900 process frequently reduced married women's work options to those which socially were not distinguished from housework. As part of their home-based roles, women were expected to contribute unpaid labor to a family farm or small business. If the family needed cash, the major income opportunities for women at home were to take in boarders and lodgers or to do factory outwork. We can estimate the volume of uncounted unpaid family work on the basis of the occupation of the household head, and the amount of boardinghouse work by number of families with boarders where women claim no occupation; however, it is not possible to guess when women took in wash, or did sewing or other forms of outwork at home unless they themselves so indicate. Such occupations are better counted when performed in a factory or in another's home. Thus, even this reestimate of women's work will represent a slight undercount.

Our calculations for the turn of the century are based on the actual data about individuals drawn from the manuscript census as available through the 1900 Public

Use Sample developed by the Center for Studies in Demography and Ecology at the University of Washington, and do not rely on estimates based on published aggregate census reports, as Ciancanelli (1983) did. This data set includes 100,438 individuals drawn from all over the country who are recorded in 27,069 household units. For this analysis the 29,673 women between the ages of 15 and 64 were selected, since they were not likely to be in school and were below the current retirement age.

Among these women 6,662 (22.5 percent) report employment. This figure is higher than the 20.0 percent reported by the census because our calculations are drawn from the original enumerator reports and were not subject to the verification procedures.

Next we turn to unpaid family work in a farm or business. When a household head was engaged in agricultural endeavors, 15.7 percent of the household women reported gainful employment; when the head was a merchant of goods that might involve women in sales (including boots and shoes, clothing, dry goods, groceries), 21.8 percent reported employment; but when the family head held any other job, fully 26.3 percent of household women reported work. Thus, as suggested earlier (Bose 1984), males' self-employment reduced women's recorded employment. Yet there is every reason to expect that women in farm and small business households were actually performing unpaid family work for at least 15 hours a week. In fact, of the farm wives who reported gainful employment, 71.6 percent said they were family labor or family farmers.

Among farm households, 91.6 percent had no servants or hired hands to help with the work--family members' aid was essential. Another 4.9 percent of farms had hired hands in residence to help with the work, and in this case the wives effectively had boarders to care for. Thus 96.5 percent of farm families probably needed women's farm-related labor.

If we assume that 96.5 percent of the wives of men engaged in agriculture should have reported themselves as unpaid family workers, an additional 19.7 percent (5,839) of all women would have been reported as employed. Further, if farm daughters and other adult female relatives were also working at the same level as they would when the head had a nonagricultural job--that is, 40.8 and 36.3 percent, respectively, instead of the reported 21.7 and 24.2 percent--then 592 more farm women (an additional

2.0 percent of all women) would have been recorded as employed. Thus, a minimal estimate of additional women engaged in gainful employment through farm work is 21.7 percent (19.7 percent plus 2.0 percent). A maximal estimate is obtained by assuming that all women living on family farms were gainfully employed; then 28.2 percent more of all women would have been recorded as working. Because of the large numbers of people living on farms at the turn of the century, family farm work is numerically the largest component in the undercount of women's work. It is particularly important for minority women, because 50.9 percent of them lived in households engaged in agriculture, while only 32.8 percent of nonminority women did so.

Fewer women lived in households headed by small merchants: 3.3 percent of nonminority and 0.8 percent of minority women. At the turn of the century, it was not unusual for families in these circumstances to live above or behind their stores, and to have the household engaged in sales work or bookkeeping for the business. If we assume only half of all the wives did such work, and that daughters and other resident female relatives were employed at the same rate as they were when family heads had other jobs, then an additional 284 women (1.0 percent of all women) would have been counted as employed. If a maximum of half the household women were employed in family businesses, the estimate remains at 1.0 percent for the 304 women involved. They represent a small component of women's undercounted work.

A larger component is the home-based work that brought money into the household. Taking in boarders or lodgers was probably the primary method—10.4 percent of all women reported living with boarders, the likelihood being greatest in urban areas. The actual figures might be even higher, because resident female relatives were often recorded as such, rather than as lodgers, even when contributing to family income (Bernstein 1984). Although one might expect that having boarders would decrease the probability of women reporting a job, it actually increased it (Bose 1984), and the reported job was not always boardinghouse keeper. About a third of all women living with boarders who reported a job said they were in farming occupations, another 30 percent claimed to be boardinghouse keepers, and the remainder were in a variety of jobs dominated by laundry worker, nurse, dressmaker, and servant. Thus, taking in boarders was an indicator of economic need, and nonminority women were actually more likely to be gainfully employed in ·this circumstance. (This trend was not very pronounced among racial minority women, who tended to report occupations at the same rate, whether or not they took in boarders.)

Nonetheless, large numbers of women living with boarders were not recorded as having any occupation, although this varied with marital status: only 5.4 percent of wives, but 53.5 percent of female household heads, 41.6 percent of daughters, and 42.9 percent of other female relatives are recorded with occupations when boarders are present in a nonfarm or nonsmall business setting. Thus there was a tremendous amount of unrecorded paid work related to boarders performed especially by wives. If it is assumed that all wives who resided with boarders were earning money, then an additional 3.4 percent (1,005) of all women would have been employed. If the maximum estimate includes female household heads as well as wives taking in boarders, then 1,160 (3.9 percent) additional women would have been counted as boardinghouse keepers. While this contingent is not as large as those engaged in farm work, the recount of paid home-based work would be even greater if it were possible to estimate the volume of unrecorded factory outwork.

The components of our reestimate of women's gainful employment in 1900 are summarized in the table below, illustrating minimum and maximum figures for three types of undercounted work.

Type of Work	Minimum Rate	Maximum Rate
Unpaid family farm	21.7%	28.2%
Unpaid family shop	1.0%	1.0%
Boarders and lodgers	3.4%	3.9%
Counted employment	22.5%	22.5%
TOTAL	48.6%	55.6%

If the actual rate of women's gainful employment was midway between the low and high estimates, and our assumptions are well founded, then 52.1 percent of all women were gainfully employed at the turn of the century. This result is corroborated by Ciancanelli's (1983) calculated probable rate of 48.8 percent. More important, we can conclude that the rate of female employment has not changed greatly over the course of the 20th century and that the apparent increase in that rate to 54.5 percent is due to the increased ability of women's work to be counted.

CONCLUSION: 1900 AND 1980 COMPARED

Obviously these results contradict popular beliefs. What are the implications of finding similar, rather than increasing, female labor force participation rates over the course of the 20th century? First, we have supported the theory that women have always worked and contributed to a family's income.

Second, we can identify exactly who was a part of the turn-of-the-century undercounted, hidden labor force: unpaid family workers on farms or in small business; those engaged in the "underground" or "irregular" economy of the time, taking in boarders or doing factory outwork; and, demographically, native-born white women, more than foreign-born white (ethnic) or racial minority women (Durand 1968). Their work became counted, and increased the apparent numbers of employed women for several reasons: recent changes in census definitions; the shift in much of women's remunerative work to places outside of the home where it was more likely to be counted; and the general trend of our economy away from agriculture, which resulted in increased rates of employment, especially among married women, because of the large undercount that occurs in most countries of women's family farm work (Durand 1968).

Third, while the amount of women's employment has not changed over time, the nature of that work has changed. A smaller percentage of women's work is now in family enterprises and instead involves working for others. Part-time work used to be available only to homeworkers, whose contributions were then regarded as part of their family chores; now part-time jobs also exist abundantly in firms, and more of women's part-time work occurs where it is visible. Yet these changes in the nature of work do not mean women are better off (see ch. 2). In fact, at any given point in time only about 27 percent of all adult women, but about 56 percent of all adult men, are working full-time and full-year. Thus, while more recorded women's work means that greater percentages of women are directly earning their own money, it does not necessarily imply economic independence, since so few women work full-time, year-round, and even those who do, earn an average of 60 percent of the median male income.

Finally, a study of the undercount of women's work indicates the importance of uncovering the ideology behind any census count. As we saw, the ideologies embedded in the 1900 census are different from those of the 1980 census. However, in making the 1900 census more comparable with the 1980 one, we did not remove ideology. Rather, we held it constant, so that both censuses reflected contemporary ideas. We know that the 1980 census has problems of its own and is not nonideological. Further, both censuses share some ideological components. For example, women's unpaid work in child rearing or housework is not considered labor (or even "unpaid family labor") in either time period, nor are new tasks such as installing your own phone counted. Thus elements of the dual spheres ideology remain in the 1980 census, separating unpaid domestic tasks from "work." While it is probably not possible to achieve a nonideological census, we want to understand its biases and strive for a census that does not undervalue women's economic contributions.

6

"Cogs to the Wheels": The Ideology of Women's Work in Mid–19th-Century Fiction

Amy Gilman

> The girls did not so much seem accessory
> wheels to the general machinery as mere
> cogs to the wheels. (Melville 1855, p. 245)

The emergence of working–class women as significant characters in American fiction is a subject seldom treated by
either literary critics or historians. Partially this reflects our culture's general tendency to hide or mask the
female working class and its importance in American history and culture, but it also suggests the extent to which
questions of class and gender have until very recently
been considered outside the purview of traditional 19th-
century literary and cultural studies. Yet, an examination of mid–19th-century fiction suggests that writers of
this period were actually quite conscious of women's work
and of working women, and that they attempted to integrate them into their general commentary on American
social life.

The arrival of the working woman as a legitimate
character coincides with early industrialization: the development of the factory system, the rise of the modern
city, and especially the emergence of a female working
class. By the second quarter of the 19th century, women,
both immigrant and native–born, were central to the process of industrialization already under way. In textile
centers like Lowell, Massachusetts, the famous "mill girls"
formed the basis of the labor force; in cities and towns
characterized by mixed early industrial economies, women

were similarly essential to all the processes of production. By the 1840s, thousands of women worked in factories and sweatshops producing clothing and shoes, maps and books, leather goods and hats, and many other manufactured goods. Thousands of others took piecework into their homes, ran boardinghouses and laundries, or worked for wages as domestics in families other than their own. Poorly paid and often horribly exploited, these working-class women constituted an essential part of the social portrait of early industrial America. And, for many men and women, the presence of the female worker constituted a perplexing and often fearsome consequence of industrial progress.

The working female character appears most often in 19th-century popular fiction as opposed to belles lettres. But we also find her in the works of two of the most important writers of the American literary renaissance--Herman Melville and Nathaniel Hawthorne. Not surprisingly, these two distinct traditions developed strikingly different treatments of this subject, suggesting a range of imaginative possibilities within the context of 19th-century American culture. Yet, despite their differences, both traditions offer relatively limited portraits, suggesting the extent to which women in general, and working women in particular, remain culturally, if not economically, marginal to the dominant traditions in American culture and society.

The purpose of the following discussion is to examine the treatment of the working-class woman in both traditions in antebellum American literature. I have not attempted a comprehensive study, but instead have tried to pick representative examples of the subject under study. I am interested in the ways in which the working woman was and was not integrated into American fictional literature of the period, and how this integration expressed a complex mixture of ideas, attitudes, and cultural meanings about the roles of women and work in American society and culture.

THE POPULAR NOVEL

The arrival of the poor and wage-earning woman as a legitimate literary subject parallels the rise of the sentimental novel, increased literacy, and an expanded, and largely female, readership.[1] The presence of this character reflects the general concentration of women (of all classes) within the expanded corpus of popular novels in the first half of the 19th century. It also coincides with the increased bifurcation of "highbrow" and "lowbrow" culture, and with the tendency to exclude women and women's concerns from the corpus of classic American literature, the works of Hawthorne and several tales of Melville being notable exceptions.[2] Usually, therefore, the working woman is found in what Nina Baym (1979) terms "women's fiction," "novels which are written about women, are addressed to women, and tell one particular story about women" (p. 22). This fiction also tended to articulate a domestic ideology that upheld separate spheres for men and women, the significance of family life, and the belief that women, operating from the household as wives and mothers, were the source of Christian values for the society as a whole. Moreover, the working woman usually appears in stories that represent a blend of reform and domestic ideology (such as espousing temperance or prison reform), a genre that found its finest expression in Harriet Beecher Stowe's Uncle Tom's Cabin (1857).[3]

Much has been written about the cultural meaning of this domestic literature. Critical debate has centered on whether it was in any sense oppositional or alternative, to use Raymond Williams' (1973) criteria, to mainstream American culture (p. 10), or whether it merely reflected and ultimately enhanced the values of the dominant patriarchal and early industrial capitalist culture. Sentimental literature, as Mary Kelley (1979) writes, is seen from either of two general critical perspectives. One view, best articulated by Ann Douglas (1977), faults such literature for its sentimentality and its popularization of bourgeois values, which, she maintains, inhibited the social and political roles of women, sentimentalized children, and reinforced strict gender divisions in American culture. The second perspective on sentimental literature suggests that while it upheld the domestic dream of the bourgeois life, it also harbored a discontent with many of the characteristics of the new social and economic order. Critics such as William R. Taylor, Helen Papashivly, Catharine Sklar, Nancy Cott, and Nina Baym maintain that in the glorification of the female-identified values of charity, piety, community, and maternity, and in the longing for the return to the traditional values of a mythic earlier society, domestic feminists rejected the competitive, individualistic, and materialistic values they associated with the social and economic

transformation occurring in their midst.[4] In this literature, Kelley (1979) argues that the writers perceived the
distance between the realities of everyday life and the
dream of domestic happiness, and expressed "an undercur-
rent of dissatisfaction and despair" with the status of
women (pp. 434-436).

The characterization of the wage-earning woman
moves us once again into the center of this debate about
the meaning of sentimental literature. Because of societal
ambivalence about the existence of the woman who worked,
her role and significance within popular literature were
problematic for 19-century writers. Yet novels about women
and work are interesting precisely because they confront
questions of reality, social class, and gender within the
context of bourgeois domestic values. By dealing with the
social and literary problems posed by these new women
through sentimentalization, the authors of popular fiction
turned the working woman into an idealized bourgeois her-
oine--a symbol of virtue and victimization. Within this
predominantly bourgeois domestic framework, the virtues of
home and hearth were often interwoven with an awareness
of and sympathy for the changing lives of American women.
That work and domesticity were intertwined in this fiction
suggests that popular novelists reflected the very real
connection of these two strands in the contemporary culture. Moreover, the fusion of these two apparently anti-
thetical dimensions of 19th-century life--domesticity and
working-class life--had important implications for the development of American attitudes about class and gender.

Charles Burdett, a New York journalist and the
author of many popular urban novels, was typical of many
authors who saw their fiction as having a definite social
and moral purpose. All of his works had a specific message, urging temperance and Christian charity, or chron-
icling the dangers of quickly made fortunes. Burdett's
preface to The Elliot Family, or The Trials of New York
Seamstresses (1850) is instructive because it provides us
with information about his motivation for writing as well
as his feelings about the novel.[5] Inspired by such English
social novelists as Charlotte Tonna, Burdett was convinced
that the problems of working English women were shared
by American women. He hoped a female author would write
an American version of Charlotte Tonna's bitter Wrongs of
Woman (1843-1844), but since no one had done so, he took
up the task himself. In the preface, Burdett stated that

his purpose was "to show the public the utter inadequacy of the compensation paid for female labor." He hoped that "some means may be devised whereby the conditions of some thousands of female operatives in the city may be ameliorated" (p. vii). The Elliot Family was written specifically to publicize the conditions of seamstresses.

Other novelists, both male and female, were equally straightforward about their purposes. In Ernest Grey, or the Sins of Society: A Tale of New York Life (1855), Maria Maxwell advocated both prison reform and improved conditions for female labor. Interwoven in her complex tale of mistaken identity, romantic love, and the evils of the prison system is a steady thread of narrative describing the life and work of two lower-class women in New York City during the 1850s:

> True labor is excellent, is honorable, is
> necessary, but it must have limits--human
> beings have other and higher faculties to
> cultivate, and there must be something
> astray when woman, socially restricted and
> naturally unfitted for some pursuits, is
> forced to labor sixteen hours a day of the
> twenty four to obtain a mere subsistence,
> soul and mind stinted in their growth,
> while man, by a few hours of labor, can
> support in comfort not only himself, but
> his family; and this is because woman is
> weak on all points save one--unhappily for
> herself--she is strong on endurance.
> (p. 18)

Similarly, Sara Parton (who wrote under the name Fanny Fern) used her novels occasionally to protest the conditions and limited opportunities for working-class women. In Ruth Hall (1855), the story of a woman who seeks and achieves financial and emotional independence, Fern deplores the conditions of work for female factory operatives in the garment trades.

In the fiction dealing with working women, the authors used the novel as a vehicle for informing the reading audience about women's work. The processes of work, as well as the common practices of the trade, are explained. Wages and information about rent, food, housing, and daily care tend to form an important part of the novel's content. The depiction of reality, however, is often limited to such specific information, reflecting both contemporary ambivalence about women's work and the limitations of the author's imagination. For example, working female characters like the Elliot women seem always to work as seamstresses. Indeed, "seamstress" became a generic term for many kinds of female labor, rendering her a stock character in popular literature and graphics: "seamstress" thus becomes a metaphor for female suffering and the degradation of women's waged labor.

The problem of social class and relationships between men and women of different classes is central to the popular urban novels. Whether the author affirmed the American dream of social mobility, or whether he or she used social class as a metaphor to confront problems of morality, the depiction of collective class behavior runs through almost all 19th-century popular literature. In these American novels the issue of class provides the central tension, since both the story line and the moral of the tale revolve around the juxtaposition of class relationships.

Among urban fiction, The Elliot Family is again a good example. The story opens with a glimpse of two households: that of the Elliot wife and two daughters, Clara and Laura, in a deathwatch around the bed of the father and husband; and that of a materialistic and nouveau riche middle-class family, the Simmonses, in the parlor of their house. As in so many novels of this type, the two families offer the reader a study in contrasts, one family a distorted reflection of the other. Both families have two daughters, and we follow the daily existence of all the principal characters until their death or marriage. The dying Mr. Elliot is a respectable mechanic, his daughters pious, selfless, and warmhearted. Mr. Simmons and his wife, by contrast, have scrambled their way up the economic ladder by deceit and trickery, and finally attain not only money and fine china, but also the mortgage of the Elliot family house. The death of Mr. Elliot plunges his wife and daughters almost instantly into poverty. Stripped of virtually all their possessions, and most of their friendships as well, these women, without men, are without any social position; and, because of their gender, they lack the power to preserve any prior social status. Most of all, they lose their respectability and marriageability in a social world dominated by both patriarchal and commercial values.

Burdett is remarkably sensitive to the nuances of class behavior as well as to the details of social and economic life in New York of the 1840s and 1850s. He chronicles for us the transformation of the garment trades, and the quick rise in fortune of those who seized the opportunity and rode the wave of the developing factory system. Mr. Simmons, the middle-class patriarch, is a fine, if somewhat caricatured portrait of the new manufacturer who exploits his female labor while showing a kindly and charitable public demeanor. New factory owners like Simmons (who closely resembles Bounderby in Dickens' Hard Times) are the culprits in the social novels: it is they who have turned their backs on their humble origins, victimized the needy, and exploited the new factory workers, particularly women. They are distinguished from the old wealthy merchants who maintained a benevolent public pose. Justice prevails in the course of the novel, however, and Simmons receives his due when his business fails and his life-style disintegrates.

Burdett's message about the Simmons family and what they represent is clear and also typical of other sentimental and domestic novels: the pitfalls of American life at midcentury were vast; money quickly gained was just as quickly lost; and those who made it immorally would reap their just reward. The belief that wealth and social status were not fixed only helped to underscore the sense of danger and transience in American life. True "class," however, was not linked to cash--only false values and acquired tastes were. The women in the Simmons family, totally dependent on paternal money and its fruits, ultimately suffer more than the man. Without their father's money and connections, they, like other dependent women, lose their home and possessions, and are stripped of their position in society. Mr. Simmons, despite his setback, is left relatively untouched by his changed situation. False women are, in the reckoning, treated worse than evil men.

The theme of identity in this popular urban fiction is interwoven with questions about social stratification and the portrayal of reality. Appearance and reality motifs, the clearest expressions of this theme, predominate in many of the tales and are used to explain events otherwise difficult to comprehend. [6] In The Elliot Family, the women are poor and in need of employment because of the deaths of their husbands and fathers. Although never wealthy, the Elliot women were the wife and daughters of a skilled artisan who lived according to proper bourgeois domestic values. All members of the family were presumably American-born, so the issue of immigration and ethnicity did not have to be tackled by the author. Similar patterns are established in other novels. In Timothy Shay Arthur's Lizzie Glenn, or The Trials of a Seamstress (1855), Lizzie and her father are the sole survivors of a shipwreck—a typical event in popular novels. Her father becomes deranged and no one believes their true identity. Lizzie takes her father to an insane asylum outside of Boston and tries to find work for herself as a seamstress in that city. In the end, of course, true identity is revealed and Lizzie, really Eugenia Ballantine, a southern belle, is finally allowed to give up her needle and marry her long-lost fiancé.

As in The Elliot Family, the usual explanation for the woman's low social position was widowhood or the death of her father. Often the unsuspecting widow or daughter finds herself done out of her inheritance by some evil relative, guardian, or business associate. In Sarah Parton's Ruth Hall, (1855), nasty relations refuse her help because of her strong, independent spirit. More common was the situation in Chances and Changes (1845) or Lilla Hart (1846), both urban novels by Burdett, where the women are nefariously, if temporarily, deprived of their money. In all these cases the women are victims, and their poverty an accidental or inadvertent event that has no relation to their own actions.

Whatever the causes of deprivation, the author usually informs the reader that although the women are poor or working as seamstresses, their true identity is disguised. In Lilla Hart, the orphaned Lilla is described as "different" from the usual poor. In Chances and Changes, mother and daughter reveal their real social class by their tone, manners, and behavior; and well before the reader realizes that they were the victims of fraud, he or she can observe their grace and delicacy. In Arthur's Lizzie Glenn (1858), Lizzie is described as having "a taste and appearance that showed her to be one who had moved in a circle of refinement and intelligence" (p. 29). And, in general, a variety of euphemisms and descriptions serve as a code to indicate to the reader that a particular female character is indeed truly worthy or respectable. For example, their hands are described as delicate or their clothing is noted as worn and old but of fine quality. Where visual symbols fail, manner and tone in the dialogue suffice to clue in the reader. And, of course, Christian charity and the avowal of religious concerns are the best indications of all.

English novels seldom shied away from vivid descriptions of the working classes. In the novels of Tonna, Gaskell, or even Dickens, it was possible for lower-class characters to be respectable and good while legitimately poor. In American literature, even that which was intended to educate, there was little space for the working classes. Those who were poor and worthy not only were expected to conform to middle-class definitions of behavior and manners, but also were, in the long run, denied their class identity and ethnicity as well.

Because of this peculiar reconstruction of events, the portrayal of class in these novels is nullified from the start. All of the characters are ultimately "middle class," and class differences become only temporary and superficial. In confronting the problem of class, particularly as it applied to women, a curious paradox is thus constructed that allows one to read about the poor, to sympathize with their situations, and even to urge reform while never having to really accept the notion of class distinctions within American culture. This paradox—the admission and denial of class within one framework—is characteristic of novels that contain working female characters.

This framework also allowed the reader some degree of consolation in a society that seemed to offer no real protection from a sudden loss of wealth or fortune, and it also helped to establish and reinforce the mythic notion that America, unlike England, was a classless society and that most Americans were middle-class. Perhaps most important, these ideas removed women as a social threat by creating an ideology that perceived working-class women as victims. Once the issue of class identification was established, and once the principal working-class female characters could be identified as victims rather than as threats, popular authors were freed to construct a working-class heroine who conformed to very special specifications. Working-class women came to take on all the characteristics of the finest and purest bourgeois heroines; they were pure, pious, and hardworking. Moreover, an entire subculture was created of poor women in fiction, a subculture that provided an idealized mirror image of middle-class domestic life.

Significantly, their poverty and sex excluded these working-class characters from ordinary society. Like

Hawthorne's Hester in The Scarlet Letter, they were forced
by circumstances to create a world unto themselves; unlike
Hester, however, they create a complex social world, one
that is exclusively feminine and in which men seldom, if
ever, intrude or intercede. Here women and children, des-
perate though they are for the meager necessities of life,
always help one another. They work, live, and die in
close quarters, sharing what little they have and never
turning on one another or rejecting friendship. While
their material existence bears little resemblance to domestic
feminine middle-class culture, the women of this feminine
subculture of poverty reflect all of its ideal values. Poor
women are the repositories of goodness, charity, and cooperative behavior. In fact, they are more likely than
their middle-class counterparts to behave according to true
Christian principles.

Most of the women in the novels of working-class
life have lost their original or nuclear families. They
create new "families," without men or fathers, and these
reconstructed families are in many ways idyllic. Although
they are established out of economic or social necessity,
the economic and emotional relationships contained within
them are pure. Housing, food, and the necessities of daily
life are automatically and cheerfully shared. Even money,
so often the source of domestic difficulties in popular tales,
is freely shared by those in need. In T. S. Arthur's
Lizzie Glenn (1858), Lizzie establishes an important friendship with Mrs. Gaston, a poor widow whom she refers to
as her "more than mother." And in Maxwell's Ernest Grey
(1855), the two principal female characters establish a
friendship that sustains them through their difficult and
good times. They, in turn, befriend the wife and child of
the ill-fated Ernest Grey and leave no stone unturned to
aid him. The two women live and work together, sharing
their lives and feelings as well as their material existence.
After the marriage of Lizzie Roberts to the good Richard
Kane, her dear friend comes to live with them, remaining
an essential part of their domestic married life. In Burdett's Chances and Changes, a similar friendship emerges.
Here Jane, the poor daughter of a milliner (and once
wealthy matron) marries happily and brings her friend
Anna to live with her and her new husband.

In general, men are present in these stories only
at the beginning and the end of the narrative, and are
always outside the principal action of the story. This

construction works well as a literary device, since it re-
moves men from the scene and allows the author to focus
primarily on women. The exclusion of men, and the emphasis on female community and female friendship, clearly
serve other and more important functions as well.

Smith-Rosenberg (1975) has chronicled the importance
of female friendships and relationships in 19th-century
America. What is interesting is that these relationships
should be idealized in fictional descriptions of the poor.
By creating what is essentially a female "culture of poverty" in an American urban environment, 19th-century
authors articulated very particular ideas about sex, class,
and poverty in an emerging capitalist and industrial culture. They not only came to idealize female cultural
values and the implicit sexual segregation of economic
roles and social function, but also saw the fullest reali-
zation of these ideals in a world of poverty and deprivation.

If the emotional and spiritual lives of women like
Clara and Laura Elliot remain intact, the physical toll
they sustain is tremendous. What happens to women in
novels such as these suggests what their alternatives were
in 19th-century urban culture. Marriage, the happy end-
ing for all good Victorian heroines, was bestowed upon
relatively few working-class women. In Burdett's Lilla
Hart and Chances and Changes, marriage, when it does
occur, serves a dual purpose: it resolves the problem of
personal identity for the female character, and it relieves
her of the necessity to work. Those women who do marry
in popular novels, and who are also initially seamstresses
or poor, raise their class status through marriage. Lizzie
Roberts in Ernest Grey becomes domestic and middle class,
as do the characters in Chances and Changes and Lilla
Hart. In those novels where the women were originally
upper-middle-class, as in Arthur's Lizzie Glenn, the resolution of the story lies in the reclamation of upper-class
status and a long-lost fiancé. And since women often
took their best friends with them into their new households,
two women were saved by the marriage of one. The new
household thus came to be dominated not so much by a
man and woman as by two women who maintained their
friendship and shared the new household responsibilities.

For other important female characters there are less
happy endings. Again The Elliot Family provides a fine
example. In the course of the novel Mrs. Elliot and her

two daughters die. Their deaths are painful, slow, and ultimately merciful. They are also logical. Within the framework defined by Burdett, such women had only two possible alternatives: death or marriage. Because of their respectability, their chastity, and their moral purity, there was no other way to resolve their lives within his limited imaginary framework. Their physical decline becomes a metaphor for their economic deprivation and victimization. Their deaths reflect their powerlessness to resist the social isolation and economic privation to which society condemned them. The poor seamstresses could not survive in New York City.

MELVILLE AND HAWTHORNE

Melville

Although the character of the working woman is usually found in popular fiction, both Hawthorne and Melville utilize different versions of "working women" to explore contrasting dimensions of 19th-century culture. Melville's "The Tartarus of Maids" (1855) is an inseparable companion piece to his "The Paradise of Bachelors." Both stories share a central character, a male figure, "a seed seller" who journeys to the Knights-Templars, an exclusive men's club of the old order, in the first story, and to a paper factory in the Vermont hills in the second. In London, this American, along with nine bachelors, is served an elegant and plentiful dinner that "was the very perfection of quiet absorption of good living, good drinking, good feeling, and good talk . . ." (p. 236). In "The Tartarus of Maids," our narrator is far removed from London, traveling past "Mad Maid's Bellow's Pipe, and into a rocky gorge, commonly called Devil's Dungeon," where "Blood River" runs (p. 239). He arrives at a paper mill that manufactures the envelopes he uses for his seed business. The setting is bleak; the factory, a classic example of the "machine in the garden" (Marx 1964, pp. 15-16). In the midst of the January snow he sees the factory: ". . . a large white-washed building, relieved, like some great whited sepulcher, against the sullen background of mountain side firs, and other hardy evergreens, inaccessibly rising in grim terraces for some two thousand feet" (pp. 239-242). Upon his arrival he exclaims to himself,

"This is the very counterpart of the Paradise of Bachelors . . ." (p. 243).

The narrator soon comes upon the workers in the paper factory--a series of pale, shivering girls. Amid the hum of the machinery, "that vaunted slave of humanity . . . the girls did not so much seem accessory wheels to the general machinery as mere cogs to the wheels" (p. 245). It is precisely the juxtaposition of these two worlds, one exclusively masculine and the other feminine, that gives the stories their importance.

In these two stories, Melville explores contrasts: male and female, wealth and poverty, city and country, life and destruction, luxury and deprivation, the exploiter and the exploited. Together they shape his indictment of technology, the new factory system, and the life of the factory operative. More important, they raise questions about the nature of exploitation and the workings of a system that denies all participants their humanity, life, and sexuality.

All the principal characters are unmarried and victims of their respective cultures: even the owner of the factory, a bachelor, is analogous to the London bachelors of the first story. The factory operatives, however, are all maids, leading the narrator to wonder out loud: "Why is it sir, that in most factories female operatives, of whatever age, are indiscriminately called girls, never women?" The owner replies:

> Why, I suppose, the fact of their generally
> being unmarried . . . for in our factory
> here, we will not have married women:
> they are apt to be off-and-on too much.
> We want none but steady workers: twelve
> hours to the day, day after day, through
> the three hundred and sixty five days,
> excepting Sundays, Thanksgiving and Fast-
> days. That's our rule. And so, having
> no married women, what females we have
> are called girls. (p. 254)

Upon realizing that all the women he had seen, young and old, are maids (virgins), the narrator is overcome with emotion; he pales and hastily leaves the dungeon. "Then shooting through the pass, all alone with inscrutable nature," he exclaimed--"Oh! Paradise of Bachelors! and oh! the Tartarus of Maids!" (p. 254)

Melville employs the factory girls to describe the bleakness of the new industrial and capitalist age, the victimization it creates, and the contrasts that are its essence. The bachelors in the first story are all prosperous and comfortable, the unspoken owners of the new technology, who are removed from, if not untouched by, the immediate damage the new technological system creates. The women, by contrast, are all poor, quickly aging, and slaves to the machinery they tend. Indeed, their lives are so awful that the narrator is unable to endure the contrasts between the two worlds he has experienced.

Aside from the general theme of woman as victim, which is sparsely but effectively employed here, Melville uses these women to portray isolation and loneliness, particularly that brought about by human detachment from nature. Sexual imagery expresses this theme throughout. The factory, like its female workers, is virginally white; simultaneously it is also deathly, a "sepulcher." The women are all forever maids, while the men inhabit a completely masculine and equally sterile, if more luxurious, environment.

The sterility of the new age is again underscored by the process of paper production. The women tend machines that are driven both by their own life force and by the waterpower of "Blood River," yet they produce only blank white paper. The surrounding terrain yields no flowers, not even bachelor buttons, only gold buttons for "Old Bach," the owner of the factory. The women, who are both virginal and ghostly, symbolize Melville's fears about the destructiveness of the coming industrial age. Virginity here gives way to sterility and is tied inexorably to the promise of spiritual, sexual, and social death.

The women in this story remain anonymous, uniform, and almost ghostlike. They are all victims because their lives as women, and as sexual and human beings, are denied them. Their virginity is not becoming; it is horrifying, deathlike, instead of pure. We find no popular notions of women as domestic symbols; here they are empty vessels, the handmaidens of machinery that strips them of their youth, their sex, and their life, yielding only blank paper in return. Melville has drawn on all the themes common to sentimental novels about women—victimization, virginity, and the isolation and separation of the masculine and feminine spheres—but he has not glorified or sentimentalized women. We are left with a world divided between men and women where neither is fulfilled, and both are entirely isolated and ignorant in their isolation.

Hawthorne

Unlike Melville, who dealt with the loneliness of working women as a community, Nathaniel Hawthorne uses Hester Prynne in The Scarlet Letter to portray isolation of a different sort. Hester's isolation, sexuality, and intelligence, in addition to her womanhood, push her outside the boundaries of American society. Her passion, feeling, and thoughtfulness place her with the other artistic figures in Hawthorne's universe. Yet Hester's sex is equally instrumental in creating her physical and moral isolation. Hester, seamstress, nurse, and midwife, is symbolic of all women, but her consciousness points to the particular dilemma of American womanhood—that of being both part of, and yet outside of, the dominant culture:

> A tendency to speculation, though it may keep woman quiet, as it does man, yet makes her sad. She discerns, it may be, such a hopeless task before her. As a first step, the whole system of society is to be torn down and built up anew. Then, the very nature of the opposite sex, or its long hereditary habit which has become like nature, is to be essentially modified before woman can be allowed to assume what seems a fair and suitable position. Finally, all other difficulties being obviated, woman cannot take advantage of these preliminary reforms until she herself shall have undergone a still mightier change; in which, perhaps, the ethereal essence, wherein she has her truest life, will be found to have evaporated. (1851, pp. 165-166)

Hester's feminine role is underscored by the kind of work she performs. Rejected by New England society, alone and with a child, she is forced to depend upon that same society for her livelihood. Typically she turns to sewing, creating garments of value for important occasions and shrouds for the dead. Hester's work, if not her person, comes to be a highly valued commodity and "she had ready and fairly requited employment for as many hours as she saw fit to occupy her needle" (p. 82).

Interestingly, like women in the sentimental novels, Hester belongs to no discernible social class. Her work is transformed into art, her economic dependency into asceticism, and her isolation into alienation. In creating a strong woman, and in celebrating female values, Hawthorne shared more than he realized with the "scribbling women" he disdained. He elevates Hester's work to a higher level, for her needlework is so fine that it is really art. It alone survives the ravages of time, to be found in the Custom House many years later and provide the occasion for the narration of the tale. The scarlet "A," the symbol of Hester's work and art, and the label of her oppression, defies time and forms the bridge between Hawthorne's two worlds of the 17th and 19th centuries. Women, like artists in Hawthorne's universe, are able to expose and transcend the evils of their society.

Throughout her life, Hester never abandons her feminine role. She is a seamstress and a mother; she performs acts of charity and tends the sick. Her detachment from society allows her the humanity and even the social commitment that her neighbors, so subsumed within their culture, are unable to express. Hester's gender, like her sexuality, shields her from the crowds, the damning masses of New England society. Her "true womanhood" is what condemns her, but it is also what Hawthorne cherishes about her, and ultimately it provides her salvation. Hester, existing on the fringes of a culture that both uses and rejects her, comes to represent the situation of all women. In the end she is allowed to survive intact, if not unhurt, by her community. Her distance has given her solitude, and that in turn allows her to remain whole.

CONCLUSION

Hawthorne's seamstress and Melville's "maids" are similar in many ways to their counterparts in domestic popular fiction. All of the writers discussed use women—particularly those who exist on the outskirts of society because of their social and economic class—to explore the themes of isolation and victimization. Like the popular

novelists, Hawthorne and Melville idealize the feminine
role, identifying it with traditional and humanistic values,
and use it as a counterpoint to the male-identified, individualistic arenas of work and public life. Moreover,
each of these writers uses the wage-earning woman as a
vehicle for social criticism. Ironically, the popular novelists were the most willing to deal with issues of class and
work; however, having unmasked the beast, they were unable thereafter to deal with its true visage. Hawthorne
shared the anti-materialist and anti-individualistic philoso-
phy inherent in the ideology of domestic feminism but rejected by treatment of social class. Indeed, the lack of
sentimentality in Hawthorne's depiction of his female characters is closely linked to this stance. Because he was
unwilling to pity his female characters, Hawthorne was
able to ennoble them and to create multi-dimensional beings out of his heroines.

Melville comprehended the link between sex and
class in industrializing America. He used the factory operatives, the "maids," to illustrate the starkness of contemporary life and to delineate the developing class relationships inherent in 19th-century society. As in most
American fiction, there is little overt or expressed conflict
between the two groups he portrays. But there is tension,
a profound tension that is underscored by the sexual differentiation and stress between the two groups: the bachelors and the maids. Their economic and social separation
from each other is therefore one of class as well as of sex,
the women functioning as the proletarians of the coming
industrial age as well as its victims. Unlike the popular
novels, however, where women are also often poor, victimized, and single, in Melville's story their victimization
is not sentimentalized; instead, it is truly horrifying.
Melville was able to confront both the changed position of
American women resulting from the new factory system and
the serious damage it brought upon them.

Popular novels posited women and women's values
as correctives to an emerging commercial and acquisitive
culture. But, unlike Hawthorne or Melville, the sentimental novelists never confronted the causes or the depths of
the social maladies they feared. Instead, they helped to
create a series of myths about the nature of that system,
its values, and its functioning that masked the real problems and their causes. This sentimentalization of the poor
working woman arose out of, and helped to refine, a set
of beliefs that denied the reality.

The poor heroine thus takes on a special function in middle-class popular literature of the mid-19th century. She is "womanhood" in its purest and most unadulterated form, providing a middle-class readership with a moral lesson in worthy values, ideal feminine behavior, and true piety. Indeed, because poor women, unlike poor men, seemed to exist on the periphery of active social life, separated physically and socially from the mainstream of bourgeois life, their physical and social separation allowed the writer to use them as a mirror image of middle-class womanhood. The image served as a corrective, reminding the reader of the true ideal of feminine virtue and be-havior. Of course, the kind of purity and morality granted to poor women was sustained only as long as they held to Victorian moral codes. Thus, they were locked into an entirely middle-class definition of behavior; an alternative mode of behavior was never allowed or even considered, only a more refined version of that defined by middle-class norms and propriety.

This description of female behavior had several re-sults, not the least of which was that any genuine class identity—ethnic, economic, or cultural—was denied. The lowly position of women was sentimentalized and their col-lective poverty heavily idealized, thereby implying that corrective measures were at best a risky venture. Endur-ance became by extension every woman's province. In short, the popular culture helped to legitimize (unwitting-ly and ironically) the feminization of poverty and the cul-ture's acceptance of the secondary status of women.

By 1850 bourgeois domestic values permeated all as-pects of popular culture. A "respectable working-class woman" was a contradiction in terms, just as a permanent female proletariat was an inadmissible possibility. The lines were already drawn by midcentury: those who were permanently poor and female should be either unworthy or foreign-born. Native-born women like Clara and Laura Elliot were allowed only a temporary excursion into the world of poverty and work, and if their lives could offer no respite from their suffering, then their deaths were in-evitable. With their death knell there emerged a set of beliefs that denied the working-class American woman a legitimate status or tradition in American popular culture. Perhaps the rigor with which she was excluded and hidden testifies to the importance of her role during these years of cultural transformation.

NOTES

1. For a discussion of female readership and literacy, see Ann Douglas, The Feminization of American Culture (New York: Knopf, 1977), pp. 61–66; Helen Waite Papashivly, All the Happy Endings (New York: Harper Bros., 1956), pp. 36–46; and Kenneth Lockridge, Literacy in Colonial New England (New York: Norton, 1974), pp. 38–42, 57–58.

2. For a discussion of this, see Leslie Fiedler, Love and Death in the American Novel, rev. ed. (New York: Stein and Day, 1966), pp. 23–31; and G. J. Barker-Benfield, The Horrors of the Half-known Life (New York: Harper Colophon, 1977), pp. 8–18.

3. Although outside of this discussion because of its subject matter, Harriet Beecher Stowe's novels generally fit within this tradition.

4. William R. Taylor first set forth this interpretation of the cultural meaning of domesticity in his discussion of Sarah Hale and Daniel Webster in Cavalier and Yankee (New York: Harper Torchbook, 1969), pp. 177–222. See also Catharine K. Sklar, Catharine Beecher: A Study in American Domesticity (New Haven: Yale University Press, 1973), esp. pp. 151–167; Nancy Cott, The Bonds of Womanhood (New Haven: Yale University Press, 1971); and Papashivly. Nina Baym, Women's Fiction (Ithaca, N.Y.: Cornell University Press, 1979); and Mary Kelley, Private Woman, Public Stage: Literary Domesticity in Nineteenth Century America (New York: Oxford University Press, 1984), reflect the most recent comprehensive scholarship on this fiction. See especially Kelley's preface, pp. vii–viii.

5. Another, and again better-known, novel dealing with women's work is Louisa May Alcott's Work (1875). It chronicles a variety of women's trades, and is both reformist and sentimental. Since it was written largely after the Civil War, it is beyond the scope of this discussion. Interestingly, however (and probably because of when it was written), this novel ends on a decidedly feminist note, concluding with an interracial group of women, rich and poor, sitting around a kitchen table.

6. Henry Nash Smith writes that what he calls the "appearance, reality trick" was characteristic of dime novels about the American West written during the same period. Virgin Land: The American West as Symbol and Myth (Cambridge: Harvard University Press, 1950), pp. 126–135.

PART II

LINKS BETWEEN THE PUBLIC AND PRIVATE SPHERES

7

The New Patriarchy

Carol A. Brown

The years since the late 1970s have seen the culmination of major long-term changes in the societal relationship of men and women. A new form of patriarchy is becoming evident. The kind of work done in the family and in economic institutions, the familial relationships between the sexes and the generations, and women's social position within society as a whole have altered to such an extent that we can no longer depend on traditional concepts to analyze women's place. American society is still patriarchal, but the newly emerging form of patriarchy differs in important particulars from the old. The family basis of patriarchy has declined; a publicly centered patriarchy that uses women's labor directly, through industry and government instead of through male-headed families, has expanded. These changes and their implications for women are the subject of this chapter. The specific focus will be on women's work, particularly women's place in the family and in the paid labor force.

First I discuss the concept of patriarchy. I then discuss the distinction between private or family-centered patriarchy and public or industry-centered patriarchy. I posit that control of women's labor is moving from the private patriarchy of individual men within families to the public patriarchy of hierarchical, male-dominated work institutions that are part of the profit-making system (Brown 1981). I then describe the current situation of women's work in the paid labor force and the extent to which it conforms to the concept of public patriarchy. I also

consider institutions outside the profit system, in particular human services and the welfare state, that uphold
public patriarchy and to some extent replace women's
home-based labor. I then examine the implications of the
change for different groups of men and women. It appears
that higher-class men benefit and lower-class men lose.
There is a controversy about whether women as a class
are better off under public patriarchy. I argue that they
are.

PATRIARCHY

Patriarchy is the "rule of the father." As the concept has developed in recent years, patriarchy has come
to refer to a system of social relationships in which males
dominate females in certain ordered hierarchical ways.
The system is socially structured (Omvedt 1986) and materially based (H. Hartmann 1981b). Patriarchy is not
merely an ideology or a psychological struggle, although
these are important components of any patriarchal system.
In my analysis, patriarchy is based on a set of material
relationships involving money, goods, services, labor,
market exchange, production, and reproduction that enable
men as a group to obtain material benefits from women as
a group through the hierarchical structure. Patriarchal
systems also include religion, ideology, psychology, culture, and other aspects I will not analyze. A society is
more or less patriarchal to the extent that the domination
of men over women is more or less strong and important to
society. The ordering of the relationships between men
and women is usually (but I will argue not necessarily)
based on kinship.

No system of patriarchy gives unfettered freedom to
men to do as they wish. Although they have privileges
over women, men are expected to carry out responsibilities,
sometimes onerous, to their families and to society. Like
women, they stand in different places in the class structure, and have greater or lesser privileges and oppressions based on class.

The relationship between patriarchy and capitalism
is the subject of extensive academic debate. Some analysts
argue that family-based patriarchy is the primary locus
of exploitation and oppression of women. In this analysis,
other social and economic forms, however important they

may be for the exploitation of men, are less significant in structuring women's lives (Delphy 1984). Others argue that the economic class structure, particularly capitalism,[1] is the only important form of exploitation for both men and women (Vogel 1983). In such analysis, patriarchal family relationships exist to assure reproduction of human beings, without which production and exploitation would not be possible.

Analysts of both types tend to see the family as patriarchy, and the rest of the social and economic relations of society as not-patriarchy. The public, nonfamily areas of life are seen as capitalism or socialism or whatever. In such analyses, what patriarchal aspects there may be to law, religion, market economy, and so on are there mainly to uphold the family patriarchy.

My analysis is different. The area outside family patriarchy is equally my concern. The area outside the family is as much patriarchy as the area of life inside the family (H. Hartmann 1981b; Sokoloff 1980). I agree with Stacey (1983, 1986) that gender and economy are systems that often "operate via compatible processes that are difficult to distinguish" but that can, and at times must, be analyzed separately. Although capitalism may be patriarchal, and American patriarchy may be capitalistic, capitalism and patriarchy are different systems. (For critique and comments see Sargent 1981.) This chapter concentrates on patriarchy, although the interconnection with capitalism will be evident.

That part of patriarchy which functions inside the family will be called private patriarchy; that part which functions outside the family in the society in general will be called public patriarchy. I do not argue that the "private" home is unconnected to the rest of society, as feminist theory is sometimes criticized as doing (Kelly 1979; Rapp 1982). All patriarchal systems are total social systems including family and extrafamily elements. My distinction between private and public is for the sake of analyzing the changing balance between them.

PATRIARCHY AND WOMEN'S LABOR

Patriarchy is a social system that includes the family relation and to a large extent defines it. All patriarchal systems have both private and public aspects. The

balance between them may differ in different systems, and
may change over time. Women's work is patriarchally determined to the extent that women work under the auspices
of and to the benefit of men. The meaning of control over
women's labor differs, depending on the balance between
private and public patriarchy. We can speak of the private aspect of patriarchy when referring to the relationships between individual men and women found in the family. In this socially patterned, legally sanctioned institution, the individual husband has traditionally had, and
continues to have, various forms of rights over his wife.
Two of the most important are his right to her daily labor,
both productive and reproductive, and his right to the
product of one type of labor, her children. In many societies the marital relationship gives the husband the right
to have his wife do the housekeeping and child care, and
gives him the custody and control of the children.

The public aspect of patriarchy is the control of
society and of social institutions—the economy, religion,
government—by men collectively. In this public life outside the family, men collectively uphold men's rights.

When private patriarchy dominates the patriarchal
system, the family-centered control by husbands over their
wives' daily labor is the main way in which women's labor
is brought into society. When this is the case, public
patriarchy is less obvious and largely indirect. Male
dominance over, and often monopolization of, jobs, property, family law, and welfare policies tend to prevent
women from public participation and to assure their dependence on the family. For example, property rights or
inheritance may be restricted to men only; women may be
excluded from the priesthood or from serving in government; laws may directly grant rights to husbands and remove them from wives. Domestic obligations in turn tend
to assure women's inability to challenge men's public predominance.

When public patriarchy dominates a patriarchal system, the elements of the public patriarchy are quite different. The family system is less important. Public patriarchy does not so much restrict women from public participation as it encourages public participation under conditions of inequality. The public patriarchy comes to
have more direct control over women's daily labor. Women
still work under the auspices of men, but they more often
work directly in the social institutions outside the family,

for men who are not their husbands. More of the benefit
of their work goes to their employers, clients, customers,
or coworkers, and to society in general. The legal, religious, welfare, and governmental systems are oriented less
to maintaining the relationship of husbands and wives,
and more to regulating the positions of men and women as
publicly defined groups. For example, birth control and
abortion laws may have no reference to marital status or
rights of husbands. Women do less of their work within
male-dominated families and are less dependent financially
on male heads of households. Women may still do the
majority of housework and child care.

In both types of societies just described, public
patriarchy and private patriarchy coexist. Each upholds
the other, although at times each may conflict with the
other. The difference is in which type of patriarchy dominates the system.

In the 19th and much of the 20th century, private
patriarchy dominated. The work that women did in the
family, tending past, present, and future workers, was,
in most analysts' view, their major contribution to the
economic system.

Today in the United States the public aspect of patriarchy has increased dramatically, although it is far
from total domination. The extent of its increase and the
decline of private patriarchy have shifted the balance of
the patriarchal system. Out-of-home paid work for women
increasingly takes the spotlight. Women live relatively
public lives in schools, in work places, in popular and
elite culture, and in political life.

Public patriarchy is no longer primarily oriented to
providing women to the private patriarchy, that is, keeping women at home. Most laws giving husbands rights
have been abolished. However, women continue to provide
the vast majority of unpaid domestic work without which
the paid economy could not function. They may be doing
so in homes without husbands; they are probably doing so
in the evening, when they come home from their paid work.
A greater portion of care for the elderly, children, and
adult workers is done outside the home, by women who are
paid, albeit poorly, in formal organizations such as schools
or hospitals. Although the family remains an important
social institution, housewifery is not the only focus for
women's lives. Women's contribution to the economy is
more likely to be direct, as a paid worker.

The division of labor between the sexes is increasingly carried out primarily in the labor force; the conditions limiting or expanding women's place in society are set less by husbands or for the sake of husbands, and more by employers and public policy makers for the sake of male-dominated society in general or specifically for the sake of profit-making employers. Productive labor that was once the province of the housewife is more often performed in factories. Clerical work in offices is almost entirely women's work. Service work takes over much that was previously considered familial reproductive labor. The work of women in childbearing and child rearing is increasingly oriented to state policies, public support, and professional caretaking. I would go so far as to assert that male-headed families are no longer needed to maintain patriarchy (C. Brown 1981).

I contend that the changes that have taken place in women's work can best be understood as changes in the balance of control over women from the private patriarchy of individual husbands within families to industry- and government-centered public patriarchy of a high-technology, monopoly capitalist economy.

WOMEN'S WORK: HISTORICAL CHANGES

Prior to the beginning of U.S. industrialism in the early 19th century, the majority of women in the United States worked within families, holding their primary economic and social positions as wives, mothers, daughters.[2] If what we now call housework and child care were included in the definition of work, then almost all American women have always worked. The lady of leisure was a largely unattained Victorian ideal. If housework and child care were excluded from the definition of work, as they were and still are by most analysts, most women were nevertheless not ladies of leisure in the 19th century. Ciancanelli (1983) has shown that when all the work women did involving money is included in the calculus—wage labor, small business, taking in boarders, engaging in cottage industry, or working as unpaid family workers in a money-making family enterprise—then about 60 percent of adult women could be defined as in the labor force. This percentage is not very different from the labor force participation rate as currently defined (59 percent) (see ch. 5).

Yet it is obvious that the conditions of women's work today
are very different from what went before. Then, the majority of women worked in their homes, often combining productive labor with household labor. Doing household labor
in other women's homes was a major part of waged labor.
Today the majority of women work in offices, factories,
schools, hospitals, and other formal institutions, then return home at night to do significant amounts of (unpaid)
housework and child care if they are married or are
mothers.

Women's participation in the U.S. paid labor force
has grown since the mill girls flocked to Lowell in the
1830s, and has increased particularly since World War 11.
Despite the continued importance of women workers in a
few industries, such as textiles and garments, the expansion of capitalism in the 19th century depended to a much
larger extent on male workers. Men of all classes became
part of the factory- and office-based economy, whereas
paid work for women was more often limited to poorer
women. In the 20th century the growth of monopoly capitalism came increasingly to include the work of women of
all social classes (see chs. 2 and 3).

By the beginning of the 20th century, profit-making
enterprises took over much of the production previously
done at home (such as home canning or sewing), and
women often became the workers in the growing factories.
The development by profit-making corporations of domestic
electricity, sliced bread, fast foods, household appliances,
and other goods and services potentially decreases the
need for many aspects of housework.[3] Goods such as telephones and television sets cannot be produced at home;
family members, including wives, must work in the labor
force for wages to obtain these goods (C. V. Brown 1982).
Other economic developments within the profit-making sector
made work available that was considered suitable for
women. The expansion of office work took place largely
after World War 1; the expansion of service work, after
World War 11 (J. Smith 1984). As Oppenheimer (1970)
showed, women have wanted to work for pay throughout
the 20th century; the development of these economic sectors
made paid work for women possible.

As the ability of families to provide services to
their members declined, in good part because of the growth
of capitalism, government and public agencies increasingly
provided reproductive services such as physical and health

care; public education; child guidance; monetary support for the unemployed, ill, or fatherless; and money and services for the retired elderly. Such expansion has been particularly strong since World War II (Piven and Cloward 1971). The rise of human services increases the possible number of jobs for women and decreases the necessity of family membership for survival.

In monopoly capitalism, the vast majority of workers work as individuals in corporations rather than as members of family firms that have to provide their own labor force. As family-based enterprises have declined, the economic value of children to individual fathers has decreased along with the economic value of women's child-rearing labor (C. Brown 1981; Rotman-Zelizer 1985). The decreasing centrality of the family to the economy leads to easier divorce, decreased child-bearing, and the willingness of men collectively to accept the abolition of laws and customs that upheld husbands' rights. The decreasing demand by husbands for women's home-based labor makes housewives and ex-housewives into an available labor force.

The ability of women to enter the paid labor market, albeit in an inferior position, was enhanced by other social changes. Legally these included the removal of a variety of laws that had given husbands legal rights over their wives' labor and property, and the removal of legal restrictions on women signing contracts. Other changes included the development of more reliable, legalized birth control, and the increasing acceptability and availability of nonmaternal care for young children. Corporate policy and eventually federal law abolished marital status and motherhood as criteria for a woman's employment. Such changes began in the 19th century and accelerated in the 1970s, largely as a result of the women's movement. Despite the changes, women still retain heavy home responsibilities. The changes diminish the inequalities of private patriarchy but do not negate them.

The growth of women's employment was not on a basis of equality with men's work. Rather, women's paid employment has been accompanied by corporate and state policies that maintain women's inferiority. These include occupational segregation, lower wages for women than for men in the same jobs, protective legislation that raises the cost of employing women and therefore makes them less valuable to employers, and child care policies that make women less able than men to take certain types of heavy work, overtime work, or jobs involving travel.

At the bottom of the economic ladder these problems may push women out of the labor force entirely. Many poor mothers without husbands or job skills or alternative child care are unable to obtain wages that can support their families; they rely on AFDC or other public programs for economic support.

WOMEN'S WORK AT PRESENT

Today the majority of working-age women (18-64) are in the labor force. Single and divorced women tend to have higher labor force participation rates than married or older widowed women, but marital status is having a decreasing effect on women's chances of working for pay. Although giving birth has traditionally been a reason for women to drop out of paid work and begin full-time home-making, as the labor force participation rate for women has increased, the rate for mothers of young children has increased even faster. By 1983, half of all mothers of two-year-olds were in the labor force, and the proportion of women working increased with the age of the youngest child (Waldman 1983). Over their lifetimes, virtually all women will spend more years in the labor force than as child rearers.

Most women, like most men, work as individuals for large or small companies and agencies; the family enter-prise has virtually disappeared. The last holdout, the family farm, has largely gone under in the 1980s farm crisis. In 1983, 93 percent of employed women were wage and salary workers, working neither for themselves nor in family businesses, but for companies and businesses (U.S. Census Bureau 1985, p. 395). Women workers are important to all industrial sectors. Women are more than 50 percent of the workers in retail trade; finance, insurance, and real estate; and services, particularly entertainment, health, hospitals, elementary and secondary education, welfare, and religion. Only in agriculture, mining, and construction are women less than 20 percent of the workers.

Fox and Hess-Biber (1984) have summarized the ex-tensive body of research on women workers: The occupa-tions held by women are concentrated in the secondary labor market--jobs characterized by low wages, poor working conditions, little chance for advancement, lack of stability, and personalized employer/employee relations conducive to arbitrary and capricious work discipline. "By 1980, 75% of all working women were in occupations where women are the majority" (p. 70).

Berch (1982) and Sapiro (1986) have listed the ten jobs employing the largest number of women in each decade since 1880. The occupations show "remarkable continuity. . . . Overall, the lists contain the same types of jobs year after year. Women clean, cook and serve food, sew, teach and do clerical and sales work; in other words, much of the work women do for pay is the same kind of work they are expected to do as wives" (Sapiro 1986, pp. 384-385). My own examination of the occupations of employed women in 1981 shows that about 30 percent are in paid occupations that almost directly replicate the work of housewives.

Although there has been some limited decline in sex segregation since 1970, the work world remains basically segregated into men's jobs and women's jobs. Even the slight decline appears less positive when examined closely: women tend to be able to enter previously male work when those occupations are declining in power and status and males are able to find better jobs elsewhere (Carter and Carter 1981; Hacker 1979; Sokoloff 1987). On the whole, women have been able to increase their numbers in the labor force because the occupations and industries into which they are segregated have been expanding their need for labor.

The barriers to occupational change are extensive, and involve both public and private patriarchy: childhood socialization of boys and girls to want different work, discriminatory practices of career counselors and employment firms, corporate personnel practices, harassment by male coworkers, failure of government to require affirmative action, reluctance of women to face the battles and hostilities that would result from their entering nontraditional work, child care responsibilities, and the refusal or inability of husbands to share housework and child care equally.

Women are segregated vertically as well as horizontally. Taking only year-round, full-time workers in 1982, women averaged 63 percent of men's earnings. The majority of such men earned more than $21,000 in 1982; the majority of such women, less than $14,000. If all persons

with income are included, the median income for men in
1982 was $13,950; and for women, $5,887. Women's income
averaged 42 percent of men's (U.S. Census Bureau 1985,
p. 452). Women are less likely to have paying jobs, less
likely to have full-time paying jobs, and less likely to
have high-paying jobs than are men.

Women's wages tend to be lower than men's even
within the same occupational groupings, whether these are
professional subspecialties or blue-collar work (Matthaei
1982, p. 197). On the whole, women and men do not work
in the same occupations. The expansion of women's paid
work since World War 11 has been less in professional or
highly paid technical work, and more in service occupations characterized by low pay and lack of promotion opportunities.

In some cases the hierarchical relationship of men
and women is built directly into the work structure of individuals. The relation of an executive secretary to an
executive is that of an "office wife" (Glenn and Feldberg
1984). In other cases the hierarchy is occupational.
Staff doctors, predominantly male, leave orders for hospital nurses (predominantly female) to carry out.

Management of the labor force is a white male pre-
rogative. Although low-level management positions may be
filled by women, 96.5 percent of persons making $50,000 or
more in executive, administrative, or managerial positions
in the 1980 census were males; 94.9 percent were white
males. Among members of professional specialties making
$50,000 or more, 96 percent were male and 90 percent were
white males (U.S. Census Bureau 1980, table 281).

The higher-level managers not only manage the
labor force, they also set and carry out the policies and
programs of business, public administration, education,
medicine, and other fields. Nor does government offer an
antidote to disproportionate male power. In 1982, women
were only 12 percent of state legislators and 6 percent of
mayors; in 1983 they were only 4 percent of the U.S. Congress (U.S. Census Bureau 1985, pp. 247, 251).

An increasing amount of control over women's daily
labor is held by employers, not husbands. Husbands may
willingly accept, even urge, wives to engage in less home-
making and child care in recognition that what women can
buy with the money they earn working may be more valuable than what they can produce through their unpaid
labor at home (Weinbaum and Bridges 1979; C. V. Brown

1982). What they can buy depends on what goods and services companies offer; in other words, what employees are paid to do.

The social division of labor is maintained. Women do women's work and men do men's work, both in the home and in the paid work place. Women's work is low-paid or unpaid; men's work is higher-paid, enabling men on the whole to buy women's work both at home and in the market. Control over social policies remains in the hands of men.

CLASS AND RACE

The goods and services that are produced, the conditions of the work that produces them, and the market relations under which they are offered to clients and customers are all hierarchically ordered. American society is capitalist. The increase of public patriarchy is an increase in the power of corporate managers and the upper class. It is an increase in the power of higher-level men at the expense of the erstwhile privileges of lower-level men. Upper-level men continue to have stay-at-home wives and in addition have women employees, whereas lower-level men have either no wives or working wives and are themselves employees. They obtain goods and services to the extent that the decision-making elite considers the provision of such goods and services to be in the interest of the elite, and to the extent that the men's wage levels or other statuses permit.

Although the benefit is largely to the upper-level men, it is not only to them. The jobs of many working women are oriented to giving "service with a smile," making life nicer for men at all levels (Hochschild 1983). Examples range from television entertainers, provided free by advertisers to everyone with access to a television set, to airline flight attendants, provided by airlines to those who can afford to fly. It could be said that under public patriarchy, women are provided as a public good for all men. Poorer men who could never afford homemaker wives may now receive the services of working women, albeit at a much lower level. For example, men in some public chronic care hospitals have their beds made and rooms cleaned by women workers.

Women's benefit from public patriarchy depends on their economic class and their family status. Although women's wages are well below men's, professional women's wages are higher than unskilled women's wages. Clearly, what can be bought can be bought better by those with more income. The career woman combines freedom and income to a greater extent than other women except those with clear title to inherited wealth. Those who perceive themselves as powerless and fit mainly for motherhood will reject policies and practices connected with public patriarchy (Luker 1984). These particulars may be less matters of income and more matters of education and class background.

Low-income women may be better off under the programs of the welfare state than under the power of low-income husbands. Women may get both jobs in the public sector and services from the public sector. Services to low-income people are provided to women as well as men (such as free television or Medicaid hospital beds).

Married women at most levels of the class system may enter the welfare system when they become divorced (Weitzman 1985). Compared with husbands, public agencies may be more reliable, more amenable to negotiation, and less likely to become violent while drunk.

Minority women are differentially affected by the change. Black men and women have always been subject to a patriarchy originating outside of, and destructive to, their family structure (Hooks 1981). In the early stages of the women's movement some feminists seemed to envy black women their freedom from the private patriarchy of black husbands, without recognizing the oppression they suffered from the public patriarchy of white, male-dominated society. For black women and for other minorities, the family can be both a source of oppression and a protection against the worst excesses of capitalism (Humphries 1977; see also ch. 3). At the same time, some of the struggle of minority women has been to obtain the benefits of public patriarchy (such as medical care or AFDC) that were, and sometimes still are, denied them on racist grounds.

HUMAN SERVICES

Human services are very important in this changing emphasis from private, family-based patriarchy to public, industry-based patriarchy. Women's labor in patriarchal families was oriented not merely to producing goods and services that can be translated into profit-making industries, but also to reproducing human beings as citizens, soldiers, and workers. Cooked food and clean clothes, education and job training, the inculcation of morality and aspirations, as well as health care, old age security, entertainment, child care, and other services are needed by individuals as well as by society.

The family as an institution remains important to the extent that it is a major source of these various forms of reproduction. Women continue to provide unpaid labor that helps the capitalist system to survive. Yet in various ways capitalism undercuts the family. One way is by undercutting family-owned businesses and creating a nation of employees. Another is by making childbearing and child rearing incompatible with employment when employment is a necessity. Retirement pensions that aid labor peace decrease the elderly's need to depend on children. Low wages decrease the ability of families to aid unemployed members. The lack of family businesses and the necessity to work for companies carry endless implications for childbearing, schooling, and old age security (Folbre 1986; C. Brown 1981).

The demographic transition to small families was taking place in the United States by the end of the 19th century. A recognition that families were "not doing their jobs" (as the job was defined by the upper-middle and upper classes) was behind a variety of reform efforts beginning in the same era. Among the reformers' complaints were children running unsupervised in the streets, fathers deserting their wives and children, and adults refusing to aid their elderly parents (Johnson 1925; Stewart 1893). These tended to be problems of working-class and poor families. The solutions tended to be public programs directed by the middle class or the rich.

In the United States the establishment of the welfare state in the 1930s resulted from the obvious inability of families to take care of their members under the conditions of capitalist depression. Despite economic recovery, both the governmental welfare state and associated profit-making, nonprofit, and governmental services have expanded over time. The presence of such services transfers yet more influence from the family to the public sector.

Some services replace the family with out-of-family care, such as nursing homes for the elderly and day care for children. These in effect replace the housewife with working women (thus enabling women to leave home for paid work, perhaps in services). Such services did not necessarily develop for the purpose of enabling women to work. They may have originated in a concern for the welfare of the recipients, such as neglected children or abandoned elderly.

Other services maintain women in traditional roles. AFDC and other programs recognize the impoverishment of mothers without husbands. Various public funds and services for female-headed families presume the woman to be at home, her husband replaced by "The Man," as welfare departments are sometimes called. Although such women are in traditional roles, they are not in traditional families. Their work at home is under the auspices of public patriarchy. (See Folbre 1986 for an analysis of the economic underpinnings of child rearing under public programs.)

Some of the human services that have developed since World War II are large-scale replacements for work that was done on a minor scale or in a few families whose members had talents in the area. Child psychology in the form of school social workers and psychologists, mental health clinics, and family counseling may be seen as an outgrowth of the concern for raising mentally healthy children, but parents, neighbors, and Dutch uncles never gave the time and attention that these professional services do.

Some services that have developed in the 1970s and 1980s came about as a result of the increase in working women. Evening hours in supermarkets and after-school programs in public schools increased as more mothers worked out of the home. In most communities day care for children changed from a minimal service provided to "at risk" families by the welfare department to a service available to all comers, usually on a sliding fee scale, by nonprofit and profit-making agencies for the same reasons.

Work that was previously domestic continues to be performed, but to be performed out of the home to a greater extent than previously. When work passes out of the home, control of the work and the setting of standards also pass out of the home. Decisions about what services are to be provided by whom and to whom are made not within families but within agencies; they are made by professionals using such criteria for other people's welfare as they consider important. The professionals have partially taken over the substance and control of what remains of family work (Sussman 1971; Weinbaum and Bridges 1979). Ehrenreich and English (1978) argue that the rise of professionals and their advice undermined the autonomy of women in families and women's networks in communities. Families that can pay for services retain more influence over the services than those who depend on third-party payments or those who retain the work within the family. Working-class families are less likely to buy services, and more likely to depend on third-party payments. Although agencies give some credence to parent or client control, such control can most often be exercised only in the decision to use or not to use the service. The content of the service is decided by the professional or the agency. For example, one family may pay for a private child psychologist and another may use the child psychologist at a community mental health center, but both depend on the psychologist to decide what therapy the child needs.

When families lose control over their members, the male heads of family lose power.[4] It could be argued that female-headed families suffer as much diminution of power as male-headed families, and that therefore the change has little to do with patriarchy. This would be an incorrect reading of the situation. Female heads of families have never had social power; male heads have. It would be more correct to say that with the increase in public control of family services, male heads of family lose power and female heads of family fail to gain power.

WOMEN'S WORK AND PUBLIC PATRIARCHY

The increase in working women and the increasing importance of public patriarchy have various implications for men and women. Lower wages and job segregation for women assure the continuation of male domination. Speaking of the relation between women's low wages in public and their subordination in the family, Heidi Hartmann (1981b) says, "The lower pay women receive in the labor market both perpetuates men's material advantage over women and encourages women to choose wifery as a career. Second, then, women do housework, childcare, and perform other services at home which benefit men directly. Women's home responsibilities in turn reinforce their inferior labor market position" (p. 22). Thus public patriarchy continues to uphold private patriarchy even as it undercuts and changes it.

The inferiority of women in the labor market does not merely assure men's dominance in the family. Women's low-paid reproductive work serves men, women, and children outside the family. Men can obtain women's services without being married to them. This in itself is not something new. When private patriarchy was more important, men obtained women's services outside the family through servants, prostitutes, and boardinghouse keepers. What is new is the extent to which the family is replaced by services provided by organizations to the general public. Waitresses, nurses, and housecleaners are among the effective replacements for workers within the home. Women's work in the family becomes less important to individual men. The collective labor of women becomes more important to men collectively. When the government, for example, seeks to assure that a particular human service is available to all, it counts on low-paid women workers to do the job. When private industry makes goods and services available in the marketplace, low-paid women can produce them cheaply enough for others to afford, and better-paid men are better able to afford more of them. Some production is carried out by extremely low-paid women in Third World countries (Ehrenreich and Fuentes 1983).

Although public patriarchy provides women's services to men, it gives individual men less power over individual women. The man who is living with a woman does not have the legal or traditional power over her that a husband had over his wife. Husbands might have been better off maintaining the traditional powers they had over their nonworking wives, had it been possible for them to keep the powers and to keep their wives at home. On the other hand, it can be argued that women won their freedom from the legal power of husbands only because husbands no longer valued that power enough to defend it, and that this came about because the change from a family-based to a corporate-based economy decreased the value of women's home labor. Today full-time housewives are most often found among ruling-class families that can afford the luxury of a member not producing income (Ostrander 1984). Higher-class people have most access to women's home labor, as they do to other kinds of labor.

The years since the late 1970s have seen a continuation of the ideological power of the "traditional family"
and an increase in the political pressure from the new
right to restore legally sanctioned male domination in families. This has taken place along with increasing career
training and labor force participation by mothers and
other women. It demonstrates that patriarchy and capitalism as systems may have conflicting needs for women's
labor: the former to have women at home serving husbands
and family, the latter to have skilled and educated women
working in the labor force. The increase in public patriarchy is an adjustment to these conflicting needs that
contains its own conflicts. The Republican cutbacks in
the welfare state do not send women back into the home,
but merely assure that they will remain deprived under
public patriarchy (Folbre 1986).

In many ways women collectively are better off with
increasing public patriarchy. Jobs with pay are more
available. Careers are open to the best-educated; interesting work is not impossible to find (Petchesky 1985).
Even relatively low-paid work has advantages. Having a
chance to work gets women out of the house, away from
domestic oppressions and into potential friendships. Women
have some ability to support themselves, giving them security in case their husbands leave or they want to leave
their husbands. They live better by buying their goods
than they could have by making them. There is increasing personal freedom and more economic power within marriage for the working wife (see ch. 8) than for the stay-
at-home wife, even though the working wife may have more
hours of labor when paid work and housework are combined.
Men have not increased their share of housework to equality; mothers and married women often have a "double day"
of paid work and housework.

The availability of services produces a better quality of life even for less affluent women. In the profit-
making sector, McDonald's can produce meals more cheaply
and with less labor than a woman could produce on her
own. Higher-quality steak houses are available for the
more affluent families. A variety of human services (such
as mental health counseling, job information and counseling) are provided as part of the welfare state, and are
available to women who cannot afford to buy them and
cannot produce them at home. Dale and Foster (1986, p. 3)
argue that family policies were included in the welfare

state in part because feminists campaigned for a recognition of the importance to society of the work that mothers did at home (see also Zaretsky 1982, p. 191). The result is not merely AFDC financial support to mothers at home but also public provision of services to women and to their families. Services produced by women who are paid for their efforts produce jobs for the female workers and services for the female clients. The federal effort to decrease such welfare services is intended to strengthen private patriarchy but so far has been unsuccessful.

As the private family becomes less necessary or attractive, men may remain single or may become and remain divorced, leaving women to cope with financial support and housework for themselves and their children. Women carry out family work without being members of families. Research shows that men's disposable incomes increase after divorce because the women take on the financial burden of the children (Weitzman 1985). In living-together arrangements, the woman may pay her own bills and do all the housework as well. The increase in teenage nonmarital childbearing is another case of men not having to take on responsibility as husbands and fathers. However, it should not be assumed that marriage is necessarily preferable for the mother. Just as men have choices outside marriage, so do women (though more limited ones); they also have the opportunity to avoid the worst excesses of a bad marriage. They may choose to marry or remarry for love or for higher incomes, but at least they have the choice. (See Petchesky 1985 for an extended discussion of this point.)

The feminization of poverty that is such an obvious result of recent economic and social change must be considered in historic context (Pearce and McAdoo 1981). Married women without income of their own have traditionally been absolutely poor. Their poverty was hidden by their husbands' incomes. It is assumed that the majority of wives shared their husband's standard of living and class advantage; if the class was high enough, the wives could live well. How much redistribution took place within the family is not clear. Husbands were not legally required to provide anything but the barest necessities. In public patriarchy, women become dependent for incomes on welfare and transfer payments or on their own, often ill-paying, jobs. Sharing of a man's income is not built into the system, although many women live with men or accept various forms of financial support in exchange for services. Until more research is done, it will not be clear whether women are actually poorer under a patriarchy that is predominantly public or one that is predominantly private. Perhaps the major change is that women's poverty has now become overt where it was previously covert.

Women who remain unmarried and have jobs or careers do not avoid patriarchy. They avoid private patriarchy but are subject to public patriarchy.

Patriarchy as a system is not good for women. Historically, women individually and through collective movements have looked to the state for protection against individual men and for alteration in the terms of private patriarchy. Women wanted equality; they got public patriarchy. Public patriarchy is less harsh and easier to organize against than private patriarchy. It may better enable women to find male allies. Public patriarchy may be less bad than private patriarchy, because there is more freedom and more opportunity to negotiate one's relationships, but how much less bad depends on a variety of factors, such as one's ability to take advantage of the opportunity. Patriarchy as a system benefits men, but does not benefit all men equally. The benefit of the transition to relatively greater public patriarchy may be uneven for men as well as women.

The question remains of the future, especially in light of the rightward trend in public life. I have asserted that the direction of change continues to be toward a greater emphasis on public patriarchy. I believe that despite conflicting trends, the emphasis on public patriarchy will continue. The conservative policies of the federal government in the 1980s have been oriented to upholding and restoring the traditional male-dominated family, but they do not appear to be successful. Despite cuts in spending for particular programs, the welfare state is here to stay. Cuts in benefits do not send women back into the home, but merely assure that women will remain deprived under public patriarchy. Making public patriarchy harsher does not re-create the structural factors (such as 19th-century capitalism) that upheld the nuclear family of private patriarchy.

Capitalism in the 20th century has not decreased its efforts to sell goods and services to individuals and families. Entrepreneurs have responded to changes in the family by providing commodities and out-of-home services that may have the effect of decreasing people's dependence on families.

Women's labor force participation remains high for all ages and marital statuses. But past experience has made it clear that employment in occupations may expand or contract with economic change. There is evidence that the high-tech economy will automate some of the services and clerical work that have been the mainstay of women's employment. One possibility is that decreased employment will send women back into the home. "Housewife" has often been a euphemism for "unemployed," and may become so to a greater extent. It is not clear, however, that unemployed women will in fact become housewives supported entirely by their husbands. Private patriarchy declined in part because many men did not see a benefit to themselves in supporting a wife. Perhaps unemployed women will become divorced unemployed women. Perhaps they will become welfare mothers subject to a particularly important part of the public patriarchy. Perhaps they will find jobs in newly developing industries.

The traditional family with the dependent wife, which is the basis of private patriarchy, has been pronounced dead many times but continues to show vitality because of its usefulness to patriarchal capitalism and its ideological power. It is less widespread than the ideology would have it, and has shown decline (U.S. Census Bureau 1985, pp. 40-48). When old forms fail, people invent new forms that they hope will provide security, equality, and happiness. The 1980s have seen the rise of living alone, living together by heterosexual couples and same-sex roommates, female-headed families, three-generation families, created families, group homes, and other ways of living. Husbands and wives who have children have struggled to create egalitarian marriages. These new forms of family are a response to the decline of the traditional family. They form as they do because of the rise of public patriarchy. Given the change in opportunities and necessities outside the home, people can create new forms of private life. We can expect the new forms to be less than perfectly egalitarian because the society is less than egalitarian.

CONCLUSION

I have argued that the changes in women's work are best understood as changes in the primary locus of control over women from the private patriarchy of individual husbands within families to industry- and government-centered public patriarchy of a monopoly capitalist economy. I have argued not that private patriarchy has disappeared, but that the balance has altered toward the public. I believe it will continue to alter in that direction. Although there are some benefits of public patriarchy to working-class and poor men, there are also severe losses. The benefits tend to accrue to the higher-class men. Women as a category are better off under public patriarchy, although women with higher educations and job skills benefit more.

The male-dominated family can no longer be taken as the source of women's oppression or as the standard of patriarchy. Private, intimate relations continue to exist, but they will take different forms in the new patriarchy. Research should concentrate on the development of new forms of patriarchy within the public arena of government, industry and business, and human services. Analysis needs to integrate the mode of production (advanced capitalism, socialism) into an understanding of patriarchy. Political action that concentrates on the public arena in such areas as abortion and birth control laws or comparable worth is particularly important in diminishing public patriarchy.

NOTES

1. Capitalism is one form of class society. Most analyses of patriarchy have concentrated on the relation of capitalism and patriarchy because most analysts are concerned with their own (capitalistic) societies. Other forms, such as feudalism in the past and socialism today, have their own relationships with patriarchy. See, for example, Judith Stacey's (1983) work on patriarchal socialism in China.

2. The large exception was slaves, who worked in a white male patriarchy. Slave women worked primarily for the white owners and were expected to do the housekeeping and child care of the slave community (Hooks 1981).

3. Whether housework in fact decreased is open to question. As housework became easier, standards rose and women were expected to do more of it. Data show that the full-time homemaker of today puts in as many hours as the full-time homemaker of the early 20th century with the

same size family. However, women today do not have the same size families and are not as likely to be full-time homemakers. Wives and mothers with paid jobs do significantly less housework than those at home full-time.

4. Zaretsky (1982) argues that the welfare state did not undermine and invade family life but, rather, enabled family life to survive under the invasion of capitalism. 1 would suggest that state policies may have upheld the family-based household as a private economic unit, useful as a consumption element under capitalism, but that such policies did not uphold the rights and powers of males to dominate families (the private patriarchy).

8

The Struggles of Superwoman

Myra Marx Ferree

Everyone knows what a superwoman is. The mass media are full of portraits of women who combine employment, marriage, and children into a far more than full-time career, professing all the while that they make no compromises in any of these areas. Their children receive "high quality time" to make up for any loss of quantity, their husbands are given all the attention and even deference they expect, and their performance on the job is exceptional (Shaevitz 1984). Popular magazines seem to play upon women's aspirations for this role, offering advice about how to manage stress and organize time so that women can "have it all" (Weil 1986; Harris 1985). The idea that this supercommitment of time and energy is the essence of women's liberation remains a popular stereotype of feminism.

The superwoman ideal actually has little to do with feminist hopes for a transformation of society. It sidesteps crucial questions about the dynamics of power or the higher value placed on maleness in favor of a frantic attempt to accommodate women with families to an employment

My greatest appreciation is expressed to my colleague Michael Gordon, for his share in the effort of collecting the data, and to Elaine J. Hall, for her help in running the statistical analysis on which this chapter is based. Thanks also are expressed to the University of Connecticut Research Foundation, which provided a small grant to support the initial stages of this project.

system that assumes a male worker with a support system at home. Rather than encouraging a change in the level of practical social support for women, it presents women's struggles with an unsupportive environment as the standard. While the popular literature may suggest that men make some changes in their own family or work roles, or describe the social policies of nonsupport for mothers that aggravate the difficulties women face in carrying multiple roles, there is little hint of how dramatic and far-reaching the changes in both these areas would have to be to reduce significantly the burden women now carry. Instead of seeking political change, women are encouraged to make the best of a bad situation by improving their own time-management or delegation skills.

The superwoman ideal evident in these magazines is more than theoretical; there is some evidence that women attempt to achieve it (Hewlett 1986, pp. 18–47; cf. Shaevitz 1984). An indication of the generality of this pattern can be found in sociological studies of the division of labor in the home. It has become commonplace to note that men whose wives are employed do little if any additional house-work and take on no significantly greater share of the more arduous or unpleasant tasks of child care (Berk 1985; Michelson 1985). However, it is also noted that employed wives generally express little dissatisfaction with this highly unequal division of responsibilities in their families (Berk 1985, ch. 7; J. Pleck 1985, ch. 4). If the division of household labor is not changing, while women's share of the paid work load increases steadily, why are employed women not reporting a pervasive sense that this is unjust? Why is their level of reported dissatisfaction with men's share apparently not rising?

While the superwoman ideal is not the only ideological justification available for the double or triple day of labor expected of women, it provides one influential model encouraging acceptance of the status quo. By defining the successful woman as one who is happily carrying this multiple burden, and in addition suggesting that it was women who sought this change, the superwoman ideal de-legitimates discontent. While it defines women's paid employment as perfectly acceptable and appropriate, it continues to put household labor in first place as a morally prior responsibility for women. If women find paid work "in addition" to their other work to be too great a burden, their first recourse is to quit their paid job. If they wish to continue their paid work, they are ideologically defined as wanting this "extra" job and willingly taking on the double day it demands; if they would prefer to quit but cannot afford to do so, they are pitied for the struggle that is their lot because they are poor. In neither case is the public/private, male/female division of labor called into question. Women who "want to work," women who "have to work," and women who "choose to stay home" are pitted against one another rather than against the social arrangements that make the double day a condition of all women's employment.

Feminists have not been successful in disassociating themselves from this superwoman ideal in the public mind. The demand for women's economic and social independence from male control has often been simplistically translated into an appeal for more and better-paid jobs, which in practice has had the immediate effect of increasing women's burdens. Unfortunately, the women who personally feel that trying to be a superwoman is not liberation, but see no practical alternatives presented by the women's movement, are likely to be co-optable by anti-feminists. It seems significant that a recent university-sponsored symposium on dual-career families was headlined with a quote from Lily Tomlin: "If I had known that having it all was this much work, I would have settled for a lot less."

The backlash fueled by disappointment with the realities of "having it all" seems to have begun. Hewlett (1986), for example, calls women's liberation a myth and castigates American feminists for not having provided European-style support systems that make combining family and career less exhausting: generous maternity leaves, good child care outside the home, time off to care for sick children. She treats the superwoman ideal as the creation of feminist ideology rather than recognizing the absence of social services for families as a consequence of the capitalist ethic. The American "free market" ideology of choices is used to buttress the claim that women have willingly accepted the undeniable difficulties of the double day by opting to have both children and jobs. Thus, the conflict between paid employment and child rearing becomes a problem for individual women to solve. The gender division of labor traps all employed mothers, even feminists, in the struggle to be superwoman.

However, while all women face the ideological demand to do it all, some women may be less willing than others to accept the popular definition of their paid work as an "extra" challenge added on to their continuing responsibility for approximately 80 percent of the housework. These women struggle to achieve some greater equality at home. While even full sharing of the burdens of housework and child care between husband and wife will not make the work load manageable without supporting services (paid child care, take-out food), a more equitable division of labor at home would both ease some of the practical difficulties and undermine the legitimacy of women's double day. It is therefore important to explain how and when women are moved to resist.

Explanations for women's willingness to accept the double day without complaint or challenge fall in two general categories. On the one hand, materialist perspectives tend to emphasize the significance of earned income for family power and to base predictions about resistance on the available resources for successful struggle. Seen from this angle, one would expect the women who actually try to achieve a more equitable division of family labor to be those who are more significant family breadwinners. Since women's paid work is more likely to be a major source of financial support for working-class families, these women have more opportunity to resist a one-sided division of labor. As Benenson (1984) shows, the wage gap between husbands and wives is greater in high-income families because even when the women's earnings are relatively high, their husbands earn proportionally more. Moreover, having better jobs, the wives are more susceptible to having their paid work defined as personal luxury or selfishness, something they chose to "add" to their prior responsibility for housework. Such women may be pressured by guilt to compensate their families by being overachievers at home as well as on the job. Unlike women whose paid work provides a major share of the family income and who may therefore be more able to demand "help," women whose earnings are less consequential may be able to take paid employment only if they promise--explicitly or implicitly--that nothing will change at home (cf. Ferree 1984).

On the other hand, attention to the importance of values and attitudes in shaping family structure would suggest that middle-class women have the most incentive to strive for change and the best chances of achieving it. Some researchers suggest that equality in the household is a less valued goal in working-class families (Harding

1981). Because better-educated women may have a more
egalitarian ideology about the work that is appropriate
for men and women to do in general, they might therefore
be expected to want more shared responsibility in their
own homes. These attitudes would then appear to be good
predictors of women's willingness to struggle against a
one-sided division of labor, even if their power to change
it is not sufficient to make much difference in who does
which chores (Hiller 1980; Huber and Spitze 1981). Unlike
the materialist perspective, the focus on values and attitudes would suggest that middle-class women are more likely than working-class women to challenge the superwoman
ideal and attempt to resist the double day.

Most of these inferences about the sources of women's
willingness to struggle and their implications for class
differences in domestic inequality have not yet been tested
directly. While there are many studies focusing on who
does what work in the home, there has been little attention
paid either to the processes by which the work is allocated
or to women's responses to the burden they carry (but see
Hood 1983; Lein 1983). The present study is an attempt
to explore the validity of these diverse explanations for
the amount of struggle over housework that takes place in
different families. Unlike studies focused on the outcome--
who does what housework--this research attempts to illuminate the process by which sharing is negotiated and when
women define the outcome as fair or unfair. By defining
themselves as having a right to expect more housework
from their husbands, women distance themselves from society's demand that they be superwomen, whether or not
they actually succeed in increasing their husband's share.
Examining this question is an attempt to bring to the surface a nearly invisible issue in the voluminous literature
on the division of labor in the home: the role of women's
struggle for change.

THE SAMPLE

The present study makes several crucial but contro-
versial methodological assumptions. First, paid employment
is not seen here as exceptional, deviant, or in need of
explanation when women engage in it. Therefore, the primary question is how employed women understand their jobs
and integrate them into their lives rather than how they

differ from full-time housewives. Thus, the most useful comparisons are not between women who hold paid employment and those who do not, but among women who interpret and deal with their employment in different ways. This sample therefore includes only women who work at least ten hours a week.

Second, using desire for change as a dependent variable directs attention to the family context and personal meaning of paid employment and housework as women experience them. Because the issue is not one of determining the "objective" distribution of household tasks but of understanding the women's perceptions and responses to inequality, there was no attempt to get data from both spouses on who does what in the home or how they both feel about the existing division of labor. This does not mean that the women's accounts can be taken as necessarily accurate or objective, but it implies that their own perceptions of the situation will be most significant in shaping their choices. For example, if a woman believes that her husband is unhappy about her employment, this perception is assumed to directly influence her willingness to push him for more participation in housework, regardless of how he himself might answer a survey question about his attitude toward her work.

Third, because the focus is on how women cope with the role overload arising from paid employment, marriage, and motherhood combined, single mothers and childless wives were screened out of this sample. This means that the sample is far from representative of the whole population of employed women, even though it was selected randomly before these filters were used. Some losses are particularly regrettable. For example, black women are a significantly lower proportion of this sample than they are of the population of the metropolitan area. Nonetheless, the screening procedure makes possible a closer look at the amount of struggle over the division of labor in roughly comparable families. Households without husbands or children have different demands for housework to be done as well as different persons available to share it.

The data for this study were gathered through telephone interviews using a structured questionnaire. The sample was randomly drawn and households were then screened by telephone to discover if they included a married couple with children under 18 at home and if the wife was employed at least 10 hours per week. Of 1,152 households called, 19 percent (224) refused to answer the screening questions, and of the remainder only 11 percent (105) met the screening criteria. The interviews with the resulting sample were conducted between March and June 1984.

In total, 103 employed married mothers completed interviews. Their median age was approximately 35 years, and they had been married about 12 years to their present spouse (15 percent were previously divorced). The women had an average of two children at home; 18 percent had one or more children under age three, and 23 percent had children between three and five years old. Their paid jobs were quite diverse: 30 percent were in clerical occupations, 26 percent in blue-collar, and 44 percent in other white-collar jobs. However, the majority (55 percent) were in female sex-typed occupations, jobs in which 80 percent or more of the workers are women. The median family income fell in the category of $30,000-$40,000; the women themselves reported personal earnings averaging $12,000 in the previous year. Twenty percent of the wives reported providing half or more of the family income; 24 percent contributed 10 percent or less. About a quarter (27 percent) of the women had worked for pay without interruption at least since their first child was born. The average break for the remaining three-quarters was six years out of the labor force. Husbands' occupations were overwhelmingly male sex-typed (66 percent) and white-collar (74 percent). Although only 9 percent of the husbands moonlighted in second jobs, almost half (47 percent) were reported to work more than 40 hours a week every week.

As other studies have found, these employed women carry the bulk of the responsibility for housework. They reported spending a median of 3 hours a day (approximately 21 hours a week) on housework in addition to their paid employment. Part-time workers—those with jobs less than 35 hours a week—were 40 percent of the sample. About a quarter of the part-time workers (28 percent) did 5 or more hours of housework a day—35 hours a week, the equivalent of a full-time unpaid job. Among those with full-time paid jobs, 13 percent had a full-time unpaid job, too, doing 5 or more hours of housework daily. In contrast, husbands and children were reported to do much less. The men were said to do a median of 4 hours a week, and all the children combined to do a median of

4.5 hours weekly. On average, therefore, the women reported their own share of housework time at 73 percent of
the total, which is consistent with prior studies (J. Pleck
1985; Berk 1985).

Specific chores were reported to be always or typically done by the wife in most instances: cooking (76 percent), cleaning the house (68 percent), washing clothes
(73 percent) and dishes (49 percent), doing the grocery
shopping (63 percent). Taking these traditionally female
chores together, we find that 24 percent reported doing all
5 chores always or typically, while 50 percent carried the
responsibility for 4 or more. Women with full-time paid
jobs carried somewhat less responsibility at home: 62 percent of the part-time workers and 43 percent of the full-
time workers always or typically did 4 or more of the
traditionally female chores, but approximately equal proportions did all 5 (21 percent vs. 26 percent).

As a consequence, a majority (57 percent) of wives
with full-time jobs have a total workweek, paid and unpaid labor combined, of 61 hours or more, while only 13
percent of their husbands do so much work. The number
of hours of paid employment was strongly associated with
women's total workweek—a majority (55 percent) of part-
timers worked 50 hours or less, but only 13 percent of
full-timers did. However, about two-thirds (64 percent) of
all husbands were reported to work 50 hours or less.
Thus, only for wives with part-time jobs is the total load
of work perceived to be roughly comparable with that of
their husbands. Virtually all the women with full-time
jobs were struggling with some degree of overload.

WHAT IT MEANS TO BE A SUPERWOMAN

In order to identify the women who most accepted
our culture's definition of housework as a morally prior
responsibility that a woman owes her family, whether she
has a paid job or not, I asked two related questions.
The first asked women if they agreed or disagreed with
the statement "When I am at home, I try to make up to my
family for having a job." This attitude, called "guilt,"
was expressed by exactly half of the women. The second
question was directed to the idea that women who work
remain personally responsible for maintaining a certain
level of housework. The specific statement was "I make

every effort to ensure that everything around the house is done as well now as when I was home full-time"; 59 percent of the women concurred. This attitude is referred to as "maintaining standards." Feeling guilty about working for pay and trying to maintain the same housework standards are positively related, but only weakly. About a third of the entire sample expressed both superwoman attitudes.

The extent to which these women actually acted like superwomen is not simply a result of these attitudes but also in part a function of circumstances. The first issue is whether housework is shared. There are two specific ways of measuring how the labor at home is divided: by the time spent and by the tasks done. Both are used here, as the wives reported the number of traditionally female chores they do always or typically, and the number of hours of housework they estimate their husbands do weekly. Women who feel that they do a higher proportion of the housework (report less sharing) are judged to be performing like superwomen, whether or not this is their preferred role. The second type of behavior that conforms to the superwoman ideal is carrying an objective overload of work, as indicated by the total number of hours of both paid and unpaid work the wife does weekly. Related to this is her subjective sense of being overloaded, expressed by feeling rushed. Nearly half (45 percent) of the women reported always feeling rushed. I call both the objective and the subjective indicators "overload," and treat them as a measure of stress of combining dual roles.

While doing the housework single-handedly and experiencing a greater degree of stress and overload can both be seen as ways of living out the superwoman ideal, it does not follow that the same women are experiencing both. In fact, there seems to be little or no relationship in practice between the sharing measures (the husband's hours of housework and her responsibility for fewer traditional chores) and the measures of either objective or subjective overload (the wife's total workweek and her sense of time pressure). This is not as surprising as it might seem, because the wife's degree of overload reflects the impact of both paid work and housework on her alone, while sharing measures only the contributions of family members to housework. Since such sharing is in any case relatively low, it may not contribute substantially to reducing her overload. What contribution there is also may be offset by a tendency for family sharing to be greater when her overload is higher.

Ultimately what we are interested in measuring is neither being stuck in the role of superwoman nor simply agreeing with the values underlying the superwoman ideal, but the wife's willing acceptance of a seriously unequal division of labor. Unless a woman is prepared to define her husband's contribution as less or much less than she has a right to expect, she can hardly be expected to struggle to increase his share. Thus women who say that the amount of housework their husbands do is "more" or "as much as you have a right to expect" have taken on the most central feature of the superwoman ideal.[1] This perceived fairness will also be referred to here as a lack of desire for change in his share. Overall, 19 percent of the sample felt that their husbands did much less than they had a right to expect and 28 percent said they did a little less, while a majority (53 percent) accepted their disproportionate burden of housework as fair.

The relationships between the different aspects of trying to live up to a superwoman ideal are also interesting. Feeling guilty about having a job seems to be somewhat associated with having a longer total workweek and feeling always rushed, but also with more perceived unfairness. Trying to maintain the same standards of housework seems to undercut sharing: wives who try to keep up the same standards experience less participation by the husband and more sole responsibility for tasks. But maintaining one's standards for housework does not seem to increase the wife's subjective or objective overload, nor to reduce her desire for change. Sharing, however, is itself related to the desire for change: when more sharing actually occurs, the husband's share is less likely perceived as unfair. (See Table 8.1 for correlations.)

WHO ARE THE SUPERWOMEN?

One purpose of this study is to identify the situations in which women are most or least likely to try to conform to the superwoman ideal. I expect the most crucial factor to be the women's own material circumstances. This I take to be the extent to which the wife plays the role of breadwinner in her family. I call her financial support role that of a breadwinner if she says that needing the

Table 8.1. Correlations among Superwomen Measures and Four Key Predictor Variables

	GUILT Make Up For Job	HOUSEWORK STANDARDS Maintain Standards	SHARING a)Husbands Hours Many	SHARING b)Wife Does Few Trad. Chores	OVERLOAD a)More Total Hours Worked	OVERLOAD b)Feels Always Rushed	DESIRE FOR CHANGE Husband Does Much Less Than Expected
I. Superwomen Measures							
1. Housework Standards	.18*						
2. Husband Hours	-.12	-.20*					
3. Traditional Chores	-.10	-.28**	.55**				
4. Total Hours	.16	.10	.06	-.12			
5. Feels Rushed	.29*	.01	-.03	-.16	.29*		
6. Desire for Change	.16	.13	-.35**	-.39**	.20*	.19*	
II. Financial Support (high=more significance)							
Role of Wife							
1. Need $	.01	-.13	-.07	-.03	.10	.31**	.24*
2. Support Family	.11	-.19*	.04	.06	.21*	.19*	.28*
3. Great Impact	.12	-.29*	.17*	-.13	.23*	.20*	.19*
4. Defer Purchases	.08	-.19*	.01	-.01	.32**	.17*	.21*
5. His $ Inadequate	.03	-.26*	-.01	.06	-.02	.08	.07
6. Her Income %	-.02	-.23*	-.20*	.12	.29**	.14	.19*
Financial Support Scale	.08	-.27*	.07	.07	.24*	.25*	.26*
III. Conflict Over (high=more conflict)							
Her Job							
1. Husband's Attitude	.22*	.03	.06	-.03	.22*	.21*	-.00
2. Kids Attitude	.31**	-.06	.10	-.06	.23*	.40**	-.21*
3. Fewer Arguments	.16	.07	-.00	.01	.19*	.23*	-.01
Conflict Scale:	.33**	-.02	.08	-.05	.30*	.42**	.10
IV. Feminist Attitudes (high=more feminist)							
1. Toward Movement	-.01	-.05	.09	.18*	-.14	.26*	.12
2. To Shared Roles	-.20*	-.25*	.25*	.22*	-.22*	.17*	-.03
V. Class							
1. Blue Collar H	-.00	-.11	.04	.06	-.02	.11	-.07
2. Blue Collar W	.13	.07	-.18*	-.17*	.11	.03	.04
3. Education H	-.01	-.06	-.04	.09	-.05	.00	-.08
4. Education W	-.03	-.09	.01	.10	-.06	.14	.00
5. Family Income	-.06	-.00	.02	.02	-.06	.05	.10
Class Position Index:	-.02	-.03	-.03	.08	-.06	-.00	.02

* = p < .05
** = p < .01

money and supporting the family are important reasons for her working, if loss of her job would have a serious impact on her family and require putting off major purchases, if she perceives her husband's income as less than adequate to support the family, and if the percentage of total family income she contributes is high. Because women who are breadwinners control significant family resources, they are expected to be able to negotiate for a more equitable division of labor than women whose earnings are more peripheral to the family's standard of living.

A second, competing explanation stresses the importance of the values and attitudes the woman holds. I chose to consider two different sets of feminist attitudes here. The attitude I call "feminism" is an orientation toward the women's movement in general and consists of three questions. Women who say they favor most efforts to change women's status, are willing to apply the label "feminist" to themselves, and say that the women's movement had an impact on their lives are counted as feminist. The second attitude, which I call "egalitarianism," is an orientation toward role segregation in the family in the abstract. Answers to three questions—agreeing in principle that raising children is mother's work, that men ought to be the primary breadwinners, and that mothers of young children should stay home if they can—are used to indicate less egalitarian values. Both types of feminist attitudes are expected to lead to demands for greater male involvement in the family because they imply less acceptance of gender segregation as natural and inevitable.

Third, both values and economic circumstances are expected to influence the amount of conflict the wife's employment produces in the family. Higher conflict would probably tend to reduce women's desire for further change in their husband's role. Individuals receive a high family conflict score if the wife perceives that her husband would prefer that she did not work, that her children would prefer that she did not work, and that there would be fewer arguments at home if she were not employed. Family opposition is expected to increase the difficulty women face in combining paid work and housework, and to make it more likely that they would attempt to be superwomen whose paid work is not allowed to reduce their family's claims on their time.

Finally, there is social class, which might be expected to have some effect on all of the previous aspects of the women's situation--but the expected relationships between class and actual sharing or the desire for change are unclear from the existing literature. Higher social class may produce positive effects on feminist and egalitarian attitudes, and negative effects on the significance of the wife's income for the family standard of living, as discussed before. If working-class men are particularly threatened by their wives' assumption of a major piece of the breadwinning role, an important aspect of contemporary men's definition of self-worth, there may be more conflict over wives' employment in working-class families. I use measures of the husband's and wife's education and occupation, and total family income as the indicators of class position.

HOW WOMEN END UP TRYING TO BE SUPERWOMEN

Looking at the breadwinning role, feminist attitudes, family conflict, and social class of women workers suggests some interesting differences between the women who tend to adopt certain aspects of the superwoman ideal and those who resist. (Table 8.1 presents a summary of the correlations discussed here.)

When women who are breadwinners for their families are compared with those whose financial contributions are less significant, we find that the breadwinners are just as likely to feel guilty about their employment but are significantly less likely to try to maintain the same housework standards. They are also more likely to experience overload and to want their husbands to do more housework but, surprisingly, they are not significantly more likely to get help at home.

Women who favor shared family roles in principle are less likely to feel guilty about working for pay; they also tend to lower their standards for housework. These women report getting more help from other family members and do fewer traditionally female tasks alone. Perhaps as a result, they are not more likely to feel that their husbands' contribution is unfairly low. Surprisingly, they report feeling more rushed even though they work fewer total hours than average. In contrast, attitude to the women's movement in general has little relationship to any aspect of the superwoman phenomenon. The only significant effects are that feminists are more likely to feel rushed and to do fewer traditionally female chores.

Women who face more opposition to their paid employment from their families are more likely to feel guilty about working, and they, too, experience a greater degree of overload. But these women are not more likely to try to maintain their standards for housework nor less likely to expect their husbands to do more, as one might have expected them to be. As with the breadwinners, women who face family conflict over their jobs are neither more nor less likely to actually get more help from their husbands and children than are women in general.

Finally, with regard to the various measures of class, it is striking how little total effect is found in any dimension. The only statistically significant effect is that wives in blue-collar jobs get less help in the aggregate than other employed wives receive. Class does have consequences, however, for the other family relationship variables we have just examined. Wives of men in blue-collar jobs are more likely to be breadwinners for their families, as are women married to less well educated and less affluent men; and, as we have already seen, women whose earnings are more significant for their families lower their standards for housework, experience more overload, and think their husbands do less housework than they have a right to expect. Women who are better educated are more likely to endorse shared family roles in principle and to support the women's movement. More egalitarian attitudes in turn contribute to less guilt and lower standards for housework, more sharing, and feeling more rushed. Wives married to better-educated men are less likely to be significantly supporting their families with their earnings, but they are also less likely to face substantial opposition to their paid employment. These diverse effects of class apparently cancel each other out, leaving no net relationship between class position and overload, sharing, or desire for change.

Taking these various interrelationships together and considering their simultaneous effects through a statistical technique known as path analysis, we can single out key aspects of the pattern outlined above. First of all, it is the breadwinning role of women that produces most of the effects seen in the model. Women whose earnings are most significant in supporting their families report their jobs produce more family tension (and such conflict increases guilt feelings as well as overload). The women who are more significant breadwinners are also more likely to lower their standards for housework, to experience more overload, and to want more of a contribution from their husbands, regardless of how egalitarian their attitudes. In contrast, when the effects of being a breadwinner are taken into account, support for shared roles in principle has only one significant effect, that of reducing guilt (see Figure 8.1).

Figure 8.1

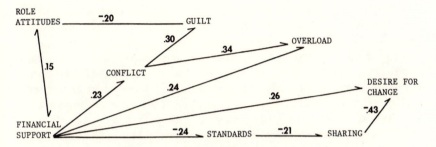

It is therefore evident that the belief that family roles should be shared in the abstract is not enough to produce either the reality of or the desire for greater sharing of housework in women's own families. Women who believe in shared roles are less likely to feel guilty about having a job; but their lesser guilt, however much it helps them enjoy their lives, does not contribute to reducing their daily overload or to creating a more equal division of housework. The role of significant breadwinner, on the other hand, has diverse and substantial effects on the woman and her family. It imposes certain burdens, particularly the greater degree of overload it demands and the family resistance it provokes.

But being a family breadwinner also conveys two important advantages to women workers. First, women who contribute more financially through their paid work feel less compelled to maintain the same level of contribution of unpaid housework, which promotes a greater level of participation in housework from other family members. Second, the greater their breadwinning role, the more the women perceive their husbands' contributions to housework as unfairly low. This seems to reflect their ability to define their work as an important contribution to the family, and thus to see the burdens of the double day as something both husband and wife should carry. In contrast, when the husband continues to carry out the main financial support role, the wife is likely to excuse him from housework, regardless of the hours of paid and unpaid work she has to put in. While one might expect women who are breadwinners to seek more help because their paid work is so demanding, it does not appear to be their experience of overload that leads to a greater desire for change but, rather, their relative financial contribution that leads these women to define their husbands' share of housework as too low.

Our second major finding is that measures of social class appear to have no direct effects on any of the measures of adherence to the superwoman ideal. All of the effects of class are felt indirectly, through both attitudes to shared family roles in the abstract and the likelihood of being a major family breadwinner. The general effect of higher social class is to increase ideological support for shared roles while decreasing the material base from which such sharing can be negotiated. It is the less affluent and less educated women who are contributing a greater share of family income. These women, as family breadwinners, are seeking greater housework contributions from their husbands, and feeling that the share the men do is less than they have a right to expect. In contrast, women in a higher social class are more likely to be egalitarian in principle, but the only observed effect of this is to reduce their feeling of guilt about working.

In sum, class has two sets of effects anticipated in the literature. On the one hand, working-class families are more likely to rely on the wife's earnings, and her significant role in supporting the family tends to produce a greater sense of entitlement as well as a less perceived need to maintain the same level of housework herself. On the other hand, support for shared roles in principle is lower in working-class families. However, this has less practical consequence than expected. For example, the amount of opposition to their employment that women perceive is not affected by either their own attitudes to shared roles or their social class directly; the greater conflict observed in working-class families appears to result entirely from the greater likelihood of working-class wives being in the role of significant breadwinner. Thus, insofar as working-class husbands are especially threatened by their wives' work, this seems to be entirely explained by the greater significance of their wives' earnings to the

family and the consequently greater real loss to them of
the masculinity-defining breadwinner role.   Men in higher
social classes are more relaxed and supportive of their
wives' employment only insofar as the women are not
breadwinners.   The idea that working-class families are
less egalitarian holds only in terms of abstract beliefs;
even though principles about shared roles differ, women's
desires for a fairer division of labor in their own homes
do not reflect these general expectations so much as their
role in supporting the family.

CONCLUSIONS

The analysis here has attempted to move away from
a simple description of who does the housework in order
to begin clarifying the process by which most women continue to accept the burden of the double day.   We know
that most women continue to do the vast majority of the
household labor; the problem is to explain why they do
so, for the most part, without complaint.   This has required attempting to explain the circumstances under which
women will define their husbands' share of the housework
as unfairly low.   This leads us to three basic points.
First, this explanation emphasizes the extent to
which women themselves accept the demand that they be
superwomen who can just "add on" paid employment to
their morally prior "family responsibilities."   The idea
that women should not let their jobs have an impact on
their families, measured here as feeling guilty about working and trying to maintain the same standards of house-
work--the superwoman ideal--has been shown here to contribute to the actual struggle to be superwomen in prac-
tice--a greater overload of work and less help from the
rest of the family for employed women.
Second, we have focused on women's stated perception that the share of housework their husbands contribute
now is all they have a right to expect.   We define women's
willingness to expect more housework from their husbands
as their effort to resist the superwoman ideal.   We find
that the primary factor explaining such resistance is the
significance of the women's own earnings to the family
standard of living, what we have called a breadwinner
role.   The desire for change in the husband's share of
housework appears to be predicated directly upon this

financial support role, increasing women's sense of being entitled to a contribution of housework from their husbands to offset their contribution to family income. When taking the number of hours of paid and unpaid work into account, we find that it is not how much paid work women do, but what that work means to the family, that gives women the perceived right to look for change at home.

In contrast, neither the woman's own attitude to shared roles in principle nor her perception of how her family feels about her work does much to explain her desire for greater participation from her husband in carrying the burden of the double day. While women with egalitarian role attitudes and those whose families are more supportive feel less guilty about working for pay, they still seem trapped in the struggle to handle an overload of work with little practical support from other family members, and they are no more likely than other women to define this situation as unfair.

This means that the materialist explanation for family equality--her stronger financial position vis-à-vis her husband--overshadows the idealist view that women who support equality in principle will struggle to achieve it in their own homes. This does not mean that women are unconscious pawns of economic circumstances, but it does suggest that the position of breadwinner is an empowering one, with rights and responsibilities recognized by all family members, including the woman who holds a paid job. Insofar as she shares that breadwinning role with her husband, she feels entitled to demand a greater share of housework from him. Women with egalitarian attitudes but few breadwinning responsibilities seem to discount their own hours of paid work in assessing the family division of labor. Apparently the significance of housework is measured in hours alone, but the significance of paid employment is in dollars earned and in the meaning of those dollars to the family standard of living.

Third, we have tried to identify the effects of social class on women's response to the superwoman ideal. Contrary to some expectations, there are really no direct effects of class. The apparent significance of social class can be accounted for by the greater probability that less affluent and less educated women workers will be carrying some of the breadwinning role for their families. Such women--who "have to work" to help support their families-- are most likely to define their continuing sole responsibility for the housework as inappropriate. Even when their attitudes about role-sharing in principle are more conservative, these women feel entitled· to expect their husbands to do more at home to an extent that women whose work is more economically optional do not.

In contrast, higher social class, particularly as measured by education, does lead women to endorse more general statements about family role-sharing as an ideal and to support feminism in principle. Thus, while they may themselves be willing to concede that their personal position in the family is economically secondary, and so express no discontent with their husbands' small share of housework, they may be more effective in seeking equal treatment in the work place. As the significance of being a breadwinner shows, women's economic position in the labor market will have to change in order to create the conditions for real equality at home.

While no women, regardless of class, are able to free themselves individually from the pernicious effects of the superwoman ideal, the women whose earnings play a major role in supporting their families are at least in a position to challenge the prevailing assumption that women should do it all. The women in this study who "have to work" seem to be the pioneers who are struggling not only to have a paid job but also to bring their family into the kitchen to work with them. If and when their wages rise to fairly reflect their work, they will have gained an important lever with which to produce family change.

Ultimately, it is this sort of economic change that is required for women's employment to benefit them individually as well as to better support their families. Only as family breadwinners do women seem to have a chance to achieve equity within the home. Unless women have the economic leverage to expect equality at home as their right and to struggle to achieve it, "having it all" will be too much work to continue to be mistaken for liberation.

NOTE

1. The willingness to see inequality as just, rather than a seemingly more direct question about whether the wife was satisfied with the amount of housework her husband did, captured more of the sense of her sentiments. Both questions were asked in the pretest, but the satisfac-

tion item was dropped when it became clear that even women who complained vociferously throughout the interview still said they were "satisfied." Such women were, however, willing to say that what their husbands did was "a little less" or "much less" than they had a right to expect.

9

Reconceptualizing Family, Work, and Labor Organizing: Working Women in Troy, 1860–1890

Carole Turbin

INTRODUCTION

Since the late 1970s the view that work and family life
are systematically related and overlapping dimensions of
existence has become an important framework for the study
of working women and the family. This view, which has
displaced the earlier concept of work and family as distinct and mutually exclusive spheres, is a part of the
growing literature on links between private life (women's
world of family and household) and public life (men's
world of business, industry, politics, and professions).
Scholars have argued that family life and work place experience are interconnected and that the relationship between them is dynamic (Tilly and Scott 1978; Kelly 1979).
Shifts in the work process related to industrialization
changed the family, but family ties also influenced the
organization of work, work rhythms, and who worked with
whom and where (Hareven 1977; Dublin 1979). More recently researchers have questioned the idea that women's work
was transferred from home to factory in a unilinear manner; they have developed a new analysis of how industrialization transformed household production and, consequently, the relationship between family life and work experience (Dublin 1981; Blewett 1981, 1983).

This essay on women collar workers in Troy, New
York (1860–1890), examines a neglected aspect of the relationship between work and family life: the bearing of
these relationships on women's labor militancy.[1] Troy

offers a good opportunity to study these relationships.
The mid-19th century was not only a period of rapid industrialization but also a time when the nation was de-
bating the rights of blacks and women, and the right of
wage earners to organize. At the same time the suffragists were organizing, the labor movement was developing a
national organization. Troy played an important part in
these developments. The city was the home of the Emma
Willard School, the first women's secondary school that
provided a traditional men's curriculum. As a major industrial center with a strong labor movement, the city led
the movement to establish producers' cooperatives. Two
industries dominated Troy: the iron industry, which was
a major producer of the region's iron goods, such as
stoves, bells, and nails, and the shirt, collar, and cuff
industry. Troy earned its nickname "Collar City" because
it produced 90 percent of the nation's detachable collars.

In 1860 the collar industry employed over 3,000
women, largely of Irish background; by 1880 the number
had grown to over 8,000. Collar women included factory
operatives who stitched men's detachable collars and laundry workers who washed, starched, and ironed newly manufactured goods before they were sold to retailers. In
addition, uncounted numbers of women from Troy and surrounding communities did finishing work at home.[2] Although collar sewers, ironers, and starchers initiated
strikes that involved all or part of the industry at various
times, it was the laundresses, particularly the ironers,
whose organization was so impressive. In 1864 collar
ironers formed a union of about 500 members that lasted
until the end of a three-month strike in 1869. In 1886
laundresses and collar sewers formed the Joan of Arc Assembly of the Knights of Labor and, again led by the
ironers, engaged in a major strike.

In this well-organized labor community, the Iron
Molders' Union No. 2 was the collar women's close ally.
The local was one of the strongest in the Iron Molders'
International Union, which was one of the nation's most
prominent unions. Several events highlight this alliance.
In 1864 iron molders helped collar laundresses organize a
union, and in subsequent years they continued to offer
support. In 1866, during the molders' "Great Lockout,"
the laundresses reciprocated (and demonstrated their own
financial solvency) by donating the immense sum of $500
to the molders' strike fund. Molders again provided

crucial support during the collar ironers' spring 1869 strike. Partly because this strike concerned the workers' right to organize, a central issue in the molders' 1866 strike and in the labor movement in general, the collar ironers' struggle became a cause célèbre for New York State's labor movement. The 1866 lockout involved a similar issue. Molders and collar women were again linked, but the Knights of Labor in general, rather than molders in particular, were the women's allies.[3]

Most studies of women's unions explore the question of why a smaller proportion of women than men formed sustained labor organizations.[4] Links between family life and work experience are examined in order to shed light on an important part of the picture: how women's family roles discouraged them from forming permanent organizations.[5] However, too often this analysis is presented not as a partial explanation but as a framework for understanding all of women's labor activity. This is misleading not only because it fails to explain organizations like the collar laundry union, but also because it does not contribute to an accurate, comprehensive understanding of women's labor activism and their consciousness of their shared interests as workers. A full analysis of women's unions must ask a question few researchers have explored: Considering the barriers to permanent organizations for women, under what conditions were some women able to form relatively successful, permanent unions, develop an awareness of shared interests, and form strong alliances with male workers?[6]

Studies that focus on the question of what factors discouraged women's organization tend to overemphasize contrasts between women and men wage earners. This approach tends to view women workers as a homogeneous group and to stress specifically female characteristics, such as passivity. In previous work I have argued that analyses of women's unions must take into account factors similar to those considered in studies of men's labor movements, including status in the labor force and the community, level of skill and earnings, and identification with occupation (Turbin 1979). This chapter will summarize these points and discuss further implications. It will also take the analysis a step further by considering a dimension that has been suggested by studies of women and has only recently been considered in analyses of men: the relationship among family and community ties, household economy, industrial structure, and work place experience. These relationships have a bearing on the consciousness and labor activity of both women and men--indeed, on the development of an entire labor community.

RETHINKING WOMEN'S WORK PATTERNS AND CONSCIOUSNESS

Viewing women as a homogeneous group tends to lump them together on the lowest level of the working class and to ignore crucial differences in female occupational groups, types of activism, and levels of consciousness. An examination of distinctions between groups of working women, including those in the same industry, reveals previously unstudied facets of the relationship between work and family that are central to understanding the labor activity of both women and men. One of these facets is the extent to which women were temporary workers. This section will closely examine differences in the labor force participation of Troy collar women who were at different stages of the life cycle and from various household economies. Turning the conventional question on its head, the chapter will explore how women's consciousness as workers reflects the extent to which their wage work was permanent. Examining the different forms of this permanency reveals that some individual women were permanent workers and some were part of social and ethnic groups that were a permanent and continuous segment of the labor force.

A look at collar laundresses' ages, marital statuses, and employment patterns reveals that the roles of many working-class women included that of provider.[7] Census data and contemporary reports challenge the popular view that the majority of women wage earners were young, single girls who were not dependent on their income for survival, and cite evidence that a larger percentage of collar women worked because they had to. Like other female occupational groups not all collar women were young and single. In 1870, 18 percent of collar laundresses were widows with small children who boarded, or they lived alone or with parents or other relatives. Of the remaining 82 percent who were single, not all were young; 45 percent were 25 years or older.[8] According to Augusta Lewis, leader of New York City's female typographical union, and Susan B.

Anthony, many collar laundresses had other relatives dependent on them for income (New York Sun, July 5, 1869). The laundresses' president, Kate Mullaney, supported her mother and two younger sisters (New York World, February 12, 1870).

Collar women's employment patterns also challenge popular assumptions.[9] Although women's work patterns were different from men's because their life cycle was different, the relationship between women's labor force participation and life cycle cannot be summed up with an ideal picture of young women working for only a few years before marriage. In keeping with working-class families' assumptions that family members would contribute to making a living, employment for women like Troy's laundresses was a familiar experience at every stage of life. Daughters who entered the labor force when they reached a suitable age had more than a few years of work ahead of them,[10] and those who did not marry remained in the labor force much longer.[11] Many women who left employment for marriage continued to earn money through homework or taking in boarders. The percentage of women who were widows or separated indicates that even young women who did not work before marriage might have to work later if their husbands died or deserted them.[12] Some collar women were employed for a good part of their lives, and others worked at one time or another, or during several stages of their lives either within or outside of their homes.[13]

Evidence suggests networks of women who worked in the collar laundries, and in later decades in the collar industry as a whole. Collar work seems to have been a tradition in some families, partly because collar laundry work was especially attractive to women from Irish working-class families. There were other opportunities for work in Troy but, as we shall see later, in the 1860s and 1870s collar laundry work was a good niche in the occupational structure for women of Irish descent. Just as sons often entered the same occupation as their fathers or older brothers, sometimes daughters followed their mothers or other female relatives into the same occupation, often working side by side in the same shop. Networks included more than family members. In Troy's closely knit Irish working-class community, workers recruited friends, neighbors, and other relatives; women's networks must have included sisters-in-law, aunts, and other female relatives.

Contacts at work influenced community, ethnic, and family ties, and vice versa.[14] Family financial needs, the expectation among working-class families that women would contribute to making a living, and the fact that the collar industry provided stable employment for Irish working-class women combined to make the social group from which collar women were drawn a permanent part of the labor force. Although not all individuals were permanent workers, collar women were part of a social group that supplied the labor force of the collar laundries in these decades.

There are good reasons to conclude that women in this segment of the labor force perceived themselves as part of this group. The existence of networks suggests that individual women knew others with similar or different work histories. At any given time female relatives in the same household or neighborhood probably worked for wages in the collar laundries, and others had worked there in the past or expected to be employed in the future. Moreover, the fact that collar laundresses' activism mobilized most of the workers in the industry and was sustained over long periods of time, rather than being tied to particular labor struggles, indicates that group awareness was continuous and not limited to sporadic periods of activism. A combination of close family ties and shared experience as workers and activists suggests that collar women were conscious of their shared interests as workers.

Speculation about women's perception of themselves as a group suggests that differences in household economy and stage of life cycle may explain some variations in women's labor militancy. Since Anthony's observation that "nearly all" the laundresses were supporting aged parents and younger siblings was based on a visit with the union's leadership,[15] her comments indicate that Kate Mullaney's family was not atypical (New York World, February 12, 1870). Other leaders were also the only wage earners in their households. This suggests that women who were dependent on wages because of their household economy and stage of life were more likely to be conscious of their shared interests and to translate their awareness into activism. The large proportion of collar women whose households included male wage earners had other reasons to be committed to unionism (which will be discussed later), but it is possible that they were less active in the union's daily operations. Women who were more dependent on wages to support themselves and others for an extended period of time probably formed an important part of the leadership.

This analysis suggests rethinking some conventional ideas about women workers and women's and men's labor activism and consciousness. Dichotomizing women and men workers glosses over distinctions in the work patterns of women in different stages of life and various family economies, and in localities with different industrial structures and populations. Just as obstacles to women's labor organizing do not constitute a framework for understanding women's activism, so working women should not be assumed to be temporary workers lacking identification with their work or awareness of their common interests as workers. Group consciousness does not stem only from work-related factors and the type of labor force participation experienced by men. In part because of ties to networks of family members and neighbors who shared similar identity, perceptions, and experiences, individual women who may have been temporary workers were conscious of themselves as part of a group who shared common interests as workers, although their self-perception may have taken different forms. Examining the interrelationship among family life, community and ethnic ties, and (as we shall see later) work place experience contributes to understanding variations in the activism of workers of different industries, and differences in consciousness and commitment to collective action among organized workers in the same industry.

A POSITION WORTH DEFENDING

Further examination of conditions contributing to women workers' ability to form sustained labor organizations sheds light on other similarities and differences among female occupational groups and between women and men wage earners in the same industry. Comparisons with less well-organized female workers, such as sewing women, show that among working women, collar laundresses were relatively privileged. In fact, collar laundresses, particularly ironers, shared many of the characteristics of male workers who organized successfully. Labor historians argue that in this period, as in other decades, the best-organized workers were highly skilled wage earners in the highest levels of the working class. This was partly be-

cause workers in occupations that retained the characteristics of skilled crafts strongly identified with their trades
and had a stake in defending their relatively high position on the social scale. Also, their labor was a comparatively scarce commodity that could be withheld in order to
bargain with employers. Earning higher wages than most
workers, they possessed the financial resources to weather
hard times, including strikes (Montgomery 1967). While
collar laundresses' situation differed from that of male
workers, they shared an identification with their occupation and a relatively high status in the working-class community, and they had good reasons to protect their rights
as workers.

What was the position of Troy's collar laundresses
in the community and the industry? Like many industrial
workers, collar laundry women were largely of Irish descent. Immigration patterns in the United States partly
explain the overwhelming proportion of Irish women employed in the laundries. Many Irish immigrants found
their way to Troy because the Hudson River provided convenient transportation from New York City, and Troy's industries promised employment. But the position of Troy's
Irish population differed from that of other urban centers,
where Irish immigrants were concentrated in the lowest
levels of the working class. Walkowitz (1974) reveals that
many of Troy's Irish immigrants achieved relatively high
status through employment in the skilled branches of the
city's growing iron industry.[16] Census data indicate that
while many collar laundresses came from families of unskilled workers, an even larger group came from skilled
workers' families. Their family status was consistent
with both the low status of Irish workers in general and
the relatively high status of many Irish families in Troy
(Turbin 1979).

However, collar laundering was low on the occupational scale. Occupations reserved for women were judged
to be unskilled partly because manual dexterity and other
abilities necessary for work such as sewing and ironing
were considered natural female attributes (Elson and Pearson 1981; Phillips and Taylor 1980). Since training was
through long hours of work at home rather than in formal
apprenticeships, the learning process was invisible and
thus unrecognized. But collar laundering had even less
status than sewing because it had the added disadvantage
of being unladylike. While women from prosperous families

may have done their own fine needlework, they rarely did their own laundry. People invariably compared laundry work with taking in washing, which was one of the most menial and poorly paid women's occupations.

Thus, although laundry work was an industrial occupation, it was considered less genteel and respectable than dressmaking, millinery, or even routine hand stitching. Moreover, although laundering was probably not any more fatiguing and health-impairing than sewing and factory work, working conditions involved heavy physical labor, which was distasteful to many women. Esther Keegan, the collar laundresses' vice-president, reported that laundresses were on their feet for almost all of their 11 to 14 hours of labor. In her shop 12 women worked in a space of about 16 square feet where temperatures reached the "nineties" in the winter. In the summer it was so hot that they often had to "forgo their work for two to three weeks at a time from sheer inability to perform it." Ironers were required to continually lift hot, heavy irons, and starchers' fingers became sore from constant immersion in starchy water. Keegan asserted that because of these conditions, laundresses frequently contracted consumption: "None but the strongest could stand it." Women from American backgrounds who had more options for employment probably preferred the more ladylike occupations of sewing and light industrial work (Turbin 1979).

While collar laundering was not attractive to women of American background who could get other work, it was a good occupation for Irish women who wished to escape employment in service occupations.[17] Working-class women considered the work of cooks, chambermaids, and housekeepers degrading because it involved serving or cleaning up after others and offered less personal independence. Collar laundering not only had the advantages of industrial wage work, but it also provided relatively regular employment and high earnings, in part because of the union. Combining the disadvantages of unladylike labor with the advantages of industrial work, it attracted women from lower levels of the working class who sought to avoid domestic service, and those from higher levels who were willing to endure hard physical labor for high wages (Turbin 1979).

Collar ironing was the most pretigious of the laundering steps, and ironers were the best organized. Although it had lower status than other women's work, ironing in commercial laundries required a combination of manual dexterity and physical strength that could be mastered only with two to four weeks of intensive training. Proud of their ability to endure harsh working conditions and to handle hot, heavy irons for hours, collar ironers boasted that not every woman was equal to the task.[18] Several incidents corroborate ironers' claims and indicate that the difficulty of finding good workers contributed to their ability to bargain successfully with employers.[19] During the ironer's major strike in the spring of 1869, laundry proprietors could not maintain full production levels even while scab workers were being trained. As the employers admitted, it took "some time to teach the newcomers the business." Even with a few weeks of training, the inexperienced workers' abilities were not equal to the dexterity and speed of the striking ironers (Turbin 1979).

Partly because of this centrality in the production process, ironers could demand higher wages than starchers and washers—and, indeed, than most other women wage earners. In 1872 the average earnings of working women were $299 per year, or $6.96 per week, while the average working man earned $611.33 per year, or $13.44 per week. Collar ironers earned from $10 to $12 per week, about twice as much as the average working women and nearly as much as some working men. These relatively high earnings contributed to ironers' identification with their work and to establishing their status within their occupation and the community. High wages also provided resources that contributed to the union's strength and members' ability to weather strikes and hard times (Turbin 1978, 1979).

A strike over the introduction of ironing machines suggests that ironers were willing to take risks to preserve their jobs and skills. With the goal of raising production levels and replacing the piecework system with wages based on average output, in February 1886 the firm of Miller, Hall, and Hartwell installed ironing machines in their laundering department. Ironers were put to work running the machines and folding finished collars and shirts.[20] A spokeswoman for the 200 folders and machine operatives who walked off their jobs rejected the employer's claim that mechanization and the new form of payment would benefit workers because they could earn as much as in the past for much less taxing work. She said that the strikers' goals were to protect the jobs of those who might be dismissed because of the machines' increased output and to preserve the ironers' expertise. The latter concern took the form of protest against the decrease in the more able workers' advantages.

Expressing pride at expert ironers' accomplishments mixed with resentment that less able hands might earn much more under the new system, she said, "Of the two girls who have been running these machines the past week, one is a first class ironer who thoroughly knows her business and the other cannot work so fast or so neatly. . . . Yet they both earned nearly the same wages on these machines" (Troy Daily Telegram, February 22-24, 1886). The ironer's cooperation in this conflict indicates that protests were aimed at employers who sought to eliminate ironer's skills rather than at less expert workers who earned more under the new system. At stake were not only technological changes and leveling of wages, but also ironers' source of status, relationship to the production process, and control over the work process and earnings.

Collar laundresses had good reasons to protect their interests as workers, but ironers were in a better position to defend them. Ironers took a special pride in their work that resembled the attitudes of men in trades requiring skill and strenuous labor, and like well-organized male workers they possessed financial resources and could bargain relatively effectively with employers. Perhaps because of ties of family and ethnicity as well as bonds resulting from cooperation with other workers in small shops, ironers' greater resources and prestige did not lead to deep divisions among those who performed different tasks in the laundering process. Instead, like molders in the iron industry, ironers took the lead. Their leadership was probably a crucial ingredient in the labor activism of the entire industry.

FAMILY, ETHNICITY, COMMUNITY, AND INDUSTRIAL STRUCTURE

Since collar laundresses were not craft workers whose labor was a scarce commodity, their strategies depended on the support of Troy's well-organized, Irish-dominated labor community. It was partly because of this tightly knit labor movement that in Troy more relatively

unskilled workers were organized than in some other industrial centers. Workers for whom there are barriers to
organization (women and less skilled workers in general)
are more likely to organize in a community with a strong
labor movement (Montgomery 1967). As leaders of this
community, iron molders not only lent resources to less
skilled neighbors but also articulated grievances and provided examples of success. Some groups who benefited
from this support were day laborers, sewing women, and
women who ironed newly manufactured collars for commercial laundries (Walkowitz 1974; Turbin 1978).

Women faced more barriers to organization than did
other less-skilled workers. Despite male union officials'
encouragement of women's unions, many men believed that
women took men's jobs and reduced their earnings, and
that the household, not the factory, was woman's "proper
place." At best male unionists viewed women's unions as
irrelevant because unmarried women were temporary workers and the goal of unions was to raise men's wages to a
level sufficient to enable their wives to devote themselves
to hearth and home.[21] However, in Troy some male wage
earners had more reasons to encourage women to organize
than to be hostile or indifferent. Since most of Troy's
industrially employed women were single or widowed, and
the employment of daughters and widows without men to
support them was congruent with working-class families'
expectations, the city's female industrial labor force was
not a threat to traditional family structure.[22] Moreover,
the sex segregation of Troy's industrial structure fostered
a firm alliance between important groups of women and
men wage earners: iron workers and collar women. Employed women may have threatened men's perception of
themselves as their families' breadwinners, but since the
iron industry employed only men and collar factories employed predominantly women, women workers as a group
were not perceived as a threat to men's source of livelihood. In fact, well-organized women contributed to male
unionists' goals of economic security and a strong labor
movement.

Evidence indicates that from the 1860s to the 1880s
collar laundresses (and sewers in the 1880s) provided an
important contribution to iron molders' households. As we
have seen, while many collar women were the only wage
earners in their families, a larger proportion lived in
households that included male wage earners. In many

cases they were the daughters, sisters, or in-laws of iron molders.[23] Sharing the burden of their families' economic support with men, they may have had attitudes toward the union and male unionists different from those of women like Kate Mullaney, whose families were entirely dependent on their earnings. But their family relationships gave them other reasons for having a stake in a strong and permanent union, and provided one basis for cooperation between workers of different genders.

Family relationships do not always lead to cooperation. Daniel Walkowitz and Barbara Abrash's film The Molders of Troy suggests that among Troy's Irish working-class families, commitment to unions was part of family lore, and the household and community were places where union matters were discussed and sometimes resolved. But family tradition can work against labor organization just as it can reinforce it.[24] Family members who were loyal unionists did not always agree on strategies or attitudes toward union struggles. Strikes, lockouts, and other work-related emergencies called forth animosities as well as co-operation. In Troy, alliances between women and men were based on other factors fundamental to Troy's industrial and social structure.

The 1886 collar women's strike highlights the complex mix of factors that encouraged these alliances. Collar laundresses and sewers joined forces to form a local of the Knights of Labor in 1886, shortly before the ironers struck against machines in February (Troy Daily Press, February 11, 1886). In June about 200 starchers and ironers in the laundry department of George Ide's firm initiated another major strike by demanding an equalization of wages with other companies. The increase amounted to from 0.5 to 1 cent per piece, depending on the type of collar. When the women refused to return to work, the employer responded by combining with other manufacturers to form an association and closed down all the shirt and collar factories in the city. The result was an industry-wide lockout that involved 33 establishments and about 8,000 women, including home workers in Troy and vicinity. Although manufacturers and employees agreed on a compromise on wages in Ide's laundry within a few days, the lockout continued because employees insisted that the manufacturers' association recognize the Knights of Labor as the workers' representative. The employees won part of the increase they sought, but the demand that the Knights represent the collar women was rescinded (Troy Daily Times, Troy Daily Press, Troy Daily Telegram, May 15–June 23, 1886; New York World, May 15–June 22, 1886; John Swinton's Paper, May 15–June 29, 1886).

Family ties between iron molders and collar women seem to have played a role in determining events. Locking out the entire industry over a demand for a small increase in one shop that was resolved fairly quickly makes sense only when the significance of the Knights' demands for recognition and some crucial events in the iron industry are considered. The collar women's five-week strike coincided with a four-month strike in the iron foundries. The strikes ended within a few days of each other, and both involved the Knights of Labor. Collar manufacturers, who sought to stem the influence of the Knights, were probably concerned that the newly formed Joan of Arc Assembly would extend the Knights' influence into yet another segment of the labor force. But the fact that the molders' and collar women's strikes ended within days of each other suggests other relationships between the conflicts besides their association with the Knights. Labor leaders and other observers argued that the collar manufacturers were in league with the foundry owners; manufacturers locked out their employees because during the molders' strike, families were dependent on the income of collar women who were molders' wives and daughters. Manufacturers hoped that throwing the women out of work would pressure iron molders to reach a settlement favorable to the foundry owners.[25]

Observers claim that the factory owners' use of family ties to break the molders' strike supports the conclusion that family relationships, in conjunction with Troy's industrial structure, encouraged cooperation between workers of different genders. Since the city was dominated by two industries, one employing women and the other employing men, when men went out on strike, they could rely on the earnings of female family members in the other industry and vice versa. Earnings of female family members were relatively certain, since the collar industry employed thousands of Troy's women as both home and factory workers. Similarly, the iron industry employed a large proportion of Troy's male labor force (Walkowitz 1978). In both industries wages were relatively high and work steady, although there were slack periods. While this is not the only reason for Troy's high level of labor militancy, the

relationship between industrial structure and family patterns is an important part of the explanation for Troy's
strong labor community.

Ethnic and community ties also strengthened collar
and iron workers' ability to hold out during strikes and
hard times. Not all workers could depend on the earnings
of relatives in the same household during strikes. Those
who were the only wage earners in their families probably
depended on the resources of relatives in different households in the same or different neighborhoods, on friends
and neighbors, and on benefits provided by the union's
strike fund or on contributions (New York World, July 3,
1869). Living in the same neighborhoods and participating
in Irish political and nationalist organizations, Troy's
laundresses and iron molders were linked through community and ethnic ties as well as through family relationships.[26]

Examining shifts in the labor activism and alliances of collar sewers underlines the influence of family and ethnic ties on labor militancy. Collar sewers engaged in little activity before they organized with laundresses in the 1880s, and on one occasion when they did
strike, they refused help from the molders' union (Troy
Daily Times, February 10, 1864). Two factors contributed
to this change. First, by the 1880s collar laundries were
incorporated into collar factories, and sewers and laundresses were employed in the same establishments and faced
the same employers.[27] Second, shifts in the ethnic composition of collar sewers resulted in closer ties to Troy's
working-class community. In 1865, 19 percent of sewers
were born in Ireland, in contrast with 79 percent of laundresses. Five years later the percentage of Irish women
employed sewing collars had more than doubled. In 1870,
44 percent of sewers were Irish, compared with 80 percent
of laundresses.[28] In the 1880s collar sewers were part of
the same industrial establishments as laundresses, and a
larger percentage of sewers were linked to laundresses and
iron molders through family, community, and ethnic ties.

Other work supports the view that family relationships have a bearing on the characteristics of labor struggles. Mary Blewett's (1979) study of shoe workers in mid-
19th-century Lynn, Massachusetts, argues that tensions between women workers' ties with male family members and
ties with other women workers militated against firm alliances between women and men. Unlike Troy, Lynn and

surrounding areas were dominated by one major industry employing both women and men. In keeping with the strict sexual division of labor in which women worked as shoe binders at home or as stitchers in all-female shops, women and men belonged to separate labor organizations. While women factory workers were part of a mobile labor force recruited from surrounding areas, home workers were largely wives or daughters of male shoe workers. Blewett's (1979) work on Haverhill suggests that factory operatives from other communities were not regarded as outsiders; coming from backgrounds and localities similar to that of the families with whom they boarded, strong ties developed between the young women and Haverhill's residents.

As in Troy, family relationships and women's contributions to the household economy were crucial ingredients in the web of alliances. In the 1860 regional shoe strike, women factory workers (whom male workers had helped to organize) argued that improving women's wages was as important as improving men's. Also, they sought to form an alliance with female homeworkers. Blewett argues that the male-dominated strike committee refused to acknowledge the women factory workers' demands because they feared the decline of homework, on which their families depended. Since the strike leadership ignored their demands, the female factory operatives' support was lost, although homeworkers continued to participate in the strike. The conflict ended in April with the issue of wages unresolved (Blewett 1983). Blewett's analysis and the example of Troy indicate that the influence of the relationship between family ties and industrial structure on labor organizing is a fruitful area of research for understanding labor militancy in 19th-century cities.[29]

CONCLUSIONS

These conclusions have important implications for understanding working women in general. Avoiding stark contrasts between women and men, and looking at conditions under which some women were able to organize successfully, reveals subtle differences between male and female workers, and among women workers in the same and different industries, occupations, and communities. Moreover, while studies that focus on barriers to women's organization emphasize women's isolation from each other and lack of concern with common interests, the laundresses' experience suggests conditions under which some working-class women may be conscious of their interests as a group. Consciousness takes different forms in different circumstances and may not always result in sustained organization, but it is important to see it as a possibility emerging from shared experience. Broadening the focus of labor history to include an examination of women who formed successful unions and perceived themselves as a group contributes to a comprehensive understanding of working women and their organizations.

The preceding analysis also suggests a new perspective on the study of women, work, labor organizing, and the family. It indicates that an area formerly thought of as especially suited to understanding women's work, the family, is also key for analyzing labor activism--indeed, the entire labor movement in a community or region. This perspective reveals the limitations of looking at women's work force participation and labor activism mainly in terms of their family roles while analyzing men's employment and union activity largely in terms of work-related factors. Reserving family life for understanding women and work experience for analyzing men leads to a narrow understanding of both sexes and neglects links between family, work, and industrial structure that contribute to an understanding of a community's complex social life.[30] Analysis of these links will contribute to a reconceptualization of women's and men's labor activism and consciousness.

NOTES

1. The discussion of Troy in the 1860s immediately following is based on material that originally appeared in Turbin (1979). Discussion of the 1880s is based on research completed since publication of that essay.

2. Estimates are unreliable, since homeworkers often do not appear in the manuscript census, but observers agreed that in the 1880s at least 3,000 women did homework in Troy and vicinity.

3. The discussion of the iron molders and Troy's labor movement is drawn from Walkowitz's important work on Troy (1972, 1974, 1978).

4. For example, Kennedy (1979) and Tentler (1979) stress factors that militate against women's sustained col-

lective action. Studies of working-class communities such as Dawley (1976) and Walkowitz (1978) discuss women's activism as well as barriers to organization, but they do not systematically examine specific conditions under which women organized successfully.

5. Kessler-Harris (1975, pp. 217-242; 1979) discusses ways in which male unionists' attitudes toward working women discouraged organization.

6. Tilly (1981) analyzes this question systematically.

7. This argument appeared in Turbin (1979). Also see Groneman (1977, pp. 83-100).

8. Percentages are drawn from 1865 New York State manuscript census schedules and 1870 federal manuscript census schedules. These data are discussed more fully in Turbin (1978, pp. 197-206).

9. The question of the extent to which women were temporary workers is complicated. Maintaining that women's work was a temporary stage before marriage was a means of reconciling contradictions between the ideology of domesticity and the economic reality that compelled women to work. Related to this is the undercount of working women in the census. Women may have been reluctant to identify themselves as wage earners; enumerators may have failed to inquire about women's occupations. See Bose (1984; see also ch. 5) for a discussion of the undercount of employed women in the census.

10. The youngest working women in the census were 14, but sources suggest that children left school for wage work after age 12. See Walkowitz (1978, p. 115) and Kaestle and Vinovskis (1978) for a discussion of school leaving.

11. One unmarried woman who appeared in the 1860 census as a collar laundress when she was 25 was still working in the laundries in 1870, when she was 36.

12. Some widows left the labor force when their children were old enough to support them.

13. See Turbin (1978, pp. 198-200; 1979, p. 206) for further discussion.

14. Analysis of Troy's closely knit Irish working-class community is based on Walkowitz (1978). Hayner's (1925, pp. 635-636) suggestion that grandmothers, mothers, and daughters were employed in the same collar shops, often working side by side in the same room, is reinforced by documentation of this pattern in other communities (Dublin 1979; Hareven 1977, p. 195; Wallace 1978, pp. 59-61.

15. Anthony's report was based on a visit to Troy in 1870. Delayed between trains, she took the opportunity to visit the union's failing cooperative laundry and meet with its managers, including Kate Mullaney and Esther Keegan, who had been dismissed by employers after the 1869 strike. Harper (1898, pp. 999–1000) notes that Anthony referred to this visit in speeches about the ballot's importance for women's bargaining position with employers. She argued that if women were enfranchised, the collar laundresses would have won their strike.

16. Men of Irish descent constituted the largest numbers of workers in each of the largest skilled branches of the iron foundries: molders, puddlers, and heaters and rollers.

17. For Irishmen, skilled iron work also had more status than for American and British working men (Walkowitz 1974).

18. Penny's (1863) compilation of employers' reports from the early 1860s includes comments by proprietors of commercial laundries that good ironers were scarce and commanded high wages.

19. For example, having given in to demands for wage increases since 1864, in 1869 laundry proprietors tried to undermine the union by persuading nonunion ironers in the city's largest laundry to train new hands to replace workers in union shops. The owners would not have tried to weaken the union in this way if they could simply have fired the union ironers and replaced them with new hands. Kate Mullaney reported that the employers' tactics failed because the nonunion ironers, "seeing what the results would finally be, for their own protection, joined the union in a body." The owners' need for experienced labor enabled the ironers to strengthen the union even further (Turbin 1979, p. 210).

20. Manufacturers may have abolished the piecework system in order to increase their control over wages and the work process. Stone (1975) argues that piecework gave employees more control over wages, although it was also a source of division among workers.

21. For a discussion of the family wage, see H. Hartmann (1981b, pp. 25–27), Barrett and McIntosh (1980), and May (1982).

22. The small percentage of industrially employed married women was probably due to the collar industry's extensive homework system, which enabled women to earn

income at home.   Homework in Troy is described by Greeley
(1873, pp. 614–615) and Weise (1877, p. 265).

   23.   Preliminary analysis of census data indicates
that more collar laundresses were members of iron molders'
families than were women in other industrial occupations.
In 1865, 14 percent of the laundresses' male relatives
were molders.   In contrast, molders constituted only 8
percent of collar sewers' male relatives, and 5 percent of
sewing women's male relatives.   Although these figures
are modest, they indicate that slightly more laundry women
than other working women were related to molders (Turbin
1979).

   24.   Conflicts between family members during the
laundresses' 1869 strike are described in the Troy Daily
Whig, June 23, 1869.   See H. Hartmann (1981, pp. 367–368)
for a useful analysis of conflicts and struggles that take
place within families.

   25.   The argument that collar manufacturers were
in league with iron foundry owners appears in New York
Bureau of Labor Statistics (1887, pp. 44–77); New York
World, May 19 and 20, 1886; Troy Daily Times, May 26,
1886; John Swinton's Paper, May 23 and June 23, 1886.

   26.   See Walkowitz (1974, pp. 433–435; 1978) for an
insightful analysis of Troy's ethnic, political, and community networks.

   27.   The organization of the collar industry from
its inception to the 1870s is fully described in Greeley
(1873, pp. 614–615).

   28.   Discussion of these shifts is based on census
data and on reports from the Troy Daily Press, Troy Daily
Times, and Troy Daily Telegram, May 15–June 23, 1886.
Changes in the proportion of Irish collar sewers seem too
great to be due to errors related to the small size of the
population or limitations of census data.   If sewing was
more genteel, although less remunerative, than ironing,
the increase in Irish collar sewers may indicate Irish upward mobility or that by the 1880s changes in collar sewing made the occupation less desirable to women of American background.

   29.   See Benenson (1982), Foster (1974), and
Humphries (1977) for an analysis of the role of family
patterns in labor organizing.

   30.   This argument has also been made by Feldberg
and Glenn (1979b).

10

A Living Wage Is for Men Only: Minimum Wage Legislation for Women, 1910–1925

Susan Lehrer

INTRODUCTION

From the beginning of the 20th century through World War I, protective legislation for women workers was a major focus of liberal social activity. These laws were passed during the "sweatshop" era, with the support of a wide spectrum of reform groups, including suffragists, labor reform organizations, and the Socialist Party. The reformers fought for passage of state laws that would limit the hours of women workers (for instance, to 10 per day or 60 per week), prohibit night work for women, bar women from certain occupations, and provide other protections deemed important for women workers. Throughout this period, the constitutionality of all forms of labor legislation was in flux; however, the trend was to find laws that protected wage workers against employers increasingly acceptable. This was especially true concerning laws that applied to women workers. The one exception was minimum wage legislation for women. Until the New Deal (when the law affecting both men and women workers was upheld), minimum wage laws for women failed to gain a secure legal foothold. The reason for this failure can be understood only by examining the connection at the societal level between women's work in the labor force and her domestic labor in the home, and the way the state intervened in this arena. This chapter explores why minimum wage legislation for women failed to gain legitimation at a time when other forms of sex-specific labor laws were being upheld as constitutional.

Protective legislation for women established a special legal status for women workers, which appeared to be responding to their needs as women; it did this, however, by leaving the major premises about women's position in the home intact. These laws that regulated women's work lives were in fact reinforcing the traditional assumption that woman's place is properly in the home; the laws then regulated her work force participation to accord with this. Minimum wage rates set under these laws necessarily took into account prevailing wage structures at a given place and time; they incorporated existing lower wage rates for women as a matter of course. Therefore, through minimum wage laws the state was maintaining and reinforcing the sex-based hierarchy of labor, in which women were paid less than men because they were women.

This chapter will first look at the legal issues surrounding the passage of labor legislation during this period, including the employers' laissez-faire position that the laws were a violation of the wage bargain and freedom of contract, and proponents' contention that women as a group were in special need of protection, and therefore the state could legitimately intervene in the "wage bargain." Next, I will examine their views of the wage structure as a whole--what determines the price of labor, because minimum wage legislation interferes directly with the "wage bargain." Employers argued that labor was a commodity with a price determined by its worth like any other commodity, and that minimum wage laws amounted to a kind of price-fixing; supporters argued that the "price" of women's labor bore little relation to its "value"--if indeed that could be determined. Finally, the emergence after World War 1 of a principled, feminist opposition to all forms of protective legislation for women will be examined to see why feminists' views about the position of women led them to support the first equal rights amendment in spite of the sharp criticism they received.

Protective labor laws applied mainly to women in industrial employment. In some cases, they were applied where women predominated in a trade, while in others there was a high proportion of women in "male"-centered trades (such as printing). They did not apply to waitresses or other female jobs such as nursing, and almost never covered occupations that employed black women (except for laundries), since black women were excluded from industrial jobs until World War 1.

Although some of the reasoning behind these laws appears archaic, and certainly the laws themselves are now presumptively improper under Title VII of the Civil Rights Act of 1964, the same issues have resurfaced in the 1980s debate over comparable worth (equal pay for jobs of comparable value); the idea of whether there is a "work-worth" determined by the "value" of labor is again at issue.

HISTORY OF MINIMUM WAGE LAWS

In the United States, regulation of wages was seen as a remedy only for exceptionally low-paid work, and then only for women, not men. Labor unions and the American Federation of Labor (AF of L) were not particularly interested in getting legislation passed; they viewed all forms of labor legislation as a threat to unionizing because they felt it would decrease workers' reliance on their own efforts. Since women workers were considered harder to unionize, this might justify legislation on their behalf. Samuel Gompers, AF of L president, stated his position regarding legislation as follows: "The AF of L is in favor of fixing the maximum number of hours of work for children, minors, and women. It does not favor a legal limitation of the workday for adult men workers. . . . The AF of L has apprehensions as to the wisdom of placing in the hands of the government additional powers which may be used to the detriment of the working people" (American Federationist 21 [1914]: 544).

In this country, it was not until 1912 that Massachusetts established a commission to study industrial conditions and set wage rates. Minimum wage boards were set up in several states from 1912 on, but although there was a Supreme Court case that challenged the constitutionality of minimum wage legislation in 1917, the Supreme Court merely let stand lower courts' approval (Baker 1925, p. 80). Therefore, in 1923, it came as a surprise to both sides when the Supreme Court declared the Washington, D.C., minimum wage law for women unconstitutional (Adkins v. Children's Hospital, 261 U.S. 525, 1923). Past decisions had been increasingly favorable to protective legislation: the Supreme Court upheld a "no night work" law for women in 1923 (Radice v. People), as well as hours limitations that prohibited women from working long or dangerous (night) hours. These kinds of laws were becoming another fact of industrial life that employers grudgingly accepted as inevitable. But the wage contract was another matter altogether. Arguments surrounding this will be looked at next, to contrast employers' assumptions about wages with the arguments in support of the laws.

EMPLOYERS' VIEW OF THE WAGE BARGAIN

Employer's primary objection to minimum wage laws was based in part on the arguments they used against other labor legislation in the past—that it was an infringement on the right (of a woman) to contract the conditions of (her) labor, and that it was class legislation favoring one group at the expense of another, thereby violating "due process" and "equal protection" clauses of the Constitution. Legal arguments did not distinguish between men and women workers on this point.

Speaking specifically about the wage issue, the lawyer for the employers in the 1917 Oregon minimum wage cases argued that the law:

1) fixes a wage based solely upon the individual needs of the employee, measured not by anything which has relation to the fact of employment or to the particular occupation in question, but measured solely by the individual needs of the person employed . . . .

2) it puts the burden on the employer to supply individual needs to the extent that the money required therefore is in excess of what the employee earns, or can earn or is worth . . . . (R. Brown 1917, pp. 477–478)

The problem with minimum wage laws, he continued, is that they assume that every individual has a "generic right" to receive not just mere subsistence, but the "full means of living in health and comfort, including reasonable expenditure for pleasure and diversion." And if the individual cannot earn this, the law then demands that it be paid from "outside sources," specifically, "by the one who happens to have that individual on his pay-roll," even if it has to come out of his profits or, if that is not possible, then out of his capital. If the owner cannot support this, he will have to go out of business and also be charged with being a "parasite" because he cannot pay this "forced contribution to the individual needs of its employees" demanded by the minimum wage (R. Brown 1917, p. 480).

The employers here were arguing that the wage bargain must be considered in isolation from the social conditions of reproduction of the labor force and, therefore, they could not be held responsible for providing a living wage to any worker, male or female. "The need to any person of a 'living' is an <u>individual</u> need. It exists before employment, and during employment, and after employment. Such need is, indeed, diminished, or supplied, during employment to the extent of the wage actually paid. . . . The need itself is one which is a natural or purely individual need and has no origin in the fact of employment" (R. Brown 1917; p. 480).

This contrasts with the Marxist position that wage labor and capital constitute a socially defined relation, in which the wage rate is the outcome of a struggle between the class of workers and capitalists. One of the contradictions that arises in the course of capitalist relations of production is that capitalism both depends upon and tends to destroy the creator of surplus value, the worker. As individuals, however, capitalists stand to benefit from low wages; thus, the employers argued that "price-fixing" of labor was "a new expression of the paternalistic and socialistic tendencies of the day. . . . It is consistent with the orthodox socialist creed, but it is not consistent with the principles of our government which are based upon the protection of individual rights" (R. Brown 1917, p. 486). By contrast, Marx pointed out the effects of continued overwork on the working class as a whole; legislation designed to mitigate some of the worst abuses (such as the English Factory Acts) simply provided the conditions by which capital can continue to function while being real concessions to the working class.

Social reformers tended to accept the premise that a wage was a social relationship; employers refused to see the wage bargain as anything other than an individual relation between employer and employee. In addition to the individualistic, laissez-faire position used by employers to argue against <u>all</u> labor legislation, regardless of whether it affected men or women, employers had to counter the arguments that women were in special need of protection, and therefore legislation could be permitted when it would not be if the law were directed at men.

In the employers' brief before the Supreme Court in
Stettler v. O'Hara, counsel argued that the minimum wage
statute for women was in principle no different from one
applying to men: "One right which nature has conferred
equally on men and women is the right to work for a living at such wages as he or she shall deem satisfactory,
and at such employment as he or she shall choose if it be
not harmful to others or to himself or herself" (Fulton
1916, pp. 25-26). That right was unquestioned regarding
men, and there was no reason to distinguish men from
women in their need for protection, he argued. He made a
distinction between minimum wage laws and laws regulating
the hours that women may work, which are based on the
public's interest in "the preservation of a vigorous race
and in preventing citizens from becoming dependents on
public charity" through ill health. (These laws generally
were being upheld as constitutional by 1916; lawyers are
nothing if not realists in that respect.) Since "women are
more delicately organized than men, and hence a woman's
health may be injured when and where a man's would not,"
such laws might legitimately go further in regulating
women's work than men's (Fulton 1916, p. 52). But a
minimum wage law involves different principles entirely,
concerning the value of the commodity labor. This value
depends on the law of supply and demand like any other
commodity; unlimited price-fixing by the legislature would
be simply preposterous.

In the Oregon case, the lower court's decision pre-
vailed because of a split Supreme Court (one justice did
not participate). (Brandeis had just been appointed to
the court, but was involved in preparing the brief for
counsel.) Similar legislation was initially upheld in other
states as well. Courts made it plain that they were not
passing on the wisdom of such laws, which would become
clear only with time, but solely on the issue of whether
it was "reasonable" to think that detrimental conditions
exist that might be remedied by the laws passed by the
legislature.

In summary, employers argued against minimum
wage laws by claiming that the wage bargain was a private matter to be decided by individual employers and employees; any interference with this was an infringement on
their rights to freedom of contract. They claimed that
wages represented the "worth" of the worker and that the
employer was under no obligation to provide for the full

support of a worker. Since wage labor was a commodity
with a "price" and a "value" like any other, minimum
wage laws were a kind of price-fixing. Employers denied
that any circumstances differentiated women workers from
men in this respect.

THE SOCIAL REFORMERS' VIEW
OF THE PRICE OF LABOR

The controversy over minimum wage legislation
focused on the question of what determines a wage. As
shown, employers contended that there is a "value" of
labor that is determined by the same market conditions
that determine the value of other commodities; however,
proponents of the legislation countered that "competition
leads to a wage; but it does not necessarily follow that
it leads to an 'economic' wage or to a 'fair' wage" (Groat
1925, p. 77). The "wage bargain" is affected by the relative powerlessness of one party, and therefore the going
wage need bear no necessary relation either to the work's
worth or to the employer's ability to pay. One critic of
the adverse decision on minimum wage laws asked:

> And would the learned Justice [Sutherland]
> furnish the scale for ascertaining and
> measuring what this "worth" [of the labor
> performed] might be! The range of opinion
> swings all the way from that of the Marxian
> socialist who maintains that the whole
> product and nothing less is the "worth"--
> the true equivalent of the laborer's toil
> . . . to that of the most hard-fisted of
> employers, who maintains that in hard
> times they are worth nothing and in good
> as little as he can possibly pay. (Grimes
> 1925, p. 116)

Thus, proponents of the minimum wage argued, it is a fal-
lacy to claim that each employee has a "work-worth."
Minimum wage laws "would not compel employers to make
any contract that in their judgment is not remunerative";
rather, these laws are "opposed to the theory that there is
a constitutionally guaranteed right to make the most advan-
tageous bargains which one's economic position permits"
(Powell 1917, p. 6).

Because women workers were not effectively able to demand a "fair" wage, the price of labor was not the result of fair competition but reflected their lesser bargaining power, just like other aspects of the employment contract. Wages paid therefore did not reflect the "value" of labor to the employer; instead, "The rates of wages depend to a large degree upon the personal equation of the employers and upon the helplessness of their employees, and to a very inexact degree upon the cost of labor in relation to the cost of production" (Holcombe 1912, p. 36). In fact, according to one Boston study, the wage scale did not vary because of the quality of the goods, and "in general there appeared to be no relation between wages and prices" (F. Kelley 1912, p. 1008).

Proponents of minimum wage laws argued that the "wage bargain" must not be seen in isolation from the social conditions that give rise to it; the employer is responsible not only for paying for work done, at the rates he can command, but also for the reproduction of the labor force. This is not "paternalistic" or a compulsory redistribution of property, it was argued; the statute simply says to the employer: "If you choose to seek profit from the labor of a woman, you must pay what it costs to keep her in condition to furnish that labor. If it is not to your advantage to pay for labor what it costs to produce it, you need not employ that labor" (Powell 1917, p. 3).

The employers' contentions that they bear no responsibility for the living conditions of the worker, and that the worker's needs and wants are irrelevant to the employer, were also disputed, on the grounds that "during employment the need to the employee of a living is likewise a need to the employer. And the statute deals with the employer only during employment" (Powell 1917, p. 7). The law is prohibitory rather than compulsory in nature, Brandeis had argued earlier. He commented: "How potent the forces of conservatism that could have prevented our learning that like animals, men and women must be properly fed and properly housed, if they are to be useful workers and survive" (Brandeis 1915, p. 494).

A legal minimum wage becomes necessary because wages are below the cost of living and the employer becomes, in effect, a parasite on the community. For women who are paid starvation wages (such as young girls in unskilled jobs with an oversupply of available labor) this difference is made up either by the family or by charity (including the subsidized boardinghouses and lunchrooms that were common during the period). Or, as one writer pointed out, they die of malnutrition and sickness, or turn to prostitution. The minimum wage, then, "does commit organized society to a more responsible attitude toward the whole labor problem" (Seager et al. 1913, p. 89). According to this line of reasoning, which was also used in the Brandeis brief of Stettler v. O'Hara to develop a substantive justification for the minimum wage law, industries that underpay their employees are subsidized, in effect, either by the workers' families or by society as a whole, which bears the rest of the cost of maintaining them.

Since wages are not fixed by the "worth" of labor, but by the desperation of the "marginal" female worker, competition from other employers will force even the "fair" employer to squeeze wages down. In this case, as in other social issues, such as health regulations, where the "public" can take a hand in regulating the "social bargain," the purpose is "to safeguard the community." Both the physical degeneration of the workers and the social unrest that would be averted were used as practical reasons why a minimum wage was in the community's best interest. Far from leading to socialism (as critics of the measure asserted), it would be more accurate to say that "this and other needed social reforms tend to make outright socialism undesirable and unnecessary" (Seager et al. 1913, p. 88).

Social reformers, whether labor-oriented or women's suffragists, accepted the prevailing notions that women's wages were not comparable with men's; it was the shockingly low rates of the most poorly paid women that minimum wage laws were aimed at. They saw that women's low wages could not be accounted for simply by their lower productivity or "work-worth," and felt that in the prevailing legal climate the laws could be legitimated in the courts like other forms of protective legislation for women workers. How that minimum wage was arrived at, and why it ultimately failed to gain acceptance throughout this period, will be looked at next.

SETTING A MINIMUM STANDARD OF LIVING

From the preceding discussion, it is clear that minimum wage legislation raised a basic issue concerning how the price of labor is determined in a competitive, capitalist society. Although those who favored the law argued that a wage ought to be sufficient to ensure subsistence both for the individual worker and for the future generation of workers, that had to be translated into a specific standard for it to have any meaning. Whether a minimum rate is fixed by statute for a given occupation, or for all women, some means must be used to determine what would be a "reasonable" minimum. The laws expressed this in various ways: "necessary cost of proper living and to maintain the health and welfare" (California); "necessary cost of living, maintain them in health, and supply the necessary comforts of life," as well as consider the "financial condition of the business" (Colorado); "experienced adults, $1.25 a day" (Utah) (Andrews 1914, pp. 22–23).

It is obvious that fixing the dollar amount ultimately depends upon two things: the specific standard that is set (whether stated or assumed), and the amount of money it takes to achieve it. In the period immediately preceding the passage of these minimum wage laws, studies of family budgets were done under various auspices (Hughes 1925; Chapin 1909; More 1907; Anthony 1914). Many were conducted by charities, settlement houses, or universities, while others were done by state or federal agencies, including the Department of Labor and the Bureau of the Census. Many of the studies were done specifically to document the wretched living conditions of the majority of workers in a given locale, and to argue for ameliorative measures, including protective labor laws and workman's insurance. These studies were used as evidence presented to the Supreme Court to demonstrate the need for legislation. "Brandeis brief" is a kind of legal argument that was developed in an earlier case (Muller v. Oregon) involving legislation for women workers. This kind of argument depends upon concrete, substantive economic data (rather than an appeal to legal precedent) to establish the need for the law. Therefore, findings of these various studies were crucial in documenting the legal case, especially for hours laws and minimum wage laws.

Earlier studies (those done between 1900 and the start of World War I) were often done with an eye to determining what level of income was required to prevent a family from falling into "dependency," and often contained moralistic pronouncements about the life-styles of the families studied. One case study of 200 families living in the

immediate area around Greenwich House in New York City
deliberately excluded the "dependent class," on the grounds
that "the very poor are not representative of the normal
workingman's family" (More 1907, p. 5). Of those studied,
comparatively few families were completely dependent upon
the husband's income, unless there were young children.
As the children grew a little older, the mother could contribute financially to the family's support, but More noted,
"As soon as he [the husband] sees that the wife can help
support the family, his interest and sense of responsibility
are likely to lessen, and he works irregularly or spends
more on himself" (More 1907, p. 87). As the children grew
still older, they worked and the mother could again stay
home.

The case-study method used by More reveals judg-
ments by the interviewer about the character and competence of the wife, and the responsibility and morality of
the husband, although primary emphasis was still placed
upon income level. The woman may be "an attractive, am-
bitious wife," but unable to do well because of the low or
irregular income of her husband due to illness, "lack of
enterprise," or intemperance. Similarly, if the woman is
"improvident and shiftless, the standard of the family"
suffers (More 1907, p. 137). This study clearly showed
how close these families were to the subsistence level; the
average wage earner's family was "continually on the
verge of dependence," and half of the families studied had
been dependent (More 1907, p. 47). This study, it will be
recalled, specifically excluded families considered already
below the poverty level, and although it did include
female-headed households, the even lower level of women's
wages was not mentioned.

THE LIVING WAGE: FOR MEN ONLY

All of the budget studies and standard of living
studies for families or single women demonstrated the extremely low wages of women workers throughout this period.
One study of working conditions of mothers by Katherine
Anthony, done as part of the Russell Sage West Side Studies (New York City), using a case-study method covering
370 wage-earning mothers, found that the average income
of those families with both parents working ($705) was
barely enough to support them. Fully one-third of the

women studied were widows, the chief cause of death of their husbands having been tuberculosis (35.4 percent) (Anthony 1914, pp. 15–16). This study described the long hours these women worked (nine hours a day or more) and the low wages, which were generally about half those of men. Anthony did not attribute this to differences in intelligence or skill required, but to the general practice of paying women less (Anthony 1914, p. 108). She was critical of the patronizing, moralizing attitude of social agencies, and stressed the heroism, determination, and courage of these women, concluding, ". . . not one of the mothers could afford not to earn. They had become wage-earners in obedience to the most primitive of maternal instincts. Their children would have suffered seriously" otherwise (Anthony 1914, p. 199).

Almost never was a woman's wage alone sufficient to support a family, and frequently women did not earn enough to support themselves. Another study, which focused mainly on single women, emphasized the reliance of families on the wages of their women workers, 86 percent of whom turned over their total earnings in an unopened envelope to the family household manager. By contrast, "It was not unusual to find families in which the sons were not giving a cent to the support of the house" (Odencrantz 1919, p. 21). In these families, wage earning did not contribute to the woman's independence, and her wage earning was considered a necessary evil. The author commented, "In this way, the women are kept in the paradoxical position of simultaneous wage-earning and dependence" (Odencrantz 1919, p. 176).

Another, less systematic set of case studies of "self-supporting women living away from home in New York [City]," done for the National Consumers' League (a women's reform organization), described a number of different women's living situations, including one 17-year-old who had been working in retail stores; she lived variously with an aged grandmother, with an aunt, and in a dormitory of a charity-supported home for working girls (Clark and Wyatt 1911, p. 11).

From the preceding, it is clear that while men's wages were hardly adequate (studies also demonstrated the reliance of families on multiple sources of income, including women's), women's did not begin to approach subsistence for a family. The assumption on which relative wage structures for men and women were based was that every man was the wage earner in a family, and his wage alone ought to be enough to support it. As one study put it, the wife's function then is supposedly to "produce economic and spiritual values within the home." This implies "First, every man's wage is a family wage and, second . . . a woman's place is in the home. . . . According to this theory . . . every woman is regarded as dependent upon the wages of some man, either husband, father or brother. When she finds it necessary or expedient to work outside her home she is regarded as a temporary worker with no one but herself to support" (Hughes 1925, p. 10). However, Hughes noted, "The struggle to live on the husband's wage, in most industrial families, is a failure" (1925, p. 13). A number of different reasons were advanced to account for this, including woman's "comparative inefficiency," her "physical limitations [which] make her a less efficient worker than man in certain occupations, [h]er lack of trained skill," and "the fact that . . . industrial employment [is] a temporary makeshift rather than a life career" (Bosworth 1911, p. 7).

The "solution" to the "problem" of women working outside the home, then, was clear, according to some observers: ensure a living wage for men. Testimony was given to that effect by a number of authorities before the New York State Factory Investigating Commission. One physician stated that, rather than emphasize health issues concerning working women and childbearing, the best thing to do "is to give a decent living wage to the woman's husband." When asked, "You think a man's wages ought to be enough to support his wife and children?" the doctor answered, "Yes, emphatically." Florence Kelley (a noted social activist) testified that a woman should not be allowed to work for at least three months after childbirth, and went on to generalize:

> Well, it is done largely through a mistaken idea of thrift on the part of the family, or by the shiftlessness and selfishness of the husband drinking up the family earnings, and largely encouraged by the manufacturers . . . for the purpose of reducing the wages by having both heads of the family and all the children contributing to the family purse. . . . A man who is in the position of head of the family . . . ought

to be held up by the community rigidly to
his duty in supporting his wife and children. (New York Factory Investigating
Commission 1912, p. 1599)

When asked what would happen if he could not do it, she
replied, "I think he ought to go to the workhouse . . ."
(New York Factory Investigating Commission 1912, p. 1599).
In an article titled "How Nightwork of Women Is Menacing
Maternity," one writer commented, "Women do not work in
the mills at night because they want to, but because they
have to, because their husbands are getting so little"
(de Luna 1921, p. 86).

These views explicitly argued that a man's wage
was the relevant one in discussions about the low standard
of living of workers, and that women's chief contribution
as keeper of the home needed to be protected. Hours limitations and "no night work" laws clearly fit this aim;
these laws restricted women's participation without completely eliminating them from the work force. But minimum
wage laws raised the possibility of increasing a woman's
ability to support herself or a family independently; her
role as maintainer of the home was no longer considered
to take precedence over her work outside it. That this
was a threat to prevailing views of the proper family
structure is clear from the above examples.

The notion of a family wage was sometimes used to
critically judge the system by its own standards, as Scott
Nearing did. He looked at the results of a number of
budget studies, and stated, "Nothing could show more con-
clusively the frightful inadequacy of American wages"
(Nearing 1915, p. 18). He opposed the whole wage system,
but argued: "Under the present social system, a man's
wage must be a family wage. The home is looked upon as
the basic social institution. Each man is expected to
make a home, and having made it, to earn a living sufficient to allow the wife to devote her time and energy to
the care of the home and of the children" (Nearing 1915,
pp. 157-158). The problem with this approach, even when
it is used to criticize, is that it ignores the issue of
women's wages completely, and the assumption that the
man is the head of every family goes unexamined.

Another writer, Susan Kingsbury (1920), agreed that
discussions of budgets and wages should not assume a
man's wage ought to be a family wage, that is, ought to

support a family. However, Kingsbury cautioned that employers did argue that a very low minimum was adequate even for men, precisely because there were other family members contributing. Therefore, she argued, those who want to determine the wage rate by whether the worker supports a family "avoid the real issue of wage for service, or wage as a fair proportion of production in a competitive economic system. If the world is advancing to a cooperative place, then these questions will indeed be justly pertinent" (Kingsbury 1920, pp. 142-143). In contrast with reformers who argued for a family wage for men, she concluded: "The proper basis [is] equal wage for equal time and equal service . . . the amount necessary to maintain a family in health and at least the minimum comfort should be regarded as the minimum wage for every adult wage-earner, and no allowance should be made for contributions from other family members" (Kingsbury 1920, pp. 157-158). The issues raised by minimum wage legislation, then, ultimately concerned the position of women in the family and how that was to be related to their ability to participate as self-sufficient members of the work force.

POSTWAR FEMINIST OPPOSITION

After World War 1, probably partly because of women's experiences in war work, as well as the successful suffrage campaign, the terms of the debate broadened. Although social reformers, including suffragists, had accepted the need for special legislation to protect women workers, and had made it a major focus of their activity, after the war a new kind of argument began to appear against laws that applied only to women. When employers argued for the right of their "girls" to work 10 or 14 hours a day, that was one thing, but when former suffragists argued for equality before the law, and no special legislation for women workers, that was a qualitatively new kind of opposition. We will now consider these feminists, and the way in which their arguments opposing legislation for women were incorporated into the employers' briefs, successfully, to oppose the minimum wage law but not, at this time, other "protective" laws.

Following the passage of the suffrage amendment in 1920, and after several years' deliberation, some suffragists decided to support an equal rights amendment that

would end sex-based legislation in all spheres. Before
the suffrage amendment had passed, many of these women
had worked _for_ passage of protective legislation for women,
arguing that one of the expected benefits of suffrage for
women would be to promote beneficial legislation for women
workers and children. After women got the vote, and with
the experience of the war effort (in which women workers
were utilized when needed, and generally fired afterward
to protect men's jobs), the National Women's Party decided
to support equal rights for men and women. This put
them in the position of opposing all of the labor legislation they had struggled for and passed, if the law did
not apply equally to both sexes. The proposed ERA evoked
a storm of debate among former suffrage allies. Many reformers, including suffrage activists, opposed the "blanket
amendment," as the ERA was called, specifically because
it would do away with special protections for working
women.

The National Women's Party (NWP) developed its
position against special legislation for women workers
clearly and consistently. The declaration of principles
stated: Women shall no longer be barred from any occupation, but every occupation open to men shall be open to
women, and restrictions upon hours, conditions and remu-
neration of labor shall apply alike to both sexes (_Equal
Rights_ 1923, February 24). They argued that legislation
applying only to women workers would not protect women,
but would handicap them in their efforts to compete with
men in skilled occupations. Although they recognized the
inequalities that existed in women's wage structures, they
felt that legislation only for women would not remedy the
situation. In an article on the minimum wage campaign
(for women) in New York State, they noted the "almost un-
believably low wages" for women that the state Industrial
Commission had found. However, they pointed out that the
minimum for men was estimated not for an individual alone
but for an individual with dependents, while this method
was never followed when estimating women's needs. Yet
"Women workers almost as invariably as men have dependents. A minimum for them should be made on the same
basis as the minimum for men" (_Suffragist_ 1919, February
15).

By 1920, the wisdom of protective legislation for
women had begun to be questioned. The NWP, in its newspaper _Suffragist_, posed the problem as follows:

How to protect their right to earn a livelihood and at the same time their lives while
they are earning it, is the question confronting women in industry. Protective
legislation has proved in many instances
to be a boomerang, with the ultimate effect
of guarding women against injury in industry by keeping them out of it or of so
limiting their occupations that they could
not earn enough to live any life, however
safe. (Suffragist 1920, February)

The NWP consistently held the position that women
were to be considered adults before the law, and not
classed with children, as in need of special regulation.
It argued:

If minimum-wage legislation is to remedy
low wages and sweatshop conditions, it
must apply to men as well as women.
Labor legislation which links women with
children will not solve the low-wage problem. It does not adequately regulate
child labor. . . . The protection women
need is equal pay for equal work, and
they will never achieve this as long as
they are put in a special class by labor
legislation. (NWP n.d.)

It is not surprising that this kind of opposition to
labor legislation from within the ranks of feminist groups
would be utilized by employers in their opposition (for
very different reasons) to labor legislation. In argument
before the Supreme Court against the minimum wage laws,
one justice noted the opposition of women to these laws,
and asked: "Can it be that the women of this country
favor such laws, and especially for them alone? . . .
All over the country today thoughtful and progressive
women are contending for industrial equality which follows
as a natural and logical sequence to political equality"
(Ellis 1923, p. 5). He specifically cited the NWP position
opposing labor laws for women, as well as several other
women's groups, including the Equal Rights Association,
the National Women's Suffrage Association, and the Federation of Business and Professional Women's Clubs (Ellis

1923, pp. 6–7), all of which were on record in opposition to minimum wage laws and other labor legislation for women only. The brief also referred to the circumstances of passage of the law by the U.S. Congress (since it was a Washington D.C. law), quoting one U.S. senator at length:

> Do women need protection? Are women un-
> able to take care of themselves? . . . In
> one breath you are standing here telling
> us they are capable of performing all the
> duties of citizenship; . . . and in the next
> breath you say they need guardians and
> commissions to look after their wage.
> Where now are the knightly ladies whose
> flaunting banners have recently been borne
> back and forth in this ignominious classi-
> fication with infants. . . . (Ellis 1923,
> p. 16)

THE SUPREME COURT REJECTS THE MINIMUM WAGE FOR WOMEN

In 1923 the Supreme Court struck down the District of Columbia minimum wage law. Choosing its precedents carefully, the court in its decision made no mention of the minimum wage law in Oregon that it had let stand in 1917, but instead invoked a much earlier decision that had struck down a ten-hour day law for bakers in New York (Lochner vs. New York, 198 U.S. 45, 1905) and had been allowed to lie unnoticed throughout the upsurge of protective labor legislation in the interim. (It was not until 1937 that a minimum wage law was upheld by the Supreme Court, and then, in a kind of belated vindication of the NWP's position, the law applied to both men and women. This is the form of wage regulation that has now become standard.)

The new position of women and individualistic, laissez-faire principles were both used in the majority opinion by Justice Sutherland in striking down the law. He found the extensive two-volume "Brandeis brief" (prepared by Felix Frankfurter with Mary Dewson of the National Consumers' League) "only mildly persuasive" (Adkins v. Children's Hospital, 261 U.S. 525, 1923:560). He accepted the employers' view of the "wage bargain" in their brief against the law:

> [A minimum wage] compels him [the em-
> ployer] to pay at least the sum fixed in
> any event, because the employee needs it,
> but requires no service of equivalent value
> from the employee . . . it amounts to a
> compulsory exaction from the employer for
> the support of a partially indigent person,
> for whose condition there rests upon him
> no particular responsibility, and therefore,
> in effect, arbitrarily shifts to his shoulders
> a burden which, if it belong to anybody,
> belong to society as a whole. (Adkins v.
> Children's Hospital, 261 U.S. 525, 1923)

He stated that the law in question was "simply and exclusively a price-fixing law, confined to adult women . . .
who are legally as capable of contracting for themselves
as men" (Adkins v. Children's Hospital).

His views on the legal equality of women called
forth favorable comment from the NWP, which quoted from
his decision at length in its journal, Equal Rights:

> The ancient inequality of the sexes other-
> wise than physical, as suggested in the
> Muller case, has continued with "diminish-
> ing intensity." In view of the great—not
> to say revolutionary—changes which have
> taken place since that utterance, in the
> contractual, political and civil status of
> women, culminating in the 19th Amendment,
> it is not unreasonable to say that these
> differences have now come almost if not
> quite to the vanishing point. (Equal
> Rights 1923, April 21, p. 76)

The NWP approved of the reasoning in the Court's decision
(including the defense of liberty of contract regarding
women), and noted:

> The courts are among the last places to
> express changes in popular opinion. When
> one finds the Supreme Court of the U.S.

> beginning to realize . . . that women
> should be "accorded emancipation from the
> old doctrine that she must be given special
> protection . . ." one can feel that at last
> the world is beginning to realize that
> women are adult human beings. (Equal
> Rights 1923, April 21, p. 76)

By contrast, the dissenting opinion of Justice Holmes stated: "It will need more than the 19th Amendment to convince me that there are no differences between men and women, or that legislation cannot take those differences into account" Adkins v. Children's Hospital, J. Holmes dissent, 261 U.S. 525, 1923:570).

As Kessler-Harris (1982) pointed out, these early proponents of the first equal rights amendment were in the strange position of opposing ameliorative labor laws that progressive forces had struggled for years to get passed. They also accepted employers' arguments that the right of workers to individually contract the conditions of their labor was being violated by labor legislation. They came under sharp attack for this apparently reactionary stand from former suffragist allies and labor reform groups, but did not retreat from their principled opposition to all laws that applied to one sex only.

CONCLUSION

The debate on minimum wage legislation, by touching directly on the "wage bargain," reveals the tensions between the desire of employers to treat wage labor as a commodity, without regard for the health and reproduction of the workers as a class, and the demands of social reformers that conditions of life be improved, at least for the lowest sector, under pain of its possible extinction, or of social disorder and revolution. Reformers argued that if maximum hours were important protections for women and had been legitimated by the courts, then a minimum wage also could be set. They presented volumes of evidence demonstrating the low standard of living for workers and the particularly low wages of working women. Against this, employers put forth the principle that had been increasingly eroded in previous Supreme Court decisions: that any interference with the employer-employee relation was a violation of freedom of contract. When it came to a minimum wage, however, the Court accepted the employers' view. Thus, the failure of minimum wage legislation for women workers cannot be explained by looking at purely formal legal principles. The use of legal precedent and substantive evidence (real, economic conditions) to establish the constitutionality of labor legislation allowed the Court to continue to uphold hours and "no night work" legislation (for instance, in Radice v. People, U.S. 292, 1923) while disallowing minimum wage laws.

Because of the social reformers' limited views of possible solutions to the problem of women's low wages and overwork, and their unwillingness to question the ideology of the male-headed family structure, the reformers' arguments stressed women's special need for protection because of their physical weakness, as well as women's lack of labor organization, and emphasized the importance of women's maternal functions. These laws also set women apart from men in their need for protection, reinforced the dependent position of women as primarily wives and mothers, and contributed to segmentation of the labor force by limiting women's participation in it.

Minimum wage laws affected women workers, whose wage scale never approached subsistence. But this was not the primary way in which women contributed to reproduction of the labor force. Although, as wage workers, women helped support the family, their wage labor never was supposed to make them self-supporting; where minimum wage scales for women were set up, they did not even pretend to ensure the support of a family, and generally not even of the woman herself. On the contrary, it was felt that an equitable wage structure was one that would allow the man to support a family unaided, and women's wages were sometimes considered a potential deterrent to this. The state thus contributed to the maintenance of the subordinate position of women through its support for a certain kind of family structure and unpaid domestic labor of women, and through maintaining the gender-based wage structure as well.

PART III

CONSCIOUSNESS
AND
RESISTANCE

11

Searching for the Causes of Sexual Harassment: An Examination of Two Prototypes

Peggy Crull

It hardly seemed necessary to ask the question "What causes sexual harassment?" when women's organizations first began their advocacy work on the issue in the mid-1970s. The public recognition that sexual harassment was a problem for working women followed the feminist outcry and organizing against rape by a number of years. Activists and theorists on working women's issues simply borrowed the idea that rape is an act of aggression, not sexual attraction, and applied it to sexual harassment. They pointed out that in the work setting, the ability to express that aggression comes from economic rather than physical power. For example, Working Women's Institute's educational materials drew on a shorthand description of status differences at work to explain the origin of this phenomenon: "What factors contribute to sexual harassment? A glance at the position of women relative to men in the economic hierarchy reveals that men hold most of the positions with authority to hire and fire while women are relegated to lower level jobs. Too many men abuse their power by making sexual demands on women workers" (Working Women's Institute 1986).

Most theoreticians in early writings adopted similar assumptions. For example, in her historical notes on sexual harassment Bularzik opens her analysis thus: "As in many forms of violence against women, the assertion of power and dominance is often more important than the sexual interaction. Sexual demands in the workplace . . . become even more coercive because a woman's economic

225

livelihood may be at stake" (1978, pp. 25-26). Several longer works looked in more detail at some of the ways women's subordinate status in the world of work interacts with sexual harassment (Farley 1978; MacKinnon 1979). More recently MacKinnon (1982) has argued that rape, sexual harassment, and pornography demonstrate that violence, sexuality, and power are inseparable in a male-defined society.

On occasion, the idea that sexual harassment is an abuse of economic power has been incorporated into research hypotheses. For example, speculating that the women who have the least power in the work force would experience the most harassment, researchers have tested to see if women in the lower-status jobs in a particular work place, or women in low-status occupations such as clerical and service occupations, more frequently report harassment (Gruber and Bjorn 1982; Gutek and Morasch 1982; U.S. Merit Systems Protection Board 1981; and Working Women's Institute 1985). Their results have been mixed and, in fact, show a trend slightly to the contrary; lower-status women in specific work places do not necessarily report more harassment, and women in lower-status occupations report less harassment than do women in male-dominated, higher-status occupations.

The failure of the research to confirm the hypothesis that greater power differences lead to greater harassment is what forced me to lay aside any rhetorical intent and ask with sincere curiosity, "What causes sexual harassment?" I broke this question down into two complementary subquestions. Recognizing that all men are not equally powerful in relation to all women at work, my first question became "Can we account for different amounts and types of sexual harassment by different amounts and types of male power at work?" Assuming that even defining male power in all its complexity might not explain the occurrence and variations of sexual harassment, my complementary question was "Do we need to consider other forces operating inside and outside of the work place in order for our explanations to be complete?"

Applications of these questions to many different types of information have uncovered complexities that are not captured by the statement "Sexual harassment is an abuse of power." It is the goal of this chapter to unravel some of those complexities through analyzing two prototypical sexual harassment situations. I will first describe the behaviors in these situations that have been labeled "sexual harassment" and summarize research on them. Then I will look at the different power relationships between the women and men involved that appear to produce those behaviors. Having developed a theory of how power configurations at work lead to specific types of harassment, I will suggest other constructs that need to be added. Finally, I will trace the implications of this analysis for future activism and research in this area.

It is important to understand the major source of the speculations of this chapter. While the analytic framework is, of course, influenced by the psychological, sociological, and legal literature on sexual harassment, the material against which I tested it was conversations with, letters from, and counseling records of women who came to Working Women's Institute for assistance, as well as complaints, depositions, and court proceedings in scores of legal cases. Although this kind of information frequently is more resistant to analysis than material gathered in a scientific manner, it provides a particular richness of possibilities. In addition, I have drawn on studies and theoretical papers that touch on the origins of sexual harassment.

In beginning to answer the question of what causes sexual harassment on the job, I hope to provide some insight into a much larger issue, the relationship for women between work and sexuality. It is my contention that sexual harassment is only the "tip of the iceberg." What lies beneath is a whole system of assumptions, practices, and structures through which sexuality negatively affects women's position in the marketplace. It is that system which, I suspect, will prove to be one of the most critical hidden aspects of women's work.

TWO PROTOTYPES OF SEXUAL HARASSMENT

Even though a single label has been used in public discussion of this phenomenon, sexual harassment is many behaviors. The common thread that links them is that they are all in some sense "sexual," and they all interfere in some way with the ability of the person who is their target to work, or they make that person feel uncomfortable or frightened. Two specific patterns of sexual harassment have received the most legal and popular attention.

Called quid pro quo harassment (MacKinnon 1979), the first pattern came to the attention of the public and the courts in the early 1970s.[1] These situations boiled down to a boss who says, in essence, "Sleep with me or you're fired." (In Latin, quid pro quo means "one thing in return for another.") The landmark case of Adrienne Tomkins illustrates the usual scenes of the drama (Sexual Harassment Brief Bank and Bibliography 1985, p. 292; Tomkins v. Public Service Electric and Gas Co.).[2] A stenographer for a large utility, Tomkins approached her boss to ask him for a promotion. He insisted they have the discussion over lunch at a local Holiday Inn. Once there, he drank quite a bit and refused to discuss the issue at hand but, instead, kept trying to convince Tomkins to check into a room with him. She finally left, went back to work, and complained to other company officials. The result was a demotion and eventual dismissal.

Episodes of quid pro quo harassment like that of Tomkins (and many others--see Sexual Harassment Brief Bank 1985, pp. 288-295, which includes Miller v. Bank of America, Romano v. Lehat, and Williams v. Saxbe) frequently have two distinct phases. In the first, the man lets his sexual interest be known in subtle and not-so-subtle ways. It does not always boil down to a sexual proposition, but may simply be a request for a date or dates. At this point the behavior appears to be indistinguishable from garden variety sexual attraction that we might find in a social situation. It is only when the woman ignores, refuses, or complains about the advances that the interaction seems to take on a character different from attraction. Realizing he is not going to get what he wants, the harasser retaliates by using his position as a boss to demote or fire the woman, either rapidly or through a slower series of calculated moves. Sometimes the boss does not go that far but merely denies the woman a raise or becomes especially critical of her work (Crull 1982b, 1984).

In the second prototypical harassment situation, called "atmosphere harassment" in the courts,[3] the sexual behavior is hostile and intimidating from the outset. This is the situation in which men sexually taunt women who work with them. One court case, that of Debby Ukarish, illustrates this phenomenon at its worst (Ukarish v. Magnesium Elektron, Inc 1981). She was the first woman to do production work in a rural chemical manufacturing plant. After a few weeks of unskilled tasks, she was assigned to be trained for more difficult work by a co-worker who had already made .it a point to greet her with such comments as "Do you want this rod up your cunt?" and "Do you want a belly full?" Instead of training her, he left her alone to complete dangerous tasks in which he was supposed to instruct her. Finally, one day when his taunts were accompanied by physical scuffling, Ukarish was fired for fighting while her coworker was kept on.

Frequently in atmosphere cases the behaviors include sexual graffiti and pictures in work areas and participation by several men rather than a single harasser. Often the woman's safety is intentionally jeopardized and she is ignored rather than trained. The usual source of the harassment in these situations is coworkers, but foremen and supervisors are often complicit in some fashion. Most women in these situations do not get fired but end up leaving or suffering great distress (see Sexual Harassment Brief Bank 1985, pp. 272-284; Continental Can v. State of Minnesota; Guyette v. Stauffer Chemical Co.; Kyriazi v. Western Electric Co.). Even though this behavior is labeled sexual harassment, just like the behavior in our first prototypical situation, they are really quite dissimilar. Sexual attraction in any of the senses we usually think of it hardly seems to play any part in typical atmosphere harassment. That is, the behavior doesn't appear to be intended to lead to a sexual liaison, but instead seems to be an expression of hostility. In essence, this behavior is merely harassment that happens to take the form of sexual behavior, whereas in quid pro quo harassment the harassing character of the situation does not become entirely evident until the woman refuses the sexual advances and the man begins to retaliate through work (Crull and Cohen 1984).

There is a final, but critical, distinction between these two types of harassment. Many of the quid pro quo cases that have been documented involved women in jobs that are popularly thought of as "traditional" for women. That is, the women were in an occupation that is predominantly held by women and in which the work is considered suited to women. For example, in legal cases cited earlier there are Tomkins, a stenographer; Miller, a proofing machine operator; Romano, a bookkeeper; and Williams, a public information aide. These jobs would all be classed as clerical, and at Working Women's Institute we have seen quid pro quo cases in other traditional occupations, such as teaching and nursing. On the other hand, the atmosphere cases have generally been reported by women who are in "nontraditional" occupations. That is, they are in occupations that are predominantly held by men and in which the work is considered suited to men. Often, but not always, these occupations are blue-collar. Examples of cases cited earlier (other than Ukarish, who was an unskilled operative) were Kyriazi, an engineer, and Guyette, a lab technician.[4]

RESEARCH ON THE TWO PROTOTYPES

Because most studies do not separate their findings into the categories developed here, existing research provides only sketchy information with which to flesh them out. Few studies have looked at the prevalence and types of sexual harassment in traditional settings, but several have done so for nontraditional settings. Surveys, interviews, and observational studies of women in coal mines (White, Angle, and Moore 1981), the construction trades (Wider Opportunities for Women 1982), the uniformed services (Martin 1978), and a variety of blue-collar jobs (Walshok 1981) confirm that intimidating and hostile sexual comments and actions toward women are characteristic of those settings. Of course, propositions also occur in those settings, and sometimes they are from supervisors or foremen who may threaten the woman's job (Martin 1978; White, Angle, and Moore 1981; Walshok 1981). However, the bulk of the propositions seem to serve as taunts or intimidation rather than to be actual suggestions for dates or sex. Gutek's interviews of a random sample of women and men in the Los Angeles area showed that women in male-dominated settings (by this Gutek means women in nontraditional occupations or women in traditional occupations who happen to work in mostly male settings) experienced more comments, looks, and gestures that they perceived as hostile than did women in female-dominated or integrated settings. On the other hand, they also experienced more comments, looks, and gestures that they perceived as complimentary, and they received more complimentary than insulting behaviors, according to their reports (Gutek and Morasch 1982). A study conducted by Working Women's Institute of employees for the Federal Aviation Administration's Eastern Region indicated that women in nontraditional jobs experienced more sexual harassment than did women in traditional jobs, but it is not clear which kind (Working Women's Institute 1985).

It is difficult to ascertain from the research exactly what kind of harassment characterizes traditional work settings. We can only extrapolate from several studies in which the majority of women appear to be in traditional jobs (Crull 1982b; Hayler 1980; U.S. Merit Systems Protection Board 1981). In one Working Women's Institute study where approximately 68 percent of the sample were clerical and service employees, 20 percent of women who had sought counseling, information, and referral from the Institute in a particular year reported that their harassers had made sexual overtures accompanied by a threat to their jobs. Sixty-six percent of the entire group had experienced some form of retaliation for not submitting to harassment, even when it had not been accompanied by a threat (Crull 1982b). Eighty percent of the harassers in this study were superiors with the authority to hire and fire. Two other studies, both surveys, can probably be assumed to cover mostly traditional occupations because their subjects are women who work for governments, one group in a state (Illinois) government and one in the federal government (Hayler 1980; U.S. Merit Systems Protection Board 1981). They show that from 20 percent to 52 percent of their respondents report that they were propositioned, with 37 percent of the federal women saying the harassment involved superiors. They find that a smaller proportion than in the Working Women's Institute sample feel that their jobs were threatened in such a situation. However, this can be explained by the fact that the Institute sample was of women who were seeking help and, therefore, were more likely to have had their jobs threatened. The Merit Systems sample showed a surprisingly high proportion of harassment coming from co-workers (Tangri, Burt, and Johnson 1982).

These samples of mostly traditional working women report many other kinds of behavior besides coercion into dating or sexual activity. For example, 33 percent of the women in the Merit Systems study said they had experienced sexual remarks, 28 percent suggestive looks, 26 percent deliberate touching, and 9 percent letters and calls. However, the research does not indicate whether these incidents were part of or separate from pressure for dates or sex, and, even more important, it fails to separate those which might have been of the hostile or degrading variety reported by nontraditional women from those which might have been more benign though unwanted.

The research, then, does not lead to a clear conclusion as to whether these two situations are typical, nor does it explain why they have become the legal and popular prototypes of sexual harassment. In fact, both the data and anecdotal evidence alert us to other situations—offensive comments from bosses not associated with negative repercussions, or pleas for dates from coworkers coupled with retaliation—that don't fall squarely into these prototypes. Furthermore, there are several other sexual harassment dramas that are frequently the subject of counseling and lawsuits, such as waitresses who are forced to endure the looks and touches of their customers, and saleswomen who are expected to sleep with clients to close a deal, that the research hardly touches. For the moment, however, I will concentrate on the two prototypical situations, since they represent not only very different and recognizable types of behaviors but also very different power configurations.

POWER CONFIGURATIONS IN THE TWO PROTOTYPES

Even though each case clearly represents an "abuse of power," the male players in each of the two dramas hold different amounts and types of power over the women. In several earlier papers I have described the different power relationships between the men and women in these two prototypical situations, in order to see if they could account for the different types of harassment that go on in these situations (Crull 1982a; Carothers and Crull 1984). The very essence of the quid pro quo dilemma lies in the fact that the harasser has the power to fire the woman toward whom he directs his attention. For example, Adrienne Tomkins's title of stenographer indicates that she was in a low-paid, low-status position, and the boss had a great deal of authority over hiring and firing. She was not likely to become a threat to his job or surpass him in authority. The man in nontraditional settings, the kind in which atmosphere harassment tends to occur, is in a very different position. He is often the woman's coworker and, thus, has little direct power over the economic aspects of her job except by virtue of his seniority and his ability to provide training and information. Moreover, he may feel she is actually in competition with him for the good wages that are characteristic of nontraditional jobs and, thus, a threat to his relatively high status in the job market. Debby Ukarish took a job in the Magnesium Elektron factory because it was the only well-paying work in the area.

The different types of harassment in these situations may be a function of the different levels of power. In the quid pro quo situation, the man simply uses his authority to command the woman to engage in sexual behavior, just as he uses his authority to command her to do work-related tasks. If she refuses, he uses his authority to let her go, just as if she had refused to perform a work-related task. It is as if his power has overflowed into an area where it is not appropriate. In the nontraditional situation, sexual harassment appears to serve as substitute for the power the man is losing on the job. In addition, by using sexual behaviors to intimidate the women, the men may hope to drive them out of those particular jobs altogether. Gruber and Bjorn (1982) also suggest this. They speculate that unskilled men would be especially likely to use this tactic because they have no other source of power. Surveys have shown that men in these positions actually admit or boast that they don't want women there (Wider Opportunities for Women 1981; Working Women's Institute 1985).

The analysis of the causes of harassment in the two situations needs another variable, sex-typing of the jobs, in order to be complete. In the quid pro quo harassment pattern illustrated by the Adrienne Tomkins case, the jobs of the harasser and the woman who is his target are clearly sex-typed, and each player is in a slot "appropriate" for his or her gender. Tomkins' boss is in a clearly male job (an executive or manager) and she is in a clearly female job (a stenographer). An even more complete way to conceive of their positions is to use an analogy to the patriarchal family.[5] He is in the husband/father position in the work place, and she plays the supporting wife/mother role. His harassment of her is like an overflow of his husband/father role into areas that are not job-related. Gutek (1985) uses a similar concept, which she calls "sex-role spillover," to explain sexual harassment in traditionally female jobs. In her view, because women in traditional jobs are in the majority in that occupation, their role as a sex object "spills over" into their

work role, implying that men either intentionally or unintentionally treat women in traditional jobs sexually when
they are supposed to be treating them according to their
work role. Both Gutek's and my characterization of the
origins of sexual harassment in the traditional case suggest that the reason for the harassment is that the man is
acting as if this woman is a wife because her job carries
that implication.

In nontraditional work places we have a different
configuration of roles. The male here is also in a masculine, husband/father role, in that the work he does is
thought of as masculine because it involves being outdoors,
lifting heavy objects, facing danger, or accomplishing
technical or intellectual tasks. However, the woman in
this work place is out of gender role. She is doing masculine work as opposed to supportive, wifely work. The
sexual behaviors directed at her in this setting may be a
way to remind her that she is not in her proper gender
role. Gutek's idea of the function of sex-typing here is
different from mine. Again she uses the term "sex-role
spillover" to describe what she believes causes the sexual
harassment. Since men are in the majority in these occupations, their conceptions of women as women, rather than
as workers, spill over into the women's work role. Based
on her interviews of blue-collar women, Walshok (1981) offers a third explanation for harassment, one that is similar to Gutek's. According to her analysis, men in blue-
collar occupations that are nontraditional for women lack
any common work experience with the newly entering women
and must fall back on stereotyping to fill the void.

The addition of gender roles or, more accurately,
family roles to the formula helps to give a more comprehensive view of the power configurations in our two prototypical situations. Power is not simply a matter of who can
hire or fire or who makes more money in the marketplace.
Instead, it is inextricably linked to roles in the patriarchal
family that are reflected in the work place. The power that
may be playing itself out in a sexual harassment situation
is not merely economic power but a power derived from
these patriarchal relationships. The executive has power
over the female by virtue of the fact that he hired her and
by virtue of the fact that he plays a masculine, husband/
father role in the work place. Similarly, the male in a
male-dominated job setting has power based both on economics[6] and on the "masculine" nature of his work, although

the entrance of women into his occupational category threatens those sources of power.

Given this overview of the interlocking sources of power in the work place, how can we summarize our answer to the question "What causes sexual harassment?" In the quid pro quo situation, where women tend to be in occupations that are typically held by women, the sexual behavior that is the first step in the harassment drama appears to be an outgrowth of the patriarchal nature of the work relationship. The boss treats the woman like a wife in a number of ways because her job consists of performing nurturant, supportive tasks typical of wives and mothers in the home. Treating her as a sex object is one of those ways. It does not appear that this behavior is designed to "keep her in her place," since there is very little in those traditional work relationships to suggest that the woman is likely to threaten the economic or gender superiority of her boss. The sexual behavior happens because she is in her place. Only when she refuses his sexual overtures does she seem to be out of place and in any way a threat to his patriarchal power. It is then that he must put her in her place by using his economic power and firing or demoting her, or retaliating in some other way through work.

In the male-dominated situation, however, the woman is out of place because she is performing both work that is similar to the husband's/father's work in the patriarchal family, and work that in the economy draws "good" wages, thus providing a modicum of economic power. The cause of sexual harassment here is the need to put the woman back in her place. In these situations, hostile and threatening sexual behavior is the perfect mechanism to accomplish this. It reminds the woman that she is still a woman, even if she takes on a masculine veneer through the work she does, and it leads to loss of the economic advantage provided by such work by making her unable to perform up to par or pushing her out altogether.

USING THE PROTOTYPES TO ANALYZE
A RANGE OF SITUATIONS

The analysis of these two prototypes has created a continuum against which we can compare other incidents of harassment and the work place dynamics that underlie them. At one end of the continuum are behaviors that appear to have as their goal some sexual/social interaction and at the other end hostile, threatening, and degrading acts that seem to serve as a substitute for patriarchal power. Corresponding to the sexual/social end of the continuum are situations where the harasser holds the greatest amount of economic power over the woman and where the sex-typing of the jobs are the greatest. Corresponding to the hostile end of the continuum are situations in which the man has the least amount of power over the woman and where she is violating patriarchal norms of the work place by holding a male sex-typed job.

Many dilemmas other than the ones analyzed above fall definitely on one end or the other of the continuum. For example, at Working Women's Institute we frequently counseled nurses who were harassed by doctors, household technicians[7] who were harassed by the men in whose homes they worked, and teachers who were harassed by principals. In all of these cases, the form of the harassment tended to be propositions that, when they were rejected, were followed by unmistakable retaliation. In all of these cases the women are clearly in positions that are economically subordinate and sex-typed.

On the other hand, there are several cases of women in nontraditional jobs other than the blue-collar factory and uniformed service jobs already mentioned.[8] Two that stand out are a woman who was a surgical resident in a hospital (surgery is the most male-dominated medical specialty) and two women who were technicians in a lab where only one other woman had ever worked (Lipsett v. University of Puerto Rico 1983; Sexual Harassment Brief Bank 1985, p. 279; Guyette v. Stauffer Chemical Co.). In both cases there was harassment from coworkers that consisted of intrusive sexual comments, graffiti and lewd sexual jokes about them, and statements that they did not belong there. In addition, the work environment was made inconvenient for the surgeon and unsafe for the technicians. The surgical resident's story has an extra twist to it, in that she was also being propositioned by her attending physician (her boss); this, in combination with the harassment from fellow residents, eventually led to her being drummed out of the program for "disciplinary" reasons even though she had exceptionally high academic evaluations. The two technicians eventually quit their jobs for fear of their safety. All of these women entered situations in which they had some economic and sex-role equality with the men around them.

A number of other clusters of behaviors encountered in the Working Women's Institute counseling and education activities do not fit as neatly on the continuum, but it still provides a basis for explaining them. Many of the women who have come to us for assistance are not in clerical/secretarial positions but would be classed as managers/administrators or professionals/technicals (Crull 1980). For example, one was a woman who supervised coders in a large market research firm and was being harassed by the manager of that department.[9] Another was a social worker in a large city hospital who was being harassed by her immediate supervisor, another social worker. In their cases and others like them, the behavior of the harasser was at the outset more hostile and degrading than in the traditional quid pro quo situation. For example, the social worker's harasser would refer to her breasts as "suckers" or "lollipops." The coding supervisor's harasser let her know that women couldn't really compete in market research. On the other hand, their behavior was somewhat more hesitant than the usual quid pro quo retaliation. Neither had the woman fired outright but undertook a campaign to make her look bad to other men in authority. This combination of slightly hostile, slightly hesitant behavior can be explained by the continuum.

Because these women are not considered "support" staff but, instead, hold positions that require them to independently sustain their own projects, they have somewhat more power in relation to their harassing bosses than would a woman in a clerical/secretarial position. Furthermore, they are in occupations where there is not a great deal of distinction between their jobs and those of their bosses in terms of sex-typing. Thus they fall somewhere in the middle of our continuum, and so does the harassment they experience.

Other familiar sexual harassment dilemmas are explainable by the above analysis even though the configurations of power and patriarchy are more obscure. For example, waitresses have lodged a substantial number of complaints of sexual harassment by their customers (Sexual Harassment Brief Bank 1985, p. 285; Marentette v. Michigan Host). The bulk of the advances they report are pats and grabs, sexual comments, and leers. They may also receive propositions but, due to the structure of the situation, the retaliation against them when they do not respond in the desired fashion is not firing but reduced tips or complaints to their boss. The configuration of power and roles here falls on the traditional end of the continuum even though it is more complex. The customer/harasser has economic power over the woman only through his ability to withhold tips or complain to her boss. Their positions with respect to each other are definitely sex-typed, since she is providing the nurturance of serving food to him.

There are a number of other groups of complainants who are in similar power and role configurations with their harassers. For example, nurses are often the target of sexual comments and touches from the men for whom they are providing the nurturant nursing function.[10] In this case the male boss who has the authority to act on a complaint from the patient is the doctor or a hospital administrator. A third group of women, those in lower-status sales and service positions (department store sales clerks, grocery store cashiers), have similar experiences even though their function is not always nurturant (Sexual Harassment Brief Bank 1985, p. 276; EEOC v. Sage Realty).

Until this point, it has been relatively easy to match the forms of harassment found in different situations to points along the continuum of power and patriarchy. However, there are some instances in which the form of the harassment seems incongruent with the economic and gender-role relationships. One such situation is that of women in business for themselves or women who represent their companies to major customers who are propositioned by their customers. For example, an interior decorator who came for counseling at the Institute had been summarily let go by one of her regular customers, a boutique owner, after she refused several sexual advances made in front of his employees. We have had similar cases of women in advertising sales and other sales jobs where large accounts were involved. Their harasser/customers canceled the account or complained to the woman's boss.

The direct propositions and swift reprisals here are somewhat disjunctive with the gender-role relationships of the woman and man. Because women in these jobs are doing work that was male-dominated until the 1970s, we might expect the customer/harasser to feel threatened by their presence and to employ the usual tactics of sexual hostility and degradation. However, the economic control of the man over the woman here is strong; even though he is not the person who hired her, because of the amount of business a customer of this type brings, he wields a great deal of economic power over her--much more than a coworker would in any other male-dominated situation. Apparently the economic relationship here wins out over the gender-role relationship in determining the kind of sexual behavior that takes place.

OTHER FORCES CONTRIBUTING
TO SEXUAL HARASSMENT

The first subquestion of this chapter--Can we account for different amounts and types of sexual harassment by different amounts and types of male power at work?-- can be answered "To a great extent." The analysis developed here provides an explanation for many of the forms of harassment that have been reported to Working Women's Institute, documented in court cases, and described in the research. However, there are two reasons to take a serious look at the second subquestion, "Do we need to consider other forces operating inside and outside the work place in order for our explanation to be complete?" First, there is no doubt more than one set of factors is contributing to any of the types of harassment described here. Second, there are many situations that may not be explainable by the power configurations spelled out here. This summary has not dealt with, for instance, coworker to coworker harassment in traditional situations, harassment of women by male subordinates, harassment of women by other women, harassment of men by women, or harassment of men by other men; such dilemmas will probably require additional constructs. I will quickly summarize the other forces that need to be examined in order to complete the answer to the question of this chapter.

The present analysis has been confined to the relationship of the harassing man or men to the woman or women, assuming that women are the measure of male power at work. Given the patriarchal nature of the work place, it is likely that the relationship of the harassing man to other men at work may also play a part in his behavior, since male power in a patriarchy is measured against other male power. Harassment of women may be a mode of competing with other men for power and authority, or it may be a way of displacing frustrations and dissatisfactions with the other men who have higher status than the harasser.

It is important to look beyond the work place to the marketplace as a whole to understand what causes sexual harassment. In a sense my description of how masculine or how feminine an occupation is assumes a comparison not only with the other occupations in a work place but also with those in the marketplace as a whole. For example, men who gain masculine satisfaction from having a job in construction are probably making implicit comparisons of themselves with men in feminine jobs in other parts of the marketplace, such as men in the service industries. Their harassment of women may be a way to improve their image in relation to men in other industries when they feel their industry is becoming "feminized." There are other ways in which the concept of the marketplace is important. I pointed out that men may be threatened by the entrance of women into particular nontraditional jobs. They may also be threatened by larger changes in their industry or occupation, and use the harassment of women as a way to restore some order to their work lives.

Dzeich and Weiner (1984) have explained sexual harassment of students by professors with such a construct. (Even though this is not an analysis of a work relationship, it is still relevant here.) They speculate that many professors who harass their students find it difficult to live up to professional expectations, since college teaching, particularly in the 1970s and 1980s, is not the prestigious occupation that it used to be and is not as lucrative as other occupations. They use their power over the students to gain that lost prestige. Many other industries are experiencing enormous changes due to buyouts and mergers that have resulted in power shifts and, no doubt, insecurity on the parts of many men in these industries. Sexual harassment of women in this case may be a way to restore some of the power and security that have been disrupted.

Finally, we must go beyond the marketplace to the culture at large for some answers. Men may simply find the women at work, regardless of their authority over them, a convenient target on which to take out their frustrations at having to live up to the requirements of the larger patriarchy. Several theorists who have attempted to account for the origins of sexual harassment have followed this line of thought. College professors suffer not only from erosion of prestige in their industry, according to Dzeich and Weiner (1984), but also from their own failure to live up to cultural standards of masculinity. They suggest that in some cases, the reason for the lecherous behavior is a personal crisis brought on by societal expectations that they have failed to meet. The first is the expectation, first faced in adolescence, that a boy be athletic, a quality Dzeich and Weiner feel most college professors probably lacked then and have not attained as adults. They also suspect that many of the men are middle-aged and experiencing a crisis based on that. Any or all of these conditions might push them to try to reestablish their feelings of success by attracting the attention of a young, admiring college student.

Tangri looked both to work place relationships (which she calls opportunity structures in the organization) and to sociocultural factors to develop predictions about patterns of sexual harassment. By sociocultural factors she means the patriarchal system "in which men rule and social beliefs legitimize their rule" (Tangri, Burt, and Johnson 1982). Specifically, she and her colleagues believe that societal rewards for aggressive and domineering sexual behavior on the part of males, and passivity and acquiescence on the part of females, will contribute to the existence of sexual harassment, sometimes despite organizational structures and sometimes in conjunction with them. The stories of working women in the late 1800s and early 1900s are recounted by Bularzik (1978) in order to demonstrate that one source of sexual harassment is the need to preserve women as a cheap labor force. In addition, keeping women in this position helps to maintain the patriarchal family, since women are kept dependent on men. A third theorist (Stanko 1985) links sexual harassment with rape and incest, and argues that all three are made possible by complementary social structures that condone male violence and promote female "respectability."

IMPLICATIONS OF THIS ANALYSIS FOR ACTIVISM

The inspiration for the analysis undertaken here came from an activist context. I was forced to articulate a detailed description of how power works in sexual harassment for two specific reasons. First, many of the women with whom the Institute has worked in education and counseling were not satisfied with generalizations about the origins of sexual harassment. They needed to find the precise location of their own situation before they could figure out how to resolve it. Until women can get this kind of information, they cannot begin to develop political solutions that make sense to them. For instance, once they understand that their coworkers feel threatened by them, they can help to start an education campaign and get support from their union for it.

The second reason I was pushed toward this analysis was that since 1973 there has been a need for good legal theory with respect to the origins of sexual harassment. This is especially true where judges have heard atmosphere cases. Too often they believe that women should simply accept the crude and offensive behaviors that are characteristic of male-dominated work settings, unaware that this behavior has malicious intentions. The question of the intent and effects of sexual harassment has been argued and reargued over the years. Even though the Supreme Court concluded in June 1986 that a sexually offensive atmosphere is indeed discriminatory, this conclusion can be strengthened by thoughtful research (Meritor Savings Bank v. Vinson 1986).

FUTURE RESEARCH ON THE CAUSES
OF SEXUAL HARASSMENT

The analysis of this chapter started with the discovery that there are at least two distinct types of behaviors that have been labeled "sexual harassment," and moved on to look at their sources. I bemoaned the fact that most research, however, does not clearly distinguish between those behaviors in gathering and manipulating data. It is time to start using the two categories (and some of the variations spelled out in the latter part of this chapter) for research. Several existing studies (for example, U.S. Merit Systems 1981) have data bases that could be broken down to show variations in types of harassment for women in traditional and nontraditional jobs, and new studies must be designed with such analyses in mind.

The additional forces in the work place, the marketplace, and the culture that I suggest play a part in sexual harassment are excellent places to begin to develop new research questions. We need to project, for example, how male competition with other males in different work settings might affect their sexual behavior toward women there. Tangri and her associates (1982) formulated alternative sets of predictions based on three explanatory models of sexual harassment: a biological model, an organizational model, and a sociocultural model. More work needs to be done at this level.

There are other ways to revamp our research. We need not only refinements and expansions of research questions, but also new sources for answers to the question of what causes sexual harassment. In my own research at Working Women's Institute, I have conducted interviews in which I have asked women to explain why they thought their harassers acted as they did. This has provided an extremely detailed picture of the behavior of harassers and rich clues to the reasons for harassment, many of which shaped the constructs in this chapter. Men also need to be queried about their opinions on and their participation in sexual harassment. Several studies endeavored to get input from men on why they harass (Alliance Against Sexual Coercion 1980; U.S. Merit Systems 1981; Wider Opportunities for Women 1981; Working Women's Institute 1985), but we need to be more clever in finding and interviewing male informants.

Finally, we need to expand our concerns far beyond finding out what causes sexual harassment. Several books and articles have done so by looking at the general issue of sexuality at work (Neugarten and Shafritz 1980; Gutek 1985). It is only when we have begun to understand the place of the entire range of sexuality in the work relationships of men and women that we will understand the causes of sexual harassment in their fullest sense.

NOTES

1. This is often labeled "exploitative" harassment (J. Ellis 1981).

2. The Women's Rights Law Reporter published a comprehensive listing of sexual harassment cases that will be updated periodically. The listing gives a summary of each case and sources.

3. This is also labeled "condition of employment" (MacKinnon 1979) and "generalized harassment" (J. Ellis 1981).

4. The terms "traditional" and "nontraditional" are not entirely accurate descriptors of these jobs, since the proportions of women and men in various occupational categories sometimes change dramatically over time. In addition, what is considered suitable work for women usually changes with the proportions. However, because they are commonly used and understood, I chose to use the terms "traditional" and "nontraditional."

5. This discussion is not meant to be an analysis of the ways in which the work force and marketplace can be described as sex-typed or "patriarchal." There are a number of works that address this topic; they include H. Hartmann (1976), Kanter (1977), MacKinnon (1979), Sokoloff (1980), Matthaei (1982), and Brown (see ch. 7).

6. Men in male-dominated jobs tend to make better wages than women in female-dominated jobs, and often better wages than people in many jobs held by equal numbers of women and men.

7. "Household technician" is the term that the New York-based organization of domestic workers in private homes prefers to apply to this occupation.

8. This finding diminishes the likelihood that the negative sexual behaviors we find in blue-collar situations are class-based.

9. All cases from the Working Women's Institute constituency of women who have sought assistance are altered to protect their anonymity. However, I have been careful to retain the features of their jobs and dilemmas that are important for the analysis.

10. Nurses perform scientific and technical tasks in addition to, or perhaps even more than, nurturant tasks in many cases. However, they are still seen as nurturant, perhaps because they are compared with doctors.

12

The Dialectics of Wage Work: Japanese-American Women and Domestic Service, 1905–1940

Evelyn Nakano Glenn

INTRODUCTION

The work of women has been a much neglected topic in the economic and social history of Japanese-Americans. Yet, from the moment they arrived, Japanese-American women labored alongside the men to secure their own and their families' livelihood (Millis 1915; Strong 1933). Much of their work took the form of unpaid labor on family farms and businesses. However, many women turned to wage work to supplement family income. Until World War 11, the most common form of nonagricultural employment for the immigrant women (issei) and their American-born daughters (nisei) was domestic service.

As was true for immigrant women from other rural societies, domestic work served as a port of entry into the urban labor force (Chaplin 1978). The demand for domestic help among urban middle-class families en-

---

The author is grateful to Jean Twomey for assistance in transcribing and organizing the data, to Haru Nakano for help in arranging the interviews, and to Peter Langer for comments and suggestions in the course of writing. Special thanks are also owed to the Women and Work Group, whose discussions helped crystallize some of my thinking. Amy Kesselman provided a thoughtful and careful reading, and offered many useful suggestions for this final version.

sured a constant pool of jobs, while the occupation's low status and unfavorable working conditions made it unattractive to those who could secure other kinds of jobs. Thus, the field was left open to the newcomer and the minority woman.

For European immigrants, domestic service was a temporary way station. By the second generation, they had moved into the expanding white-collar clerical and sales occupations (Stigler 1946). The Japanese, however, like blacks and other minorities, were barred from most industrial and office settings (cf. Lerner 1973). Thus, Japanese women remained heavily concentrated in domestic work even into the second generation. Only after World War 11 did institutional racism diminish sufficiently to enable the nisei and their children to move into other occupations. Involvement in domestic service was thus an important shared experience for Japanese women in the prewar years, serving as one basis for ethnic and gender solidarity (Yancy, Ericksen, and Julian 1976).

This chapter examines that experience, using the case of issei women in the San Francisco Bay area in the period from 1905 to 1940.[1] The first three sections describe the historical context in which issei women's specialization in domestic work evolved: the development of Bay area Japanese communities, the arrival of issei women, and the labor market structure they confronted. The next five sections give a detailed account of domestic workers' experiences: the circumstances leading to involvement in domestic work, the entry and socialization process, the conditions of work, relations with employers, and the interaction between the women's wage work and their unpaid work in the family.

This account illustrates the interaction among the multiple forms of oppression to which the women were subjected and the resilience they developed (cf. Dill 1979). Issei domestic workers were subjugated by institutional racism, by conditions of work in domestic employment, and by the structure of issei family life, yet they were not passive victims, but active participants shaping their own lives. Faced with oppression, issei women strived, often in covert and indirect ways, to gain control over their work and other aspects of their lives. Out of this effort, I argue, grew a sense of autonomy and self-reliance that enabled them to transcend the limitations of their circumstances and gain a measure of satisfaction from essentially menial work.

HISTORY OF BAY AREA JAPANESE COMMUNITIES

We begin by examining the historical context in which Japanese women's involvement in domestic work developed. The pre-World War II history of Japanese communities in the San Francisco Bay area can be divided into three periods--frontier, settlement, and stabilization--each demarcated by specific historical events that shaped the immigrants' lives (Miyamoto 1939).

The "frontier" period, roughly 1890 to 1910, was when the first wave of immigrants arrived. The issei were remarkably homogeneous. Most of the immigrants were young, single males from rural villages in southern Japan, with an average of eight years of education (Strong 1934). They came as sojourners expecting to work a few years to amass sufficient capital to establish themselves in Japan. They started out as unskilled wage laborers in agriculture, railroading, mining, and lumbering, or in domestic service (Ichihashi 1915, 1932). Later, as they accumulated capital and know-how, many launched small enterprises, usually laundries or stores. In place of their old kin ties, the issei men formed mutual aid associations with those from the same prefecture (kenjinkai) and organized rotating credit associations (tanomoshi) to raise capital (Light 1972).

Until 1907, San Francisco, as a port city, was one of three main centers of Japanese population.[2] The Japanese congregated in a section of the Western Addition, a district of low-rent, rundown housing that became known as Little Osaka. From San Francisco, issei spread to other cities in the East Bay. By 1910, the Japanese populations of the four main cities were San Francisco, 4,518; Oakland, 1,520; Berkeley, 710; and Alameda, 499 (U.S. Census Bureau 1913).

Growing anti-Japanese agitation led to a series of legal measures designed to reduce immigration and discourage permanent settlement. The 1907 "Gentlemen's Agreement" between Japan and the United States closed entry to laborers. Between 1910 and 1929, more men returned to Japan than entered the United States (Ichihashi 1932). However, those who remained began to think in terms of a longer stay. The "Gentlemen's Agreement" contained a loophole: it permitted the entry of wives and relatives. The issei began returning to Japan to marry and bring back wives or to send for "picture brides."

The arrival of issei women marks the beginning of the "settlement" period. Between 1909 and 1923, over 33,000 issei wives immigrated (Ichihashi 1932). This was a period of family and community building. The sex ratio became less skewed and the population came to include children as well as adults. Extensive infrastructures developed with the establishment of ethnic churches, newspapers, language schools, and business and service establishments. Ethnic enclaves formed in San Francisco's Western Addition, on the borders of Chinatown in downtown Oakland, and around City Hall in Alameda. Except for jobs, the issei could fulfill most of their social and material wants within the ethnic community. According to one observer, "Very few Japanese ventured beyond those comfortable environs" (Kitano 1960, p. 183).

Meanwhile, partly in response to more permanent settlement, anti-Japanese sentiment grew. An Alien Land Law was passed in California in 1913, prohibiting the issei, who were ineligible for citizenship, from owning land or leasing it for more than three years. The 1924 immigration act cut off all further immigration from Asia (Daniels 1973).

The end of immigration marks the start of the "stabilization" period, 1924-1940. Henceforth, the growth of population depended entirely on births. There was little room for expansion of ethnic enterprises serving a largely Japanese clientele. Thus, the issei found their opportunities shrinking and began to pin their hopes for the future on their children, who by virtue of American citizenship had rights denied their parents.

ISSEI WOMEN

Most of the issei women who arrived in the United States between 1907 and 1924 were from the same southern rural backgrounds as the male immigrants and had similar levels of education. The women in the study averaged six years, with two having no schooling and two having completed ten years, the equivalent of high school. The typical issei woman was in her early twenties and was married to a man ten years her senior who had lived for some years in the United States, working as a wage laborer or small entrepreneur (Strong 1933).

Following Japanese custom, the marriages were arranged by the families of the bride and groom through a go-between (baishakunin). Many issei men managed to save or borrow money to return to Japan to meet their prospective brides and to get married. Many others, for financial or other reasons, could not return. In such cases, the match was arranged by the go-between through an exchange of photographs, hence the term "picture marriage." The union was legalized by registering it in the husband's home prefecture.

For the most part, the women felt they had little say in the selection of a husband. Daughters were expected to go along with their parents' judgment. Yet the extent to which women felt forced or manipulated by their parents and by circumstances varied.

At one extreme is Mrs. Takagi,[3] who recalls that her father tricked her into going to stay with her adopted grandfather on the pretext that she would receive training to become a midwife:

> Otherwise, I wouldn't have gone, you see.
> I knew my mother needed help I
> stayed one week and helped my uncle [a
> doctor]. I was thinking I would stay to
> help him. Pretty soon, they took me to
> see this man. I'd never seen or heard of
> him. He was my second cousin. You don't
> know the Japanese system: they just pick
> out your husband and tell you what to do.
> So, I did it . . . I never gave my parents
> a fight.

Another issei, Mrs. Nishimura, falls somewhere in the middle of the continuum. She was only 15 when she was persuaded by her father to marry Mr. Nishimura:

> In the Japanese style, we used a go-between
> and the husband would come to Japan to
> pick up his bride. My father was rather
> new in his thinking, so he told me that
> rather than stay in Japan and attend
> school, I should come to the U.S. My
> mother told me . . . that I was too young.
> But, it's something that had to be done
> . . . I was rather big for my age, . . .

> I cried at the time, and I'll always re-
> member that. My parents felt a little
> guilty about it, almost as if they had
> forced me to come, and apparently they
> kept asking about me, about how I was
> doing, until they died.

At the other extreme we have Mrs. Shinoda, who
claims she dreamed of going to the United States even as
a child:

> I told my father that I wouldn't get mar-
> ried, unless I could come to the United
> States. [Did your parents oppose you?]
> Yes, they were all against me. [How did
> you know you wanted to come to the United
> States?] I don't know. When I was small,
> in elementary school, we had to write an
> essay on "What I Wish For." I wrote in
> that essay that I'd like to go to America.
> My friends read it and told what I had
> written. That's funny, huh?

Mrs. Shinoda was stubborn enough to hold out until her
father gave in. She didn't marry until she was 28, but
she got her way.

Despite the pain of separation and fear of the un-
known, the majority of the women said they left Japan
with positive expectations. Just as the men came to better
their lot, issei women came with their own hopes: to further their education, to help their families economically,
to seek a happier home life, and to experience new adven-
tures.

The boat trip to the United States, usually from
Yokohama to Seattle or San Francisco, normally took over a
month. The women report feelings of homesickness and
physical illness, although they also fondly recall friendships they developed with other women during the voyage.
The first shock for the picture brides was meeting their
spouses. Mrs. Yoshida, who traveled with a number of
other picture brides, recalls the responses of some of her
companions upon catching glimpses of their husbands:

> A lot of people that I came . . . with said,
> "I'm going back on this very boat." I

told them, "You can't do that; you should
go ashore once. If you really don't like
him, and you feel like going back, then
you have to have a meeting and then go
back. . . ." Many times, the picture was
taken twenty years earlier and they had
changed. Many of the husbands had gone
to the country to work as farmers, so they
had aged and became quite wrinkled. And
very young girls came expecting more and
it was natural.

As for herself, Mrs. Yoshida says she was disap-
pointed that her husband (16 years her senior) looked
much older than a neighbor at home the same age. However, many people from her village in Hiroshima had traveled to Hawaii and to the mainland United States, and she
wanted to go, too: "I didn't care what the man looked
like."

The second shock was having to discard the comfort
of kimonos and slippers for constricting dresses and shoes.
The women were generally taken straight from clearing immigration to be completely outfitted, often in a Japanese-
run store. Mrs. Okamura, who came in 1917, laughs when
she remembers her first dress: "It felt very tight. I
couldn't even move my arms. That was the first time I
had ever worn Western clothes, so I thought they were
supposed to be like that. . . . Later, Mrs. S. taught me
to sew my own clothes. She had a pattern that we all
used to make the same dress in different materials. So I
found out that first dress was too small."

As Mrs. Okamura's account indicates, earlier immigrants taught new arrivals the ropes. Living quarters
were usually secured within the ghetto. Many couples
rented rooms in a house, and shared kitchen and bathroom
facilities with several other Japanese families. Thus, help
and comfort were close at hand. Mrs. Horiuchi says the
best time in her life was when she was a new bride who
had just arrived in the United States. All of her husband's friends dropped in to welcome her and bring gifts.
Sometimes, husbands who had worked as "schoolboys" (domestics) taught their wives how to shop, cook, and clean.
Community agencies such as the YWCA and the public
schools sponsored housekeeping and English courses for
newcomers. Most of the women in the study took some of

these classes, but claimed that they were unable to continue their studies once children arrived. Partly for this
reason, most never fully mastered English. Another reason
was that the women rarely ventured outside the confines
of their ethnic community, except to do domestic work for
wages. The ethnic community provided for most of their
needs and insulated them from the hostility of the larger
society.

The issei women arrived at a time of accelerating
anti-Japanese agitation. Their arrival was itself a focus
of attack, since it signaled an intention on the part of
the issei to settle on a longer-term basis. Anti-Japanese
propaganda depicted the practice of picture marriages as
immoral and a ruse to contravene the Gentlemen's Agreement. As a result of mounting pressure, the Japanese
government stopped issuing passports to picture brides in
1921 (Ichihashi 1932).

Mrs. Takagi was outspoken about the racism of the
period:

> I think all the [Japanese] people at that
> age had a real hard time. [They had to
> work hard, you mean?] Not only that,
> they were all thinking we were slaves, you
> know, sleeping in the stable upstairs. And
> even when we'd get on a streetcar, they'd
> say, "Jap, get away." Even me, they al-
> ways threw stuff from up above. [They
> did? What do you mean?] I don't know
> why they did that. I was so scared. . . .
> One man, he was going on a bicycle and
> someone threw cement. That night he lost
> an eye. But they never sued, they never
> reported it because they didn't speak
> English. . . . I don't know what other
> people think, but we didn't have very
> much fun. We didn't have very many
> jobs. A lot of people graduated from col-
> lege and still no job, before the war.

ECONOMIC ACTIVITIES OF ISSEI WOMEN

Issei women had little time to brood about their
situations. Whether rural or urban, they were expected

to be full economic contributors almost immediately upon arrival. Like other working-class women of that era, they manufactured many basic household necessities, such as foodstuffs and clothing, as well as performing the maintenance and child care tasks (Smuts 1959). In addition, according to an early observer of the issei: "The great majority of wives of farmers, barbers and small shopkeepers take a more or less regular place in the fields or shops of their husbands, while a smaller number accept places in domestic service, or in laundries, or other places of employment. Thus, a larger percentage of those admitted find a place in the 'labor supply'" (Mills 1915, p. 27).

According to U.S. census figures, 20.8 percent of all Japanese women over 15 were gainfully employed in 1920. This is similar to the proportion of women employed in the overall population (23.3 percent). However, since virtually all Japanese women over 15 were married, the issei rate of employment was remarkably high. In the population at large, only 9.0 percent of all married women were in the labor force (U.S. Census Bureau 1975). Also, because Japanese men were concentrated in agriculture and small businesses that relied on wives' unpaid help, the extent of issei women's gainful activity is probably underestimated.

It is difficult to specify the occupational distribution of issei women. They frequently divided their time among housework, unpaid work in family farms and businesses, and paid employment. In such cases, what constitutes the main occupation cannot be pinpointed. However, there are data that indicate the range of their activities. Strong surveyed 1,797 issei women in a 1933 study of Japanese-American occupations. He classified 998 (58 percent) as housewives, 438 (26 percent) as part-time assistants to their husbands, 53 (4 percent) as full-time assistants, and 227 (13 percent) as engaged in independent occupations. He notes, however: "Undoubtedly, the last two figures are too low and the first figures too high. Accuracy in this connection was very difficult to secure because many of these women speak very little English and are unaccustomed to talk to strangers, and in some cases the Japanese men prevented or interfered in the interviewing of their wives" (Strong 1933, p. 109).

There are similar limitations to the U.S. census data. The figures in Table 12.1, which show the occupational distributions for 1900, 1920, 1930, and 1940,[4] should

Table 12.1. Occupations of Employed Japanese Women in the United States, 1900-1940

	1900		1920		1930		1940[a]	
	Number	Percent	Number	Percent	Number	Percent	Number	Percent
Total Females 10 Years of Age or Older	985		25,432		36,693			
Total females in gainful occupations	266	100.0	5,289	99.9[b]	6,741	100.0	6,693	100.0
Occupations								
Agricultural, including farm & nursery labor	13	4.9	1,797	34.0	2,041	30.3	2,525	37.7
Servants, including cooks, chambermaids and others	151[c]	56.8	1,409	26.6	1,195	17.7	690	10.3
Other personal services, including barbers, waitresses, lodging house keepers, laundry operatives	57	21.4	951	18.0	1,463	21.7	1,579[d]	23.6
Trade, including saleswomen, clerks	9	3.4	369	7.0	946	14.0	683[e]	10.2
Dressmakers, seamstresses, tailors	23	8.6	124	2.3	121	1.8	—[f]	—
Other manufacturing, mechanical pursuits	8	3.0	378	7.1	348	5.2	801[g]	12.0
Professional services (teachers, nurses)	5	1.9	145	2.7	329	4.9	214	3.2
Clerical occupations	—	—	75	1.4	271	4.0	—[h]	—
Other	—	—	41	0.8	27	0.4	201	3.0

Notes:

^aOnly foreign-born (issei) women are included in the figures for 1940. The 1940 census for the first time separated out native and foreign-born. The figures for 1930 contain some native-born (nisei), but they probably constitute only a small proportion of the total. Because of immigration patterns, most nisei were born after 1910.

^bDue to rounding.

^cIncludes some waitresses.

^dConsists of "proprietors, managers, and officials, except farm and service workers, except farm."

^eThe category is named "clerical, sales and kindred workers" in the 1940 census.

^fThis category is no longer separately reported; presumably these occupations are included below under manufacturing.

^gThis category is named "operatives and kindred workers" in the 1940 census.

^hIncluded in category of Trade; see also note e.

Sources: 1900--U.S. Bureau of the Census, Occupations of the Twelfth Census (Washington, D.C.: U.S. Government Printing Office, 1904), Table XXXV; 1920--Fourteenth Census of the United States, vol. 4, Population, occupations (Washington, D.C.: U.S. Government Printing Office, 1923), Table 5; 1930--Fifteenth Census of the United States, vol. 5, General Report on Occupation (Washington, D.C.: U.S. Government Printing Office, 1933), Table 6; 1940--Sixteenth Census of the Population, Population Characteristics of the Nonwhite Population by Race (Washington, D.C.: U.S. Government Printing Office, 1943), Table 8.

be seen as a rough estimate of the proportion of women engaged in various fields. Agricultural work, including work in plant nurseries (which was an early Japanese specialty), was the largest field of employment.[5] Domestic service was by far the most common form of nonagricultural employment. In 1900, over half of all women were so employed; however, the numbers are so small as to make the data inconclusive. By 1920, domestic service accounted for 40.3 percent of all women engaged in nonagricultural occupations. Overall, there seems to have been a trend away from concentration in domestic work between 1920 and 1940.[6]

During this same period, there was increased employment in personal service (which in the Bay area was primarily laundry work) and in retail trade. The growth of employment in service and trade reflects the move of Japanese men away from wage labor and into small enterprises, which employed women as paid and unpaid sales, service, and clerical workers. A small but steady percentage of women found work in manufacturing, primarily in food processing and garment manufacturing. With the establishment of ethnic community institutions, there was a small demand for professionals, such as teachers in Japanese-language schools.

The occupations in which Japanese women specialized share several common characteristics. The work could be fit around family responsibilities (for instance, children could be taken to work, or the hours were flexible); they were an extension of women's work in the home (such as food preparation, laundry, and sewing); they were in low-technology, labor-intensive fields where low wages and long hours reduced competition from white women; they took place in family-owned or ethnic enterprises where language or racial discrimination did not constitute a barrier to employment. Domestic service had the first three characteristics and was, therefore, consistent with the general run of occupations open to Japanese women. Because of the common characteristics of the occupations, one would expect the jobs to be highly substitutable. The job histories of the women support this expectation. The women in the study moved easily among these occupations, but never moved outside them. The 11 women with experience in non-domestic employment had worked in one or more of the following fields: farming, hand laundry at home, embroidery at home, midwifery, and assisting in family-owned cleaning store, hotel, or nursery. Domestic service, thus, can be seen as belonging to a set of occupations that constitute a distinct and narrow labor market for Japanese women.

ISSEI WOMEN'S ENTRY INTO DOMESTIC WORK

Having described the historical and economic context of issei women's wage labor in the Bay area, I turn to an analysis of the circumstances that came together in the lives of issei women to lead them into domestic service.

Unlike other immigrant groups who specialized in domestic service, these women did not have a prior tradition of service in their homeland. Generally, only indigent and unattached women became servants in Japan. Most of the immigrants who came to California were better off economically than the average rural peasant. They had sufficient resources to pay their fares, and as much cash on hand as immigrants from northern Europe (Ichihashi 1932). Thus, becoming a domestic worker meant a drop in status as well as a break with tradition. Given the lack of previous experience in wage labor generally, and a cultural prejudice against domestic service, the explanation for issei women's involvement in domestic work must lie in the situations they confronted in the United States.

One unusual historical circumstance was that the path into domestic work was paved by issei men, starting in the early days of immigration. Many had gained their first foothold in the United States as "Japanese schoolboys." This designation was reportedly coined in the 1880s by a Mrs. Reid, who enrolled a few Japanese students in her boarding school at Belmont, California. These students earned their tuition and board by doing chores and kitchen work (Ichihashi 1932). The term came to refer to any Japanese apprentice servant, whether or not he had any involvement in formal schooling. The job itself was the education: it provided the new immigrant with an opportunity to learn English and become familiar with American customs. In return for his services, the schoolboy received token wages of about $1.50 a week in 1900 ($2 a week by 1909), in addition to room and board, compared with the $15 to $40 a month earned by trained servants. It has been estimated that at the height of male immigration (1904-1907), over 4,000 Japanese were employed as schoolboys in San Francisco (Daniels 1973).

Still other immigrants earned their first wages in the United States as day workers, hiring out to do yard chores and housecleaning on a daily or hourly basis. Groups of men from the same prefecture sometimes took lodgings together and advertised their services. Millis (1915) found 163 Japanese day work firms listed in the 1913 San Francisco City Directory. In addition, issei who had their own businesses sometimes acted as agents for day workers. Ads for a Japanese nursery included notices such as the following, which appeared in the Alameda Argus in 1900: "Japanese Help. Also, first class Japanese help for cooking, general housework, or gardening, by day, week or month, furnished on short notice."

Both forms of domestic service were temporary stop-gaps. Schoolboy jobs and day work were frequent first occupations for new arrivals; after a short time, the issei moved on to agricultural or city trades (Strong 1933). In the Bay area, many day workers graduated into a special-ized branch of domestic service, gardening. The Japanese gardener became a status symbol, but the indoor male do-mestic had largely disappeared by 1930. The early asso-ciation of men with domestic service, however, established the stereotype of the Japanese domestic—a stereotype in-herited by the issei women when they arrived. The "situ-ations wanted" columns in Bay area newspapers, which prior to 1908 had been dominated by ads for "Japanese schoolboys," now began to include ads for women, such as "Japanese girl wants situation to assist in general house-work and taking care of baby. Address, Japanese Girl, 1973 P Street."

The path into domestic service was, thus, clearly marked. The issue remains, what were the personal circum-stances that launched many issei women on the journey?

The case of Mrs. Yoshida is a good place to begin. Ninety-one years old at the time of the interview, she ar-rived in 1909 as a picture bride. Her husband, 16 years her senior, had lived in the United States for almost 20 years and had managed to acquire a laundry in Alameda, which the couple ran together. Since they had one of the few telephones in the Japanese community, they began act-ing as agents for day workers. Employers called to re-quest help for cleaning or other jobs, and the Yoshidas referred the requests to the issei men who dropped by. By 1912, Mrs. Yoshida had two small children and she felt that they needed extra income:

l started to work because everyone went
on vacation and the summer was very hard
for us. The cleaning business declined
during the summer. . . . l bought a
second-hand bicycle from a friend who had
used it for five years. l paid $3 for it.
My husband disapproved of my doing day
work. He said "stupid." So, at night l
went to the beach and practiced on that
bicycle. At night nobody was at the beach,
so even if l fell down, l didn't feel em-
barrassed. And then l went to work. l
worked for half a day and was paid $1.
. . . We didn't know the first thing about
housework, but the ladies of the house
didn't mind. They taught us how at the
beginning: "This is a broom; this is a
dustpan." And we worked hard for them.
We always thought America was a wonderful
country. At the time, we were thinking of
working three years in America and then
going back to Japan to help our parents
lead a comfortable life. . . . But, we
had babies almost every year, and so we
had to give up that idea. [She had ten
children between 1910 and 1923.]

Although the specific details are unique, Mrs.
Yoshida's account reveals several common elements that
came together in the lives of issei women who entered domestic work. First, the Yoshidas' intention of accumulat-
ing a nest egg and returning to Japan was shared by
other immigrants during this period. The women in the
study all claimed that they expected to return to Japan
eventually. Many were sending remittances to support
parents or other relatives. Because the sacrifice was
seen as short-term, the immigrants were willing to work
long hours and in menial jobs. In this context, wage work
could be viewed as a temporary expedient that, therefore,
did not reflect on the family's social standing.

A second common element was the economic squeeze
experienced by many issei families, especially after children arrived. Some families managed to accumulate enough
capital to return to Japan. Those who were less well off
postponed their return and continued to struggle for day-

to-day survival. The majority of women in the study were married to gardeners, whose earnings fluctuated. As Mrs. Yoshida's case illustrates, even those who owned their own businesses found their marginal enterprises did not generate sufficient income to support a family. Some women were in even more dire straits: a husband who was ill, who refused to turn over his earnings, or who died and left children to support. Three women, facing this situation, took or sent their children to Japan to be cared for by relatives, so they could work full-time.

Mrs. Shinoda was part of this group. Her husband, a college graduate, was killed in an accident in 1928. She was 39, and had two young sons:

> I started work after my husband died. I went to Japan to take my children to my mother. Then, I came back alone and started to work. . . . My sons were ten and eight. . . . And I worked in a family. At that time, I stayed in the home of a professor at the University of California as a live-in maid. . . . I got the job through another Japanese person. She was going back to Japan, so I took her place. [What kind of things did you do?] Cleaned house, and cooking, and serving food. [Did you know how to cook and things like that?] No, I didn't at first. The lady told me.

Given the factors pushing the issei to seek wage work, what factors drew them particularly into domestic work? The basic limiting factor was the labor market situation described earlier. Race segregation, family responsibilities, and the lack of English and job skills severely limited job options. Given limited choices, domestic work offered some desirable features. Its main attraction was flexibility. Those with heavy family responsibilities could work part-time, yet during times of financial pressure, they could work extra days or hours as needed. A further pull was the demand for domestic labor. Day workers were sought by the growing number of middle-class urban families who could not afford regular servants. The demand was great enough that, as Mrs. Yoshida and Mrs. Shinoda noted, employers were willing to take on someone with no experience and provide on-the-job training.

ENTRY AND SOCIALIZATION

The know-how for obtaining and working in domestic jobs was widespread in the community as a result of the early experience of issei men in "schoolboy" jobs and in day work. The women sometimes resorted to advertisements, but the main way they found employment was through informal job networks. They heard about jobs through friends or acquaintances working as gardeners or domestics. Sometimes they inherited a position from an issei who was taking another job or returning to Japan. As the Japanese gained a reputation in domestic work, employers began to make requests through Japanese churches, businesses, and social organizations. Once one job was secured, other jobs were easily obtained through employer referrals.

Among the women in the study, two patterns of entry emerged. One was to begin as an apprentice, just as the Japanese "schoolboys" had done; in fact, some women used the term "schoolgirl" to refer to these positions. A "schoolgirl" job was typically entered soon after the woman's arrival and before she had children; she was more or less thrust into the position without a specific intention of beginning a career in domestic service. The job was arranged by a husband, relative, or friend. Wages were nominal, and in return the employer provided training in housekeeping and cooking. Many of the issei women attended classes part-time to learn English. The job was, thus, intended as part of the socialization of the newcomer. However, in many cases, it portended the beginning of a career in domestic service.

The experience of Mrs. Takagi, who arrived as a 19-year-old in 1920, illustrates the entry into domestic service by way of a "schoolgirl" job. Her husband's parents had immigrated with him, and the couple lived with them in Oakland:

> I was here 28 days, and my mother-in-law took me to the first job on the 29th day. So I didn't even know "yes" or "no." I was so scared to go out . . . [She took the trolley]. I got off at _____ Street. I just did it . . ., counting "one, two, three stops." If I lost my way home, I couldn't ask anybody. . . . I couldn't

hardly sleep at night. . . . The first time
I went, she taught me all the things I
said. . . . they had a coal stove, a big
one. Burned coal just like a Japanese
hibachi. It had a pipe inside and heated
the water from down below. I had to
bring the coal up, all the time I went up
and down. Then I had to wash diapers.
Me, I grew up on a big farm, so I never
had to do that. When I came to America,
I didn't know anything. So I just had to
cry. She said, "What happened to your
eyes?" Then she gave me $5 and gave me
a note and said to take it home. . . . My
mother [in-law] and father [in-law] said,
"Oh, that's big money." They thought it
[was] supposed to be $5 a month.

Mrs. Takagi was fortunate in having an employer
who treated her as an apprentice and encouraged her to
attend English classes: "She put a hat on me, put a
book in my hand, and gave me carfare. She said, 'Go to
school.'" After six months, Mrs. Takagi went on to a
general housekeeping job with a banker, and then with a
widow, before finally settling into day work.

The second pattern was to enter day work on a
part-time basis after the arrival of children, when family
expenses began to outrun income. Mrs. Yoshida followed
this path. In these cases, the women entered domestic
work deliberately. They initiated the job search themselves, after deciding that they needed to work to make
ends meet. The example of other issei women working as
domestics provided both the impetus and the means to secure employment. Mrs. Yoshida's account indicates that
her husband attempted to discourage her employment, yet
she persisted in her resolve. The conflicting wishes of
husband and wife are even more apparent in the case of
Mrs. Adachi. She began day work in her mid-thirties
after several years of taking in laundry:

When the kids go to . . . junior high
school, Mrs. S. said, "Why don't you go
out to work?" Other people with small
children did go out to work, but Mr.
Adachi was sickly when he was young, so

he didn't want the children left alone.
He said, "What if the children got hurt?
You couldn't get their lives back. The
children are worth more than a few dollars.
Just as long as we have enough to eat,
that's enough." So 1 went out secretly to
work in one place. And that one became
two and that became three. By three, 1
stopped [adding more jobs] because by that
time, my husband found out, and, of course,
there was still work at home, because 1
was still taking in home laundry.

Mrs. Adachi's decision to secretly defy her husband
is interesting, and illustrates the contradictory nature of
issei women's involvement in domestic labor. On the one
hand, circumstances beyond their control appear to have
ruled these women's lives. They were forced to seek employment because of economic deprivation, husbands' inability to provide adequate support, and the needs of
parents and other relatives in Japan. They had to travel
in unfamiliar neighborhoods and enter strange households
without any experience or knowledge of English. Some
confessed that they felt fearful and helpless in the beginning. Yet, on the other hand, some women actively sought
out employment, even in the face of opposition from husbands. And, among those who took "schoolgirl" jobs more
or less passively, many continued in domestic work even
without great financial pressure. These latter instances
suggest that employment, even in a menial capacity, provided some resources the women desired but lacked working
exclusively within their own families.

The most obvious resource provided by wage work
was an independent source of income. Although the women
put most of their wages into a common family pool, their
contribution was more evident when it was in the form of
money than when it was in the form of unpaid labor.
Moreover, because of informal pay arrangements and flexible work hours, the women could hide the amount of their
earnings. Some women reported keeping their own bank
accounts. They could use some of their earnings to purchase things for their children or themselves without having to ask their husbands. It is also important to note
that some women were largely self-supporting and/or were
supporting others. This was a source of considerable

pride. It was an option that married women did not have
in traditional Japanese society. This was pointed out by
Mrs. Takagi. After describing "killing myself" working 40
to 60 hours a week as a domestic to support herself and
her children, and to help her mother and her brothers,
who were able to attend high school because of her, she
concluded: "I'm glad to be able to do that. I'm so
lucky to be in the United States. In Japan, I wouldn't
have had the chance as a woman."

Going out to work also took women outside the confines of the family, away from the direct control of their
husbands. They could form outside relationships with employers. At the very least, these relationships expanded
the issei women's store of knowledge and experience.
Some employers provided material and emotional support.
Mrs. Takagi's employer visited her in the hospital when
she was sick and gave her the money to return to Japan
to retrieve her son. She credits this employer with helping her weather many personal crises. For women cut off
from kin, the ties with employers could be a valuable resource. If we recall Strong's remark that issei men prevented interviewers from talking to their wives, we can
see the significance of outside alliances to internal family
power relationships. Thus, it is not surprising that some
issei men opposed their wives' employment, even when the
extra wages were needed, and that some issei women persisted in working despite their husband's opposition.

CONDITIONS OF WORK

Domestic service encompasses a variety of specific
situations. The jobs the issei women entered were of
three main varieties: live-in service, full-time nonresidential jobs, and day work.

For most of its history, domestic service was a
live-in occupation, and until World War I, this was the
most common pattern in the United States. This merging
of residence and work place stood as a marked exception
to the increasing separation of production from the household, and the accompanying segregation of work and nonwork life brought about by industrialization. For the
live-in domestic, there was no clear delineation between
work and nonwork time. Work hours were open-ended,
with the domestic "on call" most of her waking hours. She

had little time to devote to family and outside social relationships. As other forms of wage work that gave workers
greater autonomy expanded, the confinement and isolation
of domestic service grew more onerous. Observers noted
that women preferred factory or shop employment even
though wages and physical amenities were frequently inferior (Salmon 1897; Watson 1937). Two issei in the study
had worked as live-in servants: a widow who needed a
home as well as a job, and a woman who arrived as an
adolescent with her parents and worked as a live-in
"schoolgirl" before marriage.

Their situations were unusual for issei women. Unlike European immigrant domestics, who were primarily
young and single, almost all issei domestics were married
and had children. Their circumstances were similar to
those of black women in the South, and like them, the
issei turned to nonresidential work. Until the 1930s, full-
time positions with one employer were fairly common. Some
issei women worked as general household help for middle-
class families, performing a wide range of tasks from
laundry to cooking to cleaning. Other issei worked as
"second girls" in multiservant households, where they carried out a variety of tasks under the direction of a paid
housekeeper.

The nonresidential jobs gave workers stable employment, set hours, and a chance for a private life. However, in order for the worker to provide all-around services, she had to put in an extended day, which typically
began with breakfast cleanup and ended only after supper
cleanup. The day was broken by an afternoon break of
one to three hours, during which the woman returned home
to prepare meals or do chores. Mrs. Kayahara described
her workday, which began at 6:30 in the morning, when
she left home to catch a trolley. She arrived at work before 8:00. Then "Wash the breakfast dishes, clean the
rooms, make lunch and clean up. Go home. Back at 5:00
to help with cooking dinner and then do the dishes. Come,
go, and back again. It was very hard. I had to take
the trolley four times."

Partly because of the extended hours in full-time
domestic jobs and partly because of the greater availability of day jobs, all of the women in the study eventually
turned to day work. They worked in several different
households for a day or half day each week and were paid
on an hourly or daily basis. The workday ended before

dinner, and schedules could be fitted around family responsibilities. Many women worked part-time, but some
women pieced together a 40- or 48-hour week out of a combination of full- and half-day jobs.

The duties of the day worker generally consisted of
two main sets of activities: housecleaning and laundry.
Sometimes the worker did both, but many employers hired
different workers for the two sets of tasks. Laundry was
viewed as less skilled and more menial, and was often assigned to minority women, such as the Japanese (Katzman
1978). Both cleaning and laundry were physically demanding because of the low level of household technology.
Cowan (1976) suggests that the availability of household
help slowed the adoption of labor-saving appliances by
middle-class housewives. Moreover, employers felt hand
labor gave superior results. Workers were expected to
scrub floors on hands and knees, and to apply a lot of
elbow grease to waxing and polishing. Some sense of the
work is conveyed by Mrs. Tanabe's description of her
routine when she began work in 1921:

> When we first started, people wanted you
> to boil the white clothes. They had a gas
> burner in the laundry room. I guess you
> don't see those things any more--an oval-
> shaped boiler. When you did day work,
> you did the washing first. And, if you
> were there eight hours, you dried and then
> brought them in and ironed them. In be-
> tween, you cleaned the house from top to
> bottom. But, when you go to two places,
> one in the morning and one in the after-
> noon, you do the ironing and a little
> housework.

The issei express contradictory attitudes toward the
demands of the work. On the one hand, they acknowledge
that the work was menial, that it consisted largely of unskilled physical labor. As one put it, "You use your
body, not your mind." The women also say that the reason they were satisfied with the work is that they lacked
qualifications--for instance, "I'm just a country person."
Yet one is also aware that the women are telling stories of
their prowess when they describe the arduousness of the
work. What emerges from their descriptions is a sense of

pride in their physical strength and endurance, a determination to accomplish whatever was asked, and a devotion to doing a good job. Mrs. Yoshida explains that she never found housework difficult; even today she can work for hours in her garden without being aware of it:

> From the time I was a little girl, I was
> used to working hard. I was born a farm-
> er and did farm work all along. Farm
> work is very hard. My body was trained
> so nothing was hard for me. If you take
> work at a jakujin (Caucasian) place, you
> have to work hard. There was a place
> where the lady asked me to wash the ceil-
> ings. So I took a table and stood up on
> it. It was strenuous, but I washed the
> whole ceiling. So the lady said, "That
> was hard work, but next time it won't be
> so hard." She gave me vegetables, fruits,
> and extra money, and I went home.

This kind of pride in physical strength is discussed in relation to men in manual occupations, but is rarely seen as relevant to women. Similarly, an orientation toward completing a task is seen as more evident among skilled craft workers than among those engaged in devalued work. Yet we find evidence of both among this group of older women engaged in what has been called "the lowest rung of legitimate employment" (Caplow 1954, p. 233).

The evolution from live-in service to nonresidential jobs to day work can be viewed as a modernizing trend that brought domestic work closer to industrialized wage work. First, work and nonwork life became clearly separated. Second, the basis for employment became more clearly contractual; the worker sold a given amount of labor time for an agreed-upon wage. Yet as long as the work took place in the household, it remained fundamentally preindustrial. While industrial workers produce surplus value that is taken as profit by the employer, the domestic worker produces only simple use value. In a society based on a market economy, work that produces no exchange value is devalued (Ferree 1983). Whereas the work process in socially organized production is subjected to division of labor, task specialization, and standardization of output, domestic labor remains diffuse and nonspecialized. The work consists essentially of whatever tasks are assigned by the employer. While industrial workers are integrated into a socially organized system of production, the domestic worker remains atomized. Each domestic performs her tasks in isolation, and her work is unrelated to the activities of other workers.

Because of its atomization, domestic work remained invisible and was not subject to regulation. Domestic workers were excluded from protections won by industrial workers in the 1930s, such as Social Security and minimum wages (U.S. Department of Labor 1975). While sporadic attempts to organize domestics were made in large cities, such efforts rarely succeeded in reaching more than a small minority. The issei in the study appear never to have been included in any organizing efforts. Thus, there was no collectivity representing their interests, and the issei received none of the benefits accorded organized workers, such as sick days or paid vacations.

Wages depended on idiosyncratic factors. Informants and subjects reported that the going rate for day workers around 1915 ranged from 15 cents to 25 cents an hour. The top rose to around 50 cents an hour by the late 1930s. Full-time domestics earned from $20 to $45 a month in 1915, while "schoolgirls" earned from $2 to $5 a week. I was unable to find wage data on other semiskilled occupations in the Bay area, but other studies have found that domestic wages during this period compared favorably with those of factory, sales, or other low-level female occupations (Katzman 1978; Stigler 1946).

Some of the variation in wages can be attributed to market factors. Wealthier households were expected to pay more. The rate in some communities was higher than in others, probably due to the balance of labor supply and demand. Alameda had a higher proportion of Japanese seeking domestic work and had among the lowest wages. Still, what is striking is the seeming arbitrariness of wages. Some workers were willing to work for less than the going rate, and some employers were willing to pay more than they had to.

It may be useful to examine the process by which wages were set in individual cases. Generally, the employer made an offer and the worker either accepted it or looked for another job at a higher wage. While the shortage of workers may have maintained a floor for wages, the ef-

fect was not uniform.   What employers offered depended a
great deal on personalistic factors.   Sometimes the worker
benefited, if the employer wanted to keep her for personal
reasons.   At other times, the employer used knowledge of
the worker's personal situation to push wages down.   Both
these elements are evident in Mrs. Takagi's story.   Her
employers liked her and paid her more than the going
rate.   However, during the Depression, employers cut back
on help, and Mrs. Takagi couldn't find enough work to
fill the week.   One employer knew about her situation and
offered her an extra day's work if she would take a cut
in pay:

> She said to me, "I tried another girl, be-
> cause you get the highest wages.   I tried
> a cheaper one, but she wasn't good.   She
> never put the clothes away and never fin-
> ished ironing. . . .   What do you think--
> take $3.50 and I'll keep you?   I'll give
> you two days a week."   I wanted the
> money--I was trying to save money to get
> my son [from Japan].   So I said, "Fine."
> She said, "I'll never tell anybody."   Here,
> a month later, she told every friend. . . .
> Everybody said, "You're working for so
> and so for $3.50 and here you're getting
> $4."   See, that's the way all the jobs
> were.   A lot of people worked for $2.50,
> so I was just crying.

EMPLOYER-EMPLOYEE RELATIONS

As the above incident illustrates, the relationship
between employee and employer was, perhaps, the most
distinctly preindustrial, as well as the most problematic,
aspect of domestic service.   The relationship has been described as feudal (Addams 1896) or premodern (Coser 1973).
According to Coser (1973, p. 32), unlike modern occupational roles, where the employer's claim is limited and
held in check by competing ties, the traditional servant
was expected to be "entirely committed to and loyal to a
particular employer."

While the totalism of the traditional servant-master
relationship was much reduced under conditions of day

work, relations between white employers and issei domestics retained two essential and interrelated characteristics of the earlier period: personalism and asymmetry.

Personalism pervaded all aspects of the employer-employee relationship. Employers were concerned with the worker's total person—her moral character and personality—not just her work skills. The issei domestics in the study in turn judged their employers on moral and characterological grounds—for instance, whether they were good Christians, or clean and neat in their habits. The importance of the personal can also be seen in the isseis' preference for personal referrals for job placement. Compatibility and mutual trust were important because employer and employee were thrown together in a situation with little mutual privacy. The worker had access to regions of the household where she might become privy to family secrets. The worker in turn was open to constant scrutiny by her employer.

A sense of mutual obligation, a carry-over of feudal values, also colored the tie between employer and employee. The domestic was expected to demonstrate loyalty, and the employer was expected to concern herself with the worker's welfare. This mutuality was viewed as a positive feature by some of the issei. Mrs. Shinoda recalls her first employer's concern fondly: "That lady was really nice. She would turn on the light and the heat in my room and stay up waiting for me to return. Usually, she would go to sleep early, but even if I returned late at night, she would wait up for me with the room heated up."

For some women, the tie with the employer became an extension of familial relationships. Mrs. Takagi described her second employer, Mrs. Cox, in these terms: "She was a Christian. Any time I came down with a sickness, she said, 'Call a doctor.' If I go to the hospital, she came every day. She was almost a second mother. If I didn't have her help, I would have been badly off. I went to Japan and she gave me help with that."

Despite the intimacy, there remained an insurmountable barrier of status, reinforced by cultural and racial differences. Thus, the familial attitude of the employer usually took the form of benevolent maternalism. Even Mrs. Takagi, who formed close and long-lasting ties with her employers, recognized the employer's need to perform acts of noblesse oblige. She said she had learned to accept gifts, including old clothes and furnishings, even

when she didn't want them. Otherwise, the employer was
apt to feel the worker was "too proud," and would withhold further gifts and bonuses.

Thus, the second main feature of the relationship
was its asymmetry. The traditional mistress-servant relation exhibited in pure form the relation of superior to inferior. This aspect, though modified with the advent of
day work, continued to stigmatize the domestic as a menial
and "unfree" worker. In extreme cases, the domestic was
treated as a "nonperson." Mrs. Takagi recalls being offered a lunch consisting of asparagus stalks whose tips
had been eaten by the employer's son. This kind of treatment was probably rare, at least according to the women
in the study. However, less direct expressions of asymmetry
are common. For example, in an asymmetric relationship,
the lower-status person has to be attuned to the feelings
and moods of the higher-status person. Mrs. Nakashima
provided an insight into this aspect when she described her
approach to domestic work:

> I concluded, after working for a while,
> that the most important thing in this type
> of job is to think of and be able to pre-
> dict the feelings of the lady in the house.
> She would teach me how to do certain
> things in the beginning, but after a month
> or two, I gradually came to learn that
> person's likes, tastes, and ideas. So I
> try to fulfill her wishes--this is only my
> way of doing it, of course, and so, for
> example, I'll change the water in the
> vase when it's dirty or rearrange wilting
> flowers while I'm cleaning house. In that
> way, I can become more intimate with the
> lady of the house in a natural way and
> the job becomes more interesting.

Although her employers may have appreciated Mrs. Nakashima's aesthetic sensibilities, it is doubtful they were as
aware of and responsive to her thoughts and feelings as
she was of theirs.

The personalism and asymmetry in the employer-
employee relation were complementary. The supposed inferiority and differentness of the domestic made it easy
for the employer to be generous and to confide in her.

The domestic was not in a position to harm her or make excessive demands, and secrets were safe with someone from a different social world. An informant suggested that the language barrier, though it hampered communication, may have contributed to the smoothness of relationships. The issei could not "hear" insulting or denigrating comments. One worker confirmed this by saying she had never minded being a domestic, but added that had she understood English, she might have gotten into quarrels with her employers.

Ultimately, however, the personalism and asymmetry created contradictions in the employer–employee relationship. As Coser (1973, p. 36) put it: "The dialectic of conflict between inferior and superior within the household could never be fully resolved, and hence the fear of betrayal always lurked behind even the most amicable relationship between master and servant." The fear is evident in issei women's complaints about employers who distrusted them. Mrs. Takagi once found money left under the corner of a rug. She carefully replaced the rug without touching the money or saying anything about it; she had been warned by her father-in-law that employers sometimes tested the domestic's honesty by leaving valuables about. Mrs. Nakashima indignantly reported an incident in which she was suspected of dishonesty: "There was a place I was working temporarily. They asked me whether I had seen a ring. I didn't know what kind of ring they meant, so I just told them no. I hadn't seen any ring while I was vacuuming. They sounded a little skeptical, saying it's strange I hadn't seen it. I felt insulted then, as though they were accusing me of something."

The conflict took its most concrete form in a power struggle between employer and employee over control of the work process. On one side, the employer attempted to exercise as much control as possible. Mrs. Noda echoed the sentiments of many of the issei when she said that her greatest dislike was an employer who was yakamashi (noisy, critical): "Indeed, where they don't say too many things, the work is better. If they ask, 'Have you done this? Have you done that? Do you understand?' There is that sort of place. Most people don't say such things because they know [better]."

Some employers seemed to assume the worker would loaf or cut corners if she was not watched. Mrs. Nakashima said she quit one job because her employer spied on her.

She said most of her employers left the house while she worked; if they returned, they announced themselves loudly. In one case, "The Mrs. would come in very quickly without warning, so it made me feel as if she were spying on me to make sure I wasn't doing anything wrong. I disliked that a great deal."

Another arena of conflict was the amount and pace of the work. Employers sometimes engaged in the household equivalent of work "speedup." If the worker accomplished the agreed-upon tasks within a designated period, the employer added more. In order to finish everything, the worker was forced to "do everything fast." Employers were thus able to exploit the issei worker's conscientiousness.

The issei had only limited resources to resist employers' attempts to control their work and the conditions of employment. Yet, within their capabilities, they strove to wrest some degree of control over their work and their lives. The choice to shift to day work can be seen as one means to gain greater autonomy. By working for several families, the domestics became less dependent on one employer. Work hours could be adjusted to fit in with the workers' other interests and responsibilities. As Mrs. Tanabe said about her change from full-time work with one employer to day work, "You're freer to yourself."

Within the structure of day work, the issei maneuvered the situation to increase control over the work process. One way was to minimize contact with employers. Mrs. Adachi deliberately chose employers who went out during the day: "I liked it best when nobody was there. The places I worked, they went out. The children were in school, and I was all by myself, so I could do what I wanted. If the woman was home, she generally went out shopping. I liked it when they didn't complain or ask you to do this or that. The places I worked, I was on my own. It was just like being in my own house, and I could do what I wanted." Her sentiments were seconded by Mrs. Noda, who said, "I don't like it when people stay home. It's more easy to work—everything is smooth [when they go out]."

Mrs. Adachi retained her autonomy by adopting a utilitarian orientation toward her employers. She "picked up and dropped" jobs on the basis of convenience, rather than becoming attached to particular employers:

Sometimes I gave the job to someone else
and looked for something else. I changed
from job to . . . job. If I had to walk
too far to the bus, or the people were too
messy, I kept the job until I found a better one, and then I changed. [How did
you find the other job?] When they're
playing cards, they talked about the help.
If someone knew who is a good worker,
they would give the other ladies my name,
and they would call me. Then I'd go and
see. If I like it better than the other
places, I'd quit the other and move to the
new one.

Some women maintained control over the work by
defining and enforcing their own standards; they insisted
on working on the basis of tasks rather than time. The
job was done when the tasks were accomplished to their
satisfaction. If they worked extra time, they did not want
to be paid; if they finished in less time, they reserved
the right to leave.

The last recourse in the face of a recalcitrant or
unreasonable employer was to quit. This was a difficult
step for the issei. They felt it was a loss of face to
complain about mistreatment, and furthermore, they felt
employers should know how to act properly without being
told. Thus, when they quit, they did so in a way that
was designed to maintain both the employer's and their
own dignity. If an employer asked why they were leaving,
the issei usually made up an excuse that avoided any
criticism of the employer. Mrs. Adachi was typical when
she said, "I wouldn't say I didn't like it, so I would
say I was tired or sick." Yet their own pride was also
important. Mrs. Yoshida reported this incident when she
quit: "There was one place that no matter how much you
do, that person would let you do more. So I thought I
would quit. That day I did a lot of work--more than
usual--and finished up everything she gave me." By meeting the challenge, no matter how unreasonable, Mrs.
Yoshida was able to leave with her self-respect intact.

WORK AND FAMILY LIFE

Issei women's experiences in domestic employment
cannot be understood without considering the relationship

between wage work and family roles. Some of the connections between work and family life have been alluded to in earlier sections, but I will now examine the dialectics of this relationship more systematically.

When they came to the United States, the issei left an economy based almost solely on household production (Nakane 1967) and entered one in which wage labor was becoming the predominant mode. The majority of issei families found "preindustrial" niches in farming and small business enterprises. In these families, the traditional system of household labor, as well as the old role relationships, were transplanted more or less intact (Yanagisako 1975). Many issei families, however, especially those in Bay area cities, adapted to the urban economy by turning to multiple wage earning. Husband, wife, and older children were individually employed, mostly in marginal, low-paying jobs. Each worker's earnings were small, but the pooled income was sufficient to support a household and to generate some surplus for savings, remittances, and consumer goods.

This strategy was in many ways consistent with the values of the Japanese household (ie) system. Because multiple wages were needed, the economic interdependence of family members was preserved. Moreover, the employment of women was consistent with the assumption that women were full economic contributors. In other ways, however, the strategy was inconsistent with the traditional ie structure. Wage work represented a form of economic organization in which the individual, rather than the family, was the economic unit, and in which work and family life were separated, rather than integrated. Women working outside the home violated the principle that men had exclusive rights to, and control over, their wives' labor.

Perhaps because of this duality, issei men were divided in their attitudes toward their wives' participation in the labor force. As noted earlier, some men opposed their wives' employment on the grounds that their services were needed at home. In contrast, other men expected their wives to pull their full weight by being employed, regardless of the women's own inclinations. Thus, while Mrs. Adachi said she was defying her husband's wishes by going out to work, Mrs. Uematsu indicated that she felt compelled to seek wage work: "My husband didn't bring in enough money, so I went out to work. I didn't even think twice about it. If I didn't take a job, people would have started calling me 'Madam' [accusing her of thinking she was too much of a lady to work] . . . . It was like a race; we all had to work as hard as possible."

The duality is further mirrored in the contradictory impacts of wage work on women's position in the family. On the one hand, to the extent that the traditional division of labor and the structure of male privilege persisted, wage work added to the burdens and difficulties experienced by women. On the other hand, to the extent that wage work reduced women's economic dependence and male control over their labor, it helped the women transcend the limitations of traditional role relationships. Evidence of both tendencies emerges from the women's accounts; the increased burdens are greater and more obvious.

Among the women in the study, the major share of housework and child care remained with them even if they were employed. All but two of the women claimed their husbands did no work "inside" the house. Mrs. Nishimura explained:

> No, my husband was like a child. He couldn't even make tea. He couldn't do anything by himself. He was really Japan-style. Sometimes, I had too much to do, so although I would always iron his shirts, I might ask him to wait a while on the underwear, but he'd say no. He'd wait there until I would iron them. People used to say he was spoiled. He was completely a Japanese man. Some people divorce their husbands for not helping around the house, but that never entered my mind. I though it was natural for a Japanese.

While Mr. Nishimura might be viewed as extreme, even by other issei, there was unanimous agreement among the women that Japanese men expected to be waited upon by their wives.

The result was that the women experienced considerable overload. The men worked long hours, often at physically exhausting jobs, but the women's days were longer. Their days began earlier than those of other members of the household, with the preparation of a morning meal, and ended later, with the preparation and cleanup of the evening meal; in between, they had to fit in laundry and cleaning. Some women were endowed with natural vitality. They could maintain an immaculate household and do extras, such as making clothes for the children. Mrs. Nishimura described her schedule during the years she was doing seasonal garment work:

> Since I had so many children, I asked my
> mother-in-law to take care of the children.
> I would get up at 5 o'clock and do the
> laundry--in those days we'd do it by hand--
> hang up the laundry, then go to Oakland.
> I would come home, and since my husband
> didn't have much work then, he'd get
> drunk and bring the children home. I
> would cook and eat, and then go to sleep.
> They all asked me how long I slept at
> night. But, since I was in my twenties,
> it didn't affect me too much.

Others, like Mrs. Uematsu, were exhausted at the end of the day and had to let things slide: "My house was a mess. I went to work in the morning, and when I came back from work, I'd cook a little and then go to sleep, and that's about all."

As Mrs. Nishimura's account indicates, an additional problem was created by wage work that did not exist under the family work system--the need for separate child care. Employers sometimes allowed domestics to bring a young child to work. As more children arrived, other arrangements had to be made. Friends, neighbors, older children, and husbands were recruited to baby-sit. Women with older children often set their work hours to correspond to school schedules. When no other means was available, and employment was a necessity, the issei sometimes resorted to sending their children to Japan to be raised by relatives, as three of the women in the study did. They planned to return to Japan and rejoin their children. In all three cases, the women stayed in the United States, and the children returned as adolescents or adults.

Despite the prevalence of male privilege, role relationships sometimes underwent change in response to new circumstances. The most common adjustment was for husbands to take on some child care responsibilities. Even Mr. Nishimura, the "completely Japanese man," transported and minded children when he was out of work. One woman,

Mrs. Nomura, claimed that her husband did quite a lot around the house, including drying dishes: "He was considerably Americanized. He was young when he came over and he was a schoolboy, so he was used to the American way of doing things. Even when we quarreled, he wouldn't hit me, saying it's bad in this country for a man to hit a woman, unlike Japan. In Japan, the man would be head of the family without any question. 'Japan is a man's country; America is a woman's country,' he often used to say."

Some respondents and informants reported cases of role reversal between husband and wife (although not among the women in the study). Role reversals occurred most often when the husband was considerably older than the wife. Since many issei men were married late in life to much younger women, they were in their fifties by the time their children reached school age. As laborers, their employment prospects were poor, while their wives could easily find domestic jobs. Mrs. Tanabe, a nisei raised in Alameda, recalls that her husband "retired" while she was still a young girl: "The Hiroshima men in Alameda were the laziest men. Their wives did all the work. My dad raised me while my mother went out and did domestic work. He did the cooking and kept house and did the shopping and took me when I went to work. So, he didn't do much really. But, in Alameda, they're known for being the lazy ones--most Hiroshima men are--so no one's rich." One reason for this pattern may be that domesticity was considered appropriate for older men. Mrs. Yamashita, another nisei, reported that her father, a widower, acted as a housekeeper and baby-sitter while she and her husband went out to work.

In addition to the division of labor by sex, the traditional Japanese family was characterized by what Bott (1957) has called segregated conjugal role relationships; husband and wife had a considerable number of separate interests and activities. This pattern seems to have been maintained by the issei to a marked degree. Leisure time was rarely spent in joint activities. Women's orbit was restricted to the home and the domestic world of women; men engaged in a wider range of formal church and community activities. Informal socializing, including drinking and gambling, were common male activities. The men's drinking seems to have been a source of conflict in many families. Two women's lives were tragically affected by their husbands' drinking. Mrs. Takagi's husband got into frequent accidents and spent much of his earnings on alcohol. Mrs. Shinoda's husband was killed in a judo mishap that occurred while he was intoxicated. Perhaps a more typical story is Mrs. Kayahara's, who described her husband in these terms: "Not so much nice, but not so bad. [Was he old-fashioned?] Just like a Japan boy! So, I did everything--cook, wash, keep house. My husband drank. He drank so much, his stomach went bad. Once we were married, he would have five or six drinks every day--sake. All his life, he did that. But, he did work hard."

The extent of drinking among issei men can be gauged by the fact that women whose husbands did not drink thought it worthy of comment. Mrs. Nomura feels her life was much easier than other women's because her husband was straitlaced: "Yes, I've been lucky. I worked, of course, and encountered social problems [discrimination], but . . . I didn't suffer at all with regard to my husband. He didn't smoke, drink or gamble. . . . Very serious Christian with no faults. Everyone else was drinking and gambling. Park Street was full of liquor stores, and so they all go there; but my husband led such a clean life, so I was lucky."

Overwork and poverty exacerbated conflicts generated by gender division in the family: the discrepancy in power and privilege, the unequal division of household labor, and the separation of male and female emotional spheres. Far from being passive, the women actively fought with their husbands. Mrs. Nakashima had to send her three children back to Japan and work in a laundry to support herself because her husband was sickly: "My life in the U.S. was very hard in the beginning because my husband was ill so much and we have such totally different personalities. We were both selfish, so we had many problems. But, after I started going to church, I became more gentle. So we had fewer quarrels. I think that is a gift from God."

Mrs. Nishimura also reported that she and her husband quarreled a great deal: "Well, he was rather short-tempered . . . there were times when I thought he was stubborn, but we were far apart in age, so I would attribute our differences to that. Being apart in age does create quite a lot of differences."

Thus, while the issei women express the traditional Japanese attitude that women must bear up under hardship, it is evident that they did not always do so quietly!

CONCLUSIONS

This chapter has analyzed the contradictions in issei women's involvement in domestic work before World War II. This approach has highlighted several aspects of their experience.

First, it draws attention to conflict as an underlying dynamic in women's relationship to paid and unpaid work. The attention to conflict makes it possible to see issei women as actors striving to gain control and self-respect, rather than as passive targets of oppression. The contest was obviously uneven; they had few resources for direct resistance, and they lacked collective strength in the form of worker organization or female kin networks. Thus, there is no evidence that they directly confronted their employers or their husbands, that they expressed militance, or that they engaged in collective action. If these are the criteria, it is easy to overlook the women's resistance to control by employers and husbands.

The strategies the issei adopted reflected their relative lack of power; they engaged in indirect forms of resistance, such as evasion. They maximized autonomy in employment by choosing work situations in which employers were absent or inactive. In the family, they went out to work secretly or withheld part of their wages as a means of gaining control over disposable income. Another strategy used in both employment and family life was to define their own standards and goals. The issei had internalized criteria for what constituted a good day's work; some women defined their jobs in terms of tasks accomplished, rather than hours, for example. They also set their own priorities in relation to housekeeping, education for their children, and the family's standard of living. There is evidence that they gained satisfaction from meeting their own standards, irrespective of the employer's or their husband's evaluations.

Second, as the previous discussion indicates, the analysis highlights the interconnectedness of different aspects of the women's experiences, particularly between paid and unpaid work. In both employment and family

life, women were in a subordinate position where their role
was defined as service to another. The content of activities in both spheres was similar. The structures of employment and family life were, therefore, mutually reinforcing. The parallel structures in turn contributed to a
similarity in the strategies used to cope with subordination.
The reliance on indirect strategies in conflicts with employers, for example, can be related in part to issei
women's experience of subordination in the household and
the community, and their inability to directly confront
their husband's authority. By contrast, black women domestics resisted or defied their employers more openly and
were less subordinate in the family (Dill 1979).

Coping strategies are usually conceptualized as
situationally specific, that is, as growing out of and being
confined to a particular setting (cf. Goffman 1961). In
this case, at least, the strategies appear to form a coherent whole. This is to be expected, in part because of
structural parallels in women's positions in work, family,
and community life and in part because of internalized
cultural attitudes, such as the value of hard work, which
carried across situations. Perhaps more important, the
process of striving in one area developed orientations that
carried over into others. Thus, the theme of self-suffi-
ciency pervaded all areas of the women's life and has persisted over time.

Finally, the analysis points to the contradictory
implications of employment for issei women's status. The
issue has often been framed in either/or terms. Some
theorists, including some Marxists, have viewed employment as a liberating force, arguing that women would
gain status in society by becoming producers in the market economy, rather than remaining nonproductive household workers. By contributing income and gaining a role
outside the family, women would increase their power in
the family. More recently, analysts have argued that employment, far from contributing to equality, actually reinforces women's oppression. They point out that women
are relegated to low-status, routine, and low-paying jobs;
that women remain responsible for unpaid domestic work
and are, thereby, saddled with a double burden; that in
both realms women are subjugated by male authority (H.
Hartmann 1976; Sokoloff 1980). While the present account
shares this recent perspective and documents the multiple
forms of oppression faced by issei domestic workers, the

focus on issei women as active agents makes it possible to see oppressive and liberating consequences as interrelated. Issei women were constrained by the larger economic and political system that forced them to seek employment while limiting them to the most marginal jobs. The conditions of domestic work subjected them to further oppression. But, out of these conditions, issei women gained advantages that enabled them to achieve certain goals, such as helping their families in Japan and providing extras for their children, to become less dependent on the ability or willingness of husbands to provide support, and to form ties outside the immediate family group. And, despite the menial nature of their employment, the issei achieved a sense of their own strength and, in some cases, superiority to employer and husband within their own area of competence.

NOTES

1. Data for this discussion come primarily from in-depth interviews of 15 issei women who worked as domestics and, for comparison, 12 nisei (American-born) and 7 kibei (American-born and Japanese-educated) women. These interviews were supplemented by informant interviews of 30 older issei and nisei members of the prewar Bay area Japanese community. Information on the economic and social background was obtained from census material, early surveys, newspaper files, community documents, and secondary sources.

2. The other areas of concentration were the Sacramento Delta and upper San Joaquin Valley (Daniels 1973).

3. This and all other names in the text are pseudonyms. Sometimes identifying details have been changed to preserve anonymity.

4. Data for 1910 are missing because compilers aggregated occupational data for Chinese and Japanese.

5. This figure is lower than would be expected from geographic distributions. From 1900 to 1930, more than half of the Japanese population resided in rural areas, according to a survey conducted by the Japanese consulate (Strong 1933). The discrepancy suggests that unpaid agricultural labor was undercounted.

6. If data for issei and nisei are combined, the percentage of Japanese-American women in domestic service increased in 1940, due to the heavy concentration of nisei in domestic work.

13

Hidden Resistance: Women Shipyard Workers after World War II

Amy Kesselman

Researchers studying the postwar fate of women employed
in industrial trades during World War II are confronted
with paradoxes that have yet to be fully explained.   Wartime polls throughout the United States indicated that most
women industrial workers wanted to continue in the trades
in which they had been trained during the war.   In the
postwar world, however, they were excluded from the industrial work force, and the growing numbers of women
joining the labor force in the 1950s were concentrated in
traditionally female, low-paid fields of work.   Some researchers have argued that the patterns of the postwar
world should be "seen as a choice by women," and point
out that few women workers made a "public show of their
displeasure" during the reconversion period (Degler 1980,
p. 434; Campbell 1984; Clive 1979).   Others have discovered
women who protested the violation of their seniority rights
after the war, and have argued that systematic harassment
and intimidation prevented women from organizing against
the sex discrimination of the reconversion period (Gabin
1980; Anderson and Tobias 1974).

      Most studies of the wartime experience of women
workers end their analysis with demobilization, leaving
the impact of the war to speculation. It is usually assumed
that whatever active discontent existed in the reconversion
period had been dissipated by the cultural consensus that
women's primary roles were as wives and mothers.

      In seeking to explain the quiescence of women dur-
ing the 1950s, historians have cited the ideological and

cultural assault on women's aspirations as individuals, the disappearance of the last traces of feminism (or at least their invisibility), the conservative nature of the propaganda used to mobilize women workers during the war (Rupp 1978; Honey 1984), the craving for "normalcy" generated by the previous two decades of depression and war (Anderson 1981), the deeply held family-centered values of the wartime generation (Campbell 1984), and the general conservatism of the postwar period—a period in which the price of nonconformity and dissent was particularly high (S. Hartmann 1982).

Women remain shadowy figures in much of this analysis, while social economic forces occupy center stage. Recent analysis of poll data has generated some useful information about women's attitudes (Campbell 1984), but more research is necessary to understand consciousness—how women saw themselves and their choices, and the ways in which various influences interacted in their daily lives. Sherna Gluck, in her study (1982) of women who had worked in the Los Angeles aircraft industry during the war, suggests that oral history can illuminate changes in women's consciousness and the forms such changes took as they were translated into daily life. This kind of research will help to remedy a fractured view of the history of wage-earning women in the 20th century and to suggest answers to questions such as the following: Did the wartime experience have any lasting impact on the lives of women industrial workers? Was the increase in the numbers of women who joined the work force in the 1940s and 1950s accompanied by changing attitudes toward waged work? Were there instances of women wage earners refusing to accept the limits they found in the postwar world and, if so, what form did they take? An inquiry of this kind requires sensitivity to the variety of responses that lie between acquiescence and political action.[1]

The following discussion brings these questions to bear on a case study of women who worked during the war in shipyards in Portland, Oregon, and Vancouver, Washington. It will explore women's individual acts of resistance, acts that did not involve conscious collective action but nevertheless were an important part of the postwar world of wage-earning women. It focuses primarily on reconversion but dips briefly into the experience of some former shipyard workers in the postwar world. The study uses interviews with women who worked in the shipyards (who will be called narrators) as well as archival material, particularly the records of the U.S. Employment Service (USES) and the U.S. Department·of Labor's Women's Bureau. These sources indicate that many of the women who had been industrial workers in the Portland-Vancouver shipyards resisted the reconstitution of the low-paid female work force after the war. Their resistance, however, was individual and unorganized, and therefore has remained hidden. Interviews with former shipyard workers suggest that in the postwar world as well, there were women who challenged the limitations they encountered. Their stories suggest the need for more research about the experience of employed women in the 1950s.

Most of the research that explores women's responses to demobilization focuses on the industries organized by the United Automobile Workers. While the UAW colluded with management after the war in the violation of women's seniority rights, it had promised protection of women workers during the war, and established a Women's Bureau within the union to address the women's problems. It is not surprising that the flickers of protest should occur in an industry in which women had some expectation that their rights would be defended by their union after the war (Gabin 1982; Tobias and Anderson 1973; Goldfarb n.d.).

The shipbuilding industry in the two adjacent communities of Portland and Vancouver was a much more conservative environment. The craft unions that consolidated their power in the shipyards early in the war did not disguise their hostility toward either female or black workers, and did nothing to encourage the expectation that they would defend the rights of women. Several unions resisted admitting women workers as long as possible, some admitted women only in special categories, and some issued temporary memberships. Despite this hostile environment, over half of the female industrial workers in the area's three largest shipyards reported in 1943 that they wanted to continue skilled industrial work after the war.[2]

After V.J. Day any remaining uncertainty about the position of women in the postwar industrial world vanished. The metal trades unions made it clear that they supported the retention of men rather than women for the shrinking pool of jobs. All of the shipyards in the area pursued a policy of laying women off before men. Between July 15 and September 1, 1945, the number of workers employed by the shipbuilding industry in the area declined by 30 percent, and the number of women shipyard workers by 41 percent.[3]

Women shipyard workers had a variety of responses to the abrupt termination of their wartime jobs. Many experienced the war as a time of suspension in which normal rules didn't apply. For these women, reconversion brought a sense of being jolted back into reality. Some expected the layoffs and prepared for them, but found losing a job frightening despite all the preparation and resignation. "You kind of get a sunken feeling in the pit of your stomach 'cause that was your job," said Virginia Larson.

Most of the metal trades unions terminated women's memberships after the war, on the grounds that they had been temporary workers. "They let us in," said Nona Pool. "They let us pay dues, but if we'd have tried to get a job in the Boilermakers, we'd have gotten laughed off the face of the earth." Pool's withdrawal card read "for the purposes of housewife."

There is no record of women shipyard workers organizing against their exclusion from the union. Some, however, expressed their anger in small ways. Loena Ellis and Betty Cleator, for example, took stands on the issue of withdrawal cards. Ellis would have liked to stay in machinist's work, but "they were not allowing women to retain their status in the machinists' union." She did, however, confront the business agent of her union, who refused to issue her a withdrawal card, on the assumption that she would never want to rejoin the union, so she might as well leave without an official withdrawal. Knowing that this would mean a hefty fee if she ever did want to rejoin, Ellis insisted on her withdrawal card.

Betty Cleator had the opposite reaction. She worked as a draftsman and would have liked to continue after the war. It was clear to her, however, that there was no chance of continuing in drafting, so when she was charged a fee for a withdrawal, she responded, "You can give me an honorable withdrawal through my last payment, or you can forget it, because I've paid all the money to this union I'm going to. You can't get me a job, you can't even get me references to one."

THE TAMING OF THE FEMALE LABOR FORCE

As peacetime industries began hiring, the barriers between men's and women's work appeared to be as sturdy

as ever. Most plants that had hired women in traditionally male jobs during the war were replacing them with male
workers. Women were almost completely excluded from the
newly available skilled jobs, even in industries where
shortages of male workers were reported, such as railroad,
logging, and aluminum fabrication.[4]

The women shipyard workers who looked for jobs
during this period found themselves confronted with the
following choices: (1) they could stay in the labor force
and work in canneries, poultry and egg processing, textiles, sales, or services; (2) they could retrain themselves
to qualify for the available jobs in skilled clerical occupations; or (3) they could drop out of the work force.
Cannery work was seasonal, and in 1945 was paying $.66
per hour for women and $.80 to $.85 per hour for men;
domestic work paid a maximum of $75 a month plus room
and board. Clerical salaries ranged from $.75 to $1.40 an
hour, depending on skill and experience. Among the highest salaries available to women were those paid to power
machine operators in textile mills. These jobs were piecework, and it was possible to earn $10 to $12 a day, but
many women avoided them because of the intense pressure
and monotony of the work.[5]

Oral history recollections of women who looked for
employment after the war vividly illustrate the situation
confronting women workers. "When the shipyard was over,"
said Jean Clark, "that was it. There was no other place.
You went back as . . . a waitress or worked in an office
or something like that. . . . Nobody would have hired a
woman to weld anything after the shipyards. I don't care
how many years of experience you'd have. Nobody would
have hired you. That was a man's job."

In January 1946, the USES reported a problem match-
ing applicants with available jobs. The majority of jobs
available (75 percent) paid wages below the prevailing
rates in the community, and some of them were even considered "substandard." The remaining jobs (25 percent)
were for machinists, mechanics, stenographers, engineers,
and electricians, but they could not be filled because employers had become very specific about qualifications.[6]

Mr. Kerrick, supervisor of the Portland USES, contended that "a very lenient attitude has been assumed in
determining whether or not a job opening was 'suitable'
employment and whether or not the claimant could rightfully
be considered 'available' for work."[7] On the other hand,

he made it clear that war-acquired skills were not taken seriously into consideration in determining the "suitability" of jobs for men or women.

According to the placement director at the USES, there were two categories of women workers that presented problems to USES because their expectations had been raised unrealistically by the war. One group was composed of young women who had entered the work force after quitting or graduating from high school during the war. After the war they had difficulty finding jobs because they had insufficient training. In the other problem group were women who had left other jobs to work in the defense industry and were reluctant to return to their former occupations. According to the USES placement director, "These women present a major problem and the USES has not been able to do too much in adjusting these women to the reconversion period. The counseling service of the USES has been used by this group, but so far the bulk of these women have not adjusted to peacetime conditions and employment opportunities."

This group of women included a substantial number of black women and women in the "higher age brackets" (over 35) who had particular problems finding jobs. Black women's choices in the Portland area were even narrower than those available to white women. About half of the black population left the area after the war, and those who remained faced widespread discrimination by employers and unions. The USES did not force employers to hire black workers because the employers threatened to find workers elsewhere.

Black women of course faced double discrimination. Only two Portland-area manufacturing establishments registered with the USES would employ them: a garment factory and a bag factory that had two buildings, one of black workers and the other of white workers. When black women sought the help of the USES or the Urban League, they were urged to take work as domestic servants. The Urban League reported the reluctance of black women to return to domestic work because of the low wages and undesirable working conditions.

Margaret Kay Anderson, the Northwest field representative of the Women's Bureau, referred to women over 35 as workers "whose services in the labor market are no longer needed." Nationally, women over 35 comprised 45 percent of the wartime labor force. Almost three-quarters

(74 percent) of the women filing unemployment claims at the beginning of 1948 in the state of Oregon were over 30, and 44 percent were over 40. At the same time there was an accumulation of "hard-to-fill" jobs in stenographic, office, and clerical work because applicants were unable to "meet the rigid employer specifications as to skill, experience and age, particularly the latter requirement." "A high percentage of job openings," reported the Portland-Vancouver Unemployment Bulletin for December 1948, "now specify that applicants should not be over 35 or 40 years of age."[8]

Women remained 25 percent of the unemployed in the Portland-Vancouver area during the three years after the war ended. The labor market in the area remained unbalanced throughout this period. At the end of 1948, USES was reporting that many workers were still looking for jobs in trades in which they had been trained during the war, but were not acceptable to employers because they did not satisfy the requirements for "all around journeyman." Simultaneously, many jobs were unfilled because "of such features as low wage scales, long hours, or the lack of guaranteed wage scales." Although the USES did not specifically mention women, the jobs enumerated were sales, domestic, and janitorial work—two of them historically "women's work."[9]

Meanwhile, inflation was straining the resources of working women. Between 1946 and 1947, the cost of living increased 15 percent while the salaries for most jobs available to women paid under a dollar an hour (Postwar Readjustment and Development Commission 1947, in the Planning Files, City of Portland Archives).

The interviews with women who looked for work after the war tell the human stories behind the "unbalanced" labor market statistics of the late 1940s. Most women eventually found jobs in clerical, sales, service, and textile work but, as the USES records indicate, they did not adjust easily to the limited opportunities they faced.

Nell Conley's husband didn't return from the service for seven months after the war ended, and she had a young child to support. During the war she had believed that it was most important to get the ships built and inappropriate to worry about postwar problems. But as she began to look for other work, she became angry at the union's exclusion of women shipyard workers and the contracting options for women in the work force. "There were very few places," she recalls, "very few jobs women could take where their salary was anywhere near what a man's would have been for the same kind of work, and there were many, many kinds of work that were simply out of bounds for women."

Office work was one of the few expanding fields for women. During the 1940s and 1950s it still offered some opportunities for advancement and attracted women who were looking for a career. Betty Cleator, for example, had obtained a degree in landscape architecture before the war but found that the field was closed to women on all levels. There were few jobs doing actual landscape architecture, and there was "a lot of discrimination" against women. Most landscape architects, according to Cleator, entered the field by working in greenhouses--work inaccessible to women. "The only thing women did in greenhouses," she said, "was to decorate the poinsettias for Christmas." When she was unable to find a job, Cleator's father paid for a two-month course at a business college. "I made my living punching a typewriter ever since." The war period, when she worked as a draftsman, was the only time in her life when she used any of the training from her college career.

Loena Ellis' postwar dilemmas illustrate what the USES described as having difficulty "adjusting to peacetime conditions and employment opportunities." Ellis remembers the period after the war as one of unrest for many people who couldn't decide "what direction to take. And in a way, I was in that boat, too, because I definitely wasn't going to go back to the factory, and the machinist work was gone, so it was sort of starting over fresh for me." She did try for a short time to find a job in which she could use some of her training as a machinist, but all she could find was in camera repair, which seemed too physically and psychologically confining to her. She therefore decided "it couldn't hurt to learn about the business world," and attended business college for a year to study bookkeeping. Virginia Larson, also realizing there was no opportunity for women machinists, used her shipyard savings to go to business college and learn secretarial skills and bookkeeping. Both Larson and Ellis saw office training as a means to escape the assembly line.

USES officials attributed the failure of women to be attracted to service work to the low wages in most of these

jobs. Marie Schrieber and Betty Neiderhaus found jobs in
department stores, but they, too, had difficulty "adjusting
to reconversion." "After the shipyards were over," Schrieber
said, "then you have to take a big cut in pay. It kind of
hurt. . . . You were back to women's wages again, you
know . . . practically in half."

The largest unfilled need in the Portland–Vancouver
area for women workers throughout 1946 was for power machine operators in the textile industries. The postwar consumption boom had boosted business in the region's garment
industry, creating a critical labor shortage. There were
6 large textile mills and about 15 small manufacturing companies in Portland and Vancouver. Most of these operated
on a piecework system. Although experienced operators
could earn wages that compared favorably with those typical of women's work, textile work did not attract workers.
Several of the women interviewed ended up working in the
textile industry in the 1950s because they found no other
jobs, but only two took these jobs immediately after the
war; and all of them commented on the tedium and pressure
involved in mill work.

Both the statistical evidence and the oral history
material demonstrate that the reconversion period was one
of enormous difficulty for women who had worked in industrial jobs during the war. Suddenly the respect women
had experienced in the shipyards vanished, and their options contracted dramatically. For these women the idea
that "both sexes gratefully went back to normalcy, [and]
gratefully resumed the deferred middle class dream of family, security and upward mobility" is a serious distortion
(Filene 1975, p. 169). For them the middle–class dream was
not easily accessible, and the return to "normalcy" made
it less so.

In the Portland–Vancouver area, women shipyard
workers who were denied the opportunity to use their
wartime-acquired skills in the postwar world did not
storm union headquarters, sue discriminatory employers, or
march in the streets. But neither did they acquiesce in
the re-creation of the "pink collar ghetto." They avoided
the low-paid, tedious, high-pressure work that depended
on female labor as long as they could, attempting to find
work that was better-paying and more satisfying. Protest
against the contracting options for women in the postwar
world was manifested in women's stubborn refusal to "adjust to reconversion."

FEISTY WOMEN AND THE POSTWAR WORLD

By 1950 the occupational distribution of employed women in Portland–Vancouver had resumed its prewar contours. The major change in the female work force since 1940 was the dramatic increase of married women. In 1940, only 17.5 percent of all married women in Portland were employed; in 1950, 27.4 percent were working for wages. Although some married women had left the work force after the war, many returned soon after and many others began working later in the decade. The predicted retirement of the "housewives turned welders" did not materialize.[10]

The range of options for employed women remained narrow. Carl Degler, claiming that opportunities for women widened in the postwar period, notes that in 1950 the number of women welders in the country as a whole was four and a half times larger than it had been in 1940 (Degler 1980). A different perspective emerges when we consider that the numbers of women welders was so small in 1940 and the number of women workers who were trained in this craft had increased so markedly during the war. In Multnomah County and Vancouver, for example, the number of women craftsmen, foremen, and kindred workers almost doubled between 1940 and 1950, growing from 461 to 878, but in both years they represented only 1 percent of all working women and their percentage of all craftsmen grew only from 2.5 to 3 percent. When one considers that there were over 20,000 women working in industrial crafts during the war, these figures do not indicate much of an advance. Degler reproduces the sexism of the 1940s by analyzing the figures as if the wartime industrial employment of women should not be expected to have any lasting impact on the occupational picture. According to wartime surveys, well over 9,000 female industrial workers wanted to continue in their wartime trades but under 1,000 women could be found doing industrial work in 1950. For the thousands of women unable to use their skills in the postwar world, the opportunities had not "widened enormously"; they had narrowed drastically.[11]

Oral history interviews reveal another form of hidden resistance, the individual rebellion of some women who either remained in the work force or rejoined it later. While these women may not have been typical, they were, I would argue, significant. Their individual acts of rebellion, invisible beyond their immediate environment, are indications that beneath the quiescence of the 1950s, tensions were mounting.

Nona Pool said of her shipyard experience, "It made an industrial worker out of me." She changed jobs 19 times, trying to find industrial work that used her mechanical ability and paid decently. She stopped working in 1959 but returned ten years later, when her husband became terminally ill. When Pool's husband first became sick,

> He said, "All you'll be able to get will be a baby-sitting job or housekeeping job, you know, after you've been off work that long." I says, "You wanna bet?" [laughs]. So I got me a telephone book and I found all the same manufacturers and I'd asked them, "Do you manufacture your product on site?" and I called up asking 'em, "Here I am all bright-eyed and bushy-tailed. You need me to help you do that work down there?"

Pool worked at a variety of jobs, mostly poorly paid and unskilled. Sometime in the late 1950s she approached someone at Freightliner Corporation, the company that eventually hired her. "'How about giving me a job welding?' And the guy, he turned around and looked at me, and he kind of laughed and he says, 'I wouldn't doubt you're a good welder, but we don't have facilities for women.' I say, 'I'll bring my own potty, just bring me a curtain.'"

These stories convey Pool's sense of the absurdity of excluding women from skilled industrial work. They also capture her image of herself as she navigated through the frustrations of the postwar job market. She saw herself as a "go-getter": persistent, resourceful, and good-humored. While Pool maintained her desire to return to welding throughout this period, she at no time pursued organizational solutions. She had no hope that the union would help her, since her shipyard experience had convinced her that it protected male privilege. She knew of no other organizations or legislation; the 1950s was not a period in which women thought of collective strategies. Like most women, Pool's approach to her problems was an individual one. Her individual perseverance did, however, eventually converge with legal and social changes that loosened restrictions against women welders. In the late 1960s she got a job building radiator grills at Freightliner. She "kept asking them to go to welding and one of the guys said, 'Well, over my dead body will you get to be a welder.' So I went to welding school again at the community college." When she finished her course in 1975, she was hired as a welder at Freightliner and welded until her retirement in 1978.

Reva Baker was one of a growing minority of white women who entered or reentered the work force while their children were still of preschool age. By 1950, 20 percent of all women with children under five were employed as compared with 6.5 percent in 1940 (Bancroft 1975). In contrast, the figures for nonwhite women remained fairly constant, 19.9 percent in 1940 and 20.9 percent in 1950. Baker's early departure from the shipyards had been precipitated by her foreman's refusal to pay her for the inspecting work she was doing. She got married during the war, then went to work as an operator for the telephone company. When her son was born, she quit to stay home until he was two and a half. She then returned to the telephone company, leaving her son first with a neighbor and then with her mother (who had moved into her community).

Baker remained with the telephone company all her working life, working her way up from an operator into a variety of jobs. Like Pool, she was able to reenter skilled crafts in the 1970s, doing frame and central office work, both of which she described as "men's jobs." "When I first told my boss that I wanted the frame job, he told me I wouldn't like it because it was dirty work, and I said, 'I've done dirty work all my life, I'm not afraid of dirt.' And he says, 'You'll get so tired running up and down those ladders,' and I said, 'I've been up and down ladders before.'" Baker convinced him, and her last two jobs at the telephone company were her favorites. When she retired, she arranged, over some opposition, to reproduce on her retirement notice a picture of a woman with a plow, accompanied by the caption "Back then you could pick the field of your choice." She added, "Today the field of choice requires that you pull your own strings."

Kay Baker's attempt to break through the barriers to skilled work was less successful than those of Reva Baker (her sister-in-law) and Nona Pool. Baker credits her shipyard experience with her conviction that "women did have a place in the working world, certainly, and that if old Ed Kaiser could do so well paying these women as much as he paid his men—it certainly put that kind of idea in my head." Baker got a job doing office work at Precision Cast Parts after she had worked as a grocery clerk for many years. Women in the plant, according to Baker, worked either in the office or in wax molding. She noticed that they used welders in the salvage depart- ment, and asked the salvage foreman if he had ever hired any women.

> He said, "No, I never heard of anyone
> wanted to." "Well," I said, "I've done
> welding before, a lot of years ago. I
> imagine, with a little brush-up course to
> get acquainted with the type of metal that
> you're working with, I don't see why I
> couldn't." He said, "I wouldn't have any
> objection to having a woman work here,
> but I don't think the manager would buy
> it." I spoke to him again a week or two
> later, and he said, "Absolutely not, no
> way." You kind of got the feeling it was
> because welding paid X amount of money
> and women didn't get paid that kind of
> money.

Kay Baker complained about the sexism at Precision Cast Parts until she retired, criticizing pay differentials, the double standard for male and female performance, the exclusion of women from policy making, and the male chauvinist attitudes of the bosses. Throughout her life she clung to the conviction that "women and men should be treated equally at work," a belief that took shape in the shipyards. "I still believe that," she said. "You don't see it very many places, but I still believe it. A job is a job, and some day those same boys are gonna pay for it, one way or another, they'll pay for tramping women down under their feet." After she retired, the women in Baker's plant filed a sex discrimination suit that included her; they told her that "they never could have done it if it hadn't been for me." Kay Baker's image of herself was as "the most famous rebel that ever worked" at Precision

Cast Parts. "They're still suffering from me," she commented with pleasure.

The stories of Nona Pool, Reva Baker, and Kay Baker represent the form that female rebellion took in the postwar period before the reemergence of feminism. All three women were acting as individuals: Nona Pool, resourceful and persistent; Reva Baker, assertive and determined; Kay Baker, angry and defiant. Nona Pool captured the spirit of their approach to work: "What you've got to do is say, 'I'm this wide and I'm gonna push a hole in there just the right size for me, and if you don't like it, that's tough stuff.'" They acted in isolation, without support, and they left a legacy for their daughters and coworkers. (One of Nona Pool's daughters became a harness builder and also works for Freightliner.)

These individual go-getters and rebels add a new wrinkle to the debate about continuity and change in the postwar period. Certainly the 1940s and 1950s was not a period of militant action on the part of wage-earning women, and I would not argue that World War II initiated a transformation in women's work patterns. I would suggest, however, that a growing number of women were identifying as workers as well as family members (Kesselman 1985); many of these women seized opportunities available during World War II; some attempted in whatever ways they could to hold on to them as the war ended. Some of these women, emboldened by their wartime experience, pushed against the limits they found in the postwar work world, and developed patterns of individual rebellion that reverberated in their work places and families. Further research will enable us to fully assess the scope of the resistance that lay submerged beneath the apparent domestic consensus of the postwar world and the ways in which it may have helped to create an atmosphere that was receptive to the feminist challenges to sex discrimination of the 1970s.

NOTES

1. Oral history interviews used in this chapter come from interviews conducted by the Northwest Women's History Project, 1980-1981, in the Portland and Vancouver area.

2. This figure is based on the reports of a comprehensive survey of workers in the three Kaiser yards conducted by the city of Portland in January 1944. The survey was an attempt to discover the postwar plans of shipyard workers. In response to the question "Do you intend to continue in industrial work after the War?" 9,257 out of 16,322 female industrial workers responded positively. Portland Area Postwar Development Commission, "Shipyard Survey," Summary Tables, Portland City Archives, Planning Files, Box 20.

3. Multnomah County Day Care Committee, Minutes, August 22, 1945; "Trend of Employment in Reporting Establishments, Portland, Oregon," September 1945, USES Records, U.S. Department of Labor, RG 183, Box 304, Washington D.C., the National Archives.

4. Margaret Kay Anderson to Frieda Miller, November 19, 1946, Women's Bureau Records, RG 86, Box 1410; "Field Report," June 1945, USES Records, U.S. Department of Labor, RG 183, Box 304, Washington D.C., the National Archives.

5. Bos'n's Whistle, August 24, 1945; Oregon Labor Market Information, January 1947, USES Records, RG 183, Box 304; Margaret Kay Anderson to Frieda Miller, November 19, 1946, Women's Bureau Records, RG 86, Box 1410; interviews with Edna Hopkins (May 28, 1981), Betty Niederhaus and Marie Schrieber (May 17, 1981), and Pat Koehler (June 18, 1981).

6. Commerce, September 17, 1946; "Field Report," January 1946, USES Records, RG 183, Box 304.

7. Kerrick's comments, and the following discussion of the activity and observations of USES officials, is based on a lengthy memo by Margaret Kay Anderson to Frieda Miller, November 19, 1946, Women's Bureau Records, RG 86, Box 1410.

8. Margaret Kay Anderson to Frieda Miller, November 19, 1946, Women's Bureau Records, RG 86, Box 1410; Mary Elizabeth Pidgeon, Changes in Women's Employment During the War, Women's Bureau Special Bulletin no. 20 (Washington, D.C.: U.S. Government Printing Office, 1944), p. 23.

9. Oregon State Unemployment Compensation Commission, "Reports," May 1947, January 1948, December 1948, USES Records, RG 183, Box 305. See Karen Anderson (1981) for similar evidence in Seattle, Detroit, and Baltimore.

10. U.S. Bureau of the Census, 16th Decennial Census, Characteristics of the Population, vol. 11, part 5, p. 1001 and part 7, p. 398; U.S. Bureau of the Census, 17th Decennial Census, Characteristics of the Population, vol. 11, part 37, p. 75 and part 47, p. 53; Gertrude Bancroft, The American Labor Force: Its Growth and Changing Composition, New York: 1958, pp. 70, 216, 226.

11. Characteristics of the Population: 17th Census, vol. 11, part 37, p. 155; Characteristics of the Population: 16th Census, vol. 11, part 5, p. 1001, and part 7, p. 398; Characteristics of the Population: 17th Census, vol. 11, part 37, p. 75, and part 47, p. 63. The figure of 29,000 is an estimate based on wartime figures from War Manpower Commission, Survey of Shipyard Operations in the Portland, Oregon, Metropolitan Area, vols. 1-111 (Portland, OR: 1943).

14

Women and Trade Unions: Are We Asking the Right Questions?

Roslyn L. Feldberg

INTRODUCTION

For years, virtually everyone has acknowledged that the relationship of women to trade unions is problematic. While perceptions of the problems have changed with the organization of work and family life, different groups have posed different questions. Unions have typically asked whether women could be organized at all, and if so, what could be done to get more members; scholars have tried to explain women's relative absence from organized labor and, within organized labor, from positions of leadership; and working women have asked in a variety of ways "Should I join?" In my reading and in talking to women employed in clerical and service sector jobs, I am struck by the combination of their desire for collective

An early version of this paper was presented at the Society for the Study of Social Problems, Washington, D.C., in August 1985. Thanks to Carol Brown for presenting it. This research was supported in part by funds from the Andrew W. Mellon Foundation, given by Radcliffe College for research at the Henry A. Murray Research Center of Radcliffe College. The Women and Work Study Group offered comments and suggestions throughout the development of this chapter. Special thanks are due to Carole Turbin, Peggy Crull, and Amy Kesselman for detailed comments. Ronnie Steinberg and Hal Benenson provided extensive notes for revision, and Mary Fillmore read every draft.

power and their belief that unions are unlikely, perhaps even unable, to provide what they are seeking.

Underlying all of these questions are fundamental puzzles of why more women are not members of or activists or leaders in unions, and what can be done about it. Since 1970, feminist scholars and union activists have begun to assess women's historical and contemporary relationships to trade unions in increasingly complex and sophisticated ways (see chs. 9, 13). Their work provides a much stronger theoretical framework for understanding both women's employment and trade unions. This chapter builds on their work to ask some new questions. Instead of assuming that women should be active in unions, I ask what unions would have to be like for women to play a more active role in them. In other words, how would unions have to change to enable women to be active, involved members? What would a "women-centered" trade union look like?

The answer that emerges is that the unions have to change their structures if they are to be institutions through which women articulate and realize their needs and wants. At present, women remain "absent from the agenda" of most unions, even those which count large numbers of women among their members (Glassberg et al. 1983). I argue that women's absence or limited place results in large part from the exclusion of "women's culture" from the unions.

By "women's culture" in the work place I mean the ways of getting things done that women value, their sense of honor, the obligations they acknowledge to coworkers, and the connections they make between their work and their womanhood.[1] I argue that unions have to be transformed to include and support "women's culture" in the work place if they are to be revitalized as institutions that truly represent the working people of the United States. What possibilities there are, or were, for working from "women's culture" shift from period to period, from context to context. Surely one major factor is the presence or absence of a feminist movement that pushes all organizations to rethink their approaches to women and offers groups of women the opportunity to become aware of taken-for-granted aspects of their own lives. But "women's culture" is present in the female-dominated areas where most women have always worked, whether it is self-consciously feminist or not. I suggest that its place in the unions prepares the way for a more sensitive response and more appropriate approach to women workers even when the larger context does not support fundamental change.

This chapter is a beginning. It offers a sketch of the argument and some thoughts about processes by which "women's culture" in the work place might come to be an integral part of union structure. As such it will raise as many questions as it answers.

I begin by asking what kinds of attempts have been made in the past to increase women's participation in unions. Next I ask what happened with those attempts and analyze why those which did not work were unsuccessful, arguing that, among other things, they did not make room for "women's culture." Finally, I discuss what has happened where union activities did take "women's culture" into account and analyze the results of those cases. (I am not addressing instances in which unions specifically excluded women or self-consciously sought to limit their involvement by organizing them into separate auxiliaries.)

UNIONS AND THE ORGANIZATION
OF WOMEN WORKERS

Despite the long history of U.S. unions' failure to come to terms with women's employment, women's presence in the work force has always been part of the picture and unions have always responded to it. At times, the response has locked women out of the labor movement; at times, it has made overtures; but always unions have had to deal with women. In every period some unions have given special attention to women workers, largely in response to their activism. During the ascendancy of the craft unions, when women were generally excluded from membership, the Cigar Makers Union and the Typographical Union accepted women members. Beyond that, at the turn of the century, unions such as the United Cloth Hat and Cap Makers Union and the United Garment Workers hired women organizers to assist them in attracting women members. In certain industries, most notably garments and related apparel, many crafts were practiced almost entirely by women. Here the International Ladies Garment Workers Union (ILGWU), which had its origins in the crafts, stands out as one of the first to undertake large-scale organizing of women workers.[2] Encouraged by the activism of the women themselves, the

ILGWU organized large numbers of women in less than ten years, largely through the work of committed women organizers.

Throughout the early 1900s, working women were viewed as different from working men. It was recognized that organizing women required some special resources and appeals. The Women's Trade Union League (WTUL) assisted in dramatizing the plight of working women, especially during strikes, and protections for employed women were won in the legislature and upheld in the courts. Union leaders accepted the idea that women responded to a different set of priorities than those which mobilized men; local organizers repeatedly argued that a union must be concerned with principles of justice for all workers, and with assistance to those not yet organized, if it was to maintain a loyal membership among women. But "different" meant "less than equal." While the unions recognized and responded in some measure to women's differences, these differences were taken as evidence that women were less valuable union members than men. They were seen as a separate class of workers and usually organized as such. As a result, the unions typically put few resources into fighting for women's wages and were less responsive to their concerns.

By the 1930s American society had changed in its industrial structure and its style of consumption. The new industrial unions that developed in this context were founded to organize all workers in a single industry. Oriented to an archetypal industrial worker who was male and headed a family with a wife at home, whatever his immigrant status, ethnicity, or skill level, the industrial unions concentrated their energies on industries that had high proportions of male workers. While clearly more inclusive than the earlier craft unions, the industrial unions and their leaders continued to view women as interlopers in the labor force and as less desirable union members. Women's presence in industrial work required that they be organized, but they were not a priority category. Little attempt was made to accommodate their differences; women were organized as workers alongside men or not at all.

The industrial unions organized women in industries from printing, garments, and textiles to automobiles and electrical work. Of these unions, the one that became best-known for its progressive position on women's issues was the United Automobile Workers' Union (UAW).

The organizing of women in the General Motors Ternstedt plant through the UAW represents the possibilities and limits of one industrial union's relationship to women in the 1930s (Meyerowitz 1983, 1985).[3] Ternstedt was unique among the Detroit-area auto plants in 1936 in that it was large (12,000-16,000 workers) and half the workers were women. Its organizing was accomplished despite the belief of the UAW leadership that a plant that was half women could not be organized. The convictions and dedication of one male organizer, who had previously organized women cigar makers, and of several women rank-and-file organizers, who were pro-union before the campaign began, were critical ingredients in the victory.[4] Despite the activism of these women, they did not have a vision of how to organize so as to take into account special issues of importance to women workers. "Women's culture" did not shape the campaign. The class issue took precedence. There was little attention to the special needs or concerns of women workers, and little awareness of their unique contributions.

Interestingly, although the organizers made no attempt to operate differently because the plant was half women, they did use an unusual tactic in their fight for recognition that may have attracted the women's support. Unable to call a sit-down strike because of a "no strike" clause in a master UAW-General Motors agreement, the organizers developed a plan for a "slowdown." This tactic, which called on the workers to remain on the job during their usual hours while working at an exceptionally slow pace to cut production, allowed the workers to continue to earn their hourly wage and interfered little with their outside activities; it drew on their patience, discipline, and social cohesion to demonstrate their power over production.

As important as their contribution was to the victory, the women rank-and-file organizers did not become union leaders. No systematic attempts were made to keep them active in the union, and their role in building it was never fully acknowledged.

Immediately after World War 11, women's hopes for equal treatment in the UAW were shattered (Gabin 1982; Milkman 1983). Women who had worked throughout the war, and even those who had been members of the union before the war, found themselves displaced from particular jobs or from employment altogether as employers, male coworkers, and the union cooperated to "give the jobs to men." Such treatment led most women to withdraw into "women's jobs" while a few continued to fight for their jobs and to bring formal complaints against their union. Ironically, this failure to represent women members began shortly after the UAW established its Women's Bureau to address the particular concerns and problems of women members. The Bureau's effectiveness in resolving women's complaints was hampered because it had no independent authority, and had to work through the local union presidents and regional directors, whose attitudes were often the source of the problems (Meyerowitz 1980; Gabin 1985). Yet it did succeed in involving some women more actively in the union through leadership training programs specifically designed for women, and in doing so it became a model for other industrial unions.

Since 1970, many unions have made new attempts to organize women workers. Most have followed the industrial model, trying to add women to the existing union structure with the help of at least one woman organizer on each campaign. In addition, many unions have given closer attention to the issue of moving women into leadership positions within the existing structures.

This new attempt to move women into leadership positions has had limited success. It founders on the dilemma that has plagued the industrial unions' approach to women since their beginning. Even at this late date, the industrial unions are trying to increase women's involvement while treating women as if they were lesser men, by not addressing the additional barriers women face from the structure of union activities and the attitudes of its male leadership. They are complemented in this attempt by the Coalition of Labor Union Women (CLUW), an organization for women trade unionists that also aims to increase women's visibility as leaders throughout the labor movement.[5] Here, too, the emphasis is on motivating and training women to aspire to leadership positions without regard to the constraints of womanhood in a patriarchal (or single-parent) family. According to Milkman's recent analysis,

> CLUW's approach [and by implication that
> of the unions in which its members are
> active] presumes that the key difference
> between women and men is that women lack

leadership skills, self-confidence and therefore, power. While taking into account the
fact that women [1 would add many, but
not all] have "family responsibilities" that
obstruct their union activity, CLUW does
not view this as the basis for a critique
of established organizational forms within
the labor movement, but rather as an additional handicap which women must somehow
overcome . . . the solution is for women
to equip themselves to compete more effectively, on the established terms, for leadership. (Milkman 1985, p. 313

Not taking womanhood into account is an established pattern in the relationship of women leaders to the
labor movement. For example, in Wertheimer and Nelson's
(1975) classic study, the women activists characterized the
relationship between children and union activity by saying
that children were "not a problem." Of 39 women activists,
more than half had young children when they began their
active union work. Only one of these women reported that
her husband always took responsibility for the children.
When husbands did not, the women made arrangements for
other women to look after their children (p. 137).
　　Despite its limitations, it is significant that CLUW
is an organization for women. It has at times articulated
a vision of more far-reaching changes than those it works
for on a daily basis, but that articulation contributes to
the possibility of future change. Moreover, its presence
within the labor movement provides a vehicle for addressing women's concerns to the still almost exclusively male
union leadership. One example of what can grow out of
such a development is the commitment of the unions to the
struggle for pay equity.

WHAT WENT WRONG? A FRAMEWORK FOR DISCUSSION

Given that over many years some craft unions and
some industrial unions have organized women workers, and
more recently have begun to involve them in leadership,
what went wrong? Why, despite these activities, are
women underrepresented among the members, activists, and

leaders of the contemporary labor movement? The answer
to these questions has two starting points. First, we must
acknowledge that the unions have not devoted sufficient
resources to this work, so that, at some level, we can
proclaim with Kessler-Harris (1975b) that it is amazing
that there are as many organized working women as there
are. Second, even at times when specific unions have put
considerable resources into this work, their approaches
have failed to take into account "women's culture," that
is, "the way women perceive and impose social order . . .
a woman's sense of 'dignity' or 'honor' at work, ordering
her perceptions of what she is willing to tolerate, and
what violates her sense of dignity" (Kessler-Harris 1985b,
pp. 118-119).

While the cultures of contemporary working women
grow out of a context that differs greatly from that of
their late-19th- and early-20th-century counterparts, in
both periods working men and working women live their
lives quite differently. Gender-based ideologies linked to
sex-segregated responsibilities at home and sex-segregated
jobs at work created differences in each period. Yet the
cultural basis of these differences in women workers' actions has long been ignored. Cultural factors unique to
men have often been recognized as part of work culture--
indeed, have often been seen as defining work. Those
unique to women have been denied cultural authenticity by
being interpreted as outgrowths of "gender roles" rather
than as part of authentic, although different, work cultures (Feldberg and Glenn, 1979b).

"Women's cultures" in the work place are forged out
of the common ground established among women coworkers
in particular settings and historic contexts, which includes
the "cultural baggage" associated with gender. Recent
analyses have described the unique features of the "women's
work culture" among department store clerks from 1890 to
1960 (Benson 1978), hospital nurses at various points in
history (Melosh 1982), contemporary garment workers in
New England and the Southwest (Lamphere 1984, 1985), and
cannery workers in California (Zavella 1985). The defining features of each "women's culture" emerge from the
interplay of particular groups of women working together
in specific contexts.

Looking at "women's culture" as a feature of the
work place suggests that women's concerns might not arise
or that they would be expressed differently by men. Unions

are thus more likely to succeed in organizing and maintaining a loyal and active membership among women where they change their ways of operating to make room for "women's culture." The failure to come to terms with it has marred whatever attempts were made to include women under both craft and industrial organization. The forms of those failures have been quite different, however.

WHAT WENT WRONG?   THE 1920s

During the Progressive era, which coincided with the continued ascendancy of the craft unions and the rise of a new, broader unionism, women's differences were assumed to be biological, not cultural, and to indicate weakness. In the 1910s there was recognition of women's special needs and problems, but not of their actual and potential contributions. This limited awareness led to an advance, so that a kind of activism developed around the organizing and protection of women workers. But the form of activism the unions supported was closely related to how women in the work force were treated in the Progressive era (see ch. 10). It meant that women were still second-class citizens in the unions.

The case of the ILGWU (1909-1924) in its relationship to New York Local 25 provides an interesting example. The ILGWU had conducted a series of impressive strikes during the period 1909-1913. These strikes had involved large numbers of women, not only as strikers but also as rank-and-file leaders. Central to the union's strategy was the women workers' appeal to the public sense of moral outrage that working women should lack decent food and face unreasonable working conditions in their jobs. As Sarah Eisenstein (1983) documents, working women had a clear notion of their own dignity and of what decent conditions of work and decent treatment involved. The garment workers conveyed images of the exploitation of women and children in the sweated trades not only to mobilize public support for their strikes but also to pressure for legislative protections that would cover women who were not part of their union. In doing this work, they forged alliances with women from the WTUL and other progressives interested in improving the conditions for all workers.

During organizing drives or strikes these extraordinary approaches and goals were generally accepted, even applauded, by union leaders as creative responses to difficult situations. But these same approaches and goals were also seen as evidence that women did not understand trade unionism--that they were naive and unreliable as union members, or were subversive.

Local 25 was the largest local in the ILGWU. Its leadership, unlike that of the union executive board, was drawn primarily from women members. In 1915, the local, with the help of a woman professor from Columbia University, extended its education program from basic trade union education to a full liberal arts program, including such topics as religion, world history, and literature.[6] The young women from the local embraced the program in large numbers, and through it developed the friendships and solidarity that made their local a vibrant and attractive one. The success of this program was not unique. Many women's groups, including the WTUL and independent unions of women clerical workers, found educational programs of particular interest to employed women. What was unique was that, on the basis of their strength in their local, the young women leaders of Local 25 developed a plan to increase the participation of the members in union decisions through a system of shop delegates.

In the 1910s the march of women organizing themselves reverberated throughout the ILGWU. As they came together in increasing numbers, the women staked out claims to issues and approaches with indisputable importance to the membership and echoing the themes of the Progressive era. The male leadership responded by encouraging the women's efforts and applauding their victories. The 1920s ushered in a period of retrenchment and conservatism. The ILGWU was engaged in internecine strife centered on Communism. The male leadership's willingness to hear what the women were saying diminished greatly. The old prejudices against women unionists, subdued during the previous decade, took on a new urgency. The result of women becoming active to the left of the leadership was to discredit all of the programs they had begun.

In this context the leadership of the international, all men with one exception, interpreted the shop delegate proposal as an attempt of Communist women to gain control of the union. They moved to dismantle Local 25 by dividing it into three separate locals and placing them under the control of the international executive board. At the same time, the meaning of trade union education was reinterpreted to restrict it to basic education about union procedures and negotiations. These changes in the program and structure of Local 25 spelled its demise. From a membership of 30,000 in 1919, its decline was so dramatic that one woman organizer claimed that the women "ran away."

People have interpreted the decline of the ILGWU during this period in many ways. What evidence is there of a "women's culture" that was destroyed in the forced reorganization? First, there are the testimonials of women associated with the local during this period of the importance of this education in their lives. Second, there are the numbers of programs and activities that the local sustained during this period, reflecting the energy and involvement of an active membership. Third, there are the analyses of women of the period, both leaders and observers, about the meaning of the educational program and the consequences of its decline (Wong 1984). Finally, there are the analyses of contemporary historians. All of these sources, with varying emphases, point to the flowering of union activity among the rank-and-file women of Local 25. Such activity wells up only when the organization that fosters it empowers a social group.

The leadership of the ILGWU failed to take "women's culture" into account because that would have involved questioning their basic assumptions about the differences between men and women, and about how unions operate. It would have raised questions such as Who were the workers? How did men and women live? What were the differences between Christian and Jewish women, and between rural and urban women? It would have meant looking closely at how the union was working and what it was producing.

The ILGWU, although not strictly a craft union, was based on a model of working men's lives and priorities that grew out of the craft unions. In contrast, there was a different model of working women's lives and priorities. These differences were elaborated in cultural themes and reinforced by the sex segregation of work in the home and in the work place. Furthermore, they were not simply variations: ideas of manhood and womanhood in the working class as well as the middle class embodied a hierarchy of power and respect that consistently subordinated women to men, despite the complex differences of ethnic/racial/ class subcultures.

The basic issue seems to be that these unions were established to serve a particular type of worker in a particular social and historical context. The programs and structures of the union reflected the issues that were most important and attractive to those workers and the ways of operating that they found at least acceptable. Those workers were predominantly men from a variety of working-class cultures that, however greatly they differed in their family customs, shared a view of men as heads of their families and as primary wage earners.

Committed, however unaware they may have been, to seeing women as fundamentally different, the male leadership of the ILGWU was unable to develop a fruitful relationship with the women members. Where the women differed from men in their approach to organizing and in the issues that mobilized them, these differences were seen not as offering a resource for the development of new approaches to union work but as evidence that women were incapable of being true union members. The women's concerns were viewed as frivolous or idealistic--in either case not a base from which unions could build. At the same time, where the women were similar to men in their organizing zeal and their courage, the similarity was ignored, because it did not conform to the male leadership's view of women, or was interpreted as evidence that the women were ideologically tainted.

The struggle within the ILGWU took place in an embattled period, punctuated by events such as the Red scares and the deportation of "Communist" immigrants. Yet the way these concerns were acted on undermined the activism not only of suspect individuals but also of women who had been loyal union members in both the rank and file and the local leadership. The programs and approaches these women pioneered were replaced with those deemed appropriate by the male leadership. The Bryn Mawr School for Working Women was one of the few places where special programs for women did survive, on the margins of the labor movement. In the end, the result was a decline in the number of women members in the ILGWU, the disappearance of women from the leadership, and the end of an era in which the ILGWU addressed for a brief time the particular concerns of its women members. The vitality that flourished briefly and that provided a glimpse of a new relationship of women to the labor movement was gone. Its rebirth 50 years later was nourished by just such places as the Bryn Mawr School.

WHAT WENT WRONG? THE 1930s AND BEYOND

If the attempts of the craft unions failed because they saw women as fundamentally different, and therefore weak, the industrial unions' efforts failed because they did not acknowledge any differences at all. Women were organized without sensitivity to their greater exploitation as workers or to the additional barriers they faced in attaining leadership positions. The union structure that was established for male industrial workers was accepted as complete. Women workers were supposed to be additions to that structure, not a reason to modify it.

While women were half of the work force at the Ternstedt plant, their unique concerns were rarely addressed, even after the union victory. They continued to earn lower wages, and most of the improvements they experienced "resulted from changes primarily designed to ameliorate conditions for men" (Meyerowitz 1985, p. 251). Equally telling was the lack of support for women rank-and-file leaders. Since child care and housework remained the responsibilities of individual women, the obstacles to activism were high. Only those without family responsibility or willing to make enormous sacrifices were able to participate fully in union work.

The Women's Bureau, established late in World War II, faced problems that paralleled those of the women it served. Caroline Davis, its director for many years, lacked the staff, the resources, and the political base she needed to operate powerfully. Early in her directorship, she wrote to the union secretary/treasurer, asking for a chair for a staffer in her office. Several weeks later she sent a reminder, and finally she asked Walter Reuther, the international president, to intervene. Only then did she get the chair. Clearly the head of the Women's Bureau did not have to be listened to. More important was Davis's attempt to establish special programs for bringing women leaders together to discuss the problems and issues they faced. A few such meetings were held and were received enthusiastically by the attending women. But the program foundered on the noncooperation of regional directors and local presidents, who refused to submit the names of women leaders or to release them from other duties to attend the program. While the international leadership was willing to endorse such programs, it was rarely willing to risk offending regional and local male leaders by pressing them to cooperate. The local leaders seemed to view these programs as both a special privilege for women and a threat to their own power bases. Without independent authority to carry out its programs, the Women's Bureau was limited to doing only what it could convince the male leadership to support.

The UAW Women's Bureau represented an attempt to come to terms with a reality that did not fit the union's underlying assumptions that what was good for male workers was good for their female counterparts. While the perception that women had special concerns and needs was not wholly wrong, it was misleading, because it located the problems in the women's character or behavior, not in the union's policies and structures. The Bureau was begun when the union had many women members and a few more active women members and local leaders, as a result of wartime opportunities. If women had become a powerful constituency within the UAW, the Women's Bureau might also have gained strength. As it was, the wartime opportunities for women to enter leadership proved to be as temporary as their expanded employment opportunities. Without that powerful constituency, the Women's Bureau lacked power. It did create a space for women, but it was a separate space—outside the centers of power in collective bargaining. Despite the goals of its staff, it served primarily to educate women to fit into the mainstream of union activities and accommodate themselves to the existing structure, not to begin the transformation of the union.

Where it was able to educate and support women within the framework of existing union traditions, the UAW Women's Bureau succeeded, as did its counterparts in other unions. Caroline Davis and others from the Women's Bureau were leaders in the fight for the Equal Pay Act of 1963 and worked hard, with the backing of their international union, for the removal of barriers to women's equality, although more easily in public than in union life.[7]

Neither the successful organizing at Ternstedt nor the separate space of the UAW Women's Bureau marked the beginning of changes in the union that might have led to

a new, vital involvement of women in their unions.
Meyerowitz (1985) argues that this was due in part to the
absence of a feminist consciousness, a consciousness that
was missing not only in the UAW but also in the larger
society of the 1930s. Yet women joined the UAW in this
period to meet their needs--so they did see possibilities.
If there had been room for these to be discussed and addressed, the presence of "women's culture" inside the
union might have provided the ground for the growth of
the feminist consciousness that was needed.[8] Its continuing absence is one outcome of the unions' inability to
make room for "women's culture," to build respectfully for
the areas of women's lives that create differences from as
well as similarities to their union brothers.

By segregating "women's culture" into a separate
space, instead of making it as integral as "men's culture,"
union leadership has maintained women's involvement as a
footnote to the basic activities of the unions. It has not
driven women out, but it has, however unintentionally,
prevented their concerns from becoming an established part
of every union agenda, and thus has prevented the women
from becoming leaders. Only the few women whose life
circumstances make it possible for them to live as men do
have gained power. By definition, these women cannot
symbolize the struggles of women who remain marginal to
the unions. The women's departments have remained political backwaters isolated from the power bases of the union,
and continue to serve a useful but limited function.

While the industrial unions came to realize that
women's life experiences prepare them differently, their
responses to these differences bogged down in trying to
educate women to be more like men. They have not yet
seized the opportunity to build unions that more fully reflect and encompass the needs of all workers.

THE LESSONS OF SUCCESS

I argue that the failure of unions to become or remain vital organizations for women members derives at
least in part from failure to come to terms with the realities of women's and men's lives. What union structures or
approaches would be more appropriate? Should differences
between manhood and womanhood be expressed institutionally in separate organizations? Should unions be structured

to embody those differences in a single organization?   If
there are separate structures, is it possible for them to be
related to each other in a way that permits unity and
solidarity?   Could unions established to facilitate men's
union activity and those established to facilitate women's
union activity be allied as equals?   Or should there be
new models of unions that incorporate the varied realities
of working womanhood as a basis of union activity for
both men and women?

      I cannot answer those questions fully.   In this
chapter, all I can do is provide examples, briefly and
unsystematically, of what has happened when "women's
culture" has been taken into account, and analyze what
made it possible for the issues and the solidarity of
"women's culture" to be a basis for union activity rather
than a barrier to it.

      When women clerical workers attempted to organize
at the turn of the century, the American Federation of
Labor (AFL) ignored their requests for assistance (Feldberg 1980).   A short time later the women found a more
sympathetic response from the WTUL.   Many of the earliest
concerns of the women were not standard trade union issues.
Stenographers in Toledo discussed the possibility of setting
up their own restaurant in that city in 1902, while those
in Pittsburgh had a "cooperative lunchroom for female
stenographers and typewriters only," no dish to cost more
than five cents.   A few years later a Chicago local of the
Stenographers Union began with 300 "girls."   The local's
aims were broad: to establish a minimum wage and to
provide a free employment agency, night school courses on
subjects related to their jobs, physical culture classes,
free medical service by women physicians, and an unemployment fund.   The minutes of various stenographers'
locals give prominent mention to schools and social events,
especially dances.

      The concerns of young women clerical workers in the
period 1900-1920 may have been far from those of the labor
movement, since the workers were primarily young, native-
born, white women who tended to be better-educated than
others in the female labor force.   Still, they show a marked
similarity to the issues that sparked ILGWU Local 25.   Most
of the clerical workers' organizations were not long-lived,
but they show that unions based on women's concerns did
attract an active membership.

Their failure to win the interest and support of the more established labor leadership may have contributed to the decline of these unions, but their autonomy forced them to build a union on the basis of their own limited resources, and the realities and dreams of working women that they knew from their own experience. Their aims indicate that while they shared with men the problems of finding jobs and getting decent wages, they approached even these common issues in a context that reflected their vision of a decent, fulfilling life for a working woman.

Although the early clerical unions are interesting as an example of the way unions grounded in women members defined and addressed issues, they do not help us to understand how the structure of a union might facilitate voicing and addressing issues of particular interest to women. To discuss how unions might change themselves to make more space for "women's culture," I turn to more contemporary cases.

The first case is from Italy. I include it because it is the only well-documented case of this type (Beccalli 1984; Cockburn 1984; Piva and Ingrao 1984). In contrast with the attempts of many U.S. women union leaders to make room for feminist influence within the existing union structure, Italian women activists moved from a feminist critique of the unions toward a more radical reconstruction. They pushed for and won the right to establish an autonomous network of women--basically a separate women's union within the trade union movement. The resulting collectives operated independently according to the methods and principles they found compelling. For example, in the mid-1970s union women allied with feminists from outside the unions to establish the "150 hours" schools, which emphasized consciousness raising, general education, developing new skills, and creating networks among women.[9] Although the schools were very successful in attracting students, the separate structures were not in themselves a long-term solution to the problems of creating unions more accessible and responsive to women. Instead, they moved women even further from the centers of power in the unions and left the latter untouched. While many women were empowered as individuals and members of small groups, in the long run this may have reduced women's power in the unions. Separatism appears to have produced not a transformed set of unions in which women are integral, but parallel networks, with the women's the smaller and weaker of the two.

The remaining cases are U.S. examples. There are several at least partially successful new organizations in the United States involved in mobilizing women for trade union activity. While these differ among themselves, they all are based among clerical workers, who are predominantly women and traditionally outside the established unions' organizing efforts. Each of these organizations has made special efforts to involve women as activists and to address their concerns. Each has been willing to raise new issues and use innovative tactics to do so. 9 to 5, the organization for women office workers, is not a union. Its founders self-consciously called it a preunion organization. Not being a union, the organization lacks the power to represent its members on the job; at the same time, it has had room to develop issues and tactics without the problems of winning elections and negotiating and administering contracts. It has pioneered in posing long-ignored issues--health and safety in offices, and sexual harassment, to name two--and in developing new tactics. It has also brought questions about appropriate conditions of work back into public debate by publicizing the practices of the best and worst employers, holding speak-outs for employed women, and mobilizing public opinion on their behalf. Many of these tactics are reminiscent of the appeals to moral outrage of an earlier generation of women activists and organizers.

Equally important, 9 to 5 has operated with a structure that encourages the development of leadership skills throughout the membership (Goldberg 1983; Milkman 1985). Members are encouraged to join committees, and training sessions are held frequently, so that every member can learn to be a spokesperson for the group. This approach, clearly reflecting the influence of the women's movement, offers women the support and opportunity to speak on their own behalf. By operating in this fashion, 9 to 5 creates a participatory democratic base within the organization-- a membership that knows how to act--and its leadership accepts the risks that such an engaged membership represents: not only loss of office but, even more, failure.

To maintain an organization of this type, members must renew their commitment regularly and new members must be recruited continuously. 9 to 5 has used some of these approaches in its development of a new union, Service Employees International Union 925, which is chartered with maximum autonomy from its international so that it can structure its own operations. The willingness of the international to enter such an arrangement is encouraging, since it indicates awareness of the importance of allowing office workers to define their own union structure. Yet SEIU 925, with its origins in grass roots organizing, its continuing tie to 9 to 5 via a shared executive director/president, and its commitment to organizing office workers, has bumped up against the limits of financial reality. While its commitment to organizing office workers in previously unorganized industries remains, the costs and difficulties of such campaigns have meant that it cannot concentrate solely on these high-risk organizing drives. It has begun to put more of its energies into organizing public sector office workers, where the costs are lower and the likelihood of success is higher, but where it is competing with more traditional and probably better-financed unions (Milkman 1985). Whether SEIU 925 can establish a firm base among public sector office workers without losing its unique character, and can go on to organize in less hospitable industries, remains to be seen. To the extent that it does, its success strengthens the argument advanced here.

9 to 5 and SEIU 925 offer examples of organizations whose structure is conducive to member involvement. The next two examples illustrate how democratic structures and practices bring forth new concerns and create space for "women's culture" even in the context of crisis situations.

The most compelling example of democratic practice I witnessed came during a strike vote of District 65-UAW (clerical and technical workers) in the midst of a hard-fought recognition campaign at Boston University in the spring of 1979. Although the union had won an election, the university refused to negotiate a contract. The clerical and technical workers had been on strike for over a week, along with faculty and librarians who were engaged in their own contract fights. The faculty had just ratified a contract and was going back to work. The clerical and technical workers had to decide whether to continue their strike or return to work to regroup. The vote was taken at a meeting that was open to everyone--not only members of the union but also anyone interested in observing. The negotiating committee, headed by the organizer, offered a resolution to continue the strike. After a few questions, the vote was taken. It was overwhelmingly in favor of continuing, but the voice response sounded tentative, as if the members were not sure of their course of action.

The organizer, Barbara Rahke, a former secretary at the university, stood up and asked that the vote be put aside. She thanked the members for their confidence in the committee and their willingness to continue a strike under very difficult conditions because the committee had recommended it. She then expressed the view that continuing the strike was a good idea only if the members really understood the options and wanted to continue. She asked for questions and comments. An animated discussion ensued. What I remember clearly is that many of the women spoke, somewhat tentatively and apologetically, about their individual concerns, and that these were addressed respectfully. (The contrast to the faculty strike, in which I participated, was telling. During faculty meetings we spoke only about strategy, never openly about ourselves.) Another vote was taken. This time the "yes" was resounding.

The strike of Local 34, clerical and technical workers, at Yale University provides a more fully documented example of creative tactics and democratic process (Ladd-Taylor 1985; Cupo et al. 1984). Once again, attention to issues of particular concern to women grew out of an emphasis on "organization building" that allowed rank-and-file women to express their ideas and develop into leaders:

> The structure of the union was based on
> the layout of Yale so that ideally every
> group of workers would be represented.
> The organizing committee consisted of over
> 400 leaders drawn from most departments
> and work groups. About 150 organizing
> committee members able to assume additional responsibility joined the steering
> committee, and leaders of that group joined
> the union staff, which eventually included
> over fifty rank and file as well as paid
> organizers. . . . Before any decision
> was made, it was discussed in small
> groups throughout the campus so that
> everyone had a chance to formulate her
> thoughts and make her views known.
> (Ladd-Taylor 1985, pp. 469–470)

Out of that structure emerged tactics such as going back to work without a settlement during the Christmas holidays, so that workers got their holiday pay and were not picketing empty buildings during the student/faculty Christmas vacation, and involving the entire New Haven community in their strike. The workers' real concerns also emerged: benefits that would meet the needs of women employees—maternity leave, affordable child care, a dental plan that covered children, a livable retirement pension, and respectful treatment by their employer based on recognition of the importance of their work to the functioning of the university.

In the case of Local 34, the approach to organizing enabled "women's culture" to be carried from the office or the laboratory into the organizing campaign and to become integral to the work of making a union. Local 34 also had strong support from Local 35, a blue-collar, male-dominated union of maintenance workers at Yale, and a firm commitment from the parent union, the Hotel and Restaurant Workers.

The above unions benefited from special relationships to their parent organizations. These relationships gave newly unionizing workers autonomy in setting up their own organizations and running their own organizing campaigns, while providing access to the financial and technical resources of the international.

CONCLUSIONS

We return now to the motivating question: How will unions have to change if they want to attract women workers as members and leaders? This question is particularly important in the present context. Some of the recent losses of the labor movement are due to shifts in the economy and to a political climate in which employers feel supported in attacking unions. But other losses are a result of unions not attracting large numbers of employed persons, men as well as women.

The AFL-CIO has acknowledged the importance of developing creative approaches and the seriousness of the problem in its report, The Changing Situation of Workers and Their Unions, which offers many suggestions for reaching out to workers in new ways, including establishing programs to teach young people in the schools about labor's contributions to American society. But it does not directly ask how unions will have to change to be more attractive to women workers. The failure to do so may limit the unions' ability to attract men as well as women.

Would new structures shaped by "women's culture" be more congenial to men as well? It is useful to consider whether union structures that developed in relation to predominantly white, male industrial workers of the 1930s, men assumed to be heads of patriarchal families, are appropriate to the contemporary way of life of men as well as women workers. The need to organize industrial workers necessitated the development of new kinds of unions that, in the end, added new models of unionism to those pioneered by the older craft unions. Likewise, the need to organize large numbers of women in previously unorganized sectors might once again give rise to new models of unionism that, in the long run, may prove more effective for many groups of unorganized workers.

Given the range of social and cultural groupings among employed women, no rigid model of a new unionism will be compelling to all of them. As Dolores Janiewski's article (1983) about the tobacco workers of the 1930s illustrates all too clearly, women have long been separated along the lines of cleavage that continue to hold sway: race, ethnicity, religion, marital status, and the presence/absence of children. The texture of daily life also differs greatly for women according to their education and social backgrounds, their incomes, whether they care for elderly parents, and, for many women, the relationships they have to the men who are important in their lives. We need unions that respect differences--that do not assume that all women have the same experiences at work, at home, or in the larger community, or that work holds the same place in their lives--while fighting for equality.

What is meaningful for contemporary women is no secret. Women who have joined unions or associations say that they seek decent earnings and respectful treatment at work--from coworkers as well as from supervisors and managers--and are attracted to organizations that offer them a chance to express their concerns and act on them. Women clerical workers at a public utility whom I interviewed in 1980-1981 had stopped attending the meetings of their local because the issues they raised were greeted so often by laughter from the male unionists.

Sexton's (1982) book on women hospital workers is filled with quotations from those working as nurses and nurses' aides, in dietary and housekeeping departments, who are angry at the disrespect they face on the job. They see that disrespect in the way they are ordered about at work; in needless, interfering supervision; in being asked to work faster than they feel a person can work; and in low wages and inadequate benefits. What they seek from the union, beyond better wages and benefits, is a respectful response to their problems, one that takes their view of the situation seriously, and works to improve and correct the aspects of it that are most disturbing to them. The women do not simply want to be "taken care of" by the union. They want to be treated as equal members, whose concerns are equally important and whose contributions are equally valued.

We return once again to our question; How would unions have to be different? They would have to make room for "women's culture" and for more meaningful rank-and-file participation, they would have to share leadership and skills, and they would have to learn to value the leadership, skills, issues, and solidarity that "women's culture" contributes. As part of that process, unions would have to adapt to most women's family responsibilities (for instance, by holding meetings at lunchtime as well as in the evenings, or at other times suggested by the members, so that women could attend without having to add new demands to their lives). At the same time, unions need to challenge their male rank and filers on two fronts. First, the men must support the union activities of women in their families by sharing family work. Second, they must struggle alongside women coworkers, reorganize paid work, and increase community social supports so that job and family responsibilities are less burdensome and more easily shared. New structures can facilitate these changes, but they cannot accomplish them. That requires a politics that affirms the goal of increasing women's involvement as full and equal members and leaders of unions, and that welcomes the transformations that will make such involvement possible.

NOTES

1. The discussion of "women's culture" in the work place has many sources. An analysis that focuses on consciousness is in di Leonardo (1985). The related topic of "differences" is analyzed in Kessler-Harris (1985a). Thanks to Ronnie Steinberg for the latter reference.

2. My account of the ILGWU is based largely on Foner (1979–1980) and Kessler-Harris (1985b). Thanks to Hal Benenson for discussion of the 1920s and the ILGWU in that period.

3. Ruth Meyerowitz shared her unpublished materials on Ternstedt and the UAW, and discussed possible interpretations of them.

4. The male paid organizer was Stanley Nowak. Among the unpaid women organizers, Irene Young Marinovich, Becky Laing Kimsley, and Martha Strong were especially active (Meyerowitz 1983, 1985).

5. See Foner (1979–1980) for the most comprehensive account of the formation of CLUW. See Meyerowitz (1980) for insights into the goals of the women leaders from the UAW who were founders of CLUW and for analysis of the pressures these women faced within the UAW.

6. For the history of the educational programs of the ILGWU, see Wong (1984). The Columbia University professor was Julia Stuart Poyntz.

7. Although not quoted directly, Dorothy Haener contributed greatly to my understanding of the progress and frustrations experienced by women leaders in the UAW.

8. See Strom (1983) for a more comprehensive discussion of feminism and "women's place" in the industrial unions of the 1930s.

9. The "150 hours" schools were set up under a 1972 collective bargaining agreement that allowed workers up to 150 hours of paid work time for public education courses (Beccalli 1984).

Bibliography

Acker, Joan, and Donald R. Van Houten. 1975. "Differential Recruitment and Control: The Sex Structuring of Organizations." Administrative Sciences Quarterly 20: 152-162.

Acosta-Belen, Edna, ed. 1979. The Puerto Rican Woman. New York: Praeger.

Addams, Jane. 1896. "A Belated Industry." American Journal of Sociology 1:536-550.

Aldridge, Delores. 1975. "Black Women in the Economic Marketplace: A Battle Unfinished." Journal of Social and Behavioral Scientists 21 (Winter):48-61.

Alcott, Louisa May. 1875. Work: A Story of Experience, Sarah Elbert, ed. New York: Schocken, 1977.

Alliance Against Sexual Coercion. 1980. "Three Male Views on Harassment." Aegis (Winter/Spring):52-59.

Almquist, Elizabeth M. 1979. Minorities, Gender and Work. Lexington, MA: D.C. Heath.

Almquist, Elizabeth M., and Juanita Wehrle-Einhorn. 1978. "The Doubly Disadvantaged: Minority Women in the Labor Force." In Women Working, Ann H. Stromberg and Shirley Harkess, eds., pp. 63-88. Palo Alto, CA: Mayfield.

American Federation of Labor-Congress of Industrial Organizations. 1985. "The Changing Situation of Workers and Their Unions." News release. Washington, D.C.: AFL-CIO, mimeo, February 21.

Amott, Teresa. 1985. "Income and Jobs for Black Women 1960-1984." Progress 6 (Spring):6-7, 10.

Anderson, Karen. 1981. Wartime Women: Sex Roles, Family Relations and the Status of Women During World War 11. Westport, CT: Greenwood Press.

_____. 1987. "A History of Women's Work in the United States." In Women Working, Shirley Harkess and Ann Stromberg, eds. Second edition. Palo Alto, CA: Mayfield.

Andrews, Irene Osgood. 1914. "Minimum Wage Legislation." 3rd Report of N.Y. State Factory Investigating Commission, appendix iii. Albany, NY: J.B. Lyon.

Anthony, Katherine. 1914. Mothers Who Must Earn. New York: Russell Sage.

Arthur, Timothy Shay. 1858. Lizzie Glenn, or the Trials of a Seamstress. Philadelphia: B. Peterson and Brothers.

Baca-Zinn, Maxine. 1982. "Review Essay: Mexican American Women in the Social Sciences." Signs 8 (Winter):259-272.

Baker, Elizabeth. 1925. Protective Labor Legislation with Special Reference to Women in the State of New York. New York: Columbia University Press.

Baker, Sally Hillsman, and Bernard Levenson. 1975a. "Job Opportunities of Black and White Working-Class Women." Social Problems 22 (April):510-532.

_____. 1975b. "Earnings Prospects of Black and White Working Class Women." Unpublished paper.

Bancroft, Gertrude. 1975. The American Labor Force: Its Growth and Changing Composition. New York: Russell and Russell.

Barbanel, Josh. 1980. "Many New Lawyers Find Practice Is Limited to Looking for Work." New York Times, November 4, p. B1.

Barko, Naomi. 1986. "The Current Boom in Temp Work Is Good for . . . Businesses, Temporary Agencies, Working Mothers?" Working Mother, May, pp. 28-31.

Barrera, Mario. 1979. Race and Class in the Southwest. Notre Dame, IN: University of Notre Dame Press.

Barrera, Mario, Carlos Munoz, and Charles Ornelas. 1972. "The Barrio as an Internal Colony." In Urban Affairs Annual Review, vol. 6, Harland Hahn, ed., pp. 465-498. Beverly Hills, CA: Sage.

Barrett, Michelle, and Mary McIntosh. 1980. "The Family Wage: Some Problems for Socialists and Feminists." Capital and Class 11:51-72.

Barron, R. D., and G. M. Norris. 1976. "Sexual Divisions and the Dual Labour Market." In Dependence and Exploitation in Work and Marriage, Diana Leonard Baker and Sheila Allen, eds., pp. 47-69. London and New York: Longman.

Baym, Nina. 1979. Women's Fiction. Ithaca, NY: Cornell University Press.

Beccalli, Bianca. 1984. "Italy." In Woman and Trade Unions in Eleven Industrialized Countries, Alice Cook, Val. R. Lorwin, and Arlene K. Daniels, eds., pp. 184-214. Philadelphia: Temple University Press.

Beller, Andrea. 1984. "Trends in Occupational Segregation by Sex and Race, 1960-1981." In Sex Segregation in the Workplace, Barbara Reskin, ed., pp. 11-26. Washington, D.C.: National Academy Press.

Benenson, Harold. 1982. "Skill Degradation, Industrial Change, and the Family and Community Bases of U.S. Working Class Response." Paper presented at the Social Science History Association, Bloomington, IN.

_____. 1984. "Women's Occupational and Family Achievement in the U.S. Class System: Dual-Career Family Analysis." British Journal of Sociology 35, no. 1 (March):19-41.

Benería, Lourdes. 1982. "Accounting for Women's Work." In Women and Development: The Sexual Division of Labor in Rural Societies, Lourdes Benería, ed., pp. 119-147. New York: Praeger.

Benería, Lourdes, and Martha Roldan. 1987. The Cross Roads of Class and Gender: Home Work, Subcontracting, and Household Dynamics in Mexico City. Chicago: University of Chicago Press.

Benson, Susan Porter. 1978. "The Clerking Sisterhood: Rationalization and the Work Culture of Saleswomen in American Department Stores, 1890-1960." Radical America 12 (March-April):41-55.

Berch, Bettina. 1982. The Endless Day: The Political Economy of Women and Work. New York: Harcourt Brace Jovanovich.

Berk, S. F. 1985. The Gender Factory: The Apportionment of Work in American Households. New York: Plenum.

Bernstein, Rachel Amelia. 1984. "Boarding-house Keepers and Brothel Keepers in New York City, 1880-1910." Ph.D. diss., Rutgers University.

Bianchi, Suzanne, and Nancy Rytina. 1984. "Occupational Change, 1970-1980." Paper presented at the Population Association of America, Minneapolis, May 4.

Blakkan, Rene. 1971. "Women Workers in America." Guardian, March 12, p. 12.

Blassingame, John. 1972. The Slave Community. New York: Oxford University Press.

Blau, Francine, and Wallace Hendricks. 1979. "Occupational Segregation by Sex: Trends and Prospects." Journal of Human Resources 14 (Spring):197-210.

Blauner, Robert. 1964. Alienation and Freedom. Chicago: University of Chicago Press.

_____. 1972. Racial Oppression in America. New York: Harper and Row.

Blewett, Mary. 1979. "The Union of Sex and Craft in the Haverhill Shoe Strike of 1895." Labor History 20:352-375.

_____. 1981. "Shared but Different: The Experience of Women Shoe Workers in the Nineteenth Century Work Force of the New England Shoe Industry." In Essays from the Lowell Conference on Industrial History, 1980 and 1981, pp. 75-85.

_____. 1983. "Work, Gender, and the Artisan Tradition in New England Shoemaking, 1780-1860." Journal of Social History 17:221-248.

Blood, Robert O., Jr., and D. M. Wolfe. 1965. Husbands and Wives: The Dynamics of Married Living. Glencoe, IL: Free Press.

Bose, Christine E. 1984. "Household Resources and U.S. Women's Work: Factors Affecting Gainful Employment at the Turn of the Century." American Sociological Review 49 (August):474-490.

Bos'n's Whistle: Official Publication of the Kaiser Shipyards. 1941-1946. (Whole issues.)

Bosworth, Louise. 1911. The Living Wage of Women Workers. New York: Longmans, Green, and Co.

Bott, Elizabeth. 1957. Family and Social Networks: Roles, Norms and External Relationships in Ordinary Urban Families. London: Tavistock.

Brandeis, Louis. 1915. "The Constitution and the Minimum Wage." Survey 33 (February 6):490-494.

Braverman, Harry. 1974. Labor and Monopoly Capital: The Degradation of Work in the Twentieth Century. New York: Monthly Review Press.

Brown, Carol. 1981. "Mothers, Fathers and Children: From Private to Public Patriarchy." In Women and Revolution: A Discussion of the Unhappy Marriage of Marxism and Feminism, Lydia Sargent, ed., pp. 239-269. Boston: South End Press.

_____. 1975. "Patriarchal Capitalism and the Female-Headed Family." Social Scientist 40-41:28-39.

Brown, Clair Vickery. 1982. "Home Production for Use in a Market Economy." In Rethinking the Family: Some Feminist Questions, Barrie Thorne with Marilyn Yalom, eds., pp. 151–167. New York: Longmans.

Brown, Jean Collier. 1938. "The Negro Woman Worker." U.S. Department of Labor, Women's Bureau Bulletin 165. Washington, D.C.: U.S. Government Printing Office.

Brown, Rome. 1917. "Oregon Minimum Wage Cases." Minnesota Law Review 1:471–486.

Brown, Scott Campbell. 1979. "Educational Attainment of Workers—Some Trends from 1973 to 1978." Washington, D.C.: Bureau of Labor Statistics. Reprinted from Monthly Labor Review (February) with supplementary tables: 54–58, A-1 to A-22.

Brozan, Nadine. 1985. "Infant-Care Leaves: Panel Urges Policy." New York Times, November 28, p. C3.

Bularzik, Mary. 1978. "Sexual Harassment at the Workplace: Historical Notes." Radical America 12 (July-August):25–43.

Burdett, Charles. 1845. Chances and Changes. New York: Baker and Scribner.

_____. 1846. Lilla Hart. New York: Baker and Scribner.

_____. 1850. The Elliot Family. New York: Baker and Scribner.

Byington, Margaret. 1974. Homestead: The Households of a Milltown. Pittsburgh: University of Pittsburgh Press.

Camarillo, Albert. 1979. Chicanos in a Changing Society. Cambridge, MA: Harvard University Press.

Campbell, D'Ann. 1984. Women at War with America: Private Lives in a Patriotic Era. Cambridge, MA: Harvard University Press.

Cannings, Kathleen, and William Lazonick. 1975. "The Development of the Nursing Labor Force in the U.S.: A Basic Analysis." International Journal of Health Sciences 5:185–216.

Caplow, Theodore. 1954. The Sociology of Work. New York: McGraw-Hill.

Carlton, Wendy. N.d. "Women Workers and Protective Discrimination: Focus on Reproductive Capacity." Unpublished MS, University of Notre Dame.

Carmichael, Stokely, and Charles V. Hamilton. 1967. Black Power: The Politics of Liberation in America. New York: Vintage.

Carothers, Suzanne, and Peggy Crull. 1984. "Contrasting Sexual Harassment in Female- and Male-Dominated Occupations." In My Troubles Are Going to Have Troubles with Me: Everyday Trials and Triumphs of Women Workers, Karen Sacks and Dorothy Remy, eds., pp. 219–228. New Brunswick, NJ: Rutgers University Press.

Carter, Michael, and Susan Boslego Carter. 1981. "Women's Recent Progress in the Professions or Women Get a Ticket to Ride After the Gravy Train Has Left the Station." Feminist Studies 7 (Fall):477–504.

Chafe, William H. 1972. The American Woman: Her Changing Social, Economic and Political Role 1920–1972. New York: Oxford University Press.

Chapin, Robert. 1909. The Standard of Living Among Workingmen's Families in New York City. Philadelphia: Charities Publication Committee of Russell Sage, William F. Fell Co.

Chaplin, David. 1978. "Domestic Service and Industrialization." Comparative Studies in Sociology 1:97–127.

Chavkin, Wendy. 1979. "Occupational Hazards to Reproduction: A Review Essay and Annotated Bibliography." Feminist Studies 5 (Summer):310–325.

_____, ed. 1984. Double Exposure: Women's Health Hazards on the Job and at Home. New York: Monthly Review Press.

Cheek, Gloria. 1958. Economic and Social Implications of Automation: A Bibliographic Review, vol. 1, Literature Before 1957. East Lansing: Labor and Industrial Relations Center, Michigan State University.

Cheng, Lucie, and Edna Bonacich. 1984. Labor Immigration Under Capitalism: Asian Immigrant Workers in the United States Before World War II. Berkeley: University of California Press.

Christensen, Kathleen E. 1985. "Women and Home-Based Work." Social Policy 15 (Winter):54-57.

Ciancanelli, Penelope. 1983. "Women's Transition to Wage Labor: A Critique of Labor Force Statistics and Re-estimation of the Labor Force Participation of Married Women from 1900 to 1930." Ph.D. diss., New School for Social Research.

Clark, Kenneth. 1965. Dark Ghetto. New York: Harper and Row.

Clark, Sue Ainslie, and Edith Wyatt. 1911. Making Both Ends Meet. New York: Macmillan.

Clive, Alan. 1979. "Women Workers in World War II: Michigan as a Test Case." Labor History 20 (Winter): 46-71.

Cockburn, Cynthia. 1984. "Trade Unions and the Radicalizing of Socialist Feminism." Feminist Review no. 16 (April):43-73.

Commerce. December 1941 – December 1946. Issued by Portland (OR) Chamber of Commerce. (Whole issues.)

Commons, John, and John Andrews. 1916. Principles of Labor Legislation. New York: Harper and Brothers.

Conk, Margo Anderson. 1978. "Occupational Classification in the United States Census: 1870-1940." Journal of Interdisciplinary History 9, no. 1 (Summer):111-130.

_____. 1981. "Accuracy, Efficiency and Bias: The Interpretation of Women's Work in the U.S. Census of Occupations, 1890–1940." Historical Methods 14 (Spring): 65–72.

Cook, Alice H., Val R. Lorwin, and Arlene K. Daniels, eds. 1984. Women and Trade Unions in Eleven Industrialized Countries. Philadelphia: Temple University Press.

Coolidge, Mary. 1909. Chinese Immigration. New York: Henry Holt.

Coser, Lewis. 1973. "Domestic Servants: The Obsolescence of a Social Role." Social Forces 52:31–40.

Counter Information Services. N.d. "The New Technology." Counter Information Report, Anti-Report no. 23. London.

Cowan, Ruth Schwartz. 1976. "The Industrial Revolution in the Home: Household Technology and Social Change in the Twentieth Century." Technology and Culture 17:1–23.

Crull, Peggy. 1980. "The Impact of Sexual Harassment on the Job: A Profile of the Experiences of 92 Women." In Sexuality in Organizations: Romantic and Coercive Behaviors at Work, Dail Neugarten and Jay Shafritz, eds., pp. 67–71. Oak Park, IL: Moore.

_____. 1982a. "Sexual Harassment and Male Control of Women's Work." Women: A Journal of Liberation 8, no. 2:3–7.

_____. 1982b. "The Stress Effects of Sexual Harassment on the Job: Implications for Counseling." American Journal of Orthopsychiatry 52, no. 3:539–544.

_____. 1984. "Sexual Harassment and Women's Health." In Double Exposure: Women's Health Hazards on the Job and at Home, Wendy Chavkin, ed., pp. 100–120. New York: Monthly Review Press.

Crull, Peggy, and Marilyn Cohen. 1984. "Expanding the Definition of Sexual Harassment." Occupational Health Nursing 32, no. 3 (March):141–145.

Cummings, Laird. 1977. "The Rationalization and Automation of Clerical Work." M.A. thesis, Brooklyn College.

Cupo, Aldo, Molly Ladd-Taylor, Beverly Lett, and David Montgomery. 1984. "Beep, Beep, Yale's Cheap: Looking at the Yale Strike." Radical America 18, no. 5: 7-19.

Dale, Jennifer, and Peggy Foster. 1986. Feminists and State Welfare. London: Routledge and Kegan Paul.

Daniels, Roger. 1973. The Politics of Prejudice. New York: Atheneum.

Davidson, Joe, and Linda M. Watkins. 1985. "Quotas in Hiring Are Anathema to President Despite Minority Gains." Wall Street Journal, October 24.

Davies, Margery. 1975. "Women's Place Is at the Typewriter: The Feminization of the Clerical Labor Force." In Labor Market Segmentation, Richard Edwards, Michael Reich, and David Gordon, eds., pp. 279-296. Lexington, MA: D.C. Heath.

Davis, Angela Y. 1971. "Reflections on the Black Woman's Place in the Community of Slaves." The Black Scholar 2 (December):3-15.

_____. 1981. Women, Race and Class. New York: Random House.

Dawley, Alan. 1976. Class and Community: The Industrial Revolution in Lynn. Cambridge, MA: Harvard University Press.

Deacon, Desley. 1985. "Political Arithmetic: The Nineteenth-Century Australian Census and the Construction of the Dependent Woman." Signs 11 (Autumn):27-47.

Degler, Carl N. 1980. At Odds: Women and the Family in America from the Revolution to the Present. New York: Oxford University Press.

De Grazia, Raffaele. 1982. "Clandestine Employment: A Problem of Our Times." In The Underground Economy in the United States and Abroad, Vito Tanzi, ed., pp. 29–44. Lexington, MA: Lexington Books/D.C. Heath.

Delatiner, Barbara. 1985. "The War Against Equal Pay for Women's Work." Working Mother, May, pp. 22–26.

Delphy, Christine. 1984. Close to Home: A Materialist Analysis of Women's Oppression, Diana Leonard, trans. Amherst: University of Massachusetts Press.

de Luna, Agnes. 1921. "How Nightwork of Women Is Menacing Maternity." American Labor Legislation Review 11:85–86.

di Leonardo, Micaela. 1985. "Women's Work, Work Culture, and Consciousness (an Introduction)." Feminist Studies 11, no. 3 (Fall):490–495.

Dill, Bonnie Thornton. 1979. "The Dialectics of Black Womanhood." Signs 4 (Spring):543–555.

————. 1983. "'On the Hem of Life': Race, Class and the Prospects for Sisterhood." In Class, Race and Sex: The Dynamics of Control, Amy Swerdlow and Hannah Lessinger, eds., pp. 173–188. New York: G. K. Hall.

"Displaced Workers: Bearing the Costs of a Changing Economy." 1985. Dollars and Sense (October):12–13.

District of Columbia Minimum Wage Cases. 1922. Supreme Court of the United States, October term #795, 796. New York: Steinberg Press.

Douglas, Ann. 1977. The Feminization of American Culture. New York: Alfred A. Knopf.

Douglas, Patricia Harriet. 1980. "Black Working Women: Factors Affecting Labor Market Experience." Working paper, Center for Research on Women, Wellesley College.

Dublin, Thomas. 1979. The Transformation of Work and Community in Lowell, Massachusetts, 1826–1860. New York: Columbia University Press.

_____. 1981. "Women and the Dimension of Outwork in Nineteenth Century New England." Paper presented at the Berkshire Conference on Women's History, Poughkeepsie, NY.

Dubnoff, Steven. 1979. "Beyond Sex Typing: Capitalism, Patriarchy and the Growth of Female Employment, 1940–1970." Paper presented at the Eastern Sociological Society meetings, New York, March.

Durand, John D. 1968. The Labor Force in the United States, 1890–1960. New York: Gordon and Breach.

_____. 1975. The Labor Force in Economic Development: A Comparison of International Census Data, 1946–66. Princeton: Princeton University Press.

Dzeich, Billie, and Linda Weiner. 1984. The Lecherous Professor: Sexual Harassment on Campus. Boston: Beacon Press.

Easton, Barbara. 1976. "Industrialization and Femininity: A Case Study of Nineteenth-Century New England." Social Problems 23 (April):389–401.

Edwards, Richard. 1979. Contested Terrain: The Transformation of the Workplace in the Twentieth Century. New York: Basic Books.

Ehrenreich, Barbara. 1984. The Hearts of Men: American Dreams and the Flight from Commitment. Garden City, NY: Anchor Books.

Ehrenreich, Barbara, and Dierdre English. 1978. For Her Own Good. Garden City, NY: Anchor/Doubleday.

Ehrenreich, Barbara, and Annette Fuentes. 1981. "Life on the Global Assembly Line." Ms, January, pp. 53–59, 71.

_____. 1983. Women in the Global Factory. Boston: South End Press.

Eisenstein, Sarah. 1983. Give Us Bread but Give Us Roses: Working Women's Consciousness in the United

States, 1880 to the First World War. London and
Boston: Routledge and Kegan Paul.

Eisenstein, Zillah. 1982. "Sexual Politics of the New
Right: Understanding the 'Crisis of Liberalism' for
the 1980s." Signs 7 (Spring):567–588.

Ellis, Judy. 1981. "Sexual Harassment and Race: A
Legal Analysis of Discrimination." Journal of Legislation 8, no. 1:30–45.

Ellis, W. 1923. Records and Briefs of the Supreme Court.
Adkins v. Children's Hospital, 261, U.S. 525.

Elasser, Nan, Kyle MacKenzie, and Yvonne Tixier y Vigil.
1980. Las Mujeres: Conversations from a Hispanic
Community. Old Westbury, NY: Feminist Press.

Elson, Diane, and Ruth Pearson. 1980. "The Latest
Phase of the Internationalization of Capital and Its
Implications for Women in the Third World." Institute
for Developmental Studies, Sussex, England.

———. 1981. "Nimble Fingers Make Cheaper Workers:
An Analysis of Women's Employment in Third World
Manufacturing." Feminist Review 7:93–95.

Equal Rights. 1923. Vol. 1. Whole issues dated February 24 and April 21.

Erie, Steve, and Harold Brackman. N.d. "Wedded to the
Welfare State: Women Against Reaganite Retrenchment."
Unpublished MS, University of California, San Diego.

Evanoff, Ruthann. 1979. "Reproductive Rights and Occupational Health." WIN Magazine (Fall):9–13.

Farley, Lin. 1978. Sexual Shakedown: The Sexual
Harassment of Women on the Job. New York: McGraw-
Hill.

Faunce, William, Einar Hardin, and Eugene H. Jacobson.
1962. "Automation and the Employee." Annals of the
American Academy of Political and Social Science 340:
60–68.

Feldberg, Roslyn L. 1980. "Union Fever: Organizing Among Clerical Workers, 1900–1930." Radical America 14, no. 3 (May–June):53–67.

Feldberg, Roslyn, and Evelyn Nakano Glenn. 1979a. "Technology and Transformation of Clerical Work." Paper presented at the Social Science History Association conference, Cambridge, MA.

_____. 1979b. "Male and Female: Job vs. Gender Models in the Sociology of Work." Social Problems 26: 524–538.

_____. 1980. "Effects of Technological Change on Clerical Work: Review and Reassessment." Paper presented at American Sociological Association meetings, New York, August 28.

Ferree, Myra. 1983. "Housework: Rethinking the Costs and the Benefits." In Families, Politics and Public Policy, Irene Diamond, ed., pp. 148–167. New York: Longman.

_____. 1984. "The View from Below: Women's Employment and Gender Equality in Working Class Families." In Women and the Family: Two Decades of Change, Beth B. Hess and Marvin B. Sussman, eds., ch. 4. Binghamton, NY: Haworth Press.

Fields, Cheryl M. 1981a. "Reagan Administration to Re-examine Federal Affirmative-Action Regulations." Chronicles of Higher Education April 6, p. 1.

_____. 1981b. "Administration Moves to Ease Federal Anti-Bias Regulations." Chronicles of Higher Education, September 2, p. 1.

Filene, Peter. 1975. Him/Herself: Sex Roles in Modern America. New York: Harcourt Brace Jovanovitch.

Fisher, Anne B. 1985. "Businessmen Like to Hire by the Numbers." Fortune, September 16, pp. 26–30.

Fisher, Lloyd. 1953. The Harvest Labor Market in California. Cambridge, MA: Harvard University Press.

Flint, Jerry. 1977. "Growing Part-Time Work Force Has Major Impact on Economy." New York Times, April 12, pp. 1, 56.

Fogel, William, and Stanley Engerman. 1974. Time on the Cross. Boston: Little, Brown and Co.

Folbre, Nancy. 1986. "The Pauperization of Motherhood: Patriarchy and Public Policy in the United States." Review of Radical Political Economics 18:72–88.

Foner, Philip. 1979–1980. Women and the American Labor Movement, Vols. 1 and 2. New York and London: Free Press.

Foner, Philip S., and Ronald L. Lewis. 1981. The Black Worker: A Documentary History from Colonial Times to the Present, vol. 6 The Era of Post-War Prosperity and the Great Depression, 1920–1936. Philadelphia: Temple University Press.

Foster, John. 1974. Class Struggle and the Industrial Revolution: Early Industrial Capitalism in Three English Towns. New York: St. Martin's Press.

Fowler, Elizabeth M. 1980. "Careers: Temporary Help Being Used More." New York Times, September 24, p. D19.

Fox, Mary Frank, and Sharlene Hess-Biber. 1984. Women at Work. Palo Alto, CA: Mayfield.

Frazier, E. Franklin. 1939. The Negro Family in the United States. Chicago: University of Chicago Press.

Fulton, C. W. 1916. Brief for plaintiff in error, Records and Briefs of the Supreme Court. Stettler v. O'Hara, October term 1916–1917, Docket #25, #26, U.S. Supreme Court.

Gabin, Nancy. 1982. "They Have Placed a Penalty on Womanhood: The Protest Actions of Women Auto Workers in Detroit Area UAW Locals, 1945–47." Feminist Studies 8, no. 2 (Summer):373–398.

_____. 1985. "Women and the United Automobile Workers' Union in the 1950s." In Women, Work and Protest: A Century of U.S. Women's Labor History, Ruth Milkman, ed., pp. 259–279. Boston: Routledge and Kegan Paul.

Garcia, Mario T. 1980. "The Chicana in American History: The Mexican Women of El Paso, 1880–1920—A Case Study." Pacific Historical Review 49:315–337.

_____. 1981. Desert Immigrants: The Mexicans of El Paso, 1880–1920. New Haven: Yale University Press.

Genovese, Eugene. 1974. Roll, Jordan, Roll. New York: Pantheon.

Geron, Lynn. 1986. "Columbia: A Taste of Union Power." Against the Current 1 (March–April):7–8.

Gilkes, Cheryl Townsend. 1982. "Successful Rebellious Professionals: The Black Woman's Professional Identity and Community Commitment." Psychology of Women Quarterly 6:289–311.

Glassberg, Elyse, Naomi Baden, and Karin Gerstel. 1983. "Absent from the Agenda: A Report on the Role of Women in American Unions." Washington, D.C.: Coalition of Labor Union Women. Mimeo.

Glenn, Evelyn Nakano. 1983. "Split Household, Small Producer and Dual Wage Earner: An Analysis of Chinese American Family Strategies." Journal of Marriage and the Family 45:35–46.

Glenn, Evelyn Nakano, and Roslyn L. Feldberg. 1977. "Degraded and Deskilled: The Proletarianization of Clerical Work." Social Problems 25:52–64.

_____. 1979. "Women as Mediators in the Labor Process." Paper presented at the American Sociological Association annual meetings, Boston, August 29.

_____. 1984. "Clerical Work: The Female Occupation." In Women: A Feminist Perspective, Jo Freeman, ed., pp. 316–336. Palo Alto, CA: Mayfield.

Glenn, Evelyn Nakano, and Charles M. Tolbert 11. 1987. "Technology and Emerging Patterns of Stratification for Women of Color: Race and Gender Segregation of Computer Occupations." In Transformations: Women, Work, and Technology, Barbara D. Wright et al., eds. Ann Arbor: University of Michigan Press.

Gluck, Sherna Berger. 1982. "Interlude or Change: Women and the World War 11 Work Experience, A Feminist Oral History." International Journal of Oral History 3(2): 92–113.

Goffman, Erving. 1961. Asylums. Garden City, NY: Doubleday/Anchor.

Goldberg, Roberta. 1983. Organizing Women Office Workers: Dissatisfaction, Consciousness, and Action. New York: Praeger.

Goldfarb, Lynn. N.d. Separated but Unequal: Discrimination Against Women Workers After World War 11. Washington, D.C.: Union for Radical Political Economics.

Goldman, Marion. 1981. Goldiggers and Silverminers. Ann Arbor: University of Michigan Press.

Gompers, Samuel. 1914. American Federationist 21 (July): 544.

Greeley, Horace, et al. 1873. Great Industries of the United States. Hartford, CT: J. B. Burr and Hyde and Company.

Greenbaum, Joan M. 1979. In the Name of Efficiency: Management Theory and Shopfloor Practice in Data-Processing Work. Philadelphia: Temple University Press.

Grimes, Barbara. 1925. "Constitutional Law: Police Power: Minimum Wage for Women." In The Supreme Court and Minimum Wage Legislation, National Consumers' League, ed. New York: New Republic.

Groat, George. 1911. Attitude of American Courts in Labor Cases. New York: Columbia University Press; reprinted New York: AMS Press, 1969.

_____. 1925. "Economic Wage and Legal Wage." In The Supreme Court and Minimum Wage Legislation, National Consumers' League, ed. New York: New Republic.

Groneman, Carol. 1977. "'She Earns as a Child, She Pays as a Man': Women Workers in a Mid-nineteenth Century New York Community." In Class, Sex, and the Woman Worker, Milton Cantor and Bruce Laurie, eds., pp. 83–100. Westport, CT: Greenwood Press.

Gross, Edward. 1971. "Plus Ca Change . . .? The Sexual Structure of Occupations over Time." In The Professional Woman, Athena Theodore, ed., pp. 39–51. Cambridge, MA: Schenkman.

Grossman, Rachel. 1979. "Women's Place in the Integrated Circuit." Southeast Asia Chronicle no. 66 (January-February). Joint issue with Pacific Research 9 (July-October 1978).

Gruber, James, and Lars Bjorn. 1982. "Blue Collar Blues: The Sexual Harassment of Women Autoworkers." Work and Occupations 9, no. 3:271–298.

Gutek, Barbara. 1985. Sex and the Workplace. San Francisco: Jossey-Bass.

Gutek, Barbara, and Bruce Morasch. 1982. "Sex-Ratios, Sex-Role Spillover, and Sexual Harassment of Women at Work." Journal of Social Issues 38, no. 4:55–74.

Gutman, Herbert G. 1975. "Persistent Myths About the Afro-American Family." Journal of Interdisciplinary History 6 (Autumn):181–210.

_____. 1976. The Black Family in Slavery and Freedom. New York: Pantheon.

Hacker, Sally. 1979. "Sex Stratification, Technology and Organizational Change: AT&T." Social Problems 26 (June):539–557.

Hall, Richard H. 1975. Occupations and the Social Struc-
    ture. Second edition. Englewood Cliffs, NJ:
    Prentice-Hall.

Hardin, Einar, William Eddy, and Steven Deutsch. 1961.
    Economic and Social Implications of Automation: An
    Annotated Bibliography, vol. 2, Literature 1957-1960.
    East Lansing: Labor and Industrial Relations Cen-
    ter, Michigan State University.

Harding, S. 1981. "Family Reform Movements: Recent
    Feminism and Its Opposition." Feminist Studies 7,
    no. 1:57-76.

Hareven, Tamara. 1977. "Family Time and Industrial
    Time: Family and Work in a Planned Corporation
    Town, 1900-1924." In Family and Kin in Urban
    Communities: 1700-1920, Tamara Hareven, ed., pp.
    187-207. New York: New Viewpoints.

Harper, Ida Usted. 1969. The Life and Work of Susan B.
    Anthony. New York: Arno Press. (First published
    in 1898.)

Harris, M. 1985. "The Three Career Life." Money, May,
    pp. 108-110.

Hartmann, Heidi. 1976. "Capitalism, Patriarchy and Job
    Segregation by Sex." Signs 1 (Spring):137-169.

_____. 1981a. "The Family as the Locus of Gender,
    Class, and Political Struggle: The Example of
    Housework." Signs 6, no. 5:366-394.

_____. 1981b. "The Unhappy Marriage of Marxism and
    Feminism: Towards a More Progressive Union." In
    Women and Revolution: A Discussion of the Unhappy
    Marriage of Marxism and Feminism, Lydia Sargent,
    ed., pp. 1-41. Boston: South End Press.

Hartmann, Susan. 1982. The Home Front and Beyond:
    American Women in the 1940's. Boston: Twayne.

Hawthorne, Nathaniel. 1851. The Scarlet Letter. Reprinted
    in the Centenary Edition of the Works of Nathaniel

Hawthorne. Columbus: Ohio State University Press, 1964.

Hayler, Barbara. 1980. Testimony before the House Judiciary 11 Committee, State of Illinois, unpublished mimeo.

Hayner, Rutherford. 1925. Troy and Rensselaer County, New York. New York: Lewis Historical Publishing Company.

Hechinger, Fred. 1980. "Affirmative Action Appears Headed for Hard Times." New York Times, December 15, p. 37.

Helfgott, Roy B. 1966. "EDP and the Office Work Force." Industrial and Labor Relations Review 19:503–516.

Herbers, John. 1983. "Census Shows Gains in Jobs by Women and Blacks in 70's." New York Times, April 24, pp. 1, 38.

Hewlett, S. 1986. A Lesser Life: The Myth of Women's Liberation in America. New York: Morrow.

Higginbotham, Elizabeth. 1983. "Laid Bare by the System: Work and Survival for Black and Hispanic Women." In Class, Race and Sex: The Dynamics of Control, Amy Swerdlow and Hannah Lessinger, eds. New York: G. K. Hall.

_____. 1987. "Employment for Professional Black Women in the 20th Century." In Ingredients for Women's Employment Policy, Christine Bose and Glenna Spitze, eds., pp. 73–91. Albany, NY: SUNY Press.

Hiller, Dana. 1980. "Determinants of Household and Childcare Task Sharing." Paper presented at American Sociological Association meeting, New York, August 31.

Hirata, Lucie Cheng. 1979. "Free, Indentured and Enslaved: Chinese Prostitutes in Nineteenth Century America." Signs 5 (Autumn):3–29.

Hochschild, Arlie. 1983. The Managed Heart. Berkeley: University of California Press.

Holcombe, A. N. 1912. "The Legal Minimum Wage in the United States," American Economic Review 2:21-37.

"Home Knitters' Victory Reported." 1981. New York Times, June 20, p. 9.

Honey, Maureen. 1984. Creating Rosie the Riveter: Class, Gender and Propaganda During World War 11. Amherst: University of Massachusetts Press.

Hood, J. 1983. Becoming a Two Job Family. New York: Praeger.

Hooks, Bell. 1981. Ain't 1 a Woman: Black Women and Feminism. Boston: South End Press.

Hoos, Ida R. 1961. Automation in the Office. Washington, D.C.: Public Affairs Press.

Huber, Bettina. 1981. "Gutting Affirmative Action—New Policy in Action." American Sociological Association, FOOTNOTES 9 (December):1, 3.

Huber, Joan, and Glenna Spitze. 1981. "Wives' Employment, Household Behaviors, and Sex Role Attitudes." Social Forces 60:151-169.

Hughes, Gwendolyn. 1925. Mothers in Industry. New York: New Republic.

Humphreys, Nancy K. 1985. The Underground Economy: An Annotated Bibliography. New York: CompuBibs.

Humphries, Jane. 1977. "Class Struggle and the Persistence of the Working Class Family." Cambridge Journal of Economics 1 (September):241-258.

Ichihashi, Yamato. 1915. Japanese Immigration. San Francisco: Marshall Press.

_____. 1932. Japanese in the United States. Stanford, CA: Stanford University Press.

Ikels, Charlotte, and Julia Shang. 1979. The Chinese in Greater Boston. Bethesda, MD: National Institute of Aging.

Jaffee, A. J. 1956. "Trends in the Participation of Women in the Working Force." Monthly Labor Review 79 (May):559–567.

Jaffee, A. J., and Joseph Froomkin. 1978. "Occupational Opportunities for College-Educated Workers, 1950–1975." Monthly Labor Review 101 (June):15–21.

Janiewski, Dolores. 1983. "Flawed Victories: The Experience of Black and White Women Workers in Durham During the 1930s." In Decades of Dissent, Joan M. Jensen and Lois Scharf, eds., pp. 85–109. Westport, CT: Greenwood Press.

Jensen, Joan M. 1980. "Cloth, Butter and Boarders: Women's Household Production for the Market." Review of Political Economics 12 (Summer):14–24.

_____. 1981. With These Hands: Women Working on the Land. Old Westbury, NY: Feminist Press.

Johnson, Julia. 1925. Selected Articles on Marriage and Divorce. New York: H. W. Wilson.

Johnson, Robert, and Laura Johnson. 1984. "The Fall and Rise of Industrial Homework: A Historical Perspective on a Contemporary Dilemma, 1910–1980." Paper presented at the Sixth Berkshire Conference on the History of Women, Smith College, June 1.

Jones, Jacqueline. 1984. Labor of Love, Labor of Sorrow: Black Women, Work and the Family from Slavery to the Present. New York: Basic Books.

Kaestle, Carl F., and Maris A. Vinovskis. 1978. "From Fireside to Factory: School Entry and School Leaving in Nineteenth Century Massachusetts." In Transitions: The Family and the Life Course in Historical Perspective, Tamara Hareven, ed, pp. 135–186. New York: Academic Press.

Kanter, Rosabeth. 1977. Men and Women of the Corporation. New York: Basic Books.

Kasarda, John D. 1974. "Structural Implications of Social System Size: A Three Level Analysis." American Sociological Review 39:19–28.

Katzman, David H. 1978. Seven Days a Week: Women and Domestic Service in Industrializing America. New York: Oxford University Press.

Kelley, Florence. 1912. "Minimum Wage Laws." Journal of Political Economy 20, no. 10 (December):999–1010.

Kelley, Mary. 1979. "The Sentimentalists: Promise and Betrayal in the Home." Signs 4 (Spring):434–436.

_____. 1984. Private Woman, Public Stage: Literary Domesticity in Nineteenth Century America. New York: Oxford University Press.

Kelly, Joan. 1979. "The Doubled Vision of Feminist Theory: A Postscript to the 'Women and Power' Conference." Feminist Studies 5 (Spring):216–227.

Kenneally, James J. 1973. "Women and Trade Unions, 1870–1920: The Quandary of the Reformer." Labor History 14, no. 1 (Winter):42–55.

Kennedy, Susan Estabrook. 1979. If All We Did Was to Weep at Home: A History of White Working Class Women in America. Bloomington: Indiana University Press.

Kesselman, Amy. 1985. "Women Shipyard Workers in Portland and Vancouver During World War II and Reconversion." Ph.D. diss., Cornell University.

Kessler-Harris, Alice. 1975a. "Stratifying by Sex: Understanding the History of Working Women." In Labor Market Segmentation, Richard C. Edwards, Michael Reich, and David M. Gordon, eds., pp. 217–242. Lexington, MA: D.C. Heath.

————. 1975b. "Where Are the Organized Women Workers?" *Feminist Studies* no. 3 (Fall):92–110.

————. 1979. "Where Are the Organized Women Workers." In *A Heritage of Her Own: Toward a New Social History of American Women*, Nancy F. Cott and Elizabeth H. Pleck, eds., pp. 343–366. New York: Simon and Schuster.

————. 1981. *Women Have Always Worked: A Historical Overview*. Old Westbury, NY: Feminist Press.

————. 1982. *Out to Work: A History of Wage-Earning Women in the United States*. New York: Oxford University Press.

————. 1985a. "The Debate over Equality for Women in the Work Place." In *Women and Work: An Annual Review*, vol. 1, Laurie Larwood, Ann Stromberg, and Barbara A. Gutek, eds., pp. 141–161. Beverly Hills, CA: Sage.

————. 1985b. "Problems of Coalition-Building: Women and Trade Unions in the 1920's." In *Women, Work and Protest. A Century of U.S. Women's Labor History*, Ruth Milkman, ed., pp. 110–138. Boston: Routledge and Kegan Paul.

Kim, Elaine. 1983. *With Silk Wings: Asian American Women at Work*. San Francisco: Asian Women United of California.

Kingsbury, Susan. 1920. "Relation of Women to Industry." *American Sociological Society, Proceedings* 15:141–58.

Kingston, Maxine Hong. 1977. *The Woman Warrior*. New York: Vintage.

Kitano, Harry H. L. 1960. "Housing of Japanese Americans in the San Francisco Bay Area." In *Studies in Housing and Minority Groups*, Nathan Glazer and David McEntire, eds., pp. 178–197. Berkeley and Los Angeles: University of California Press.

Kraft, Philip. 1977. Programmers and Managers: The Routinization of Computer Programming in the United States. New York: Springer-Verlag.

Ladd-Taylor, Molly. 1985. "Women Workers and the Yale Strike." Feminist Studies 11, no. 3 (Fall):465-489.

Lamphere, Louise. 1984. "On the Shop Floor: Multi-Ethnic Unity Against the Conglomerate." In My Troubles Are Going to Have Trouble with Me: Everyday Trials and Triumphs of Women Workers, Karen Sacks and Dorothy Remy, eds., pp. 247-263. New Brunswick, NJ: Rutgers University Press.

_____. 1985. "Bringing the Family to Work: Women's Culture on the Shop Floor." Feminist Studies 11, no. 3 (Fall):519-540.

Langer, Elinor. 1972. "Inside the New York Telephone Company." In Women at Work, William O'Neill, ed., pp. 305-360. New York: Quadrangle Press.

Lee, L. P., A. Lim, and H. K. Wong. 1969. Report of the San Francisco Chinese Community Citizens' Survey and Fact Finding Committee. Abridged edition. San Francisco: Chinese Community Citizens' Survey and Fact Finding Committee.

Lein, L. 1983. Families Without Villains. Lexington, MA: Lexington Books.

Leon, Carl, and Robert W. Bednarzik. 1978. "A Profile of Women on Part-Time Schedules." Washington, D.C.: Bureau of Labor Statistics. Reprinted from Monthly Labor Review, October, pp. 3-12.

Lerner, Gerda. 1969. "The Lady and the Mill Girl: Changes in the Status of Women in the Age of Jackson." American Studies 10 (Spring):5-14.

_____. 1973. Black Women in White America: A Documentary History. New York: Vintage.

Li, Peter S. 1977. "Fictive Kinship, Conjugal Ties and Kinship Claim Among Chinese Immigrants in the United

States." Journal of Comparative Family Studies 8, no. 1:47-64.

Light, Ivan H. 1972. Ethnic Enterprise in America. Berkeley and Los Angeles: University of California Press.

Ling, Pyan. 1912. "The Causes of Chinese Immigration." Annals of the American Academy of Political and Social Science 39 (January):74-82.

Lipsett v. University of Puerto Rico. 1983. 576 F. Supp. 1217, 1223 (D.P.R. 1983).

Long, Clarence. 1958. The Labor Force Under Changing Income and Employment, 1890 to 1950. New York: National Bureau of Economic Research.

Luker, Kristin. 1984. Abortion and the Politics of Motherhood. Berkeley: University of California Press.

Lyman, Stanford. 1968. "Marriage and Family Among Chinese Immigrants to America, 1850-1960." Phylon 29, no. 4:321-330.

_____. 1974. Chinese Americans. New York: Random House.

_____. 1977. The Asian in North America. Santa Barbara, CA: ABC Clio.

MacKinnon, Catherine. 1979. Sexual Harassment of Working Women. New Haven: Yale University Press.

_____. 1982. "Violence Against Women--A Perspective." Aegis (Winter):51-56.

Maeroff, Gene. 1980. "Shortages of Teachers Develop in Time of Layoffs." New York Times, September 29, pp. A1, A11.

Magarrell, Jack. 1983. "Job Market for College Graduates Called 'Bleak' for Rest of 1980's." Chronicle of Higher Education 26, no. 16 (June 15):1, 12.

Malveaux, Julianne. 1981. "Shifts in the Occupational and Employment Status of Black Women: Current Trends and Future Implications." In Black Working Women. Proceedings of a Conference on Black Working Women in the U.S., University of California, Berkeley: Center for the Study, Education, and Advancement of Women.

_____. 1984. "The Status of Women of Color in the Economy: The Legacy of Being Other." Paper presented at the National Conference on Women, the Economy and Public Policy, San Francisco, June.

_____. 1985. "The Economic Interests of Black and White Women: Are They Similar?" Review of Black Political Economy 14 (Summer):5-28.

Mann, Floyd C., and Larry K. Williams. 1960. "Observations of the Dynamics of a Change to Electronic Data Processing Equipment." Administrative Science Quarterly 5:217-256.

Marable, Manning. 1986. "Who's Behind 'Color Blind' Double Talk?" Guardian, March 26, p. 2.

Martin, Susan. 1978. "Sexual Politics in the Workplace: The Interactional World of Police Women." Symbolic Interaction 1, no. 2:44-60.

Marx, Karl. 1915. Capital. Chicago: Kerr and Co.

Marx, Leo. 1964. The Machine in the Garden. New York: Oxford University Press.

Massey, Douglas S. 1982. The Demographic and Economic Position of Hispanics in the United States: 1980. Philadelphia: Population Studies Center, University of Pennsylvania.

Matthaei, Julie. 1982. An Economic History of Women in America: Women's Work, the Sexual Division of Labor, and the Development of Capitalism. New York: Schocken Books.

Maxwell, Maria. 1855. Ernest Grey, or The Sins of Society: A Story of New York Life. New York: I. W. Strong.

May, Martha. 1982. "The Historical Problem of the Family Wage: The Ford Motor Company and the Five Dollar Day." Feminist Studies 8:400–408.

McLemore, Dale. 1973. "The Origins of Mexican American Subordination in Texas." Social Science Quarterly 53 (March):656–670.

_____. 1980. Racial and Ethnic Relationship America. Boston: Allyn and Bacon.

McWilliams, Carey. 1971. Factories in the Field. Santa Barbara, CA: Peregrine.

Melosh, Barbara. 1982. "The Physician's Hand": Work Culture and Conflict in American Nursing. Philadelphia: Temple University Press.

Melville, Herman. 1855. "The Paradise of Bachelors and the Tartarus of Maids." In The Works of Herman Melville, Raymond Weaver, ed., vol. 13. New York: Russell and Russell, 1963.

Melville, Margarita B., ed. 1980. Twice a Minority: Mexican American Women. St. Louis: C. V. Mosby.

Meritor Savings Bank v. Vinson. 1986. Supreme Court of the United States, no. 84–1979.

Meyerowitz, Ruth. 1980. "Women Unionists and World War II: New Opportunities for Leadership." Paper presented at the Organization of American Historians annual conference, San Francisco, April.

_____. 1983. "Organizing and Building the UAW: Women at the Ternstedt General Motors Parts Plant, 1936–1950." Ph.D. diss., Columbia University.

_____. 1985. "Organizing the United Automobile Workers: Women Workers at the Ternstedt General Motors Parts Plant." In Women, Work and Protest: A Century of

U.S. Women's Labor History, Ruth Milkman, ed., pp. 235-257. Boston: Routledge and Kegan Paul.

Michelson, W. 1985. From Sun to Sun: Daily Obligations and Community Structure in the Lives of Employed Women and Their Families. Totowa, NJ: Rowman and Allenheld.

Milkman, Ruth. 1976. "Women's Work and the Economic Crisis: Some Lessons from the Great Depression." Review of Radical Political Economics 8, no. 1 (Spring): 73-97.

_____. 1980. "Organizing the Sexual Division of Labor: Historical Perspectives on 'Women's Work' and the American Labor Movement." Socialist Review no. 10 (January-February):95-150.

_____. 1983. "Female Factory Labor and Industrial Structure: Control and Conflict over 'Woman's Place' in Auto and Electrical Manufacturing." Politics and Society 12, no. 2:159-203.

_____. 1985. "Women Workers, Feminism and the Labor Movement Since the 1960s." In Women, Work and Protest: A Century of U.S. Women's Labor History, Ruth Milkman, ed., pp. 300-322. Boston: Routledge and Kegan Paul.

Millis, H. A. 1915. The Japanese Problem in the United States. New York: Macmillan.

Mills, C. Wright. 1956. White Collar. New York: Oxford University Press.

Mirande, Alfredo, and Evangelina Enriquez. 1979. La Chicana: The Mexican American Woman. Chicago: University of Chicago Press.

Miyamoto, Shotaro Frank. 1939. "Social Solidarity Among the Japanese in Seattle." University of Washington Publications in the Social Sciences 11:57-130.

Molefsky, Barry. 1982. "America's Underground Economy." In The Underground Economy in the United States and

Abroad, Vito Tanzi, ed., pp. 47–67. Lexington, MA: Lexington Books/D. C. Heath.

Montagna, Paul. 1977. Occupations and Society: Toward A Sociology of the Labor Market. New York: John Wiley and Sons.

Montgomery, David. 1967. Beyond Equality: Labor and the Radical Republicans, 1862–1872. New York: Vintage Books.

Monthly Labor Review. 1984. "Unemployment Data." 107 (April).

Moore, Joan W. 1970. "Colonialism: The Case of Mexican Americans." Social Problems 17 (Spring):463–472.

Mora, Magdalena, and Adelaida R. Del Castillo, eds. 1980. Mexican Women in the United States: Struggles Past and Present. Los Angeles: Chicano Studies Publications.

More, Louise. 1907. Wage Earners' Budgets: A Study of Standards and Cost of Living in New York City. New York: Holt & Co.

Moroney, Heather, Jon. 1983. "Feminism at Work." New Left Review 141 (September–October):51–71.

Moynihan, Daniel Patrick. 1965. The Negro Family: The Case for National Action. Washington, D.C.: U.S. Government Printing Office.

Nakane, Chie. 1967. Kinship and Economic Organization in Rural Japan. London: Athlone.

Nardone, Thomas. 1980. "The Job Outlook in Brief." Occupational Outlook Quarterly (Spring):2–21.

Nash, June, and Maria Patricia Fernandez Kelly. 1983. Women, Men, and the International Division of Labor. Albany, NY: SUNY Press.

National Women's Party. Pamphlet on Minimum Wage, Vassar College Library. n.d.

Nearing, Scott. 1915. "The Adequacy of American Wages." Annals of the American Academy of Political and Social Science 59:111–124.

Nee, Victor, and Brett deBary Nee. 1972. Long Time Californ'. New York: Pantheon.

Neugarten, Dail, and Jay Shafritz, eds. 1980. Sexuality in Organizations. Oak Park, IL: Moore.

"New Congress, Administration, May Threaten Title IX, WEEA." 1981. Peer Perspective 7 (February):1, 5.

New York Bureau of Labor Statistics. 1887. Fourth Annual Report of the Year 1886. Albany, New York.

New York Factory Investigating Commission. 1912. Preliminary Report, vol. 3. Albany, NY: Argus Co. Printers.

New York, Secretary of State. N.d. State Census Records of Rensselaer County, 1855–1906, Troy, New York. Albany, NY: New York State Library. Records, County Court House, Troy, New York.

Noble, David F. 1977. America by Design: Science, Technology and the Rise of Corporate Capitalism. New York: Alfred A. Knopf.

Norwood, Janet L. 1982. "The Female-Male Earnings Gap." Report 673. U.S. Department of Labor, Bureau of Labor Statistics. Washington, D.C.: U.S. Government Printing Office.

Norwood, Janet L., and Elizabeth Waldman. 1979. "Women in the Labor Force: Some New Data Series." Report 575. U.S. Department of Labor, Bureau of Labor Statistics. Washington, D.C.: U.S. Government Printing Office.

Odencrantz, Louise. 1919. Italian Women in Industry. New York: Russell Sage Foundation.

Omvedt, Gail. 1986. "'Patriarchy': The Analysis of Women's Oppression." Insurgent Sociologist 13, no. 3 (Spring):30–50.

Oppenheimer, Valerie Kinkaide. 1970. The Female Labor Force in the United States. Berkeley: Institute for International Studies, University of California.

Oregonian. January 1942–December 1946.

Ostrander, Susan A. 1984. Women of the Upper Class. Philadelphia: Temple University Press.

Pachon, Harry P., and Joan W. Moore. 1981. "Mexican Americans." Annals of the American Academy of Political and Social Science 454:111–124.

Painter, Nell Irvin. 1976. Exodusters: Black Migration to Kansas After the Reconstruction. New York: Norton.

Palmer, Phyllis Marynick. 1983. "White Women/Black Women: The Dualism of Female Identity and Experience in the United States." Feminist Studies 9 (Spring): 151–170.

Parton, Sarah. 1855. Ruth Hall: A Domestic Tale of the Present Time, by Fanny Fern (pseud). New York: Mason Brothers.

Patterson, Michelle, and Laurie Engelberg. 1978. "Women in Male-Dominated Professions." In Women Working, Ann Stromberg and Shirley Harkness, eds., pp. 266–292. Palo Alto, CA: Mayfield.

Pear, Robert. 1983a. "Study Says Affirmative Rule Expands Hiring of Minorities." New York Times, June 19, p. 16.

_____. 1983b. "G.M. Agrees to Pay $42 Million to End Case on Job Bias." New York Times, October 18, pp. A1, A21.

_____. 1985a. "Justice Department Presses Drive on Quotas." New York Times, April 3, p. A6.

_____. 1985b. "Civil Rights Agency Splits in Debate on Narrowing Definition of Equality." New York Times, October 14, p. A17.

Pearce, Diana, and Harriet McAdoo. 1981. Women and Children: Alone and in Poverty. Washington, D.C.: National Advisory Council on Economic Opportunity.

Penny, Virginia. 1863. The Employments of Women. Boston: Walker, Wiese and Company.

Pesotta, Rose. 1944. Bread upon the Waters. New York: Dodd, Mead.

Petchesky, Rosalind Pollack. 1985. Abortion and Woman's Choice: The State, Sexuality, and Reproductive Freedom. Boston: Northeastern University Press.

Peterson, Iver. 1982. "For the Part-Time Worker, Slim Hope, No Choice." New York Times, April 3, p. 20.

Phillips, Anne, and Barbara Taylor. 1980. "Sex and Skill: Notes Towards a Feminist Economics." Feminist Review 6:79–88.

Piore, Michael J. 1975. "Notes for a Theory of Labor Market Stratification." In Labor Market Segmentation, Richard C. Edwards, Michael Reich, and David M. Gordon, eds., pp. 125–150. Lexington, MA: D. C. Heath.

Piva, Paola, and Chiara Ingrao. 1984. "Women's Subjectivity, Union Power and the Problem of Work." In "Trade Unions and the Radicalizing of Socialist Feminism," Cynthia Cockburn, ed. Feminist Review no. 16 (April):51–55.

Piven, Francis Fox, and Richard A. Cloward. 1971. Regulating the Poor: The Functions of Public Welfare. New York: Pantheon.

Pleck, Elizabeth H. 1979. "A Mother's Wages: Income Earning Among Married Italian and Black Women, 1896–1911." In A Heritage of Her Own: Toward a New Social History of American Women, Nancy F. Cott and Elizabeth H. Pleck, eds., pp. 367–392. New York: Simon and Schuster.

Pleck, J. 1985. Working Wives/Working Husbands. Beverly Hills, CA: Sage.

Pollack, Andrew. 1981. "Rising Trend of Computer Age: Employees Who Work at Home." New York Times, March 12, pp. A1, D6.

Powell, Thomas. 1917. "The Constitutional Issue in Minimum Wage Legislation." Minnesota Law Review 2, no. 1 December.

Power, Marilyn. 1984. "Falling Through the 'Safety Net': Wom Economic Crisis, and Reaganomics." Feminist Studies 10, no. 1 (Spring):31–58.

Progress Reports of the Postwar Readjustment and Development Commission. 1943–1949. City of Portland, Ore.

"Race Against Time: Automation of the Office." 1980. Working Women. Cleveland: National Association of Office Workers.

Rapp, Rayna. 1982. "Family and Class in Contemporary America: Notes Toward an Understanding of Ideology." In Rethinking the Family: Some Feminist Questions, Barrie Thorne with Marilyn Yalom, eds., pp. 168–187. New York: Longman.

Reinhold, Robert. 1980. "Government Takes Steps to Avert Glut of Doctors." New York Times, September 2, pp. C1, C2.

Reskin, Barbara, and Heidi Hartmann. 1986. Women's Work, Men's Work: Sex Segregation on the Job. Washington, D.C.: National Academy Press.

Reskin, Barbara, and Patricia Roos. 1987. "Women's Gains in Male-Dominated Occupations: Real or Illusory." In Ingredients for Women's Employment Policy, Christine Bose and Glenna Spitze, eds., pp. 3–21. Albany, NY: SUNY Press.

Rico, Leonard. 1967. "The Advance Against Paperwork." Ann Arbor: Graduate School of Business Administration Series, University of Michigan Press.

Rinehart, James. 1978. "Job Enrichment and the Labor Process." Paper presented to New Directions in the

Labor Process conference, sponsored by the Department of Sociology, SUNY, Binghamton, NY, May.

Roby, Pamela. 1987. "Women and Unions: The Experience of Rank-and-File Leadership." In Ingredients for Women's Employment Policy, Christine Bose and Glenna Spitze, eds., pp. 139–155. Albany, NY: SUNY Press.

Rodgers-Rose, La Frances, ed. 1980. The Black Woman. Beverly Hills, CA: Sage.

Rosenbaum, David E. 1979. "Jobs: The Skills, Then the Place." New York Times, National Recruitment Survey (sec. 12), October 14, pp. 1, 8.

Rothberg, Herman J. 1969. "A Study of the Impact of Office Automation in the IRS." Monthly Labor Review 92:26–30.

Rothschild, Emma. 1981. "Reagan and the Real America." New York Review, February 5, pp. 12–18.

Rotman-Zelizer, Vivian A. 1985. Pricing the Priceless Child. New York: Basic Books.

Rumberger, Russell. 1981. "The Changing Skill Requirements of Jobs in the U.S. Economy." Industrial and Labor Relations Review 34, no. 4 (July):578–590.

_____. 1983. "The Job Market for College Graduates, 1960–1990." Stanford, CA: Institute for Research on Educational Finance and Governance, School of Education, Stanford University, Working Papers Series, February.

Rupp, Leila J. 1978. Mobilizing Women for War: German and American Propaganda, 1939–45. Princeton: Princeton University Press.

Rytina, Nancy. 1982. "Earnings of Men and Women: A Look at Specific Occupations." Monthly Labor Review 105 (April):25–31.

Salmon, Lucy M. 1897. Domestic Service. New York: Macmillan.

Samuelson, Barbara. 1977. "Temps: The Help That's Here to Stay." New York Times, May 22, p. 13.

Sapiro, Virginia. 1986. Women in American Society: An Introduction to Women's Studies. Palo Alto, CA: Mayfield.

Sargent, Lydia, ed. 1981. Women and Revolution: A Discussion of the Unhappy Marriage of Marxism and Feminism. Boston: South End Press.

Saxton, Alexander. 1971. The Indispensable Enemy: Labor and the Anti-Chinese Movement in California. Berkeley: University of California Press.

Scharf, Lois. 1980. To Work and to Wed: Female Employment, Feminism, and the Great Depression. Westport, CT: Greenwood.

Seager, Henry, et al. 1913. "The Theory of the Minimum Wage." American Labor Legislation 3, no. 1 (February):81–91.

Serrin, William. 1984a. "Jobs Increase in Number, but Trends Are Said to Be Leaving Many Behind." New York Times, October 15.

------. 1984b. "Experts Say Job Bias Against Women Persists." New York Times, November 25, pp. 1, 32.

------. 1986. "Part-Time Work: New Labor Trend." New York Times, July 9, pp. A1, A4.

"Service Producing Industries Account for Bulk of 11 1/2 Million 1970's Rise in Jobs Held by Women." 1981. U.S. Dept. of Labor, Bureau of Labor Statistics, Middle Atlantic Region, New York, News Release. January 8.

Sexton, Patricia Cayo. 1982. The New Nightingales: Hospital Workers, Unions and New Women's Issues. New York: Enquiry Press.

"Sexual Harassment Brief Bank and Bibliography." 1985. Women's Rights Law Reporter 8, no. 4:267–295.

Shabecoff, Phillip. 1981. "Donovan Seeks to End Ban on Jobs at Home in Apparel Industries." New York Times, May 2, pp. 1, 10.

Shaevitz, M. H. 1984. The Superwoman Syndrome. New York: Warner.

Shanahan, Eileen. 1976. "Jobs in Big Banks Found Hard to Get for Minority Men." New York Times, December 13, p. 57.

Shea, John R., Ruth S. Spitz, and Frederick A. Zeller and Associates. 1970. Dual Careers: A Longitudinal Study of Labor Market Experiences of Women, vol. 1. Columbus, OH: Center for Human Resource Research.

Shennon, Philip. 1985. "Meese Sees Racism in Hiring Goals." New York Times, September 18, p. A16.

Shepard, Jon M. 1971. Automation and Alienation: A Study of Office and Factory Workers. Cambridge, MA: MIT Press.

Skold, Karen Beck. 1981. "Women Workers and Child Care During World War II: A Case Study of the Portland, Oregon Shipyards." Ph.D. diss., University of Oregon.

Smith, Henry Nash. 1950. Virgin Land. Cambridge, MA: Harvard University Press.

Smith, Joan. 1984. "The Paradox of Women's Poverty: Wage-earning Women and Economic Transformation." Signs 10, no. 2 (Winter):291-310.

Smith-Rosenberg, Caroll. 1975. "The Female World of Love and Ritual: Relations Between Women in Nineteenth Century America." Signs 1 (Autumn):1-29.

Smuts, Robert W. 1959. Women and Work in America. New York: Columbia University Press.

_____. 1960. "The Woman Labor Force: A Case Study in the Interpretation of Historical Statistics." American Statistical Association Journal (March):71-79.

Sokoloff, Natalie J. 1980. Between Money and Love: The Dialectics of Women's Home and Market Work. New York: Praeger.

_____. 1982. "The Changing Nature of Women's Work, 1940-1980: A Theoretical Contribution." Paper presented at American Sociological Association, San Francisco, September. ED 225 005. Columbus, OH: ERIC Clearinghouse on Adult, Career and Vocational Education/National Institute of Education, 1983.

_____. 1984. "The Impact of Economic Crises on Women's Employment: A Comparison of the Great Depression (1930s) and the Current Crisis (1970s-1980s)." ED 250 229. Boulder, CO: ERIC Clearinghouse for Social Science Education/National Institute of Education.

_____. 1986. "A Review of the Aggregate Sex and Race Segregation Literature: A Profile of the General Labor Force and the Professions." Paper presented at American Sociological Association meetings, New York, September 1.

_____. 1987. "Black and White Women in the Professions: A Contradictory Process." In Ingredients for Women's Employment Policy, Christine Bose and Glenna Spitze, eds., pp. 53-72. Albany, N.Y.: SUNY Press.

Span, Paula. 1981. "Where Have All the Nurses Gone?" New York Times Magazine, February 22, pp. 70-79, 96-101.

Spokeswoman. 1981. Vol. 11, January-April, December. (Entire issues.).

Stacey, Judith. 1983. Patriarchy and Socialist Revolution in China. Berkeley: University of California Press.

_____. 1986. "State Socialism, the 'Woman Question,' and Socialist-Feminist Theory." Insurgent Sociologist 13, no. 3 (Spring):20-29.

Stanko, Elizabeth. 1985. Intimate Intrusions: Women's Experience of Male Violence. London: Routledge and Kegan Paul.

Steinberg, Ronnie, and Lois Haignere. 1987. "The Under-valuation of Work by Gender and Race." In Ingredients for Women's Employment Policy, Christine Bose and Glenna Spitze, eds., pp. 157–180. Albany, NY: SUNY Press.

Sterling, Dorothy. 1979. Black Foremothers: Three Lives. Old Westbury, NY: Feminist Press.

Stewart, Charles. 1893. Disintegration of the Families of Working Men. Chicago: n.p.

Stigler, George J. 1946. Domestic Servants in the United States, 1900–1940. Occasional Paper 24. New York: National Bureau of Economic Research.

Stone, Katherine. 1975. "The Origins of Job Structures in the Steel Industry." In Labor Market Segmentation, Richard C. Edwards, Michael Reich, and David M. Gordon, eds., pp. 27–84. Lexington, MA: D. C. Heath.

Strom, Sharon Hartman. 1983. "Challenging 'Women's Place': Feminism, the Left, and Industrial Unionism in the 1930s." Feminist Studies 9 (Summer):359–386.

Strong, Edward K., Jr. 1933. Japanese in California. Stanford, CA: Stanford University Press.

_____. 1934. The Second Generation Japanese Problem. Stanford, CA: Stanford University Press.

Strumingher, Laura S. 1979. Women and the Making of the Working Class: Lyon 1830–1870. St. Albans, VT: Eden Press Women's Publications.

Stuart, Reginald. 1981. "Alabama Blacks Fear Losing the Voting Rights Act." New York Times, April 14, pp. A1, A10.

Suffragist. 1919–1920. Whole issues of February 15, 1919, and February 1920.

Sullivan, Ronald. 1982. "Medical Schools Show Big Drop in Minorities." New York Times, March 1, pp. B1, B5.

Sussman, Marvin. 1971. "Family Systems in the 1970s: Analyses, Policies and Programs." Annals of the American Academy of Political and Social Science 396: 40–56.

Tangri, Sandra, Mary Burt, and L. B. Johnson. 1982. "Sexual Harassment at Work: Three Explanatory Models." Journal of Social Issues 38, no. 4:55–74.

Taylor, Eunice. 1983. Comments delivered at the Conference on Women in the Human Services, New York University, April.

Taylor, Paul S. 1929. "Mexican Labor in the United States: Valley of the South Platte, Colorado." University of California Publications in Economics 6, no. 2 (June):95–235.

_____. 1937. "Migratory Farm Labor in the United States." Monthly Labor Review 60 (March):537–549.

Taylor, Ronald. 1976. Sweatshops in the Sun. Boston: Beacon Press.

Taylor, Stuart, Jr. 1986. "3 Bias Cases Before Supreme Court Could Reshape Law on Racial Goals." New York Times, February 23, p. 28.

Tentler, Leslie Woodcock. 1979. Wage-Earning Women: Industrial Work and Family Life in the United States, 1900–1930. New York: Oxford University Press.

The Columbian. January 1942–December 1946.

Thorne, Barrie. 1982. "Feminist Rethinking of the Family: An Overview." In Rethinking the Family: Some Feminist Questions, Barrie Thorne and Marilyn Yalom, eds., pp. 1–24. New York: Longman.

Thornton, Mary. 1983. "Affirmative Action Found to Diversify Work Force." Washington Post, June 20.

Tilly, Louise A. 1981. "Paths of Proletarianization: Organization of Production, Sexual Division of Labor and Women's Collective Action." Signs 7:400–417.

Tilly, Louise A., and Joan Scott. 1978. Women, Work, and Family. New York: Holt, Rinehart and Winston.

Tobias, Shelia, and Lisa Anderson. 1974. "What Really Happened to Rosie the Riveter? Demobilization and the Female Labor Force, 1944-1947." Module 9. (pamphlet). New York: MSS Modular Publications.

Treiman, Donald, and Heidi Hartmann. 1981. Women, Work, and Wages: Equal Pay for Jobs of Equal Value. Washington, D.C.: National Academy Press.

Tsuchida, Nobuya, ed. 1982. Asian and Pacific American Experiences: Women's Perspectives. Minneapolis: Asian/Pacific American Learning Resource Center.

Turbin, Carole. 1978. "Woman's Work and Woman's Rights: A Comparative Study of Women's Trade Unions and the Woman's Rights Movement in the Mid-nineteenth Century." Ph.D. diss., New School for Social Research.

_____. 1979. "'And We Are Nothing but Women': Irish Working Women in Troy." In Women of America: A History, Carol R. Berkin and Mary Beth Norton, eds., pp. 202-222. Boston: Houghton Mifflin.

Ukarish v. Magnesium Elektron, Inc. 1981. United States Federal District Court, District of New Jersey.

Urquhart, Michael. 1984. "The Employment Shift to Services: Where Did It Come from?" Monthly Labor Review 107, no. 4 (April):15-22.

U.S. Census Bureau. 1933. Fifteenth Census of the United States, 1930, Population, vol. 5, General Report on Occupations, ch. 3, "Color and Nativity of Gainful Workers." Washington, D.C.: U.S. Government Printing Office.

_____. 1943. Sixteenth Census of the Population, 1940: Population Characteristics of the Non-White Population by Race. Washington, D.C.: U.S. Government Printing Office.

_____. 1970. Census of the Population, Characteristics of the Population, vol. 1, pt. 1, Table 221, "Detailed Occupations of the Experienced Labor Force and Employed Persons by Sex: 1970 and 1960." Washington, D.C.: U.S. Government Printing office.

_____. 1973. Census of the Population: 1970. Subject Reports, Final Report PC (2) 1G, Japanese, Chinese, and Filipinos in the United States. Washington, D.C.: U.S. Government Printing Office.

_____. 1975. Historical Statistics of the United States, Colonial Times to 1970, bicentennial edition, pt. 2. Washington, D.C.: U.S. Government Printing Office.

_____. 1980. Detailed Population Characteristics: United States Summary. Washington, D.C.: U.S. Government Printing Office.

_____. 1983. Twentieth Census of the United States: 1980. Population, vol. 2, General Report, Statistics by Subject. Washington, D.C.: U.S. Government Printing Office.

_____. 1985. Statistical Abstract of the United States. Washington, D.C.: U.S. Government Printing Office.

U.S. Department of Justice. 1977. Immigration and Naturalization Service Annual Report. Washington, D.C.: U.S. Department of Justice.

U.S. Department of Labor, Women's Bureau. 1946. Employment of Women in the Early Postwar Period with Background of Prewar and War Data. Bulletin no. 211. Prepared by Mary Elizabeth Pidgeon. Washington, D.C.: U.S. Government Printing Office.

_____. 1975. 1975 Handbook of Women Workers. Bulletin no. 297.

_____. 1980. Job Options for Women in the 80's. Washington, D.C.: U.S. Department of Labor.

U.S. Department of Labor, Bureau of Labor Statistics. 1961. Industry Wage Survey, Life Insurance. May-

July. Bulletin no. 1324. Average Weekly Earnings, selected occupations.

_____. 1963. Impact of Office Automation in the Internal Revenue Service. Bulletin no. 1364.

_____. 1965. Impact of Office Automation in the Insurance Industry. Bulletin No. 1468.

_____. 1966. Industry Wage Survey, Life Insurance. Bulletin no. 1569.

_____. 1971. Industry Wage Survey, Life Insurance. Bulletin no. 1971.

_____. 1976. Industry Wage Surveys: Banking and Life Insurance, Table 67, "Average Weekly Earnings, Selected Occupations." Bulletin no. 1988.

_____. 1977. U.S. Working Women: A Databook. Bulletin 1977.

_____. 1980. Perspectives on Working Women: A Databook. Bulletin no. 2080.

_____. 1981. Industry Wage Survey, Life Insurance. Bulletin no. 2119.

_____. 1983. Time of Change: 1983 Handbook of Women Workers. Bulletin no. 298.

U.S. Merit Systems Protection Board. 1981. "Sexual Harassment in the Federal Workplace: Is It a Problem?" Washington, D.C.: U.S. Government Printing Office.

Vogel, Lise. 1983. Marxism and the Oppression of Women: Toward a Unitary Theory. New Brunswick, NJ: Rutgers University Press.

Waldman, Elizabeth. 1983. "Labor-Force Statistics from a Family Perspective." Monthly Labor Review 106 (December):16–20.

366 / Bibliography

Walkowitz, Daniel J. 1972. "Working Class Culture in the Gilded Age: The Iron Workers of Troy, New York and the Cotton Workers of Cohoes, New York." Unpublished Ph.D. diss., University of Rochester.

_____. 1974. "Statistics and the Writing of Working Class Culture: A Statistical Portrait of the Iron Workers in Troy, New York, 1860–1880." Labor History 15:416–460.

_____. 1978. Worker City, Company Town. Urbana: University of Illinois Press.

Wallace, Anthony. 1978. Rockdale: The Growth of an American Village in the Early Industrial Revolution. New York: Alfred A. Knopf.

Wallace, Phyllis. 1980. Black Women in the Labor Force. Cambridge, MA: MIT Press.

Walshok, Mary. 1981. Blue Collar Women: Pioneers on the Male Frontier. Garden City, NY: Anchor Books.

Watkins, Beverly T. 1981. "A 'Critical' Shortage of Schoolteachers Likely by 1985, Education Deans Warn." Chronicle of Higher Education (March 23):1, 10.

Watson, Amey. 1937. "Domestic Service." Encyclopaedia of the Social Sciences, vol. 5, pp. 198–206.

Weber, C. Edward. 1959. "Impact of Electronic Data Processing on Clerical Skills." Personnel Administration 22:21–26.

Weil, D. 1986. "Personal Priorities." Working Woman, January:114–115.

Weinbaum, Batya, and Amy Bridges. 1979. "The Other Side of the Paycheck: Monopoly Capital and the Structure of Consumption." In Capitalist Patriarchy and the Case for Socialist Feminism, Zillah R. Eisenstein, ed., pp. 190–205. New York: Monthly Review Press.

Weise, Arthur James. 1877. History of the City of Troy and the Village of Lansingburgh. Troy, NY: William A. Young.

_____. 1886. The City of Troy and Its Vicinity. Troy, NY: Edward Green.

Weitzman, Lenore. 1985. The Divorce Revolution. New York: The Free Press.

Welter, Barbara. 1966. "The Cult of True Womanhood: 1820–1860." American Quarterly (Summer):151–174.

Wertheimer, Barbara M., and Anne H. Nelson. 1975. Trade Union Women, a Study of Their Participation in New York City Locals. New York: Praeger.

Westcott, Diane Nilsen. 1982. "Blacks in the 1970's: Did They Scale the Job Ladder?" Monthly Labor Review 105 (June):29–82.

White, Connie, Barbara Angle, and M. Moore. 1981. "Sexual Harassment in the Coal Industry: A Survey of Women Miners." Oak Ridge, TN: Coal Employment Project. Mimeo.

Wider Opportunities for Women and the Center for National Policy Review. 1982. "A Territorial Issue: A Study of Women in the Construction Trades." Mimeo. Washington, D.C.: Center for National Policy Review.

Williams, Lena. 1986a. "Coalition Seeks Wider Penalty in Rights Law." New York Times, February 28, p. A20.

_____. 1986b. "County Officials Urge U.S. to Keep Hiring Goals." New York Times, March 6, p. A21.

Williams, Raymond. 1973. "Base and Superstructure in Marxist Cultural Theory." New Left Review 82:3–16.

Willie, Charles. 1981. A New Look at Black Families. Bayview, NY: General Hall.

Wolfbein, Seymour L. 1962. "Automation and Skill." Annals of the American Academy of Political and Social Science 340:53–59.

Wolfson, Theresa. 1926. The Woman Worker and Trade Unions. New York: International Publishers.

Women Employed Advocates. 1981. Bulletin 2 (April). Chicago. (Entire issue.)

_____. 1982. Bulletin 3 (May). Chicago. (Entire issue.)

Women's Research and Education Institute. 1981. "Impact on Women of the Administration's Proposed Budget." Congressional Record 127, no. 54, April 2.

Wong, Susan Stone. 1984. "From Soul to Strawberries: The ILGWU and Workers' Education, 1914-1950." In Sisterhood and Solidarity, Workers' Education for Women, 1914-1985, Joyce L. Kornbluh and Mary Frederickson, eds., pp. 39-74. Philadelphia: Temple University Press.

Working Women's Institute. 1985. "Results of a Survey on Gender Bias and Sexual Harassment in the FAA Eastern Region." Written by Peggy Crull, K. C. Wagner, and Marilyn Cohen. Mimeo. New York City: Working Women's Institute.

_____. 1986. "Sexual Harassment on the Job: Questions and Answers." Mimeo. New York City: Working Women's Institute.

Wright, Carroll D. 1900. The History and Growth of the United States Census. Washington, D.C.: U.S. Government Printing Office.

Wu, C. 1972. "Chink": A Documentary History of Anti-Chinese Prejudice in America. New York: Meridian.

Yanagisako, Sylvia Junko. 1975. "Two Processes of Change in Japanese American Kinship." Journal of Anthropological Research 31:196-224.

Yancy, William, E. P. Eriksen, and R. N. Julian. 1976. "Emergent Ethnicity: A Review and Reformulation." American Sociological Review 41:391-403.

Yap, Stacey G. Y. 1983. "Gather Your Strength Sisters: The Careers of Chinese American Community Workers." Ph.D. diss., Boston University.

Yoshihashi, Pauline. 1985. "Los Angeles Backing Equal Pay for Jobs of 'Comparable Worth.'" New York Times, May 9, pp. A1, A27.

Zaretsky, Eli. 1982. "The Place of the Family in the Origins of the Welfare State." In Rethinking the Family: Some Feminist Questions, Barrie Thorne with Marilyn Yalom, eds., pp. 188–224. New York: Longman.

Zarrella, Patricia. 1985. "'Abnormal Intimacy': The Varying Work Networks of Chicana Cannery Workers." Feminist Studies 11 (Fall):541–557.

Zimmerman, Jan. 1981. "How to Control the New Technology Before It Controls You." Ms, January:81–84.

Index

About the Authors

CAROL A. BROWN is associate professor of sociology and chair of the Department of Sociology at the University of Lowell in Massachusetts. She has written about the division of labor in the health services and about the lives of divorced mothers. Her current writing centers on issues of public patriarchy. She is a member of the Women's Research Center of Boston.

CHRISTINE E. BOSE is associate professor of sociology at the State University of New York at Albany, where she served as director of the Women's Studies Program from 1978 through 1981. She holds a joint appointment in the department of Latin American and Caribbean Studies. Dr. Bose has published in the areas of occupational prestige, gender and status attainment, women's home and paid employment at the turn of the century, and the social impact of household technology.

PEGGY CRULL is a staff associate for the City University of New York, Office of Special Programs. Between 1978 and 1985 she served as executive director of Working Women's Institute, a New York-based research, training, and consultation center on sexual harassment. Before coming to the Institute in 1978, she taught psychology at the Herbert H. Lehman College of the City University of New York.

ROSLYN L. FELDBERG is currently associate director in charge of research and education for the labor relations program of the Massachusetts Nurses Association. Previously she was a Radcliffe research scholar at the Henry A. Murray Research Center of Radcliffe College (1983-1985) and assistant professor of sociology at Boston University (1972-1983).

MYRA MARX FERREE is professor of sociology at the University of Connecticut, where she is also active in the women's studies program. Her research focuses on the family context of women's work, especially for working-class women, and on the women's movement.

AMY GILMAN is associate professor of history at Montclair State College in New Jersey, where she teaches women's history and American history. Formerly coordinator of the women's studies program at the college and a trustee of the American Labor Museum at the Botto House National Landmark, she now writes on 19th-century cultural history.

EVELYN NAKANO GLENN is a professor of sociology at the State University of New York at Binghamton. Her research, writing, and teaching interests center on issues of women and work, the political economy of the family, and the intersection of race and gender stratification.

AMY KESSELMAN is assistant professor of women's studies at the State University of New York at New Paltz. She was part of the team that produced "Good Work Sister! Women Shipyard Workers of World War 11," an oral history slide show. She writes on the history of women in the United States.

SUSAN LEHRER is assistant professor of sociology and also teaches women's studies at the State University of New York at New Paltz. Her research interests are in the area of women and work, especially current issues regarding women, work, and the family.

NATALIE J. SOKOLOFF is associate professor of sociology at the John Jay College of Criminal Justice, a unit of the City University of New York, where she teaches in the Departments of Sociology and Thematic Studies as well as in the graduate program in criminal justice. She has published in the areas of feminist theory, women and the criminal justice system, and women, work, and family. Her most recent research is on race and gender stratification in the professions.

CAROLE TURBIN is assistant professor of sociology and women's studies at the State University of New York's Empire State College at Old Westbury. From 1978 to 1980 she was an assistant professor of sociology at Vassar College. Dr. Turbin is presently working on a book that centers on the impact of the interrelationship between family life and work experience on the labor activism of 19th-century working-class women.

DATE DUE

DEC 1 1 2004			
GAYLORD			PRINTED IN U.S.A.